COUNSELOR EDUCATION
AND SUPERVISION

COUNSELOR EDUCATION
AND SUPERVISION

Readings in Theory, Practice, and Research

Compiled and Edited by

MILTON SELIGMAN, Ph.D.

School of Education
University of Pittsburgh
Pittsburgh, Pennsylvania

and

NORMAN F. BALDWIN, Ph.D.

School of Education
University of Pittsburgh
Pittsburgh, Pennsylvania

CHARLES C THOMAS · PUBLISHER
Springfield · Illinois · U.SA.

Published and Distributed Throughout the World by
CHARLES C THOMAS • PUBLISHER
Bannerstone House
301-327 East Lawrence Avenue, Springfield, Illinois, U.S.A.
Natchez Plantation House
735 North Atlantic Boulevard, Fort Lauderdale, Florida, U.S.A.

© *1972, by* CHARLES C THOMAS • PUBLISHER
ISBN 0-398-02406-5
Library of Congress Catalog Card Number: 71-184611

With THOMAS BOOKS *careful attention is given to all details of manufacturing and design. It is the Publisher's desire to present books that are satisfactory as to their physical qualities and artistic possibilities and appropriate for their particular use.* THOMAS BOOKS *will be true to those laws of quality that assure a good name and good will.*

Printed in the United States of America
P-4

To our parents
and to
Susan, Patricia, Lisa, and Lori

PREFACE

During the past decade, considerable growth has occurred in the area of counselor training. Strides have been made in the development of counselor training standards, in practices employed in the education and supervision of trainees, in systematic investigations of trainee change, in the development of innovative procedures as well as in the use of paraprofessionals in counseling and counseling-related activities. In view of these developments, we have endeavored to compile, under one cover, representative writings that appear in various publications. Our goal has been to select articles representing diverse points of view which reflect the current status of the field and offer some direction for the future.

This book is primarily designed for counselor educators and supervisors and prospective counselor educators and supervisors. In a more general sense, the book should be useful for anyone involved in the training of persons engaged in counseling activities, such as guidance counselors, rehabilitation counselors, social workers, and clinical and counseling psychologists. It can be used in courses designed to train prospective counselor educators and supervisors. Field supervisors engaged in the training of practicum and/or internship students should also find the book of practical value.

We would like to acknowledge our indebtedness to Mrs. Sylvia Newman who conscientiously read and offered critical comments concerning portions of the text, to Miss Lisa Mosher who took on the truly laborious task of typing and retyping portions of the manuscript in addition to assisting with permission requests, and to Mrs. Karen Hittson, associate editor (Charles C Thomas), whose gentle guidance proved valuable during the development of this collection of readings. Finally, we would like to express our gratitude to the authors who graciously allowed us to reprint their work.

Milton Seligman
Norman Baldwin

[vii]

CONTENTS

COUNSELOR EDUCATION
AND SUPERVISION

Chapter 1

A HISTORICAL PERSPECTIVE AND INTRODUCTION

The Emergence of Counseling as a Profession: Trait and Factor Theory

SINCE THE TURN OF THIS CENTURY, our society has witnessed a profound technological and professional development. Accompanying this development has been an alteration and growth within the profession we today know as counseling.

What began so modestly in 1908, under the direction of Frank Parsons, benchmarked a professional development that only today can be comprehended. Parsons sought to systematically analyze individual characteristics of adolescents who dropped out of the educational system, to examine the world of work with equal vigor, and then by a process of "true reasoning," to match characteristics of client and vocation (Shertzer and Stone, 1968, 1971).

Thus began the formalized process of counseling as we know it today. This cognitive matching, through expert guidance, of individual traits with environmental demands was further stimulated with the mass production of mental tests shortly after World War I. The increasing use of tests for selection, classification, and prediction led to their greater availability. Soon thereafter, tests became used as tools for more systematic application of the matching principle in counseling. Through a careful combination of data from psychological tests and vocational-educational appraisals, "trait and factor" theory provided the foundation of psychological counseling (Super, 1955; Shertzer and Stone, 1968, 1971).

The Influence of Psychoanalytic Theory

In the 1930's, the conceptualization of counseling in the United States underwent its next major transformation as psychoanalytic

[3]

theorists proposed a model which began to influence counseling theory (Schertzer and Stone, 1968, 1971). Unconscious motivation was beginning to be examined in the interpersonal dialogue between a professional counselor and his client. Counseling was more than a strictly cognitive process. It was an intense investigation of subtle but deeply significant motivation as expressed in observable behavior. The counselor was obliged to help his client understand these unconscious influences.

The Influence of Client-Centered Theory

In the meantime, Carl Rogers (1942, 1961) further extricated the dialogue of counseling from the pragmatic requirements of vocational choice. Let us focus on the client's subjective existence, Rogers advised. Let us help to clarify the client's self-awareness and assist him in achieving greater consistency between his feelings and actions. Spontaneous solutions to vexing difficulties in the client's environment or within himself would follow with patient understanding by the counselor. According to Rogers (1957), "unconditional positive regard," "empathic understanding," and "self-congruence" became key characteristics of the counseling relationship. The counselor would be of significant benefit only through an understanding of the client's private experience.

The Influence of Learning Theory

In the past twenty years yet another model has emerged, reflecting the growing understanding of technology and its applications. Under the leadership of B. F. Skinner, John Krumboltz, Joseph Wolpe, and Arnold Lazarus, professional counselors have applied the principles of behavior modification, selective reinforcement, and counterconditioning to everyday behavior (Skinner, 1957; Krumboltz, 1969; Wolpe, 1958; Lazarus, 1961).

The efficacy of these various theoretical formulations for the profession of counseling is now documented by research and clinical observation. What once was an implicit matter of offering sensible advice became transformed into a highly sophisticated, carefully conceptualized manner of helping others.

Evaluating the Effectiveness of Counseling

It was not long afterward that the issue of evaluation was brought poignantly to the fore. H. J. Eysenck proposed in 1952, and later in 1961, that systematic surveys could not establish clearly improved adaptive capacity for clients who had received the professional services of a counselor, compared with a "comparable group" of individuals who had not. As the ingredients of the counseling relationship were more carefully specified (Carl Rogers, 1957; Charles Truax and Robert Carkhuff, 1967), it became apparent that irrespective of the theoretical preference of the counselor, positive outcomes seemed to be preceded by certain qualities which were considerably less in evidence in outcomes not so positive.

Counseling theory and practice, therefore, has undergone a profound growth, marked by an "exploratory phase," a "boom phase," and now a phase of "critical evaluation."*

Early Developments in Training

The issue of training, however, has not in the past received such systematic scrutiny. At a time when counseling, counseling psychology, social work, and related disciplines have expanded so rapidly in the occupational spectrum of our society that the need for trained personnel far exceeds the supply, when universities have substantially increased the curricular emphasis in counseling, comparable attention has not been given to the issue of training.

Prior to 1955, the process was not yet clearly formulated (Arbuckle, 1965; Stoughton, 1965). Because of this essentially undeveloped level of explication before 1955, counselor training was in an "exploratory phase," much like that of counseling theory some fifty years previous. Only in the past fifteen years or so has the training process, that is, the educating of counselors in general and the supervising of them in particular, become an

---

* This terminology has been adapted for discussion of counselor education and supervision from the following text, where the terms originally refer to the development of mental testing. Thorndike, R. L., and Hagen, E.: *Measurement and Evaluation in Psychology and Education.* New York, John Wiley and Sons, 1955, pp. 5-7.

important issue. Reviews of the literature in this area are beginning to appear (Cottle and Downie, 1970; Hansen and Warner, 1971), reflecting advances in theory and research during the past ten-year period concerning the matter of training.

Recent Developments in Training

The initial impetus towards more explicit consideration of professional training was further emphasized with the passage of the National Defense Education Act in 1958, by which many professional training programs were funded (Arbuckle, 1965). The early 1960's saw the organization of the Association of Counselor Education and Supervision, the publication of the journal *Counselor Education and Supervision,* and the Wrenn report. The Wrenn report recommended seven essential components of a counselor education program (Wrenn, 1962). More recently, at their conventions, professional organizations have begun to devote a considerable portion of time to the presentation of papers relative to counselor education and supervision.*

Two issues have been dominant in many of the papers recently presented and published. The first of these is a concern with outcomes, the second with process. Outcome is the end result of an intervention. Process is concerned with the variables that produce change or improvement. Some of the questions asked pertaining to outcomes are as follows: Are counselor education programs and supervisory practices instrumental in bringing about improvement in professional skills? What literature suggests that constructive trainee changes are brought about by the supervisor or the counselor educator?

Closely associated with questions about outcomes is the matter of process—the analysis of working procedures in training. Process closely follows outcome as one of the major areas of publication. Questions pertaining to process might be: What supervisory practices result in desirable trainee change? What are the ingredients of an effective counselor education program? What techniques and strategies facilitate learning of counseling skills?

---

* The American Personnel and Guidance Association 1970 Convention, New Orleans, and the 1971 Convention, Atlantic City, The American Psychological Association 1971 Convention, Washington, D.C.

As phase two, the "boom phase" of theory and practice in counselor education and supervision reaches it peak, an increasing volume of literature is being directed toward relevant issues.

Philosophical Issues

Prior to the "boom phase," work was directed more to practice than to theory or philosophy. In 1964, Penney observed that professional educators in the field of counseling have devoted scant attention to the philosophical underpinning of their training programs (Penney, 1964, p. 379). Penney is concerned about the proliferation of training techniques and practices which in themselves are dictating goals and objectives of counselor education programs. He proposed the embedding of pragmatic issues within more broadly conceived philosophical rationales. Some basic decisions need to be made regarding the counselor educator's philosophy of man. If the educator saw man as basically antisocial and needing control and direction from others, this perspective should generate training goals consistent with this philosophical conception. If the educator saw man as fully capable of self-direction, given an appropriate growth-promoting atmosphere, this perspective should generate other training goals which were consistent with this philosophy. The latter doctrine, for example, might point to supervision as a process of enabling, facilitating, and supporting the intrinsic, natural qualities of the neophyte counselor and encouraging the growth of such qualities.

Operational Theories

In addition to philosophical issues, operational theories of educating and supervising the apprentice counselor also began to emerge. Dugald Arbuckle (1965) begins to question whether a theory of counseling could be completely transposed, without alteration, to a supervisory situation. How can the educator or supervisor implement the same facilitative conditions with the student, as the counselor with the client? Therefore Arbuckle reasons that the supervisory relationship, no matter what alterations are made in it, is in the last analysis evaluative. Evaluation involves the element of threat and there appears to be no honest way of denying this threat while at the same time maintaining the condition of "congruence," considered so important by Carl Rogers. Perhaps therefore the supervisor could be empathic and understanding without sacrificing honest feedback to the trainee, consistent with later written or more formal evaluations. Perhaps the supervisor could react with an honest expression of his personal feeling rather than make a judgment, even if his trainee interprets this response as evaluative. Perhaps the supervisor could fulfill his mandated evaluative role and still offer a facilitative, "experiential," "process-oriented" relationship. That is, perhaps facilitation and evaluation are not mutually exclusive roles.

Arbuckle argues further that the supervisor is involved with his own frame of reference, as he is experiencing and relating to the student counselor, in contrast to the counseling relationship where the client's frame of reference is paramount. There is always the possibility, therefore, that no matter how non-threatening and "process-oriented" the supervisor's comments might be, they still would come across to the student as cognitive, evaluative, and structured around content, because evaluations are, in fact, being made by the supervisor. Qualifications not withstanding, Arbuckle's position seems to be primarily based upon a facilitative relationship which the supervisor cultivates with his student.

Alternate Theories

Alternate theoretical postures have been taken by C. H. Patterson and others. Patterson (1964) argues that supervision, while therapeutically based, also contains a number of cognitive elements. He thus appears to retain the emphasis upon a facilitative relationship, but contrary to Arbuckle, he places stress upon the supervisor's obligation to teach and evaluate as well. As such, Patterson seems to take an intermediate position, somewhere between purely cognitive and experiential approaches to supervision. Cottle and Downie (1970), Hansen and Moore (1966), Wicas and Mahan (1966), and Delaney and Moore (1966), also consider supervision and training to be a counseling *and* teaching process, involving instruction, consultation, and counseling of the trainee by the supervisor or counselor educator. These authorities therefore suggest that supervision involves instruction and evaluation, in addition to a counseling or facilitative relationship.

A third theoretical approach has been taken by counselor educators who tend to subordinate the significance of a counseling relationship between trainee and supervisor and emphasize a distinctly cognitive, evaluative practice following the traditional model of teacher and student (Anderson and Bown, 1955; Mazer and Engle, 1967).

Professional Training Standards

Other major thrusts have been more directly related to practice in counselor education. One aspect of practice which has received extended attention is the matter of professional training standards. In the 1950's a number of guidelines and recommendations concerning selected aspects of graduate training were proposed by committees of several professional organizations (American Psychological Association, 1952, 1955; American Personnel and Guidance Association, 1958).

By the early 1960's, such efforts to establish definite criteria of educational programming in keeping with the highest of professional standards, began to receive more serious and formal attention. In 1960, the American Personnel and Guidance Association (APGA) began a five-year study of counselor education standards. A division within this organization, the Association for Counselor Education and Supervision, appointed a committee to develop a draft proposal concerned with standards and guidelines for the preparation of school counselors.

After progress reports which were released by this committee in 1962 and 1963, the *Standards for Counselor Education in the Preparation of Secondary School Counselors* was published in 1964. This document was further modified and then endorsed by the membership of APGA, resulting in the 1967 edition of the standards, which was and still is considered a landmark in the professional development of counselor education. Further revisions are anticipated as the criteria of counselor training change. Four major areas are examined in the education of the psychological counselor. They are (a) philosophy and objectives of the training program; (b) curriculum or program of studies and supervised experiences; (c) selection, retention, endorsement, and placement of trainees; (d) support for the counselor training program through administrative relationships and institutional resources.

In addition to the 1964 standards, the Executive Council of APGA in the same year accepted a general overview of the desired characteristics of a counselor training program. It was "concerned with the common elements in the preparation and role of all counselors rather than the total preparation and role of any specific group such as student personnel or guidance workers in colleges and secondary schools" (APGA, 1964a, p. 1). The scope of this report was therefore directed more to the preparation of a counselor, regardless of the setting in which he worked. Other organizations, such as the American Psychological Association, also developed statements relative to desired attributes of a counselor training program (Stripling, 1965).

Changes in Counselor Training Programs

The training programs suggested by the standards differ significantly from curricula offered by training programs for the psychological counselor a number of years ago (Penney, 1964; Arbuckle, 1965). Graduate education at first was pragmatically attuned to the immediate needs of the client: finding a job, getting out of the mental hospital, finding monetary support, planning an education or apprenticeship; and to the immediate needs of individuals related to the client, such as parents of the secondary school student, the spouse of a hospitalized client, or the children of a client receiving public welfare. With increasing sophistication, however, the practice of counselor education and supervision has begun to utilize basic philosophical notions, theoretical strategies, and professional standards.

Published Literature Concerned with Training

However, in spite of intensified activity, only a modest effort has been realized toward integrating this empirical data, practice, and theory under a single cover. Although a few books in the area of counseling provide a brief and a rather general overview of supervision (Cottle and Downie, 1970; Kell and Burow,

1970; Arbuckle, 1965), a compilation and classification of literature in print has until recently been nonexistent. In a sphere of activity where there is a paucity of collected resources upon which to rely, the need for more systematic organization of the literature becomes evident. At a time when the need for professional counselors has reached critical proportions (Shertzer and Stone, 1971, p. 124), it becomes apparent that an equally urgent need for techniques, strategies, and systems of supervision and training must be met. Now that counseling is becoming more publically concerned with internal professional development and is more carefully specifying the recommended content of graduate programs, a review of significant progress is timely.

The readings which follow are selected with reference to mainstream issues as they are developing at the present time. The following questions have been given particular attention:

1. What professional standards exist as guidelines for graduate training programs?

2. What qualities and skills distinguish the competent from the incompetent counselor?

3. What strategies of supervising a counselor trainee are available? What intricacies, manipulations, and unspoken assumptions develop in the supervisory relationship? What techniques and instruments are available to augment supervision?

4. What impact does the counselor educator or the supervisor actually have upon the counselor trainee's professional development? What qualities and characteristics of the trainer lead to professional growth of the trainee?

5. What are some of the more promising innovative procedures currently practiced in counselor training programs?

6. What modifications in current practice and what special considerations need to be emphasized in training the group counselor?

In summary, until the previous decade formal conceptualizations of counselor education and supervision have been rather unsystematic and incomplete. The second major developmental thrust, the "boom phase," was marked by a period when theory, practice, and research in counselor education intensified in activity, and moved into the mainstream of professional concern. Sometime in the near future a concerted effort may be made to integrate and distill the basic assumptions which appear to underlie the abundance of diverse formulations. Thus, the 1970's may reflect a phase of "critical evaluation" in counselor education and supervision (Shertzer, 1971).

This selection of readings is designed to monitor current explorations into an area whose conceptual boundaries are just beginning to crystallize. Such a survey may help readers to judge for themselves how one should intervene in helping the apprentice counselor, psychologist, or social worker become professionally qualified in cultivating facilitative relationships.

References

American Personnel and Guidance Association; Professional Training, Licensing and Certification Committee: recommendation for minimal standards. *Personnel and Guidance Journal,* 37:162-166, 1958.

American Personnel and Guidance Association: *Counselor Education: A Progress Report on Standards.* Washington, D.C., 1962.

American Personnel and Guidance Association: *The Counselor: Professional Preparation and Role.* (Statement of policy.) Washington, D.C., 1964 (a).

American Personnel and Guidance Association: Association for Counselor Education and Supervision: *Standards for Counselor Education in the Preparation of Secondary School Counselors.* Washington, D.C., 1964 (b).

American Personnel and Guidance Association: Standards for the preparation of secondary school counselors. *Personnel and Guidance Journal,* 46:96-106, 1967.

American Psychological Association, Division of Counseling and Guidance, Committee on Counselor Training: Recommended standards for training counseling psychologists at the doctorate level. *American Psychologist,* 7:175-181, 1952.

American Psychological Association, Division of Counseling and Guidance, Committee on Counselor Training: The practicum training of counseling psychologists. *American Psychologist,* 7:182-188, 1952.

American Psychological Association, Division of Counseling Psychology, Subcommittee on Counselor Selection, Counselor Training: An analysis of practices in counselor trainee selection. *Journal of Counseling Psychology,* 1:174-179, 1954.

American Psychological Association, Committee on Subdoctoral Education of the Education and Training Board: The training of technical workers in psychology at the subdoctoral level. *American Psychologist, 10*:541-545, 1955.

Anderson, R. P., and Bown, O. H.: Tape recordings and counselor-trainee understandings. *Journal of Counseling Psychology, 2*:189-195, 1955.

Arbuckle, D. S.: *Counseling: Philosophy, Theory, and Practice.* Boston, Allyn and Bacon, 1965. Chapter Four, "The Counselor: Education and Professional Relationships." pp. 118-136.

Cottle, W. C., and Downie, N. M.: *Preparation for Counseling.* Englewood Cliffs, N.J., Prentice-Hall, 1970. Chapter Twelve, "Supervision in Counseling," pp. 379-408.

Delaney, D. J., and Moore, J. C.: Students' expectations of the role of the practicum supervisor. *Counselor Education and Supervision, 6*:11-17, 1966.

Dey, G. R.: Philosophers, counselor educators, and relevant questions. *Counselor Education and Supervision, 8*:135, 142, 1969.

Dugan, W. E.: Impact of NDEA upon counselor preparation. *Personnel and Guidance Journal, 39*:37-40, 1960.

Eysenck, H. J.: The effects of psychotherapy: an evaluation. *Journal of Consulting Psychology, 16*:319-324, 1952.

Eysenck, H. J.: The effects of psychotherapy. In Eysenck, H. J.: (Ed.): *Handbook of Abnormal Psychology.* New York, Basic Books, 1961.

Glanz, E. C.: *Foundations and Principles of Guidance.* Boston, Allyn and Bacon, 1965. Chapter Seventeen, "Education for Guidance," pp. 378-394.

Hansen, J. C., and Moore, G. C.: The off-campus practicum. *Counselor Education and Supervision, 6*:32-39, 1966.

Hansen, J. C., and Warner, R. W., Jr.: Review of research on practicum supervision. *Counselor Education and Supervision, 10*:261-272, 1971.

Kell, B. L., and Burow, J. M.: *Developmental Counseling and Therapy.* Boston, Houghton Mifflin, 1970.

Krumboltz, J. D., and Thoreson, C. E.: *Behavioral Counseling: Cases and Techniques.* New York, Holt, Rinehart and Winston, 1969.

Lazarus, A. A.: Group therapy of phobic disorders by systemic desensitization. *Journal of Abnormal and Social Psychology, 63*:504-510, 1961.

Lister, J. L.: Theory aversion in counselor education. *Counselor Education and Supervision, 6*:91-96, 1967.

Mazer, G. E., and Engle, K. B.: Practicum supervision: good guys and bad guys. *Counselor Education and Supervision, 7*:147-149, 1968.

Patterson, C. H.: Supervising students in the counseling practicum. *Journal of Counseling Psychology, 11*:47-53, 1964.

Penney, J. F.: Education for guidance. In Glanz, E. C.: *Foundations and Principles of Guidance.* Boston, Allyn and Bacon, 1964, p. 379.

Rogers, C. R.: *Counseling and Psychotherapy.* Boston, Houghton Mifflin, 1962.

Rogers, C. R.: The necessary and sufficient conditions of therapeutic personality change. *Journal of Consulting Psychology, 21*:95-103, 1957.

Rogers, C. R.: *On Becoming a Person.* Boston, Houghton Mifflin, 1961.

Rogers, C. R.: The interpersonal relationship: the core of guidance. *Harvard Educational Review, 32*:416-429, 1962.

Shertzer, B., and Stone, S.: *Fundamentals of Counseling.* Boston, Houghton Mifflin, 1968. Chapter Two, "Counseling: Origin and Development," pp. 28-49.

Shertzer, B., and Stone, S.: *Fundamentals of Guidance,* 2nd ed. Boston, Houghton Mifflin, 1971, pp. 44-86.

Shertzer, B.: President's message. *Counselor Education and Supervision, 10*:197, 1971.

Skinner, B. F.: *Science and Human Behavior.* New York, Macmillan, 1953.

Skinner, B. F.: *Verbal Behavior.* New York, Appleton-Century-Crofts, 1957.

Stoughton, R. W.: APGA and counselor professionalization. In Loughary, J. W., Stripling, R. O., and Fitzgerald, P. W. (Eds.): *Counseling, A Growing Profession.* Report of the American Personnel and Guidance Association Concerned with the Professionalization of Counseling. Washington, D.C., American Personnel and Guidance Association, 1965. Chapter One, pp. 1-18.

Stripling, R. O. and Dugan, W. E.: The cooperative study of counselor education standards. *Counselor Education and Supervision, 1*:34-35, 1961.

Stripling, R. O.: Counselor education standards committee. *Counselor Education and Supervision, 2*:92-93, 1963.

Stripling, R. O.: Standards for the education of school counselors. In Loughary, J. W., Stripling, R. O., and Fitzgerald, P. W.: *Counseling, A Growing Profession.* Report of the American Personnel and Guidance Association Concerned with the Professionalization of Counseling. Washington, D.C., American Personnel and Guidance Association, 1965. Chapter Two, pp. 19-30.

Super, D. E.: Transition from vocational guidance to counseling psychology. *Journal of Counseling Psychology, 2*:3-9, 1955.

Truax, C. B., and Carkhuff, R. R.: *Toward Effective Counseling and Psychotherapy: Training and Practice.* Chicago, Aldine Publishing Co., 1967. Chapter Three, "Central Therapeutic Ingredients: Research Evidence," pp. 80-143.

Wicas, E. A., and Mahan, T. W., Jr.: Characteristics of counselors rated effective by supervisors and peers. *Counselor Education and Supervision, 6*:50-56, 1966.

Wolpe, J.: *Psychotherapy by Reciprocal Inhibition.* Stanford, Stanford University Press, 1958.

Wrenn, C. G.: *The Counselor in a Changing World.* Washington, D.C., American Personnel and Guidance Association, 1962.

Additional References

Bernard, H. W., and Fulmer, D.: *Principles of Guidance.* Scranton, Pennsylvania, International Textbook Company, 1969, pp. 235-238, 345-365.

Beck, C. E.: Ethical aspects of change in counselor education. *Counselor Education and Supervision* (special issue), 6:216-221, 1967.

Carkhuff, R. R.: A non-traditional assessment of graduate education in the helping professions. *Counselor Education and Supervision,* 7:252-261, 1968.

Chenault, J.: A proposed model for a humanistic counselor education program. *Counselor Education and Supervision,* 8:4-11, 1968.

Downing, L.: *Guidance and Counseling Services: An Introduction.* New York, McGraw-Hill, 1968, pp. 398-401.

Dreikurs, R., and Sonstegard, M.: A specific approach to practicum supervision. *Counselor Education and Supervision,* 6:18-25, 1966.

Hoyt, D. P., and Rhatigan, J. J.: Professional preparation of junior and senior college student personnel administrators. *Personnel and Guidance Journal,* 47:263-270, 1968.

Humphries, A., Traxler, A. E., and North, R.: *Guidance Services.* Chicago, Science Research Associates, 1967, pp. 385-392, 393-404.

Isaacson, L. E.: Standards for the preparation of guidance and personnel workers in colleges and universities. *Counselor Education and Supervision* (special issue), 7:187-192, 1968.

Lee, J. M., and Pallone, N. J.: *Guidance and Counseling in Schools.* New York, McGraw-Hill, 1966, pp. 493-501.

Malcolm, D. D.: On becoming a counselor. *Personnel and Guidance Journal,* 47:673-676, 1968.

Muro, J. J., and Oelke, M. C.: Guidance needs in the elementary school: cue to the preparation of counselors. *Counselor Education and Supervision,* 7:7-12, 1967.

Ohlsen, M.: *Guidance Services in the Modern School.* New York, Harcourt, Brace and World, 1964, pp. 140-144, 214-216.

Ohlsen, M.: Standards for the preparation of elementary school counselors. *Counselor Education and Supervision* (special issue), 7:172-178, 1968.

Payne, P. A., and Gralinski, D. M.: Effects of supervisory style and empathy upon counselor learning. *Journal of Counseling Psychology, 15*: 517-521, 1968.

Parker, C. (Ed.): Counseling Theories and Counselor Education. Boston, Houghton Mifflin, 1970.

Tooker, E. D.: Counselor training. *Personnel and Guidance Journal, 36*: 263-267, 1957.

Woody, R. H.: Preparation in behavioral counseling. *Counselor Education and Supervision,* 7:357-362, 1968.

Woody, R. H.: Psychobehavioral therapy in the schools: implications for counselor education. *Counselor Education and Supervision,* 8:258-264, 1969.

Chapter 2

PROFESSIONAL AND PARAPROFESSIONAL
TRAINING STANDARDS AND ACCREDITATION

IN 1967, George E. Hill wrote:

> Like the older professions, we are just starting down a long hard
> row, a path that will require many decades of struggling to de-
> velop, apply, and maintain standards both in preparation and in
> practice which will move us—probably much more slowly than most
> of us like—toward higher and higher standards of professionalism.
> Thus I start this statement with a double plea—a seemingly contra-
> dictory plea—that we be both persistently aggressive in attaining
> professional standards and wisely patient in the face of overwhelm-
> ing evidence from the histories of the other professions that our
> progress will not be smooth, nor will it be rapid [Hill, 1967, p. 131].

Hill's suggestion of a restrained but forward-looking approach
is reflected in the articles selected for this chapter. The enormous
growth of paraprofessional workers in the mental health professions represents the field's dynamic movement forward to meet
the needs of our society for increased services. The issue of accreditation, however, has been approached more conservatively
and cautiously, reflecting some deep concerns about appropriate
standards of excellence.

Professional Training Standards

Hill, in 1967, chaired the committee charged with developing
the 1967 revision of the "Standards for the Preparation of Secondary School Counselors," which is included in this chapter. Its
incorporation here, to the exclusion of other statements of professional training policies, was prompted by its comprehensive-
ness and representativeness. Readers wishing to review training
standards more specifically related to their professional affilia-
tions (e.g. elementary school counselors, rehabilitation counselors) are referred to the list of additional references at the end of
this chapter.

Accreditation

As Hill contends, movement in the area of professional standards may not be as rapid as educators and trainers of counselors would like. Progress has nonetheless occurred. Some programs have instituted self-evaluation procedures based on the 1967 revised standards, while others are considering such a move. In addition, many counselor training programs are anticipating accreditation as the logical "next step" in the historical development of the counselor education movement. This issue has resulted in considerable controversy, and the rhetoric is accelerating as the likelihood of accreditation nears. In general, proponents believe that some type of "quality control" is essential and long overdue, whereas opponents fear that accreditation will result in rigid and inflexible counselor training programs. The latter point of view is reflected in the American Psychological Association's Educational and Training Committee Report on counseling psychology:

> It is . . . possible that most of the innovative programs are not the APA approved programs, since the APA approved programs may feel inhibited in introducing new procedures which they may fear will involve risk to their APA approved status. Non-APA programs may, thus, have more flexibility in trying out new training approaches and new objectives [APA, 1970, p. 125].

In a later report, Rorer (1971) comments that precautionary measures are being taken to assure diversity and flexibility in the forthcoming accreditation of APA training programs.

Because counselor training programs are generally "housed" in departments or colleges of education, their operation has fallen under the scrutiny of the National Council for Accreditation of Teacher Education (NCATE). However, NCATE's competence to evaluate counselor education programs has been challenged on the grounds that teacher training and not counselor training represents NCATE's area of expertise. This matter of appropriate domain for certifying and accrediting organizations is critically evaluated by Stripling, as he reviews the current status and future prospects of the accreditation movement. Since it seems likely that the matter of accreditation will assume increased significance in the years to come, Stripling's informative article is offered as a reading in this chapter.

Paraprofessional Training Standards

The literature on counseling, counselor education, and supervision evidences a growing interest in the use of paraprofessionals (auxiliary personnel, technical workers, sub-professionals, support personnel, etc.). The initial impetus for this development arose from the need for more people to engage in counseling and counseling-related activities and the recognition that non-professionals can effectively contribute to the well-being of others. Unlike other innovations, where practice quickly has extended beyond empirical documentation (e.g. the encounter group movement), research has kept pace with "soft" data, suggesting that support personnel can significantly augment the functions of the professional counselor, and in some cases, successfully engage in counseling practice. This promising new dimension in counselor preparation has very definite implications for counselor educators and supervisors and thus prompted the inclusion of the American Personnel and Guidance Association publication "Support Personnel for the Counselor: Their Technical and Non-Technical Roles and Preparation."

For a more extensive discussion of the issues involved in the training and use of support personnel, the reader is urged to consider related references presented at the conclusion of this chapter as well as the selection of readings included in Chapter 8.

References

American Psychological Association: Education and training committee report. *The Counseling Psychologist,* 2:123 and 125, 1970.

Hill, G. E.: The profession and standards for counselor education. *Counselor Education and Supervision,* 6:130-136, 1967.

Rorer, L. G.: Report to the Oregon Psychological Association on APA council meetings: 1970. *American Psychologist,* 26:575-582, 1971.

Additional References

American Personnel and Guidance Association: *ACES Manual for Self-Study by a Counselor Education Staff,* based on the 1967 edition of

"Standards for the Preparation of Secondary School Counselors." Washington, D.C.

American Personnel and Guidance Association: *Standards for the Preparation of Elementary School Counselors.* Washington, D.C., 1967.

American Psychological Association: Accreditation: a status report. *American Psychologist, 25*:581-584, 1970.

American Psychological Association Committee on Counselor Training, Division of Counseling and Guidance: The practicum training of counseling psychologists. *American Psychologist, 7*:182-188, 1952.

American Psychological Association Committee on Subdoctoral Education of the Education and Training Board: The training of technical workers in psychology at the subdoctoral level. *American Psychologist, 10*:541-545, 1955.

American Rehabilitation Counseling Association: The professional preparation of rehabilitation counselors: a statement of policy. *Rehabilitation Counseling Bulletin, 12*:29-35, 1968.

Dickey, F. G.: What is accrediting and why is it important for professional organizations? *Counselor Education and Supervision, 7*:194-199, 1968.

Goodstein, L. D., and Ross, S.: Accreditation of graduate programs in psychology: an analysis. *American Psychologist, 21*:218-223, 1966.

Guidelines for graduate programs in preparation of student personnel workers in higher education. *Personnel and Guidance Journal, 47*:493-498, 1969.

Hill, G. E.: Self-study and self-evaluation of counselor education programs. *Counselor Education and Supervision, 5*:68-72, 1966.

Hoch, E. L., Ross, A. O., and Winder, C. L.: Conference on the professional preparation of clinical psychologists: a summary. *American Psychologist, 21*:42-51, 1966.

Kennedy, C. E., Danskin, D. G., Edelman, S. K., and Steffen, J. D.: The practicum in study of student development: its relation to counselor preparation. *Counselor Education and Supervision, 9*:272-276, 1970.

Miller, C. H.: Quality in counselor education. *Counselor Education and Supervision, 1*:124-130, 1962.

Van Hoose, W. H.: Conflicts in counselor preparation and professional practice: an analysis. *Counselor Education and Supervision, 9*:241-247, 1970.

STANDARDS FOR THE PREPARATION OF SECONDARY SCHOOL COUNSELORS — 1967 *

Association for Counselor Education and Supervision

The 1967 revision of Standards for the Preparation of Secondary School Counselors represents another step toward establish-

---

* Reprinted from the *Personnel and Guidance Journal, 46*:96-106, 1967, with permission of the American Personnel and Guidance Association.

ing the quality of programs for preparing secondary school counselors. In 1964 the Association for Counselor Education and Supervision, a division of the American Personnel and Guidance Association, issued the first edition of these standards. Five years of study went into that 1964 edition, study that involved hundreds of counselor educators, state supervisors, city supervisors, and school counselors. This five-year program was chaired first by Willis E. Dugan and later by Robert O. Stripling.

The 1967 edition of Standards for the Preparation of Secondary School Counselors constitutes a revision of the 1964 edition based upon use of the standards in more than one hundred institutions and reactions from more than one thousand members of the Association. The 1967 edition of the standards was endorsed almost unanimously by respondents to a mail poll of all ACES members.

These standards are intended to be used in such ways as the following:

1. For institutional self-study by counselor education staffs and their school colleagues.

2. For the evaluation of counselor education programs by state departments of education which determine what programs will be recognized as adequate to prepare candidates for certification.

3. For the evaluation of professional counselor education by appropriate accrediting bodies.

4. For use by agencies and persons conducting research in the field of counselor education.

It is the expectation of the committee—as it was of its predecessor committee—that further efforts will be made in the years ahead to continue the refinement and improvement of these standards.

Section I. Philosophy and Objectives

1. *The institution has a stated philosophy of education and has developed a set of objectives for counselor education consistent with that philosophy.*

a. Such statements have been prepared cooperatively by the staff members in counselor education.
b. Such statements are in harmony with the institution's philosophy and objectives, have been accepted by the administration, and are supported at the policy-making level.
c. State and local guidance personnel have been consulted in reviewing the institution's objectives for counselor education.
d. The statements of philosophy and objectives are reflected in pamphlets, brochures, and other publications.
e. Philosophy and objectives are reflected in the attitudes and behavior of students in the program.

2. *The objectives of the counselor education program were developed by a staff who are aware of the total secondary school program, aims, needs, and trends.*

a. The objectives reflect the staff's awareness of the structure and setting of public and non-public school education in the country.
b. Due consideration is given to developments and trends in school organization, curriculum, and program provisions.
c. The objectives include a recognition of the role of guidance services in encouraging and facilitating desirable change in education.

3. *The institution's philosophy and the objectives of the counselor education program are accepted and implemented by staff members.*

a. The counselor education program is developed, extended, and improved on the basis of the stated philosophy and objectives.
b. Philosophy and objectives are implemented on a planned basis in all areas of the program including student selection, curriculum, instructional methods and facilities, research and administrative provisions and procedures.
c. The objectives are applied in the use of staff members representing other disciplines and in the use of outside personnel and resources.

4. *The staff continues to review the objectives of the program.*

a. The objectives are reviewed in the light of the needs of youth in a changing society.

    b. The objectives are reviewed in the light of local, state, and national studies of guidance program status and needs.

    c. The objectives are reviewed in the light of studies and recommendations of local, state, regional, and national groups concerning educational needs.

    d. The objectives are reviewed in the light of significant research findings related to guidance, education, and the behavioral sciences.

5. *There is a continuous study of the extent to which the stated philosophy is transmitted and the objectives are accomplished.*

    a. There is a planned program for assessing changes in attitudes and behavior of students as they move through the counselor education program.

    b. Flexibility of assignments and experiences is provided for students with differing backgrounds of preparation and experience.

    c. Personnel in cooperating schools and agencies participate in the evaluation process.

    d. Evaluation of the effectiveness of preparation is accomplished through evidence obtained from former students, the schools in which they work, and the state departments of education. This evaluation is based upon the stated objectives of the program of counselor education.

Section II. Curriculum: Program of Studies and Supervised Experiences

A. General Program Characteristics.

1. *The institution provides a graduate program in counselor education, based primarily on the program of studies and supervised practice outlined in B and C below. The institution provides a minimum of one year of graduate counselor education. In order to fulfill the requirements of the studies and supervised practice detailed in B and C below, the institution provides at least one additional year of graduate study in counselor education either through its own staff and facilities or through cooperative working relationships with other institutions which do have at least a two-year program of counselor education.*

    a. The opportunity for full-time study in counselor education is provided throughout the academic year.

b. Flexibility is provided within the curriculum to allow for individual differences in competencies and understandings developed prior to entering the institution's counselor education program.

c. The organized curriculum for the program is published and is available for distribution to prospective students. This description includes information relating to the institutions' requirements for full-time study.

2. *There is evidence of quality instruction in all aspects of the counselor education program.*

   a. Syllabi or other evidences of organized and coordinated instructional units of the curriculum are available.

   b. Appropriate resource materials are provided.

   c. Responsibilities are assigned to or assumed by staff members only in those areas for which they are professionally qualified by preparation and experience.

   d. Provisions are made for periodic evaluation by students, staff, former students, and employers of all aspects of the counselor education program, such as course content, methods of instruction and supervised experiences both on and off campus.

   e. Evaluation is followed by appropriate revisions and improvements, if indicated.

3. *Planned sequences of educational experiences are provided.*

   a. A sequence of basic and advanced graduate courses and other associated learning experiences is defined and provided.

   b. The program provides for the integration of didactic instruction, seminars, and supervised experiences in counseling and other related guidance services throughout the sequence.

   c. Prerequisites are identified.

4. *Cooperation exists among staff members directly responsible for the professional education of counselors and representatives of departments or schools offering courses in related fields.*

   a. Cooperative working arrangements are in existence.

   b. Staff members from related areas meet with the counselor education staff for planning, implementing and evaluating the counselor education program.

   c. Course work in other areas is identified for the counselor candidate with respect to its appropriateness for graduate credit or for background work.

d. There is evidence of interdisciplinary planning with respect to both student and staff participation in designing, conducting and evaluating research.

5. *Within the framework of the total counselor education program, there are available curriculum resources as well as procedures that make it possible for the counselor candidate to develop understandings and skills beyond the minimum requirements of the program.*

a. Elective courses are available.
b. Staff time is provided for the supervision of individual study in the areas of counselor education.
c. Advisers make counselor candidates aware of such opportunities.

6. *The counselor education staff encourages the spirit of inquiry and the production and use of research data.*

a. The statement of objectives of the program reflects an awareness of the role of research in the work of the counselor and the competencies to be developed.
b. Instructional procedures make frequent use of, and reference to, research findings. Areas in which research is needed are identified.

7. *Opportunities for self-evaluation and the further development of self-understanding are provided for the counselor candidate.*

a. Opportunities are provided through such activities as laboratory experiences, supervised counseling and self-analysis through tape recordings and/or video tapes.
b. Opportunities for improvement of interpersonal relationships are provided through small group activities.
c. Counseling services provided by persons other than the counselor education staff are available to students in counselor education.

B. Program of Studies.

1. *Opportunities are provided for the development of understanding and competencies in the following:*

a. The foundations and dynamics of human behavior and of the individual in his culture.

b. The educational enterprise and processes of education.
c. Professional studies in school counseling and related guidance activities:

    (1) Philosophy and principles underlying guidance and other pupil personnel services.
    (2) The nature and range of human characteristics and methods of measuring them in individual appraisal.
    (3) Vocational development theory.
    (4) Educational and occupational information, its nature and uses.
    (5) Counseling theory and practice.
    (6) Statistics and research methodology, independent research, and familiarization with data processing and programming techniques.
    (7) Group procedures in counseling and guidance.
    (8) Professional relationships and ethics in keeping with the APGA ethical standards.
    (9) Administration and coordination of guidance and pupil personnel services.
    (10) Supervised experience (See *C* below).

C. Supervised Experiences.
1. *Supervised experiences in counseling and other guidance activities are provided as an integral part of the total counselor education program.*

    a. Settings in which such experiences are provided are appropriate for the preparation of secondary school counselors.
    b. These supervised experiences, including both observation of and work directly with secondary age youth, frequently are provided in the actual school situation.
    c. Opportunities are provided for working under supervision with parents and with a variety of school and community agency personnel.
    d. All such experiences are conducted under established ethical policies.
    e. Primary responsibility for all supervised experiences is assigned to counselor education staff members, qualified as stated in C–3–a below; secondary school counselors and advanced graduate students may be assigned subsidiary responsibilities.

2. *Three aspects of supervised experience are recognized in the coun-*

selor education program—laboratory experiences, practicum experiences and internship.

a. Laboratory experiences are provided in the first and/or second years.

   (1) Opportunities are provided for both observation and participation in activities related to the total guidance program, e.g. role-playing, listening to tapes, testing, organizing and using pupil personnel records, working with professional personnel, preparing and examining case studies, and using educational and occupational information materials.

   (2) Laboratory experiences appropriate to the counselor candidate's needs are a continuing part of the counselor education program.

   (3) Plans and procedures adopted by the staff clearly describe the integration of such experiences.

b. Practicum experiences are provided in the first and/or second years.

   (1) Practicum consists of counseling and small group work, both under supervision.

   (2) Practicum is conducted in settings which are appropriate for the preparation of secondary school counselors and which include young people with a variety of educational and vocational potential.

   (3) Practicum includes opportunity for continuing experiences in a series of counseling relationships with each of several secondary age youth.

   (4) A stated number of hours is spent by each counselor candidate in actual counseling relationships. This does not include time required for preparation and for supervisory consultations.

      (a) Counselor education students completing the two-year program spend 60 hours as a minimum.

      (b) Counselor education students completing a one-year program spend 30 hours as a minimum.

   (5) Opportunity is provided within the total workload for staff to supervise practicum experiences.

   (6) Media such as tape recorders, television and one-way vision screens are utilized in the supervision of the practicum activities.

(7) Practicum provides for a growth experience which is spread over a period of time.

(8) Supervised experiences are provided as an integral part of courses throughout the counselor education program of the student.

c. Internship may be provided. This is optional, though recommended.

(1) Internship is an advanced level of on-the-job supervised experience offered in a school setting.

(2) It is under the systematic supervision of qualified members of both the school staff and the institution's counselor education staff.

(3) It is normally a paid experience.

(4) Opportunities are provided for the counselor candidate to share responsibilities in all phases of the school guidance program.

3. *A well-qualified staff with adequate time allocated to supervision is provided.*

a. Members of the on-campus staff responsible for supervision

(1) have earned advanced degrees (preferably the doctorate) from accredited institutions.

(2) have had experience in counseling and related guidance activities with secondary age youth.

b. Secondary school staff members who supervise counselor candidates concurrently with the institution's staff should have at least two years of graduate work in counselor education or have equivalent preparation developed through long-term service and professional activity.

c. Doctoral students who supervise practicum experiences as a part of their preparation are under the supervision of staff members with appropriate advanced degrees and experience.

d. The counseling practicum is virtually a tutorial form of instruction; therefore, the supervision of five students is equivalent to the teaching of one three-semester-hour course. Such a ratio is considered maximum.

e. Supervision of internship is provided regularly by the cooperating secondary school staff and adequate staff time is allocated both for day-to-day supervision and for weekly supervisory conferences.

    f. Supervisors from the institution's staff have internship consultations and supervision assigned as part of their total workload.

    g. Time is allocated by the school system for secondary school staff members to assist in supervision of laboratory, practicum, and internship experiences.

4. *Appropriate facilities, equipment and materials are provided for supervised experiences in both on- and off-campus settings. (See Section IV.)*

D. The institution assists cooperating school systems, state departments of education, and individual school counselors with activities which contribute to in-service growth and to the improvement of the schools' guidance programs.

1. *There is a planned means of communication to encourage school and pupil personnel administrators to seek the institution's assistance in planning and conducting in-service education and program improvement activities.*

2. *The institution's staff is provided load recognition for their part in in-service and program development activities in the schools.*

3. *The institution's staff in counselor education involves its graduate students in its in-service and program development activities in the schools as a means of enriching their experiences.*

Section III. Selection, Retention, Endorsement, and Placement

1. *The institution has a procedure for identifying and selecting candidates for counselor education.*

    a. The counselor education staff has cooperatively developed criteria and procedures relating to selection, retention, endorsement, and placement.

    b. The criteria used for selection are consistent with the philosophy and objectives of the institution's counselor education program.

    c. Information about the counselor education program and about certification in the several states is available to the candidates.

    d. Qualified candidates may be drawn from various undergraduate fields and from various occupations.

       (1) Candidates who have been teachers have demonstrated superior competence as teachers.

(2) Candidates from fields other than teaching demonstrate their understanding of the secondary school and their competence to perform guidance and counseling functions in secondary schools by completing courses and supervised experiences planned for this purpose.

e. Members of the counselor education staff are available to confer with prospective candidates.

2. *The institution follows a defined procedure for the selective admission of candidates to the program of counselor education.*

   a. The candidate is assessed with respect to:
      (1) Capacity to do graduate work.
      (2) Familiarity with the objectives of the program.
      (3) Potential for developing effective relationships with youth, teachers, administrators, and parents.
      (4) Potential for engaging in research.

   b. The counselor education staff admits to the program only those candidates who meet the requirements established for admission to study in counselor education. These requirements may be in addition to those established by the institution for admission to graduate study.

   c. Decisions with respect to admission to the counselor education program are made by the staff (or by a committee) and not by any one staff member.

3. *The institution administers a planned program of selective retention, designating points within the program for evaluation of progress and informing of procedures for selective retention.*

   a. The counselor education staff has the responsibility of denying continuation in the program to any candidate whose level of academic performance and/or personal characteristics do not adequately meet institutional or professional standards.

   b. Each counselor candidate is encouraged to enter into a program of self-evaluation related to his retention in the program. To assist him in his growth in self-understanding, a counseling service separate from the counselor education program is available to him.

   c. When appropriate, cooperating school counselors and state supervisors and administrators are consulted concerning decisions about retention of candidates.

   d. Decisions with respect to retention or dismissal of a candidate are made by the staff (or by a committee) and not by any one staff member.

4. *The institution endorses successful candidates for certification and employment.*

   a. A statement of policy relating to the institution's procedure for formal endorsement has been adopted by the staff and approved by the proper administrative authority.

   b. Each candidate is informed of procedures for endorsement for certification and employment.

   c. The counselor education staff participates in this endorsement procedure.

   d. Endorsement is given only on the basis of evidence of proficiency. This implies that the candidate has completed a substantial part of his graduate work in counselor education, including supervised counseling experience, at the endorsing institution, and that his personal growth is considered to have been satisfactory.

5. *The institution provides a placement service.*

   a. Placement service organization and procedures are consistent with established principles of student personnel work.

   b. Provision is made for the participation of personnel from the state department of education and cooperating schools in the placement of candidates and their induction into the profession.

   c. Students are assisted as needed in the preparation of placement papers.

   d. Staff members utilize individual professional relationships to assist in the placement of their graduates.

   e. Assistance is provided in the evaluation of job opportunities and in the selection of positions appropriate to the individual's qualifications.

   f. The placement service provides continuing assistance to the candidate throughout his professional career.

6. *The institution maintains a program of research designed to evaluate its selection, retention, endorsement, and placement procedures.*

   a. School counselors, administrators, and state department of education personnel, when appropriate, participate in the planning and execution of the follow-up program and other evaluative procedures.

b. The program of evaluation and follow-up includes early leavers as well as those who complete the program.

c. Evaluation is followed by appropriate revisions and improvements.

Section IV. Support for the Counselor Education Program, Administrative Relations, and Institutional Resources

1. *Administrative organization and procedures provide recognition of and designated responsibilities for a counselor education program.*

   a. The program is a clearly identified part of an institutional graduate program.
      (1) There is only one unit responsible for the preparation of school counselors.
      (2) The program is oriented toward and administered through the unit responsible for graduate work in education.
   b. Cooperative relationships exist between the counselor education program and other units of the institution related to the program.
      (1) Contributions of other units to the program are defined.
      (2) Channels of communication with staff members in other units are identified and maintained.
   c. Use is made of a wide range of professional and community resources.
      (1) Sound working relations exist with state department of education, public and private schools, community agencies, and professional organizations.
      (2) Effective use is made of a wide variety of resource material and personnel.

2. *The institution provides for the professional development of the staff as well as students in the counselor education program.*

   a. Staff members are active in professional leadership and research on a local, state, regional, and national level.
   b. Staff members are participating in voluntary professional service capacities.
   c. Staff members engage in programs of research and contribute to the literature of the field.

    d. The institution provides encouragement and financial support for the staff to participate in such professional activities.

    e. The program exemplifies high professional standards in all relationships to students.

    f. Students learn about and participate in the activities of professional organizations.

3. *The institution provides adequate faculty and staff for all aspects of the counselor education program.*

    a. An individual is designated as the responsible professional leader of the counselor education program.

       (1) This individual is an experienced counselor and possesses an earned doctorate from an accredited institution in counselor education, or a closely related area.

       (2) This individual has a primary and preferably a full-time assignment to the counselor education program.

       (3) This individual's other responsibilities are consistent with and supportive of his primary obligations to the program of counselor education.

       (4) This individual is recognized for his leadership and service activities in the profession.

       (5) This individual is qualified by preparation and experience to conduct or to supervise research activities.

    b. A minimum basic staff includes the equivalent of at least three full-time qualified persons whose primary assignment is in counselor education, to insure staff depth to carry out curricular responsibilities of the professional studies and of the supervised practice and to provide program advisory service and supervision of research.

       (1) In addition to the designated leader of the staff this includes at least the equivalent of two full-time faculty members with qualifications comparable to those of the chairman, or director, of the counselor education program.

       (2) Additional basic staff members are provided in a ratio of approximately the equivalent of one full-time staff member for every eight full-time graduate students or their equivalent in part-time graduate students.

       (3) The full-time teaching load of these staff members is consistent with that of other graduate departments in the institution.

       (4) This load is modified in proportion to assigned responsi-

bilities for graduate advisement and research supervision on some formula which is consistent with established graduate school policy in the institution.

(5) Time is provided within the total workload for cooperative interdisciplinary activity with staff members in related fields.

(6) The total workload of staff members includes a recognition of time needed for professional research.

c. Faculty in related disciplines are qualified in their respective areas and also are informed about the objectives of counselor education.

d. Off-campus school personnel who supervise counselor candidates are qualified through academic preparation and professional experience.

(1) A basic policy provides for the identification and recognition of these staff members as an integral part of the counselor education staff.

(2) Such staff members have two or more years of appropriate professional experience.

(3) These staff members have at least two years of graduate work in counselor education or have equivalent preparation developed through long-term service and professional activity.

e. Graduate assistantships are provided to reduce routine demands on staff and to provide additional experiences to students in the program.

(1) Regular procedures are established for the identification and assignment of qualified students to these assistantships.

(2) These assignments are made in such a way as to enrich the professional learning experiences of the graduate assistants.

f. Adequate secretarial and clerical staff is provided in the counselor education program.

(1) Clerical responsibilities are defined and responsibility for supervision of clerical staff is clearly identified.

(2) A minimum of one full-time secretary is provided for the clerical work of the counselor education program.

(3) Additional clerical service is provided on a ratio of approximately one full-time clerical assistant for every three faculty members.

4. *For the counselor education program the institution provides facilities and a budget which are sufficient to insure continuous operation of all aspects of the program.*

   a. The institution provides a designated headquarters for the counselor education program.

     (1) This headquarters is located near the classrom and laboratory facilities used in the counselor education program.

     (2) The headquarters area includes well-equipped private offices for all professional staff members.

     (3) The headquarters area includes office space for clerical staff and graduate assistants.

   b. Practicum facilities are provided on and/or off campus in cooperating schools or other agencies.

     (1) These facilities include an adequate number of counseling offices.

     (2) Facilities are equipped with recording and listening devices for observation and supervision.

     (3) One-way vision screens are located in such a way as to provide for observation by an individual or by a whole class.

     (4) If the institution has closed-circuit television facilities, these are available to the program of counselor education.

     (5) Conference rooms are provided for tape analysis and small group conferences.

     (6) Portable recorders are available in sufficient numbers.

     (7) Seminar rooms are provided.

     (8) Ample and appropriate audio-visual and demonstration materials are available for staff and student use.

     (9) A variety of resource material is available for the demonstration and use of current information services and guidance. Included are files of educational and occupational information materials.

   c. Library facilities provide a rich supply of resource materials for both research and study in counselor education.

     (1) These include basic resources, both books and periodicals,

in guidance, counseling, personality appraisal, psychology, sociology, economics, and other related disciplines.

(2) Both current and historical materials are available.

(3) Library resources are available during both evening and weekend hours.

(4) Inter-Library loans, microfilm, and photocopy services are available.

(5) Multiple copies of frequently used publications are available.

d. Guidance and counseling center facilities are utilized on and/or off campus for the supervised experiences.

(1) Opportunities are provided for both observation and participation.

(2) These facilities provide for a broad variety of types and levels of experience and thus provide an understanding of a wide range of professional guidance and counseling activities both in and out of the school setting.

e. Testing laboratory facilities are available.

(1) Files of tests and test interpretation data are available.

(2) Space for both group and individual testing is provided.

(3) Students have access to test scoring equipment.

f. Research facilities are available to both staff and students in counselor education.

(1) Facilities include offices and laboratories equipped to provide opportunities for collection, analysis and summary of data.

(2) Calculators are provided in these offices for research work.

(3) Consultant services are available from research specialists on the institution's staff.

(4) Access is provided to campus computer centers and other data-processing laboratories.

(5) Settings are provided in which research can be conducted, including campus laboratories and secondary schools which provide enabling relationships to student and staff in counselor education.

5. *The institution recognizes the individual needs of graduate students and provides services for personal as well as professional development.*

a. Since full-time academic-year attendance is possible for most graduate students only if some form of financial assistance is available, every effort is made to develop appropriate assistantships and fellowships in counselor education.

   (1) The counselor education program is assigned a proportionate share of the total number of graduate assistantships and fellowships provided.
   (2) Part-time work opportunities appropriate for students in the program are identified and efforts are made to secure assignments for those desiring such assistance.
   (3) Loan resources are made available to students in counselor education.
   (4) Prospective students are provided information about possible sources of financial assistance.

b. Personal counseling services are available to all counselor candidates.

   (1) Available counselors are identified.
   (2) This service is available from staff members other than the members of the counselor education staff.
   (3) Patterns for referral are known to all staff members.

CURRENT AND FUTURE STATUS OF ACCREDITING COUNSELOR EDUCATION*

ROBERT O. STRIPLING

The term "accreditation" has provoked conflicting feelings among the membership of our Association during the last decade. At the same time, much professional activity has centered around the development of standards or guidelines to be used by institutions of higher education in the valuation of counselor education programs. Many people have feared that the acceptance of standards would pave the way for the adoption of criteria for accreditation which might tend to stabilize too much the content of counselor education at a time when there is a rapid expansion of concepts, such as those relating to human development, counseling and other helping relationship theories, vocational development theories, and measurement theories. Others have ex-

* Reprinted from *Counselor Education and Supervision*, 7:200-209, 1968, with permission of the American Personnel and Guidance Association and the author.

pressed concern over the possibility that the presence of more formal criteria for accreditation might cause counselor educators to become inhibited in the area of improving methods of instruction at a time when new media, such as video equipment and computers are becoming available. Still others have felt that our profession might lose control over the determination of content in counselor education through the acceptance of cooperative arrangements with accrediting agencies.

Arguments for Accreditation

During this decade, however, there has been a gradual realization that our emerging profession had an obligation to protect society, insofar as possible, from poorly prepared counselors; and perhaps the best way to accomplish this goal would be through accrediting of counselor education programs. Among the other arguments in favor of accreditation have been the following:

1. Accreditation can be used as a vehicle to improve the quality of counselor education.

2. Criteria for accreditation can include certain minimums that are quantitative in nature but essential in all counselor education programs. (For example, experience has taught us that such things as qualified staff, library materials, and physical facilities are necessary aspects of all counselor education programs.)

3. Criteria for accreditation, as well as reports of visiting teams, can be useful by college administrators in determining strengths and weaknesses of counselor education programs.

4. The process of accreditation can serve to give visibility to counselor education programs within the complexity of the college community. This is important when one recognizes that among programs of preparation in higher education, counselor education is relatively expensive and there are so many pressures on college administrators for funds to initiate and develop various programs on any campus.

5. At a time when millions of dollars of tax monies are being spent to prepare as well as employ counselors and other personnel specialists, it is important for agencies having the responsibility for the distribution of these funds to have some criteria

by which to judge the quality of counselor education programs. Frequently, agencies follow the practice of awarding monies to only those programs that are accredited.

6. Accreditation criteria can serve as guidelines to assist institutions of higher education in developing new counselor education programs during a period when there is a heavy demand for additional counselors and other personnel specialists.

Also, we have had called to our attention on many occasions during the last decade that since over ninety percent of all counselor education programs are under the direct control of departments or colleges of education, many of these programs are already being accredited by the National Council for Accreditation of Teacher Education (NCATE). This is being done even though no specific criteria for accrediting counselor education have been developed; and, in many cases, no qualified supervisor, counselor, or counselor educator is on an institutional visiting committee. With this realization in mind, ACES National Committee on Standards for the Preparation of Secondary School Counselors, in August 1963, posed the following questions to representatives of NCATE.

"*Item 1:* Counselor Education programs (and APGA) are concerned with the preparation of counselors for all educational settings (elementary through college) and for all areas closely allied to education, such as Rehabilitation Counseling Agencies and Employment Agencies.

"Question: Is NCATE's interest in standards this broad?

"*Item 2:* Counselor Education programs are graduate level programs.

"Question: Does NCATE have the authority to evaluate graduate level programs?"

"*Item 3:* While the great majority of Counselor Education programs are under the direct control of divisions of education in institutions of higher learning, a few are under the direct control of other divisions of colleges and universities.

"Question: Does NCATE have the responsibility for evaluating programs that are not directly under the supervision of divisions of education?

"*Item 4:* APGA is concerned over the fact that NCATE is evaluating Counselor Education programs even though standards in this area have not been developed by NCATE. Visiting committees, in many cases, do not include qualified Counselor Educators.

"Question: Can working relationships be agreed upon that would protect the interests of APGA in these and similar matters relating to Counselor Education?" (Stripling, 1965)

While the above questions have never been answered directly, officials of both the National Commission on Accrediting (NCA), the parent organization of NCATE (as well as other college and university accrediting groups), and NCATE have expressed a willingness to assist APGA in the development of working relationships which would lead to a more satisfactory accrediting procedure.

Limiting Factors in Accreditation Processes

Throughout these deliberations leadership in both ACES and APGA has recognized the existence of certain limitations with respect to our choices concerning accreditation. Among them are the following:

1. NCA, composed of college presidents, must approve procedure relating to accreditation in colleges and universities of the United States. While NCA has been sympathetic to the concept that different professional groups should exercise both leadership and control over accreditation in their area of specialization, there has been a realization that complete freedom for each professional group could lead to a proliferation of accrediting procedures that would be detrimental to higher education. In fact, one of the primary reasons for the establishment of NCA was to create an umbrella organization which could assume the responsibility for the coordination of accrediting in higher education. NCA does not wish to stifle the efforts of different professional groups to improve the quality of preparation, but it does

realistically recognize the fact that activities in the area of accreditation by different professional groups involved in higher education must be coordinated.

2. While the officials of NCATE have expressed a willingness to cooperate with our Association in the development of more specific guidelines for accrediting counselor education and in designating competent counselors, counselor educators, and supervisors who might serve on visiting teams, it is recognized that NCATE would resist the development of an independent agency to evaluate any aspect of programs in colleges or departments of education.

3. NCA will not enter into formal agreements relating to accrediting with professional organizations. Any independent body with which NCA or its affiliates makes formal agreements must have at least half of its membership from college professors teaching in the given area of specialization.

4. NCA and its member organizations are willing to enter into formal agreements with only groups that represent broad segments of preparation. For example, they would be reluctant, and perhaps unwilling, to reach formal agreements with a group interested only in high school counseling. However, it should be stated that in all meetings with representatives of both NCA and NCATE during the last decade, these officials have expressed a strong desire to support the improvement of the quality of accreditation in counselor education. They have recognized also that there may be wisdom in taking initial steps in improving accrediting criteria and procedures in certain aspects of counselor education, e.g. school counseling, if at the same time plans are being made to reach an eventual goal of improving accreditation in all aspects of counselor education.

Professional Groups, Standards, and Accreditation

Leaders in ACES realize that a number of professional groups, including other divisions of APGA as well as organizations not affiliated with APGA, are concerned about accrediting programs of professional preparation in the broad field of counseling and personnel work. Also, ACES has recognized the importance of working through channels of APGA in reaching agreements concerning accrediting of counselor education programs. For these reasons, both informal and formal meetings have been held during the last decade with many groups, such as:

National Association of Foreign Student Advisors
National Association of Collegiate Registrars and Admissions Officers
Association of College Admissions Counselors
American School Counselor Association
National Employment Counselor Association
National Association of Student Personnel Administrators
American College Personnel Association
Association for Counselor Education and Supervision
Association of College and University Housing Officers
Council of Student Personnel Associations in Higher Education
National Association of Women Deans and Counselors
American Association of Junior Colleges
American Rehabilitation Counseling Association
Association of College Unions

While no formal agreements have been reached in meetings with these and other groups, there seem to have emerged the following ideas:

1. The only aspect of counselor education that is now ready for more formal arrangements relating to accreditation is school counseling. This is true for several reasons. First, in the spring of 1967, the membership of ACES and the Executive Council of APGA approved "Standards for the Preparation of Secondary School Counselors—1967" (ACES, 1967). Second, the membership of ACES is expected to accept, at an early date, standards for the preparation of elementary school counselors. It is felt that these two documents can serve as bases for developing criteria for accrediting programs of preparation for school counselors even though it is recognized that it is not possible to separate all facets of school counselor preparation from other aspects of a well-integrated program of counselor education where coun-

selors and other personnel specialists for settings other than schools are being prepared.

2. It is anticipated that other areas, such as employment service counseling, rehabilitation counseling, technical school and junior college counseling and personnel work, and college and university counseling and personnel work, will have developed standards for preparation within the next several months which can be used as guidelines for self-evaluation as well as for developing accreditation criteria and procedures.

3. Long-range plans should envision the development of one set of criteria which might be used to accredit all areas of counselor education. It is recognized that much time and effort will be needed to develop such a document.

4. In order to coordinate the efforts toward the goal of developing one set of criteria for accreditation and to meet the stipulation that an accrediting group cooperating with NCA and NCATE must be independent of any association, it has been suggested that a Council on Graduate Education in Personnel and Guidance be established. The majority of the members of this council would be teaching staff in counselor education programs presently accredited by NCATE and other members of the council might be representatives of professional associations concerned with accrediting in the personnel and guidance fields. While the membership on the council would initially be composed of those directly concerned with accrediting in school counselor preparation, the membership would be expanded as other areas are ready to enter agreements concerning accreditation. No doubt, such a council would need an active executive committee which would represent different regions of the country, levels of preparation, and types of specialization in counselor education.

5. NCA and NCATE will need to reach some agreement concerning the accrediting of programs of preparation not directly under the control of departments or colleges of education. For the present, it seems feasible to negotiate directly with NCATE concerning the accreditation of school counselor education.

6. A list of qualified individuals from the personnel and guidance field who will be available to serve on visiting teams to in-

stitutions of higher education should be prepared and presented to NCATE. It would be expected that at least one person from this list would be a member of any visiting team to an institution having a program of preparation in school counseling. As other areas of preparation reach agreements about accreditation, this list would be expanded.

7. That the Executive Board of NCATE be expanded to include a representative from the proposed Council on Graduate Education in Personnel and Guidance.

8. That a close working relationship between the proposed Council on Graduate Education in Personnel and Guidance and NCATE be established and that NCA be kept informed concerning developments relative to accreditation in the broad field of guidance and personnel work.

9. There should be established, as soon as possible, an Interassociation Study Committee on Personnel and Guidance Accreditation. It would be the responsibility of this committee to develop, in cooperation with NCA and other professional groups, a long-range plan for the development of a single set of criteria to be used in accrediting all programs in counselor education. Also, the committee would have the responsibility for: (a) encouraging the development of standards for preparation in specific areas of guidance and personnel work; (b) supporting programs of experimentation where both standards for preparation and criteria for accreditation are used; and (c) assuming leadership in developing criteria and a procedure for accreditation for all of counselor education.

Projected Steps Toward Accreditation

At a business meeting during the 1967 convention, the membership of ACES voted to establish a subcommittee on accreditation which would function under the general direction of the PPS Committee of ACES. This subcommittee was charged with the responsibility of promoting the establishment of a council which would have the responsibility of providing leadership in working out procedures for accrediting counselor education programs. The committee, subsequently appointed (Paul F. Munger; Gilbert D. Moore; and Robert O. Stripling, Chairman), felt that the intent of the action establishing the committee was to provide a vehicle which would allow ACES to cooperate with both the Executive Council and the PPS Committee of APGA in promoting the development of cooperative efforts in the area of accreditation of counselor education programs. On July 2-3, 1967, this subcommittee met with the PPS Committee of APGA and reached the following agreements:

1. The PPS Committee of APGA would take the leadership in negotiating with NCATE to develop criteria and procedures for accrediting programs for the preparation of school counselors. The ACES standards for the preparation of secondary school counselors and the proposed standards for the preparation of elementary school counselors would be used as basic documents in preparing criteria to be used by NCATE.

2. The PPS Committee of APGA would prepare a list of qualified individuals to serve on visiting committees for NCATE and present this list to NCATE.

3. There would be established an interim committee which would be charged with the responsibility of creating a Council on Graduate Education in Counselor Education. It would be the responsibility of this council (a) to work with NCATE in reaching agreements concerning immediate steps in developing criteria and procedures to be used in accrediting programs of counselor education in school counseling and (b) to provide leadership in working toward the goal of one set of criteria and procedures to be used in accrediting all programs of preparation for counselors and other personnel specialists.

4. The president of the APGA would be requested to assume the leadership in gaining the cooperation of other interested professional groups in establishing an Inter-association Accreditation Study Committee. The purpose of this committee would be to develop a comprehensive plan for accreditation of programs of preparation in the broad fields of counseling and personnel work.

5. To request that the executive director of APGA arrange a meeting between representatives of the PPS Committee of APGA and NCATE for the purpose of negotiating agreements concern-

ing the accreditation of programs of preparation for school counselors.

In September 1967, NCATE accepted the following proposal from the PPS Committee of APGA:

This is a proposal for use by the National Council for Accreditation of Teacher Education of the new American Personnel and Guidance Association standards for school counselor preparation on a three-year experimental basis. These *standards* have been developed over the past ten years and have been used on a voluntary institutional self-review basis. The standards should be used for advisory purposes as a supplement to existing NCATE accreditating criteria now in force. That is, an institution's counselor education program would be appraised and evaluated in the usual manner, and the institution would also be informed of the results of the application of the new counselor education standards.

Various campuses would be selected from among those which are to be evaluated by NCATE and asked to participate voluntarily in the experimental use of the new standards. Probably, not more than ten institutions should be so involved each year. Both multi-purpose and small institutions should be included.

The period of experimental use would be three years. However, the results of the trial use of the standards would be assessed during the third year, so that evaluative use of the new standards by NCATE could begin no later than the end of the third year, if desirable.

Responsibility for conducting the experimental study would belong to an Advisory Committee on Accreditation in Counselor Education comprised of the American Personnel and Guidance Association—Professional Preparation and Standards Committee (seven members), the Association for Counselor Education and Supervision Subcommittee on Accreditation (two members), and one representative each from the National Council for Accreditation of Teacher Education, the Association of College Admissions Counselors, and the National Association of Women Deans and Counselors. The President of the American Personnel and Guidance Association would name a Committee chairman and would invite NCATE, ACA, and NAWDC to name their representatives. This Committee would assess the results of the experimental use of the standards, would report them to the APGA Executive Council and NCATE, and see agreement with NCATE about the official adoption of the standards.

The Committee would also provide NCATE with an official list of approved visitors from which one person acceptable to NCATE and the institution would be chosen as the counselor education specialist on the visitation team. The Committee would also choose three panelists who would assess the results of the use of the Standards at a particular institution.

Once appointed, the counselor education specialist would participate as a member of the visitation team just as any other member. The institution would have used the new Standards and the current ones in providing faculty descriptions of its counselor education program and the visitor would have received a copy of both reports. He would conduct the visit and make his own reports on both Standards.

The current Standards report would be integrated with the total report of the visiting team as usual, while the new Standards report would be forwarded to a three-man panel named by the Advisory Committee on Accreditation from the approved list at the same time that the visitor is appointed. The Committee would receive the assessment of the panel and the visitor's report. These would be confidential, open only to NCATE officials. These data would furnish the basis for evaluating the effectiveness of the new Standards.

Accreditation involves the process of education. It is well known that no individual or group can legislate quality programs in counselor education or in any other field of professional preparation. It is only through education and encouragement that counselor education programs can be improved. Our association, during the last decade, has only taken the initial steps in the direction of developing sound criteria and procedures for accrediting counselor education. Many challenges and much hard work lie ahead of us. Also, it must be recognized that NCATE, NCA, and other accrediting groups face tremendous problems. The question of the proliferation of groups interested in accreditation, one of the major reasons for the organization of NCA, will soon face NCATE. Such groups as the following have or will in the near future develop standards for preparation and request that NCATE negotiate concerning accreditation: school administrators, library science personnel, music educators, English educators, social studies educators, vocational and technical educators, and adult education educators. Obviously, each of the various segments of education, under the umbrella of NCATE, cannot have completely separate accreditation procedures. No doubt, NCATE will be faced with the necessity of establishing general criteria for accreditation of colleges of education and each college will be faced with the responsibility of applying specific criteria for the evaluation and accreditation of various aspects of its program. This will call for a close cooperative effort between the various professional groups involved in programs of preparation within colleges of education. As we work on standards of preparation and criteria for accreditation of programs of preparation in the broad field of guidance and personnel work, we must also prepare ourselves to work more cooperatively with other professional groups and organizations that have an interest in counselor education.

References

Association for Counselor Education and Supervision: Standards for the preparation of secondary school counselors—1967. *Personnel and Guidance Journal*, 46:96-106, 1967.

Stripling, R. O.: Standards for the education of school counselors. In *Counseling, a Growing Profession*. Washington, D.C., American Personnel and Guidance Association, 1965.

SUPPORT PERSONNEL FOR THE COUNSELOR: THEIR TECHNICAL AND NON-TECHNICAL ROLES AND PREPARATION *

APGA PROFESSIONAL PREPARATION AND STANDARDS COMMITTEE

We are pleased to present to all interested persons a statement of policy on the role, function, and preparation of support personnel for the counselor. This presentation is in recognition of the work of the members of the Professional Preparation and Standards Committee, as well as the many other individuals who contributed to the development of the statement over a period of nearly 18 months, beginning in late summer, 1965. Especially influential in initiating and expediting the project of defining the policy were Past-President Winfield Scott, President Kenneth Hoyt, former Executive Director Arthur Hitchcock, and Executive Director Willis Dugan. The policy statement on support personnel for the counselor was adopted by the National Executive Council of AGPA at its November 1966 meeting.

The statement is repeated below. We hope that counselors,

---

* Reprinted from the *Personnel and Guidance Journal*, 45:858-861, 1967, with permission of the American Personnel and Guidance Association.

counselor educators, employers of counselors, and others who are interested in and concerned about providing counseling services to the American people will read the policy statement thoughtfully. This policy is *not* intended to describe any particular occupation that may fall within the rubric of support personnel or one of its synonyms. Rather, a number of guiding principles have been set forth that should help others to define the roles and functions of support personnel in specific jobs. Similarly, it will be apparent to readers that the policy statement deals with relationships between counselors and support personnel who work with counselors, but *not* with relationships between counselors and other professionals, nor with relationships between other professionals and their support personnel. Activities of support personnel for counselors have been described for the purpose of illustrating principles. They do *not* constitute an exhaustive or definitive list of support personnel activities or duties.

We think that this statement of policy on support personnel for the counselor is timely and relevant to the needs of a rapidly changing society. The demand for more and better counseling services is spreading throughout all parts of the nation. This policy recognizes that meeting societal needs for counseling increasingly requires collaborative efforts from counselors, other professionals, and support personnel in order to be most effective. Your thoughtful reaction is earnestly solicited.

A STATEMENT OF POLICY ADOPTED BY THE AMERICAN PERSONNEL AND GUIDANCE ASSOCIATION

Rationale for Support Personnel for Counselors

The extensive forces for change in American society are having critical impact upon our educational, manpower, welfare and other institutions. A growing series of federal laws assigns a fundamental and greatly broadened role to the counseling and guidance movement in meeting the needs of additional people in a variety of life situations. The problems of helping people progress in education, and relate themselves to productive work, requires professionals and paraprofessionals to do different tasks, with various skills.

Recent federal legislation, creating greatly increased demand for personnel to provide relevant services, includes the Manpower Development and Training Act, the Economic Opportunity Act, the Vocational Education Act, amendments to the National Defense Education Act, amendments to the Vocational Rehabilitation Act, the Elementary and Secondary Education Act, and the so-called "Cold War G.I. Bill." These necessitate new approaches to the provision of services so as to make more efficient and effective use of personnel now providing these services.

This has resulted in the development of a new group of personnel positions which are variously referred to as auxiliary, technical, non-professional, paraprofessional, or support personnel. The concept of such positions is not new. It has been accepted by many professional groups. However, the systematic programming of support personnel is new in connection with the work of the counselor.

It is necessary first to consider previously published policy statements which outline the role and functions of professional counselors before we can determine the duties of support personnel. A general policy statement has been prepared by the Professional Preparation and Standards Committee of AGPA, and several of the divisions have published policy statements concerned with the work of the counselor in specific settings.

These reports and a series of related articles on counselor role and function have been published in a manual entitled *Counseling, a Growing Profession.**

It is the position of the Association that appropriately prepared support personnel, under the supervision of the counselor, can contribute to meeting counselees' needs by enhancing the work of the counselor. The appropriate use of such personnel will facilitate the work of the counselor and make the total endeavor more effective.

Guiding Principles

It is the purpose of this document to identify the principles and concepts that undergird the roles and preparation of support personnel. It provides guidelines for the development of specific functions within specific settings. There is no intention of providing detailed job descriptions for such personnel. This document, however, should provide guidelines for the development of such job descriptions.

The concept of support personnel does not refer to reciprocal lateral relationships between the counselor and collaborating occupants,

---

* Loughary, J. W. (Ed.). American Personnel and Guidance Association, 1685 New Hampshire Ave., N.W., Washington, D.C.; 1965.

such as social workers, psychologists, physicians, or placement directors.

This statement deals only with a discussion of relationships between the counselor and various support personnel. This approach is not based upon a lack of interest and/or understanding of the imporance of "reciprocal lateral relationships between the counselor and collaborating occupations." It is based upon a recognition of the importance and scope of such relationships, which means that each of these occupations may establish policies relative to support personnel, and finally that the concept of reciprocal relationships is by itself quite worthy of separate research and study.

Career patterns must also be considered in delineating between the counselor and support personnel. Support personnel jobs may or may not be terminal. In the event that support personnel wish to be upgraded to full professional status, it is to be understood that they must meet the necessary academic and personal characteristics of professional counselors.

Even though agency policy and hiring practices may ultimately determine the actual role of support personnel, the counselor must have a voice in determining what specific duties can be performed by such personnel. There are certain services, such as the establishment of a formal counseling relationship, for which the counselor must maintain responsibility and which only a counselor can provide. There are certain other services—such as orientation, outreach and recruitment activities, follow-up, development of job readiness, and improvement of personal appearance—which may be more appropriately provided by specially oriented and adequately prepared support personnel. It is essential that a coordinated pattern of professional and support services be provided.

The activities of support personnel differ from the work of the counselor in several basic respects:

1. The counselor performs the counseling function described in the professional policy statements cited above, while support personnel may perform important and necessary activities that contribute to the overall service.

2. The work of the counselor involves synthesis and integration of interrelated parts of the total range of services with, and in behalf of the counselee. The work of support personnel tends toward the particular and becomes an integral part of the larger whole only as this is developed under the leadership of the counselor.

3. The counselor bases his performance on the use of relevant theory, authoritative knowledge of effective procedures, and evaluation of the total endeavor. Functions of support personnel are characterized by more limited theoretical background and specialization in one or more support functions.

Typical Activities of Support Personnel

The role of the counselor is subtly but constantly changing, a fact that is characteristic of any dynamic profession. Since the definition of roles for support personnel is dependent on their relationship to the counselor's role, it is inevitable that support personnel roles will also change. Today, however, it is advisable to consider an analysis of the total complex of roles and responsibilities involved, in order to identify supporting activities or duties that may be performed satisfactorily by support personnel rather than by the counselor. Such activities or duties are related to specific clusters, which may be called functions, in the total complex of the professional role.

The performance of identified activities by support personnel will contribute to the work of the counselor. Sometimes the tasks supportive of counselor functions are assigned to persons who are not working in support personnel positions. It should be noted that nothing in this paper should be construed as meaning that support personnel should take the place, or responsibility, of the counselor. On other occasions, enough supporting activities can be logically related to constitute a full-time support personnel position. The counselor is, nevertheless, responsible for incorporating all such tasks into a meaningful pattern of services to the counselee.

Direct Helping Relationships

A number of support personnel activities involve direct person-to-person helping relationships, but they are not identical or equivalent to counseling as conducted by the counselor. Prominent among these functions and activities would be the following:

1. Individual Interviewing Function.

   a. Secure information from an interviewee by means of a semistructured or structured interview schedule. The information elicited would tend to be factual and limited in nature.

   b. Give information prepared in advance and approved by the counselor for its appropriateness for the interviewee.

Such information would usually be factual rather than interpretative.

c. Explain in practical lay terms the purposes and procedures involved in the services to the counselee.

d. Engage the counselee in informal, casual discussion as a means of putting him at ease and establishing an openness to counseling. Such a dyadic activity may be especially important when performed by an interviewer who is making initial contact with potential counselees who are hostile toward or apprehensive of counseling.

e. Provide informal follow-up support to a former counselee.

2. Small-Group Interviewing or Discussion Function.

a. In structured groups with a largely pre-planned program, guide discussions as a discussion leader.

b. Describe staff and material available to the group, as an information resource person, or tell the group how and where to acquire needed resources.

c. Act as recorder in a variety of small-group discussion or counseling situations, under the supervision of the counselor.

d. Observe verbal and nonverbal interaction in groups, following predetermined cues and procedures for making observations.

e. Participate in informal, superficial social conversation in a small group of counselees to help put them at ease and to establish the beginning of helping relationships that may be provided by forthcoming counseling.

f. Informally provide information and support to former counselees.

g. Perform outreach activities.

Indirect Helping Relationships

Most of the activities of support personnel appear to provide help indirectly rather than directly to counselees, even though some of these activities do involve face-to-face relationships with counselees. Among the functions and activities may be these:

1. Information Gathering and Processing Function.

a. Administer, score, and profile routine standardized tests and other appraisal instruments (nonclinical type).

b. Obtain and maintain routine information on the scope and character of the world of work with current reference to employment trends, in accordance with instructions established by the counselor.

c. Contact various sources for needed records and related information relevant to counseling.

d. Search for new sources of information about counselees, and/or the environment, under direction of the counselor.

e. Prepare educational, occupational, and personal-social information for visual-auditory verbal and graphic presentation or transmittal to others for use, in accordance with instructions established by the counselor.

f. Under the counselor's supervision, search for new sources to which the counselee may be referred.

g. Secure specific special information about former counselees upon request and under the supervision of the counselor.

h. Operate technical communications media involving printed and electronic processes on a visual-auditory nature for the counselee's benefit.

2. Referral Function.

a. Initiate general contacts with specific referral agencies.

b. Initiate contact for specific individuals with given referral agencies.

c. Aid individuals in making proper contact with referral agencies.

3. Placement and Routine Follow-up Function.

a. Through appropriate channels, establish and maintain working relationships with organized placement agencies in the community.

b. Develop specific placement opportunities (under the supervision of the counselor) for the individual cases not handled through cooperation with other placement agencies.

c. Maintain continuous surveys of placement conditions and trends as requested by the counselor.

d. Search for new placement resources that may be useful to counselees.

e. Secure follow-up information of a routine nature according to a general follow-up plan.

4. Program Planning and Management Function.

   a. Perform routine collecting and analytical statistical operations as a research assistant.
   b. Procure and prepare supplies of materials of various sorts for the counselor.
   c. Prepare standardized reports of contacts with counselees, potential counselees, and referral, placement, and follow-up agencies and persons.
   d. Maintain appropriate personnel and information records for the counselor.
   c. Supervise and coordinate the activities of clerical or other skilled personnel under the general supervision of the counselor.

The Preparation of Support Personnel

The preparation of support personnel will vary according to a number of factors. Among those that must be considered are the following:

1. People who wish to become support personnel must be selected for their potential ability to perform specific duties, and for their suitability for working with counselors and counselees in particular settings. Selection must not be restricted to those who may be capable of earning academic degrees since, in actual practice, many of these positions may be terminal in nature. Such people will come from a wide variety of educational and experiential backgrounds.

It may be possible to find people who already possess the necessary competencies, depending upon the local setting and the accumulation and organization of specific duties and/or tasks into payroll jobs. Pre-planning by supervising counselors and agency, or institutional, administrative personnel, relative to the development of support personnel payroll jobs, will be imperative.

2. The duration of pre-service preparation for support personnel will be fairly brief compared to that of the counselor, that is, a matter of weeks or months, compared to years. In-service preparation of support personnel on the job is essential to the ultimate success of the program. Such preparation should be initiated on a carefully planned basis.

3. The activities to be learned may be rather concrete and specific. In most cases this will imply an inductive approach to the development of background, theoretical, and philosophical understand-

ings. There may be a necessary emphasis upon frequent practice or drill. The preparation must utilize field settings, and/or laboratory simulations.

4. At least the final portions of a preparation program must involve opportunities to work under the field supervision of counselors. There should be supervised preparation of members of a team of support personnel.

5. The staff for support personnel preparation programs should include experienced, highly successful support personnel, counselors, and counselor educators.

6. It would be advantageous to support personnel preparation programs and counselor education programs if they could be coordinated in terms of content, time, and physical proximity.

Chapter 3

CHARACTERISTICS OF THE EFFECTIVE
COUNSELOR TRAINEE

IT HARDLY SEEMS APPROPRIATE to examine the process of counselor education and supervision without considering one of its most important components, the trainee. The history of research on this topic has been rather discouraging. Educators, uneasy about accepting empirically unvalidated selection techniques, initiated some rather ambitious efforts to predict which applicants to their program would be successful (Kelly and Fisk, 1951; Holt and Luborsky, 1958). Such efforts have not seemingly led to any dramatic changes in selection procedures. Graduate programs in psychology and counseling seem to continue the practice of selecting applicants on the basis of undergraduate grades and selected tests of academic ability. Some evidence (e.g. Wittmer and Lister, 1971) suggests a negligible relationship between counseling skill and indices of academic ability.

The situation is not as discouraging as it might seem, however, as a considerable amount of research has been addressed to the topic. This chapter offers a sample of work published over the past ten-year period.

One of the more promising approaches to the selection of counselor candidates has been the use of sociometric peer ratings (Gade, 1967; Passons and Olsen, 1969). McDougall and Reitan, in their paper "The Use of a Peer Rating Technique in Appraising Attributes of Counselor Trainees," implement this approach with students enrolled in a National Defense Education Act Institute. Significant correlations were obtained between selected peer ratings and a number of criteria, including the supervisor's rating of counseling competency, composite grade point, and Miller Analogies Test (MAT) scores.

Using a global rating of overall counseling competence made

by members of the faculty, Jansen, Robb, and Bonk reported a number of variables that were related to this criterion. Measures of intellectual ability as well as chronological age seemed to be related to rated professional competence. A number of personality variables from the Guilford-Zimmerman Temperament Survey and the Minnesota Teacher Attitude Inventory also correlated with the criterion significantly.

Asa, in his article "Interview Behavior and Counselor Personality Variables," pursued the relevance of personality variables further, using the Edwards Personal Preference Schedule (EPPS). This investigation employed a novel criterion measure—classifying responses made by counselor trainees in an interview with a coached client. Certain needs assessed with the EPPS seemed particularly relevant to the preferred mode of response in the standardized interview. It is interesting to note that Asa used a different approach compared to a number of other investigators who used global ratings of professional competence. Perhaps the reasonably strong relationship between certain EPPS variables and the criterion reflects this change in methodology.

One of the best documented predictors of counseling effectiveness seems to be rigidity or dogmatism. Tosi's investigation ("Dogmatism Within the Counselor-Client Dyad") clearly illustrates the tendency for more dogmatic, rigid individuals to respond less empathically to their clients. This particular investigation considered the client's perceptions of counselor understanding. Other investigators, using ratings of counseling effectiveness made by the supervisor (Kemp, 1962; Allen, 1967; Gruberg, 1969) report similar findings. The general rationale seems to be that the more flexible individual can dip into and attune himself to personal feelings and thereby become more responsive to the nuances of feeling expressed by a client. Preliminary findings (Allen, 1967) suggest that flexibility does not seem directly related to measures of academic ability.

A considerable amount of research seems to suggest the importance of certain counseling skills for client growth (Truax, 1963; Carkhuff and Berenson, 1967; Truax and Carkhuff, 1967; Holder, Carkhuff and Berenson, 1967). These skills refer to theoretical dimensions developed by Carl Rogers (1957, 1962) and have been labeled empathy, positive regard, and genuineness.

The importance of facilitative counselor dimensions such as empathy, positive regard, and genuineness for client self-exploration and growth is amply documented by research. Highly facilitative counselors (those offering relatively higher levels of empathy, positive regard, and genuineness) appear to differ in certain respects from less facilitative counselors.

Anderson, in her paper "Effects of Confrontation by High- and Low-Functioning Therapists on High- and Low-Functioning Clients," reports evidence indicating that highly facilitative counselors who confront their client with counselor-client discrepancies in perception, elicit significantly different reactions than less facilitative counselors who employ confrontation as a technique in counseling. High-functioning counselors elicit greater client self-exploration following a confrontation than low-functioning counselors. The author offers several explanations for this finding. One implication of the study is that the techniques and behaviors used by a counselor are rendered even more effective within a context of high levels of empathy, positive regard, and genuineness.

Recently, Foulds ("Self-Actualization and the Communication of Facilitative Conditions During Counseling") reported a number of personality variables which were related to these facilitative dimensions. Using the Personal Orientation Inventory, a number of subscales reflecting self-actualization (e.g. inner direction, spontaneity, capacity for intimate contact, and feeling reactivity) correlated positively with the level of empathy, positive regard, and genuineness offered by counseling trainees to their practicum clients. These findings certainly converge with theoretical predictions that the most self-actualized individual offers the most growth-promoting professional relationships.

A number of variables are beginning to appear which relate to effective counseling. Several characteristics repeatedly appear out of the maze of data generated by the "shotgun" approach to screening counselor trainees and the deductive approach to testing specific hypotheses. The best documented variable is rigidity or dogmatism, followed by the qualities of empathy, "congruence" or consistency of behavior with self-awareness, and interpersonal popularity as a professional peer. Other variables appear less reliable as predictors of counseling effectiveness but the variability of results may be due to different methodologies employed by different studies. Such characteristics occasionally associated with effective counseling skill include low needs for dominance and aggression, a generalized positive attitude toward other individuals, especially the client, and various aspects of self-actualization such as inner direction, capacity for intimacy, and feeling reactivity. Other characteristics show a much more equivocal relationship to counseling effectiveness. Sometimes positive associations, sometimes negative associations, and other times no associations whatsoever are found. This group of variables might include past professional experience, chronological age, academic ability, grades earned, and a hodgepodge of personality dimensions inferred from paper and pencil inventories and tests.

It does appear that prediction of the effective counselor trainee can be accomplished with increasing accuracy as specific studies of promising dimensions replace an indiscriminate and wasteful application of every selection technique available. Thus as the search narrows and the data fall into increasingly meaningful patterns, the goal of accurate selection and prediction does not seem too far distant.

A final word of caution: The predictive validity of any selection device is always relative to a criterion. It has been more or less assumed that the effective counselor or psychologist is one who can empathically understand the experiences of another individual and who can provide an atmosphere and a relationship which is growth-promoting and facilitative for his client. Therefore, certain traits which covary with these particular criteria can be used for selecting applicants to professional training programs.

But should our criteria of professional expertise change— should the effective counselor be considered an able advocate or social change agent, a coordinator of services, a professional consultant, a resource technician for assessment, evaluation, or education—then the attributes listed above might be inappropriate. To the extent, however, that the counselor educator seeks applicants who can empathically respond in a facilitative manner which fosters personal growth of a client, should the qualities discussed in this chapter be considered.

References

Allen, T. W.: Effectiveness of counselor trainees as a function of psychological openness. *Journal of Counseling Psychology, 14*:35-40, 1967.

Carkhuff, R. R., and Berenson, B. G.: *Beyond Counseling and Psychotherapy.* New York, Holt, Rinehart and Winston, 1967.

Gade, E. M.. The relationship of sociometric indices and counselor candidate effectiveness. *Counselor Education and Supervision, 6*:121-124, 1967.

Gruberg, R.: A significant counselor personality characteristic: tolerance of ambiguity. *Counselor Education and Supervision, 8*:119-124, 1969.

Holder, T., Carkhuff, R. R., and Berenson, B. G.: The differential effects of the manipulation of therapist-offered conditions upon high- and low-functioning clients. *Journal of Counseling Psychology, 14*:63-66, 1967.

Holt, R. R., and Luborsy, L.: *Personality Patterns of Psychiatrists.* New York, Basic Books, 1958.

Kelly, E. L., and Fiske, D. W.: *The Prediction of Performance in Clinical Psychology.* Ann Arbor, University of Michigan Press, 1951.

Kemp, C. G.: Influence of dogmatism of the training of counselors. *Journal of Counseling Psychology, 9*:155-157, 1962.

Passons, W. R., and Olsen, L. C.: Relationship of counselor characteristics and empathic sensitivity. *Journal of Counseling Psychology, 16*:440-445, 1969.

Rogers, C. R.: The necessary and sufficient conditions of therapeutic personality change. *Journal of Consulting Psychology, 21*:95-103, 1957.

Rogers, C. R.: The interpersonal relationship: the core of guidance. *Harvard Educational Review, 32*:416-429, 1962.

Truax, C. B.: Effective ingredients in psychotherapy: an approach to unraveling the patient-therapist interaction. *Journal of Counseling Psychology, 10*:256-263, 1963.

Truax, C. B., and Carkhuff, R. R.: *Toward Effective Counseling and Psychotherapy.* Chicago, Aldine, 1967.

Wittmer, J., and Lister, J. L.: The Graduate Record Examination, 16 PF Questionnaire, and counseling effectiveness. *Counselor Education and Supervision, 10*:293, 1971.

Additional References

Anderson, S. C.: Effects of confrontation by high- and low-functioning therapists. *Journal of Counseling Psychology, 15*:411-416, 1968.

Berenson, B. G., Mitchell, K. M., and Moravec, J. A.: Level of therapist functioning, patient depth of self-exploration and type of confrontation. *Journal of Counseling Psychology, 15*:136-139, 1968.

Bohn, M. J., Jr.: Counselor behavior as a function of counselor dominance, counselor experience and client type. *Journal of Counseling Psychology, 12*:346-351, 1965.

Carkhuff, R. R., and Alexik, M.: Effects of client depth of self-exploration upon high- and low-functioning counselors. *Journal of Counseling Psychology*, *14*:350-355, 1967.

Carkhuff, R. R.: Helper communication as a function of helpee affect and content. *Journal of Counseling Psychology*, *16*:126-131, 1969.

Carkhuff, R. R.: The prediction of the effects of teacher-counselor education: the development of communication and discrimination selection indexes. *Counselor Education and Supervision*, *8*:265-272, 1969.

Cicirelli, V. G., and Cicirelli, J. S.: Counselor's creative ability and attitude in relation to counseling behavior with disadvantaged counselees. *Journal of Counseling Psychology*, *17*:177-183, 1970.

Dole, A. A.: The prediction of effectiveness in school counseling. *Journal of Counseling Psychology*, *11*:112-121, 1964.

Hurst, J. C., and Fenner, R.: Extended-session group as a predictive technique for counselor training. *Journal of Counseling Psychology*, *16*:358-360, 1969.

Jones, J. E., and Schoch, E. W.: Correlates of success in MA-level counselor education. *Counselor Education and Supervision*, *7*:286-291, 1968.

Mezzano, J.: A note on dogmatism and counselor effectiveness. *Counselor Education and Supervision*, *9*:64-65, 1969.

Mills, D. H., and Abeles, N.: Counselor needs for affiliation and nurturance as related to liking for clients and counseling process. *Journal of Counseling Psychology*, *12*:353-358, 1965.

Pallone, N. J., and Grade, P. P.: Counselor verbal mode, problem relevant communication and client rapport. *Journal of Counseling Psychology*, *12*:359-365, 1965.

Payne, P. A.: Use of a situation test for predicting counselor performance. *Journal of Counseling Psychology*, *15*:512-516, 1968.

Rosen, J.: Multiple-regression analysis of counselor characteristics and competencies. *Psychological Reports*, *20*:1003-1008, 1967.

Spinthall, N. A., Whiteley, J. M., and Mosher, R. L.: Cognitive flexibility: a focus for research on counselor effectiveness. *Counselor Education and Supervision*, *5*:188-197, 1966.

Whiteley, J. M., Spinthall, N. A., Mosher, R. L., and Donaghy, R. T.: Selection and evaluation of counselor effectiveness. *Journal of Counseling Psychology*, *14*:226-234, 1967.

Zimmer, J. M., and Park, P.: Factor analysis of counselor communications. *Journal of Counseling Psychology*, *14*:198-203, 1967.

THE USE OF A PEER RATING TECHNIQUE IN APPRAISING SELECTED ATTRIBUTES OF COUNSELOR TRAINEES*

WILLIAM P. McDOUGALL and HENRY M. REITAN

The training and skills expected of emerging counselors are

* Reprinted from *Counselor Education and Supervision*, *1*:72-76, 1961, with permission of the American Personnel and Guidance Association and the authors.

of a type and variety which would seem to demand unique assessment. In the area of interpersonal relationships alone, the skills, understandings, and attitudes are of such nature that the more traditional evaluative techniques appear inadequate. One technique which seems to merit consideration in gaining greater insight into counselor progress and achievement is the method of rating by classmates. This paper is a report of a peer rating technique used with a group of counselor trainees enrolled in a one-semester NDEA Counseling and Guidance Training Institute.

The group was made up of twenty-five counselor trainees who were selected for the institute program on the basis of high academic records, common goals, and similar course backgrounds. All were relatively untrained secondary school counselors or teachers aspiring to engage in counseling. Their background training included at least one and not more than five graduate courses in guidance. The program for all institute participants included guidance seminars, supervised counseling practice, and courses in measurement, counseling theory, and education of the gifted student.

Since the nature of the program encouraged considerable group interaction, it presented an unusual opportunity to observe the results of a peer rating technique.

Description and Administration of Scale

During the last week of the institute, enrollees were asked to rate each classmate on four counselor behavior characteristics: contribution to class, academic understanding, self insight, and counseling potential. Academic understanding was defined as the ability to comprehend, apply, and evaluate concepts and principles related to guidance and counseling. Class contribution was described as the degree to which an institute member's contribution added to the learnings of class members. Self insight was defined as the degree to which the individual's concept of himself was congruent with the rater's view of this same person. Counseling potential was described as the degree of capability the enrollee evidenced for conducting counseling interviews, rated on the basis of the question, "To which enrollee would you most likely go or refer another person for counseling?"

Enrollees were asked to place each classmate into one of four quarters on each characteristic, maintaining an equal number of individuals in each quarter. Since each student rated 24 enrollees, it forced the distribution into six enrollees per quarter cell. The ratings on each person were assigned weights corresponding to the quarter in which he was placed. As an example, in the catagory of academic understanding, the person being rated might have two raters who placed him in the highest or fourth quarter, 2×4, twelve raters who placed him in the third quarter, 12×3, and ten raters who placed him in the second quarter, 10×2. The total weighted score for this person would be sixty-four in the area of academic understanding. This weighted score was then ranked in comparison with the weighted scores of other enrollees.

Procedure

The results of the peer rating device were examined to determine if the enrollees were rating behaviors in the four categories in a discriminating manner. The degree to which the four categories seemed to measure separate behavior dimensions was also examined.

The forced choice peer group ratings were compared with the supervisor ratings and enrollee self ratings of counseling competency. The evaluation by the counseling supervisor and by self was concerned with the ability to initiate, carry on, terminate, and evaluate the counseling interview. Utilizing a five-point scale, each of these areas was rated and a composite supervisor's rating and a composite self rating were derived. The composite ratings were ranked and comparisons made, utilizing the rank difference method of correlation.

The relationship between the peer ratings and achievement as measured by the overall grade point in institute course work was examined. Since the grade in counseling practice reflected the supervisor rating, it was excluded from the grade point average.

Additional relationships examined were those between peer

group ratings and learning aptitude as measured by the Miller Analogies Test and between peer ratings and attitudes as measured by the Minnesota Attitude Inventory.

Results

An initial examination of the peer ratings in the four areas: contribution to class, academic understanding, self insight, and counseling potential, suggested that the enrollees were not unduly influenced by the halo effect in making judgments of their classmates. This was in part evidenced by the fact that the median rating on the four characteristics indicated considerable shifting from one quarter to another. The median rating on the four characteristics showed a spread across 3 quarters for seven individuals. A spread of 2 quarters was noted for twelve individuals. For six individuals the rating stayed consistently in the same quarter. It was noted that the variation in number of rank positions for individuals on the four categories ranged from 3 to 17 with a median of 8.28 when the ratings were converted to ranks.

The degree to which the four categories indicated measurement of different behavior dimensions was examined through intercorrelations. The resulting rank difference intercorrelations appear in Table 3-I.

TABLE 3–I

RANK DIFFERENCE INTERCORRELATIONS BETWEEN CATEGORIES IN THE PEER RATING DEVICE

	Peer Rating Categories		
	Academic Understanding	*Self Insight*	*Counseling Potential*
General contribution to class	.831	.390	.531
Academic understanding		.470	.585
Self insight			.862

Inspection of the data in Table 3-I reveals the greatest relationships between general contribution to class and academic understanding, and between self insight and counseling potential. The other four intercorrelations ranging from .390 to .585 reflect greater heterogeneity.

The need for clear and systematic delineation of the behavioral characteristics being rated has been emphasized by numerous authors (Cronbach, 1949; Guilford, 1936; Wrightstone, *et al.*, 1956). The data reported in Table 3-I suggests that a more systematic investigation is needed in order to determine the kinds of behavior which should appropriately be included in this type of peer rating device. The present limited information provides at least some justification for inclusion of all four categories.

TABLE 3–II

RANK-DIFFERENCE CORRELATIONS BETWEEN PEER RATINGS
AND MEASURES OF COUNSELING COMPETENCY, ACHIEVEMENT,
LEARNING APTITUDE AND ATTITUDES

Measures	Peer Rating Categories			
	General Contri-bution to Class	*Academic Understanding*	*Self Insight*	*Counseling Potential*
Supervisor's rating of counseling competency	.708	.626	.347	.605
Self rating of counseling competency	.212	.162	.113	.209
Composite grade point	.783	.352	.375	.599
Miller Analogies Test	.348	.462	.584	.478
Minnesota Teacher Attitude Inventory	.370	.525	.188	.412

As reflected in Table 3-II, supervisor's ratings of counseling competency indicated approximately similar relationships with the peer ratings of general contributions to class, academic understanding, and counseling potential. A lower relationship was found with self insight.

The relationship between self ratings of counseling competency and the four peer rating categories was considerably lower than supervisor's ratings, ranging from .133 to .212.

The highest relationship, .783, between achievement, as reflected by grade point, and a peer group rating was in the category of general contribution to class. Lower correlations were found between the grade point and other categories.

The highest relationship found between learning aptitude, reflected by the Miller Analogies Test, and peer rating was in the category of self insight. The lowest relationship was found between the Miller Analogies Test and general contribution to class.

The relationship between attitudes, as measured by the Minnesota Teacher Attitude Inventory, and peer ratings ranged from

.188 to .525. The highest relationship was found between the Minnesota Teacher Attitude Inventory and academic understanding and the lowest between the Minnesota Teacher Attitude Inventory and self insight.

Because of the small number of cases included in this sample and the limited statistical treatment of the data, the above relationships would serve mainly to suggest areas for further study. A case in point is the discrepancy between self ratings and peer ratings for all four categories.

Suggested Uses of the Peer Rating Technique

A peer rating device may aid in the broader assessment of counselor capabilities in the following ways: (a) It may afford a means of revealing important behaviors which might be overlooked or obscured in conventional evaluative procedures. (b) Used and interpreted with discretion it gives the student an unusual opportunity to evaluate himself in the light of peer appraisal. This dimension of evaluation is needed in an area where interpersonal relationships are of paramount importance. (c) Used periodically throughout a training period, it allows for an evaluation of trainee progress, both to self and instructor. (d) It may afford a means of helping to remove psychological barriers which prevent realistic self-appraisal. (e) It may provide the instructor with an opportunity for examining his own bias in making judgments of students' behavior.

The method of peer rating which requires the forcing of classmate judgments into quarter cells seems to compare favorably with traditional ranking and rating methods.

This rating device seems to possess most of the advantages enjoyed by other rating techniques when compared to ranking methods. Among those mentioned by Guilford which seem pertinent are savings in time, wider range of application, and higher validity with judges who have had a minimum of training. The fine discrimination demanded of a student in placing his fellow students into a lengthy ordinal rank position, which may be somewhat unrealistic, is eliminated. The ranks that accrue from a ranking of the composite scores of a quarter rating seem to accomplish the same purpose.

In comparison to more conventional rating methods some of

the rating errors mentioned by Guilford are eliminated. Constant errors of leniency are precluded through the use of a forced distribution as are errors of central tendency. In addition, the rater is not asked to judge against some fixed standard the degree to which a quality or characteristic is possessed. Rather, he is asked to place his classmate into one of four quarters in relation to the fellow members of this class.

This pilot study report suggests that the peer rating technique may be useful in exploring broader dimensions in counselor trainee assessment.

References

Cronbach, Lee J.: *Essentials of Psychological Testing.* New York, Harper and Brothers, 1949.

Guilford, J. P.: *Psychometric Methods,* New York & London, McGraw-Hill Book Company, 1936.

Wrightstone, J. Wayne, Justman, Joseph, and Robbins, Irving: *Evaluation in Modern Education.* American Book Company, 1956.

CHARACTERISTICS OF HIGH-RATED AND LOW-RATED MASTER'S DEGREE CANDIDATES IN COUNSELING AND GUIDANCE*

DAVID G. JANSEN, GEORGE P. ROBB, and EDWARD C. BONK

A frequently repeated television commercial of our day claims that good and bad guys can be differentiated because "the good guys wear white hats." Unfortunately, it has proved much more difficult to distinguish between effective and ineffective counselors. In spite of the difficulty involved, considerable energy has been directed toward the delineation of the characteristics of competent and incompetent counselors.

Arbuckle (1956) compared student counselors who were chosen by their peers as potential counselors with those who were rejected by their peers. He found that the chosen student counselors were more "normal" than their rejected counterparts on the basis of scores on the clinical scales of the Minnesota Multiphasic Personality Inventory (MMPI).

* Reprinted from *Counselor Education and Supervision,* Spring 1970, 162-170, with permission of the American Personnel and Guidance Association and the authors.

Scores on the MMPI schizophrenia scale were shown to be negatively correlated with counseling effectiveness for female counselors enrolled in a counseling practicum at Purdue University by Johnson, Shertzer, Linden, and Stone (1967). They also noted that scores on the friendliness scale of the Guilford-Zimmerman Temperament Survey were negatively associated with counseling effectiveness for the female student counselors.

Counselor candidates in an NDEA Institute who were judged most effective by their peers obtained significantly higher scores on the deference and order scales of the Edwards Personal Preference Schedule (EPPS) than those judged least effective (Stefflre, King, and Leafgren, 1962). The chosen counselors obtained significantly lower scores than the rejected counselors on the abasement and aggression scales of the EPPS. Demos and Zuwaylif (1966) reported similar results for the abasement and aggression scales of the EPPS at another NDEA Institute for prospective counselors. Counselors judged most effective by their supervisors appeared to be significantly less abasing and aggressive and also less autonomous than those judged least effective. These investigators also found that the most effective counselors showed significantly more nurturance and affiliation than the counselors judged least effective.

Wicas and Mahan (1966) reported data which indicated that counselors rated effective by their supervisors and peers differed from counselors rated ineffective on four of the fifteen scoring categories of the Structured Objective Rorschach Test (SORT). The high-rated counselors tended to have higher ranks on categories related to anxiety and conformity and lower ranks on categories purported to measure persistence and emotional responsivity when compared with low-rated counselors. Thus, the high-rated counselors appeared to be more anxious, more alert and sensitive to others, more yielding to the demands of others, and more open to change than their low-rated counterparts.

Using an audio scale, O'Hern and Arbuckle (1964) observed that students in seven summer NDEA Guidance Institutes who were considered to be the most sensitive counselors were significantly younger, had attained a lower academic degree, and had been employed fewer years than those who were considered to be least sensitive. Joslin (1965) found no significant relationship between subject-matter knowledge and counseling competence either at the beginning or the end of a NDEA Counseling and Guidance Institute.

Who are the good "guys" (counselors) and who are the bad ones? Clearly any tentative answer depends upon the chosen measure or measures of counselor characteristics and the criterion of counseling effectiveness. Research using a variety of measures and criteria has yielded results which are difficult to compare and virtually impossible to synthesize.

The Problem

What is the relationship between intellective and non-intellective characteristics and competence as counselors? The present study was designed to explore this question from a somewhat different perspective than the studies reported in the literature. All students who are candidates for the master's degree in counseling and guidance at North Texas State University are required to enroll in an evaluation seminar during the final semester on campus. In the seminar, each candidate is evaluated in terms of overall competence on the basis of knowledge of counseling theories and techniques, knowledge of and ability to use test data in counseling, and counseling skill as assessed by analysis of counseling tapes. Each of the criteria is given equal weight. The question was asked, "Are there differences in intellective and non-intellective characteristics between students rated by faculty members as falling within the top 25 percent in overall competence at the end of the evaluation seminar and students rated in the bottom 25 percent?"

Procedure

The sample consisted of 34 females (17 from the top quarter, 17 from the lowest quarter) who had completed the evaluation seminar in counseling and guidance at North Texas State University during the period from September 1967 through January 1969. All of the subjects were experienced teachers, and all but one candidate in each group were certified at the secondary school level. All of the participants had completed a supervised counseling practicum.

The data used in making the ratings of overall counseling

competence were gathered at various points throughout the semester of the evaluation seminar. Knowledge of counseling theories and techniques and knowledge of tests and inventories were assessed by midterm and final objective examinations. Ability to use tests and ability to counsel were determined by analysis of individual counseling tapes. The tapes were analyzed and separate scores were obtained along the following dimensions by the seminar leader, using a seven-point semantic differential format: (a) self-concept; (b) openness; (c) empathy; (d) enthusiasm; (e) poise; (f) flexibility; (g) warmth; and (h) appropriateness of reflections, interpretations, and information.

All ratings of overall counseling competence were made by the director of the North Texas State University Counseling Center, who regularly conducted the seminar. He had never taught any of the students being rated in other classes and had no knowledge of either their test and inventory scores or their previous academic performance.

The following data were available for each subject: (a) chronological age; (b) Ohio State University Psychological Test (Form 21, 1941) raw scores; (c) Cooperative English Tests, 1962 (Vocabulary, Level of Comprehension, Expression) raw scores; (d) Guilford-Zimmerman Temperament Survey (1949) raw scores; (e) Minnesota Teacher Attitude Inventory (1951) raw scores; (f) grades in counseling practicum; and (g) cumulative graduate grade-point averages. The test and inventory data were obtained from the North Texas State University Counseling Office files, while the chronological age and grade-point data were found in the Registrar's office.

The Student's "*t*" test (Hays, 1963) was used to test for differences in mean scores on the intellective and non-intellective variables between the female students in the top and bottom quarters in the evaluation seminar course.

Results

The results of the statistical analysis of the demographic and intellective characteristics data are summarized in Table 3-III. Counselors rated high in overall competence emerged as significantly younger than those rated low. They appeared to have greater scholastic aptitude than counselors ranking low in competence on the basis of significantly higher raw scores on the Ohio State University Psychological Test and on the Level of Comprehension and Expression subtests of the Cooperative English Tests.

TABLE 3–III

DIFFERENCES IN DEMOGRAPHIC, INTELLECTIVE, AND ACHIEVEMENT CHARACTERISTICS BETWEEN HIGH- AND LOW-RATED FEMALE STUDENT COUNSELORS

Variables	Group	X	SD	t	P
Chronological age	High	28.47	6.52	4.02	.001
	Low	37.76	6.55		
Ohio State University	High	115.71	17.72	3.08	.01
Psychological Test	Low	94.00	21.94		
Cooperative English Tests					
Vocabulary	High	46.71	8.97	1.26	ns
	Low	42.59	9.57		
Level of Comprehension	High	38.88	8.76	3.80	.001
	Low	27.06	8.85		
Expression	High	62.82	11.43	2.87	.01
	Low	50.76	12.31		
Counseling practicum grade	High	3.88	0.32	6.09	.001
	Low	2.82	0.62		
Cumulative grade point	High	3.80	0.17	6.62	.001
average	Low	3.14	0.35		

As shown in Table 3-III, female counselors who were rated in the top quarter in overall competence had a significantly better mean practicum grade and a significantly higher mean cumulative gradepoint average than counselors placed in the bottom quarter. The low-rated counselors had a mean practicum grade of less than "B" (3.00) and a mean cumulative grade-point average only slightly above 3.00. In contrast, the high-rated counselors approximated an "A" average in practicum and had a very high mean cumulative grade-point average.

As shown in Table 3-IV, significant differences (at or beyond the .05 level of confidence) between the mean scores of the high- and low-rated female counselors were observed on three of the ten Guilford-Zimmerman Temperament Survey scales. The "competent" counselors appeared to be more sociable (at ease with

TABLE 3–IV

DIFFERENCES IN NON-INTELLECTIVE CHARACTERISTICS BETWEEN
HIGH- AND LOW-RATED FEMALE STUDENT COUNSELORS

Variables	Group	X	SD	t	P
Guilford-Zimmerman Temperament Survey					
General activity	High	19.41	3.27	0.63	ns
	Low	18.29	6.24		
Restraint	High	21.24	3.49	1.72	.10
	Low	19.24	3.08		
Ascendance	High	16.71	4.24	0.86	ns
	Low	15.35	4.65		
Sociability	High	23.76	3.12	2.74	.05
	Low	19.41	5.43		
Emotional stability	High	22.88	3.22	2.57	.05
	Low	18.88	5.33		
Objectivity	High	23.53	3.33	4.29	.001
	Low	17.76	4.22		
Friendliness	High	19.71	4.40	0.22	ns
	Low	19.35	4.83		
Thoughtfulness	High	20.41	3.99	1.18	ns
	Low	18.82	3.62		
Personal relations	High	23.18	3.49	1.55	ns
	Low	21.06	4.21		
Masculinity	High	11.18	3.85	0.20	ns
	Low	10.94	2.69		
Minnesota Teacher Attitude Inventory	High	69.59	21.32	4.03	.001
	Low	42.53	16.36		

others; readily establish rapport), more emotionally stable, and
less ego-involved (low scores indicate touchiness or hypersen-
sitivity) than those counselors rated low in overall competency.
A further difference, significant at the .10 level of confidence,
suggested that the competent counseling students tended to be
more restrained (high scores on R) and serious than those characterized as less competent.

A statistically significant difference of 27 raw-score points between the Minnesota Teacher Attitude Inventory mean scores of
the high- and low-rated female counselors was obtained (Table
3-IV). The mean score of the high-rated counselors suggested
that they were individuals who would be more likely to maintain
a state of harmonious and cooperative relationships in the class-

room than those counselors who were rated low. They would tend to be more open and permissive in their relationships with others than their less competent counterparts (Cook, Leeds, and Callis, 1951).

Discussion

The observation that female counselors who were rated in the top quarter of their respective evaluation seminars on the basis of overall competence were significantly younger than those rated in the bottom quarter seemed to support the results reported earlier by O'Hern and Arbuckle (1964). These investigators noted that the student counselors who were considered to be most sensitive as counselors were significantly younger and had been employed fewer years than those who were regarded as least sensitive. Apparently age is negatively related to measures of counseling effectiveness in master's degree programs in counseling and guidance, at least beyond age 30. One might assume that older candidates would bring a greater wealth of experience to the counseling program, experience which would enable them to be more effective counselors. The results do not support such an assumption.

Contrary to Joslin's (1965) finding, the present data indicated that female counselors who rated high in overall competence had significantly more verbal scholastic aptitude as assessed by the Ohio State University Psychological Test than their low-rated counterparts. The high-rated counselors also had significantly higher mean scores on the Level of Comprehension and Expression sections of the Cooperative English Tests than the low-rated counselors. Thus, there appeared to be a strong, positive relationship between measures of verbal scholastic aptitude and ratings of overall counseling competence.

The positive relationship between verbal scholastic aptitude and overall counseling effectiveness was supported by significant differences between the mean counseling practicum grades and cumulative grade-point averages of the high- and low-rated female counselors. The high-rated counselors, who scored significantly higher on three of the four measures of verbal scholastic aptitude, also achieved significantly higher grades in courses emphasizing subject-matter knowledge and in the course emphasizing counseling skill, *per se.*

Freedman, Antenen, and Lister (1967) reported relationships between personality characteristics of counselors and counselor verbal-response patterns. Certain personality characteristics inventoried by the Guilford-Zimmerman Temperament Survey (GZTS) were found by these investigators to be associated with different categories of verbal behavior by counselor candidates. The three GZTS factors (sociability, objectivity, and emotional stability) which differentiated between high-rated and low-rated female counselors at or beyond the .05 level of confidence and the one factor (restraint) which differentiated at the .10 level in the present study were all factors which accounted for three per cent or more of the total variance in verbal counseling behavior in the Freedman, Antenen, and Lister study. The results of their study indicated that sociability was associated with supportive, interpretive, information-giving, and evaluative verbal behavior by counselors. Objectivity was associated with information-giving and probing verbal responses, while emotional stability was associated with supportive and interpretive behavior. Restraint was associated with verbal activity of a probing nature.

Many counselor education programs either emphasize or require teaching certification and experience prior to acceptance for candidacy for the master's degree. The implication seems to be that the experiences gained through teacher education and classroom teaching are valuable assets for the prospective school counselor. The present data indicate that female student counselors who are rated high in overall competence have significantly higher mean scores on the Minnesota Teacher Attitude Inventory than those rated low. On the other hand, the low-rated counselors tended to be older than those rated high. Could it be that attitudes which facilitate open, permissive, harmonious, and cooperative relationships with others, whether developed through teaching experience or otherwise, are significantly related to competence in counseling, whereas teaching experience, *per se* is not? Is it possible that experience gained in the classroom by teachers over a period of years militates against the attitudes which are important in successful counseling?

Summary and Conclusions

Are there differences between "good" and "bad" counselors at the end of a master's degree program in counselor education? The data obtained and analyzed in this study suggest that there are significant intellective, non-intellective, and achievement differences between female counselors rated in the top quarter of their respective evaluation seminars in terms of overall competence and those female counselors rated in the bottom quarter. The high-rated counselors emerged as significantly younger and more intellectually capable than their low-rated counterparts. They appeared to be more sociable, emotionally stable, objective, and restrained than the female counselors who were rated low in overall competence. The high-rated counselors had scores on the Minnesota Teacher Attitude Inventory, indicative of significantly more positive, permissive, and cooperative attitudes than their less competent counterparts. Furthermore, those counselors in the top quarter in terms of overall competence achieved a significantly higher mean grade in the counseling practicum and a significantly higher mean cumulative grade-point average than the counselors rated in the bottom quarter.

When overall competence (knowledge and counseling skill) is used as the criterion for competence of student counselors, and when the rating of competence is performed by a trained and experienced counselor, the Ohio State University Psychological Test, the Cooperative English Tests, the Guilford-Zimmerman Temperament Survey, and the Minnesota Teacher Attitude Inventory appear to be useful in differentiating between the high- and low-rated individuals. Future research utilizing these and other instruments, other criteria of counseling effectiveness, and a greater number of raters is recommended. Certainly much more research is needed before counselor educators can react with any degree of certainty to the questions, Who is an effective counselor? What are the distinguishing characteristics of the potentially competent candidate in a counselor education program?

References

Arbuckle, D. S.: Client perception of counselor personality. *Journal of Counseling Psychology,* 3:93-96, 1956.

Cook, W. W., Leeds, C. H., and Callis, R.: *Minnesota Teacher Attitude Inventory Manual.* New York, The Psychological Corporation, 1951.

Cooperative English Tests: Directions for Administering and Scoring. Princeton, Educational Testing Service, 1962.

Demos, G. D., and Zuwaylif, F. H.: Characteristics of effective counselors. *Counselor Education and Supervision,* 5:163-65, 1966.

Freedman, S. A., Antenen, W. W., and Lister, J. L.: Counselor behavior and personality characteristics. *Counselor Education and Supervision,* 7: 26-30, 1967.

Guilford, J. P., and Zimmerman, W. S.: *The Guilford-Zimmerman Temperament Survey Manual.* Beverly Hills, Sheridan Supply Company, 1949.

Hays, W. L.: *Statistics for Psychologists.* New York, Holt, Rinehart and Winston, 1963.

Johnson, D., Shertzer, B., Linden, J., and Stone, S. C.: The relationship of counselor candidate characteristics and counseling effectiveness. *Counselor Education and Supervision,* 6:297-03, 1967.

Joslin, L. C., Jr.: Knowledge and counseling competence. *Personnel and Guidance Journal,* 43:790-95, 1965.

O'Hern, J. S., and Arbuckle, D.: Sensitivity: a measurable concept? *Personnel and Guidance Journal,* 42:572-76, 1964.

Stefflre, B., King, P., and Leafgren, F.: Characteristics of counselors judged effective by their peers. *Journal of Counseling Psychology,* 9:335-40, 1962.

Toops, H. A.: *The Ohio State University Psychological Test Manual.* Chicago, Science Research Associates, 1941.

Wicas, E. A., and Mahan, T. W., Jr.: Characteristics of counselors rated effective by supervisors and peers. *Counselor Education and Supervision,* 6:50-6, 1966.

INTERVIEW BEHAVIOR AND COUNSELOR PERSONALITY VARIABLES*

LELAND F. ASA

There is a constant struggle to provide improved tools of counseling, such as better tests, personal data information, autobiographies, and rating scales. As research continues for the purpose of sharpening these tools, there is another variable that may have even greater influence on the outcome of the counseling interview. This variable is the counselor himself. Generally, the different things that counselors say in the interview can be placed

* Reprinted from *Counselor Education and Supervision,* 6:324-330, 1967, with permission of the American Personnel and Guidance Association and the author.

in somewhat homogeneous categories. This study was concerned with various types of responses to the counselee verbalization of feeling and the relationship of counselor responses to the counselors' personality variables as measured by the Edwards Personal Preference Schedule (EPPS).

Problem

Counselor educators have become more and more interested in how counselor personality variables might differ from those of people in general and how different personality variables might be related to counseling techniques.

Selection of candidates for counselor education would be simplified if it were shown that individuals with a given personality profile tended to become good counselors while individuals with other kinds of personality profiles tended to become inferior counselors. However, at the present time methods of evaluation are somewhat inadequate. Studies have been made to attempt to discriminate between good and poor counselors. Predicting successful counselors on the basis of personality devices has not always been successful (Snyder, 1945). Brams (1961) and Soone and Goldman (1957) reported evidence that personality variables and effective communication in counseling interviews are related.

Extensive research has been done on counselor responses to counselee verbalization of feeling. It is generally agreed that counselor statements can be categorized into meaningful groups (Miller, 1962; Porter, 1950; Robinson, 1950). It was hypothesized in this study that if counselor personality variables varied from counselor to counselor, counseling techniques would also vary from one counselor to another.

Since researchers in the past (Brams, 1961; Campbell, 1962) have not found an extensive relationship between counselor responses and personality variables, this study was initiated to make another attempt. The problem was to determine whether counseling students engaged in graduate study in counseling and guidance possess personality variables different from those of college students in general and whether counseling students with differing personality variables would tend to react differently in similar counseling situations.

Procedure

All available male graduate students in counselor education at the University of Wyoming served as subjects. There were fifteen. One student was within one semester of the doctorate; nine were second-year graduate students; and five were in their first year of graduate preparation. The EPPS was administered to each student.

The next step was to schedule a counseling session and to expose each counselor to approximately the same situation. A professional actor was hired to play the role of the counselee. The actor (hereafter referred to as the counselee) was coached in the role that he was to play, and each counselor was given a personal data sheet containing background information. The counselee played the role of a third-year English major about to drop out of college to get married and because of the financial hardship worked on his parents by his continuing in college.

All of the counseling students were in the same area of the University, so it was not possible to keep the fact hidden that they were all counseling the same individual. Therefore, they were so informed before their interviews. It was assumed that this would not be too great a handicap after a number of the counseling students informed the experimenter that the counselee had played his role very well and that for extended periods of time they had forgotten that he was role-playing. Counseling students were not instructed to seek any specific solution.

Counseling sessions were recorded, and complete typescripts were made. Each counseling lead was categorized after Miller (1962) into one of thirty types. Next, counseling leads were collapsed into five categories: Accepting, Probing-Projecting, Interpreting, Diagnosing, and Advising. All leads which tended to be non-judgmental and did not give advice nor suggest possible causes of problems were placed in the accepting category. Leads which sought information or brought information into the interview were placed in the Probing-Projecting category. The Interpreting category was limited to depth interpretation and simple interpretation. The diagnosing category included leads which conveyed to the counselee the counselor's idea of what his problem might be. Advising leads were categorized as those the counselor could use to convey to the counselee what he should do.

To determine whether the experimenter would differ from authorities in categorizing the leads, reference was made to another research project (Asa, 1961) in which the experimenter categorized a series of counseling leads and then gave the typescripts with the definitions to two psychology professors who were asked to categorize the leads. A chi-square test was used to determine whether or not there was a significant difference in the categorization. No difference was indicated at the .05 level. Next, the experimenter re-categorized the leads of one of the typescripts of this study several months after the first categorization and without reference to the first. There was no difference at the .05 level on a chi-square test.

After the EPPS had been administered to the 15 subjects, a *t* test was used to compare the subjects and the norm group (college men) (Edwards, 1959). However, the sample was small and was not used to make inferences about counseling students in general.

Next, the frequency of the use of the five lead categories was correlated with the raw scores of the 15 variables of the EPPS. The product-moment correlation coefficient was used. The EPPS variables were labeled from X_1 to X_{15}, and the five types of lead categories were labeled from Y_1 to Y_5. The contribution of the independent variables (EPPS variables) to the type of counseling was assessed. For example, if the score on the EPPS variable Dominance was high, it could be predicted that the counselor would take initiative in directing the interview.

Finally, a regression coefficient was computed to determine the contribution of EPPS variables to the use of different types of counseling leads. It was hypothesized that some personality variables would be more important than others in determining counseling technique.

Results

There were several of the EPPS variables on which the subjects differed from the norm group at the .05 level. Difference in means between the subjects and the norm group and the direction of differences are shown in Table 3-V. It can be seen that significant differences occurred for five variables: Affiliation, Intraception, Succorance, Change, and Aggression.

TABLE 3–V

F VALUES AND *t* VALUES FOR A COMPARISON OF MEANS OF THE
EPPS BETWEEN 15 GRADUATE STUDENTS IN COUNSELOR
EDUCATION AND 760 U. S. COLLEGE MEN

	F Value	S. D.	Counselor Mean	College Men Mean	t Value
Achievement	1.13	3.89	15.81	15.66	.157
Deference	1.18	3.30	12.75	11.21	1.833
Order	1.47	3.55	8.69	10.23	−1.737
Exhibition	1.36†	4.11	15.56	14.40	1.130
Autonomy	1.26	3.97	14.00	14.34	− .343
Affiliation	1.42	2.90	17.63*	15.00	3.627
Intraception	1.52	4.24	20.56*	16.12	4.302
Succorance	1.87	3.43	7.06*	10.74	4.283
Dominance	2.80**	2.92	16.13	17.44	
Abasement	1.48	6.00†	9.56	12.24	−1.784
Nurturance	1.17	4.44	15.56	14.04	1.388
Change	1.70	3.63	17.88*	15.51	2.606
Endurance	1.21	4.81	12.13	12.66	− .445
Heterosexuality	1.27	6.18†	16.75	17.65	− .583
Aggression	1.33	3.98	10.00*	12.79	−2.802
Consistency	1.64	1.45	11.81	11.53	.769

†Table value at .05 level of significance is 2.01. Table value for all others is 2.75 at the .05 level.

*Means of study group that are significantly different from the norm group at the .05 level.

**Variance of study group is different from the norm group at the .05 level of significance.

EPPS scores for the subjects of this study were also compared with the scores of 349 National Defense Education Act Institute enrollees from 19 institutions reported by Foley and Proff (1965). Confidence intervals were placed around the mean scores for the 15 subjects. There were significant differences at the .05 level on Order, Succorance, and Change. The subjects of this study were lower on Order and Succorance and higher on Change.

After the 30 lead categories had been collapsed into five categories, the percentages of usage of each lead were figured for the subjects to determine the type of counseling leads used most. Practically every subject used leads representative of all five categories; one subject did not use any interpreting leads. The percentages of lead usage for the subjects were: Accepting 44;

Probing-Projecting 31; Interpreting 7; Diagnosing 4; and Advising 12.

Four significant relationships (.05 level) were found between counseling leads and EPPS variables. There was a significant correlation of −.56 between Accepting leads and Dominance. Probing-Projecting also correlated .67 with Dominance. There was a correlation of −.74 between Interpreting leads and Aggression. Diagnosing also correlated .58 with Aggression. Among the lead types there was one significant correlation, −.90 between Accepting and Probing-Projecting.

According to the regression coefficients, Dominance contributed positively to the use of Probing-Projecting leads and negatively to the use of Accepting leads. Intraception and Endurance contributed negatively to the use of Diagnosing leads. Achievement and Abasement contributed positively to the use of Advising leads, and Succorance contributed negatively to the use of Advising leads.

TABLE 3–VI

CORRELATION TABLE SHOWING THE RELATIONSHIP BETWEEN THE RESULTS OF THE EPPS SCORES AND TYPES OF COUNSELING LEADS USED FOR 15 GRADUATE STUDENTS IN COUNSELOR EDUCATION

	Accepting	Probing-Projecting	Interpreting	Diagnosing	Advising
Achievement	−.34	.23	−.31	.02	.41
Deference	.09	−.03	−.07	−.14	−.04
Order	−.21	.31	.10	−.43	−.18
Exhibition	.50	−.42	.42	−.08	−.35
Autonomy	.00	−.07	−.13	.11	.23
Affiliation	.48	−.41	.15	−.15	−.12
Intraception	−.35	.28	.22	−.40	.11
Succorance	.08	.01	.11	.21	−.42
Dominance	−.56*	.67*	−.27	−.29	−.10
Abasement	−.26	.12	−.04	.02	.24
Nurturance	.10	−.13	.28	.03	−.12
Change	.43	−.43	.20	.24	−.13
Endurance	−.01	.12	.00	−.37	−.15
Heterosexuality	.32	−.33	.01	.20	.01
Aggression	−.35	.27	−.74*	.58*	.39
Accepting	1.00	−.90*	.47	.01	−.36
Probing-Projecting		1.00	−.48	−.25	−.03
Interpreting			1.00	−.38	−.36
Diagnosing				1.00	.45
Advising					1.00

*Significant at the .05 level.

TABLE 3–VII

EPPS VARIABLES THAT CONTRIBUTED MOST TO FIVE TYPES
OF COUNSELING LEADS

Counseling Lead Type	EPPS Variables	
	Contributed Most	*Contributed Least*
Y₁ Accepting	Dominance (−)*	Exhibition
Y₂ Probing-Projecting	Dominance (+)	Endurance
Y₃ Interpreting	Aggression (−)	Endurance
Y₄ Diagnosing	Intraception (−)	Heterosexuality
	Endurance (−)	
	Achievement (+)	
Y₅ Advising	Succorance (−)	Change
	Abasement (+)	Heterosexuality

*The sign indicates positive or negative influence.

Discussion

This study was not designed to indicate why the subjects' scores should differ from the norm group; however, there is some reason to suppose that counselors might differ in some aspects from college students. The subjects were homogeneous in their scoring on items that seemed to relate to acceptance of people. This is not to say that all were accepting, but the group as a whole tended to be.

A counselor profile different from college men in general seems to have emerged for the subjects. The subjects tended to score lower than the norm group on Succorance and Aggression, and higher on Affiliation, Intraception, and Change.

It may be conjecture to attempt to explain the correlations between the EPPS variables and counseling lead categories. However, if it is shown that some personality variables are essential in good counseling, and if these variables can be measured, then two alternatives are open for counselor educators: (a) counseling students can be selected if they possess these personality traits, or (b) the counselor educator can attempt to manipulate personalities. It is possible that personalities (a) became different because students were enrolled in a counselor education program; (b) were different because certain types of people enter counseling education programs; or (c) were different because counseling students are able to manipulate the test and answer in a way they think counselors should answer.

It would not be difficult to exclude people who score high on the EPPS variable Dominance from counselor education programs if the counselor educators assumed that "accepting people" made better counselors and that they either could not or would not effect personality changes in counseling students. It seems evident that the subjects who scored high on Dominance did not use Accepting leads extensively but tended rather to use Probing-Projecting leads.

There seems to be some evidence from this study that individuals who scored higher on Aggression attempted to diagnose the counselee's problem. Counselors who scored low on Aggression did not attempt to diagnose extensively.

It was not possible to distinguish any trends in the use of leads among students beginning the program and students nearing the completion of the program.

Summary

The purpose of this study was to compare counselor responses to expressions of counselee feelings and their relationship to counselor personality variables as measured by the Edwards Personal Preference Schedule (EPPS). The problem was to discover whether counseling students would react differently in similar counseling situations depending on individual personality variables.

EPPS scores of 15 students in counselor education were compared with the norm group (college men); counseling leads used by counseling students were analyzed; and counseling students' scores on the EPPS variables and five categories of counseling leads were tested for correlation. Because of the small sample size, caution was urged in making inferences about counseling students in general.

A pattern of personality variables for the subjects on the EPPS differed from the norm group. Subjects scored higher than the norm group on Affiliation, Change, and Intraception, but lower on Succorance and Aggression.

As the EPPS profile varied on Dominance and Aggression, counseling techniques tended to vary as well. Subjects who scored higher on Aggression seemed to be less concerned with the counselee's analyzing his own problem.

Few patterns of lead usage appeared such as a sequence of probing, diagnosing, advising, and stopping. The subjects appeared to be rather flexible in their approaches.

References

Asa, L. F.: *A Statistical Analysis of Pastoral Recognition and Use of Transference in Counseling.* Unpublished master's thesis, Omaha University, 1961.

Brams, J. M.: Counselor characteristics and effective communication in counseling. *Journal of Counseling Psychology,* 8:25-30, 1961.

Campbell, R. E.: Counselor personality and background and his interview subrole behavior. *Journal of Counseling Psychology,* 9:329-35, 1962.

Edwards, A. E.: *Edwards Personal Preference Schedule Manual.* New York, Psychological Corporation, 1959.

Foley, W. J., and Proff, F. C.: NDEA Institute trainees and vocational rehabilitation counselors: a comparison of characteristics. *Counselor Education and Supervision,* 4:154-59, 1965.

Miller, L. L.: *Counseling Leads.* Boulder, Colorado, Pruett Press, 1962.

Porter, E. H., Jr.: *An Introduction to Therapeutic Counseling.* Boston, Houghton Mifflin, 1950.

Robinson, F. P.: *Principles and Procedures in Student Counseling.* New York, Harper and Brothers, 1950.

Snyder, W. U.: An investigation of the nature of non-directive psychotherapy. *Journal of General Psychology,* 53:193-223, 1945.

Soone, T. R., and Goldman, L.: Preferences of authoritarian and equalitarian personalities for client-centered and eclectic counseling. *Journal of Counseling Psychology,* 4:129-35, 1957.

DOGMATISM WITHIN THE COUNSELOR-CLIENT DYAD*

DONALD J. TOSI

The quality of the relationship has been emphasized as a necessary condition for achieving successful counseling outcomes (Brammer and Shostrom, 1960; Hobbs, 1965; Rogers, 1958). Research has shown that clients who demonstrate greater change in

---

* Reprinted from the *Journal of Counseling Psychology,* 17:284-288, 1970, with permission of the American Psychological Association and the author.

counseling perceive certain conditions such as empathy, congruence, and unconditional positive regard in their counselors (Barrett-Lennard, 1962; Gross and DeRidder, 1966; Kamin and Caughlin, 1963; Lesser, 1961) especially during the initial stages of counseling (Barrett-Lennard, 1962; Truax and Carkhuff, 1963).

Increasing evidence suggests that one factor contributing to the quality of the counseling relationship is the counselor's level of openness or dogmatism (Cahoon, 1962; Kemp, 1962; Russo, Kelz, and Hudson, 1964). "Highly dogmatic" or "less open counselors" are more prone to distort phenomena occurring within the therapeutic context because of greater difficulties in self-communication, that is, understanding their own thoughts, feelings, and desires, and also because of the extent to which they are cognizant and understanding of client feelings (Allen, 1967). Several studies have indicated that less open or highly dogmatic persons are characterized by more defensive behavior, insecurity, and threat under a variety of conditions than low-dogmatic persons (Kemp, 1961; Rokeach, 1960; Tosi, Fagan, and Frumkin, 1968).

While low levels of openness or dogmatism in the counselor may contribute to a favorable working alliance, Jourard (1964) has suggested that counseling relationships are in part a function of the client's and the counselor's ability to risk self-disclosure or openness. The implication is that both members of this coalition contribute equally, although perhaps in different ways, to the counseling transaction. Leary (1955), for instance, has stated that "interpersonal relationships can never be fully understood unless both sides of the interaction are studied. When only one side, the self or subject side, is studied or isolated, there is a risk of distortion [p. 156]."

While the literature is replete with inquiries focusing on the contribution of counselor personality factors to the counseling process, few studies have investigated client-counselor variables jointly (Hebert, 1967; McGowan and Schmidt, 1962). The vast majority of studies emphasizing the dyad have employed a "similarities approach," that is, counselor-client similarity on a number of personality variables (Axelrod, 1951; Carson and Heine, 1962; Cook, 1966; Hebert, 1967; Heine and Trosman, 1960; Mendelsohn and Geller, 1963; Tuma and Gustad, 1951; Vogel, 1962). In general, these studies hypothesized that high counselor-client similarity on certain personality dimensions would contribute positively to the counseling transaction. In some cases high similarity was predictive of various criterion measures, while in others medium similarity was most predictive.

While the similarities approach is useful, it does have limitations. In Vogel's study, for instance, focusing on counselor-client authoritarianism, high- and low-authoritarian dyads were combined into the same category (high similarity). Thus, the effect one dyad type could have on the criterion variable may have been cancelled out by the other. An alternative approach that would eliminate such an effect would be one that ascribes a priority to the construct under consideration and proceeds through an additive effect. A factorial analysis of variance design would permit this by simply classifying counselors and clients into high, medium, and low groups, which would then yield nine categories or dyad types. The diagonal would represent counselor-client similarity. Main effects and/or interaction effects could then be determined.

The present study examined the effects of varying levels of counselor and client dogmatism on client perceptions of the relationship following an initial encounter. The study was conducted within the interpersonal context of the dyad with special emphasis given to interviews of an educational/vocational content.

Method

Instruments

Client perceptions of the relationships were measured by the Barrett-Lennard Relationship Inventory. The scale yields four relationship components, empathy, unconditional positive regard, level of regard, and congruence, which in this study were combined into a total rating from each client. For detailed validation procedures and reliability coefficients, see Barrett-Lennard (1962). An estimated r (Spearman-Brown) of .82 for the Barrett-Lennard Relationship Inventory total scores was determined for the group of clients participating in the study.

Levels of counselor and client dogmatism were determined by the application of the Rokeach Dogmatism Scale. A discussion of the validating procedures and reliability may be found in *The Open and Closed Mind* (Rokeach, 1960). An estimated Spearman-Brown r of .81 was found for Rokeach Dogmatism Scale scores for clients. A Spearman r of .98 was obtained for Rokeach Dogmatism Scale scores for counselors.

Sample

Counselors ($N = 12$) were male trainees enrolled in their first counseling practicum at Kent State University. These counselors, prior to their practicum, fulfilled prerequisite courses in counseling theory, use of tests in counseling, and occupational information. Clients were males ($N = 40$) and females ($N = 29$) who were seeking educational and vocational counseling at Kent State University Guidance Laboratory ($\overline{X}$ age 19.5). Of the 69 clients participating in the study, 18 were in their last 2 years of high school, and 51 were university students. The use of t tests revealed no significant differences between male and female subjects with respect to their Rokeach Dogmatism Scale means and their Barrett-Lennard Relationship Inventory mean ratings.

Three procedures were instituted to assure that only clients expressing problems of an educational-vocational content participated in the study. Prior to the initial interview, clients were asked to indicate on an intake sheet their reason for seeking counseling. Clients indicating problems of a personal-social nature were excluded from the study. Second, if following the initial interview, a counselor judged a client's problem to be personal-social, that client was excluded from the study. Third, as a final check all final case reports were reviewed by the researcher at the termination of practicum.

Research Design

A 3 × 3 factorial design with repeated measures was employed. This technique reduces variability due to differences among counselors in each of three levels of dogmatism (high, medium, low) by observing each counselor under three levels of client dogmatism (high, medium, low). The three levels of dogmatism evidenced by the counselors and clients resulted in nine combinations of dyad types. Cell entries were Barrett-Lennard Relationship Inventory scores ascribed by clients to the initial interview.

Procedures

The Rokeach Dogmatism Scale was administered to counselors prior to their first interview. Counselors scoring above 140, between 118 and 139, and below 111 were arbitrarily defined as high dogmatic, medium dogmatic, and low dogmatic, respectively. There were four counselors in each of the three categories. Clients were administered the Rokeach Dogmatism Scale as part of an intake procedure. Clients scoring above 150 were defined as high dogmatic, those scoring between 121 and 149 were defined as medium dogmatic, and those scoring below 120 as low dogmatic.

Each counselor was assigned two high dogmatic clients, two medium-dogmatic clients, and two low-dogmatic clients for a total of six initial interviews. Immediately following the initial interview, clients rated the quality of the relationship provided by the counselor on the Barrett-Lennard Relationship Inventory. Clients were assured that their responses to both the Barrett-Lennard Relationship Inventory and the Rokeach Dogmatism Scale would not be disclosed to their counselors.

Results

The analysis of variance (see Table 3-VIII) revealed two significant main effects ($p < .05$), suggesting that differences in the criterion were not due to chance and could reasonably be attributed to differences in levels of dogmatism expressed by the counselors and clients. An insignificant F ratio for interaction revealed that differences in client mean ratings of the relationship could be reasonably attributed to various combinations of counselor and client dogmatism by the simple addition of the appropriate main effects ($.05 < p < .25$). That is, no combination of level of counselor dogmatism with level of client dogmatism has more or less effect on the criterion than would be expected from simply adding the appropriate single effects.

As revealed in Table 3-VIII the Newman-Keuls test disclosed

TABLE 3–VIII

ANALYSIS OF VARIANCE OF CLIENT PERCEPTIONS OF THE
COUNSELING RELATIONSHIP

Source of Variance	SS	df	MS	F
Between counselor	14,817.15	11		
Counselor dogmatism	8,235.36	2	4,117.68	5.63†
Error	6,581.19	9	731.31	
Within counselor	19,838.33	23		
Client dogmatism	10,273.53	2	5,136.76	12.49†
Client dogmatism-Counselor dogmatism	2,305.97	4	576.42	1.11
Error	7,258.83	17	426.91	
Total	34,655.48	34		

Note: Missing scores—In the final analysis of data, the two observations for each counselor within a particular cell were reduced to one by computing the mean for the two observations. This procedure reduced the total number of observations from 72 to 36, which resulted in 35 *df* for the total source of variance. Since the research design and computer program called for equal cell entrees ($N=8$), and only 69 observations were obtained for the nine cells, three scores were supplied by the author. This procedure specifically affected the *df* for the error term within counselor by reducing it from 18 to 17. The overall *df* for the total source of variance was reduced from 35 to 34 (Winer, 1962).

† $p < .05$.

that low-dogmatic clients and medium-dogmatic clients rated the relationship significantly higher than did high-dogmatic clients ($p < .05$). Low-dogmatic and medium-dogmatic clients did not differ significantly in their mean Barrett-Lennard Relationship Inventory ratings.

TABLE 3–IX

DIFFERENCES BETWEEN BARRETT-LENNARD MEANS FOR
LEVELS OF CLIENT DOGMATISM

Level of Client Dogmatism	3 (93.75)	2 (84.88)	1 (65.14)
Low (1)	28.58*	19.71*	
Medium (2)	8.87		
High (3)			

Note: Numbers in parentheses represent column means.
* $p < .05$, based on Newman-Keuls test (Winer, 1962).

The Newman-Keuls test, as indicated in Table 3-X, also revealed that low-dogmatic counselors were given significantly higher ratings by clients than were high-dogmatic counselors ($p < .05$). Differences in client Barrett-Lennard relationship mean ratings with respect to medium- and high-dogmatic counselors were not significant ($.05 < p < .06$).

TABLE 3–X

DIFFERENCES BETWEEN BARRETT-LENNARD MEANS FOR
LEVELS OF COUNSELOR DOGMATISM

Levels of Counselor Dogmatism	3 (92.58)	2 (84.29)	1 (66.93)
Low (1)	25.66*	17.37	
Medium (2)	8.29		
High (3)			

Note: Numbers in parentheses represent row means.
* $p < .05$, based on Newman-Keuls test (Winer, 1962).

TABLE 3–XI

BARRETT-LENNARD MEANS FOR ALL COMBINATIONS AND
LEVELS OF COUNSELOR AND CLIENT DOGMATISM

Counselor Dogmatism	Client Dogmatism			Counselor M
	High	Medium	Low	
High	47.00	64.75	89.00	66.93
Medium	65.13	94.25	93.50	84.29
Low	83.37	95.63	98.75	92.58
Client M	65.14	84.88	93.75	

By inspection (see Table 3-XI) certain levels of counselor and client dogmatism influenced client ratings of the relationship differently and systematically. The highest client ratings of the relationship were evidenced when low-dogmatic counselors were paired with medium- and low-dogmatic clients. In instances when medium-dogmatic counselors were assigned to medium- and low-dogmatic clients, high client ratings resulted. Comparatively speaking, the lowest client ratings were obtained when high-dogmatic counselors were paired with high- and medium-dogmatic clients. Low ratings were also revealed when medium-dogmatic counselors were combined with high-dogmatic clients.

Discussion

The major conclusion of this research is that client ratings of the relationship were increasingly higher as more openness occurred in the dyad. The two significant main effects strongly suggest that counselor and client levels of dogmatism do combine additively in terms of their effect on the criterion measure employed in this study.

The highest rated relationships were given by low- and medium-dogmatic clients interacting with low- and medium-dogmatic counselors. Conversely, the lowest rated relationships were evidenced in dyad types consisting of high-dogmatic counselors and medium-dogmatic clients and high-dogmatic clients. Similarly, medium-dogmatic counselors contributed to relationships that were given relatively high ratings by clients. In dyad types where at least one partner was low in dogmatism, client ratings of the relationship were high.

These findings also raise some questions regarding the utility of the "similarities approach" as a means of conceptualizing the counselor-client dyad. The similarities approach was not useful in describing the effects of this research. If it were, then high-high, medium-medium, and low-low dyads would have resulted in the highest client relationship ratings, with near similarities of high-medium and low-medium being next. High similarity as evidenced in low-low and medium-medium dyads did result in high client relationship ratings. High-high dyads, however, resulted in the lowest ratings. Medium counselor-client similarity found in low-medium dyads resulted in relatively high relationship ratings. In high-medium dyads, however, this was not the case. In low similarity dyads, such as low-high, moderately high client ratings were observed (see Table 3-XI).

Following an initial interview, relationships do accrue which are influenced by the dogmatism dimension in counselors and clients. Thus, differences in degree of relationships develop at the outset in counseling. The present study, however, did not answer the question of the nature of change in the relationship which may occur over several interviews. It is also conceivable that the relationship, as measured here, may be of a neurotic nature since there is no evidence to the contrary. The final outcome may not necessarily be healthy or beneficial. What may have been observed was the first step in the establishment of a series of more or less neurotic behavior or manipulation reflecting nothing more than an initial stage of seduction. The low-dogmatic counselor, for example, under conditions of threat accompanying the first practicum, could be better able to maintain more flexibility and spontaneity than the high-dogmatic counselor. This flexibility and spontaneity could be effectively used in seducing clients into perceiving him more positively. The low-dogmatic counselor's capacity to handle threat can be used to establish a relationship, but this in itself does not guarantee that final outcomes will be productive.

References

Allen, T. W.: Effectiveness of counselor trainees as a function of psychological openness. *Journal of Counseling Psychology, 14*:35-41, 1967.

Axelrod, J.: *An Evaluation of the Effects of Progress in Therapy of Similarities and Differences Between the Personalities of Patients and Their Therapists.* Unpublished doctoral dissertation, New York University, 1951.

Barrett-Lennard, G. T.: Dimensions of therapist response as causal factors in therapeutic change. *Psychological Monographs, 76 (43,* Whole No. 562), 1962.

Brammer, L. M., and Shostrom, E. L.: *Therapeutic Psychology.* Englewood Cliffs, N.J., Prentice Hall, 1960.

Cahoon, R. A.: *Some Counselor Attitudes and Characteristics Related to the Counseling Relationship.* Unpublished doctorial dissertation, Ohio State University, 1962.

Carson, R. C., and Heine, R. W.: Similarity and success in therapeutic dyads. *Journal of Consulting Psychology, 26*:38-43, 1962.

Cook, T. E.: The influence of client-counselor value similarity on change and meaning during brief counseling. *Journal of Counseling Psychology, 13*:77-81, 1966.

Gross, W. F., and DeRidder, L. M.: Significant movement in comparatively short-term counseling. *Journal of Counseling Psychology, 13*:98-99, 1966.

Hebert, D. J.: *The Counseling Relationship as a Function of Client-Counselor Personality Need and Sex Similarity.* Unpublished doctoral dissertation, Kent State University, 1967.

Heine, R. W., and Trosman, H.: Initial expectations of the doctor-patient interaction as a factor in continuance in psychotherapy. *Psychiatry, 23*: 275-278, 1960.

Hobbs, N.: Sources of gain in psychotherapy. In J. F. Adams, *Counseling and Guidance.* New York, Macmillan, 1965.

Jourard, S. M.: *The Transparent Self.* New York, Van Nostrand, 1964.

Kamin, I., and Caughlin, J.: Subjective experience of outpatient psychotherapy. *American Journal of Psychotherapy, 17*:660-668, 1963.

Kemp, C. G.: Influence of dogmatism on counseling. *Personnel and Guidance Journal, 39*:662-665, 1961.

Kemp, C. G.: The influence of dogmatism on the training of counselors. *Journal of Counseling Psychology, 9*:155-157, 1962.

Leary, T.: The theory and measurement methodology of interpersonal communication. *Psychiatry, 18*:147-161, 1955.

Lesser, W. M.: The relationship between counseling progress and empathic understanding. *Journal of Counseling Psychology,* 8:330-336, 1961.

McGowan, J. F., and Schmidt, L. D.: *Counseling: Readings in Theory and Practice.* New York, Holt, Rinehart and Winston, 1962.

Mendelsohn, G. A., and Geller, M. H.: Effects of counselor-client similarity in the outcome of counseling. *Journal of Counseling Psychology,* 10:71-77, 1963.

Rogers, C. R.: The characteristics of the helping relationship. *Personnel and Guidance Journal,* 37:6-16, 1958.

Rokeach, M.: *The Open and Closed Mind.* New York, Basic Books, 1960.

Russo, J. R., Kelz, J. W., and Hudson, G. R.: Are good counselors open-minded? *Counselor Education and Supervision,* 3:74-77, 1964.

Tosi, D. J., Fagan, T. K., and Frumkin, R. M.: Relation of levels of dogmatism and perceived threat under conditions of group personality testing. *Perceptual Motor Skills,* 26:481-482.

Truax, C. B., and Carkhuff, R. R.: For better or for worse: the process of psychotherapeutic change. Invited address: Recent Advances in the Study of Behavior Change, Academic Assembly on Clinical Psychology, McGill University, Montreal, Canada, June 1963.

Tuma, A. H., and Gustad, J. W.: The effects of client and counselor personality characteristics on client learning in counseling. *Journal of Counseling Psychology,* 4:136-141, 1951.

Vogel, J. L.: Authoritarianism in the therapeutic relationship. *Journal of Consulting Psychology,* 25:102-108, 1962.

Winer, B. J.: *Statistical Principles in Experimental Design.* New York, McGraw-Hill, 1962.

EFFECTS OF CONFRONTATION BY HIGH- AND LOW-FUNCTIONING THERAPISTS ON HIGH- AND LOW-FUNCTIONING CLIENTS*

SUSAN ANDERSON

A recent study (Anderson, 1968) has found that a therapist's ability to confront his clients with discrepancies in their ways of viewing reality is associated with increased client self-exploration (DX) following the confrontation. In the former study, the therapists whose confrontations led to increased client DX were found to be highly rated by expert judges on the facilitative dimensions of empathy, positive regard, genuineness, and self-disclosure. Thus, it was difficult to distinguish whether the effect

*Reprinted from the *Journal of Counseling Psychology,* 16:299-302, 1969, with permission of the American Psychological Association and the author.

on the dependent variable (DX) was due primarily to the presence of confrontation behavior or to the fact that the therapist was highly facilitative.

In order to differentiate the effects of confrontation from the effects of the therapist's level of functioning, this study was designed to compare the effects of confrontations by equal numbers of high and low therapists. It also differentiated the client sample into high and low functioning on the basis of expert judgments. In this way it was possible to explore the effects of confrontations by high and low functioning therapists on the DX of high- as compared with low-functioning clients.

Confrontation is defined as an act by which the therapist points out to the client a discrepancy between his own and the client's way of viewing reality. It may be directed at helping the client become more aware of his resources or constructive aspects of his personality or situation, or it may be directed toward limitations or destructive behaviors of which the client is unaware. Confrontations may be directed toward the interpersonal discrepancies, such as those between the therapist's and the client's way of viewing the client's personality, his situation, or his feelings; or they may be directed toward intrapersonal discrepancies, such as those between the client's real versus his ideal or feared self-concept, or his real as opposed to his fantasied behavior. Both the inter- and the intrapersonal discrepancies, however, are expressed in terms of a contrast between the therapist's view of the situation and the client's perception. This concept is more completely illustrated in the Anderson (1968) study mentioned above.

As in the earlier study, a high therapist was defined as one whose average rating by expert judges on the 5-point rating scales for empathy, positive regard, genuineness, and self-disclosure (Carkhuff and Berenson, 1968) was 3.0 or above, 3.0 constituting the minimal facilitative level. A low therapist was one whose average rating was below 3.0. A client was considered high if he attained an average rating scale level of 2.5 on the dimensions when placed in a "helping role" with another student acting as the "client." Level 2.5 rather than 3.0 was chosen as the cut-off point for defining high-functioning clients, since this level has been found to be above average with respect to college student populations (Carkhuff and Berenson, 1968).

Method

The therapists in the study were 16 counselors with 2 to 8 years' experience regularly employed in counseling center or student personnel activities at the University of Massachusetts. The clients were 16 undergraduate college students scheduled for relatively short-term treatment (requiring fewer than 10 counseling interviews) at the counseling center. Both therapists and clients had volunteered to participate in "some research on the helping relationship." The 16 therapists were chosen by the following procedure: Each was asked by E to submit four tape recordings of his counseling with four different college students— one of an initial interview, one of a terminal interview, and two of intermediate stages of a relationship. After listening to three randomly selected 5-minute excerpts of each of these tape recordings, two trained raters, experienced in the use of the 5-point scales mentioned above, independently rated each therapist on each of the facilitative dimensions. In order to obtain equal numbers in both the high and low categories, tapes from more than the 16 therapists chosen for the study were rated. It was necessary to rate the tapes of 23 therapists before the preplanned distribution of eight "highs" and eight "lows" was obtained.

In order to achieve the distribution of eight high- and eight low-functioning clients, 20 student volunteers were assigned to a "standard interview" situation, in which they were to talk with a person who was introduced to them as "another student who also has some problems." They were asked to meet with this person for one-half hour in the counseling center and to "try to be as helpful as possible to him." In actuality, the person to be helped was a graduate student in counseling psychology (referred to as the interviewee) who was taking the role of a client seeking help. The interviewee was instructed to simply be himself and to bring up for discussion some of his own real difficulties. The sessions were taped to allow previously trained raters to assess S's "interpersonal level" on the dimensions of empathy, positive regard, genuineness, and self-disclosure. These ratings were independently conducted by the two raters mentioned above. Ratings were based on three 5-minute excerpts, one from the early, one from the middle, and one from the latter portion of the interview. Interrater reliability coefficients were above .90 in all cases.

Once the level of interpersonal functioning had been established for all clients and therapists, four high and four low clients were assigned to the eight high therapists; equal proportions were assigned to the eight low therapists for counseling. In actuality, most counselor-client pairings had occurred prior to the completion of the rating procedures; only three pairings were delayed in order to insure equal numbers in each group.

Before treatment was begun, each therapist in the study was introduced to the concept of confrontation as defined above. Several examples were presented to the therapists as they appeared in the earlier (Anderson, 1968) study. The therapists were instructed to engage the client in two confrontations during the middle 15-minute period of the approximately 45-minute interview. This was to occur in their first and again in their fourth session, both of which were to be tape recorded. Following the interviews, each therapist was to label the points of confrontation on the tape with a piece of colored mending tape. The author reviewed the confrontation points of all therapists to insure that they were truly points of therapist-to-client confrontation. These taped interviews were then given to two trained raters (not the same individuals who performed therapist ratings) who independently rated each session for client depth of DX during the 2-minute periods before and after each confrontation point. Client DX ratings were made on the basis of Carkhuff's (1965) scale for interpersonal exploration. The ratings yielded a measure of whether or not an increase in DX followed each confrontation.

Each confrontation was also categorized by these judges according to whether it was directed toward bringing the client into greater awareness of his resources (or constructive behavior) or his limitations (or destructive behavior).

Results

The change in client DX for each of the two confrontations scored was tabulated by therapist level, client level, confrontation type, and interview number. In order to compare the effects of resources confrontations and limitations confrontations, only the data for the 12 S's who received both types of confrontations were used. An analysis of variance on the data suggests several findings:

1. Overall gain in client DX following a confrontation was higher for high-functioning therapists than for low-functioning therapists.

2. There was no significant difference in overall DX gain between high- and low-functioning clients.

3. For all clients, there was a greater amount of change in DX during Interview 4 as compared with Interview 1.

These results are summarized in Table 3-XII.

TABLE 3–XII

ANALYSIS OF VARIANCE OF DATA BASED ON CLIENT
SELF-EXPLORATION AS DEPENDENT MEASURE

Source	df	MS	F
Therapist level (T)	1	752.08	21.87**
Client level (C)	1	75.00	ns
Interview number (I)	1	252.08	8.06*
Confrontation type (R)	1	.00	ns
T × C	1	33.33	ns
T × I	1	2.08	ns
C × I	1	8.33	ns
T × R	1	75.00	ns
C × R	1	102.08	ns
I × R	1	8.33	ns
S(T × C)	8	34.37	
T × C × I	1	75.00	ns
T × C × R	1	52.08	ns
T × I × R	1	8.33	ns
C × I × R	1	2.08	ns

$* p \leq .05.$
$** p \leq .01.$

A second analysis of variance was performed on the data generated by tabulating the types (resources or limitations) of confrontations present in each interview. In some therapist-client sessions both confrontations were of the resources type (this will be called the two to nothing or "2-0" situation or treatment). In others, both were of the limitations type (this will be called the "0-2" situation); while in still others, one of each type of confrontation occurred (this will be called the "1-1" situation). The ANOVA on these data suggests the following:

1. No significant difference in type of confrontation used was found between high- and low-functioning therapists.

2. Low-functioning clients were more often given the 2-0 or the 0-2 treatment and only rarely experienced the 1-1 situation.

3. More confrontations of the limitations type occurred overall.

4. There were significant interactions between therapist level and interview number as well as between client level and interview number. These Therapist Level × Interview Number and Client Level × Interview Number interactions, however, actually appear to reflect the size of the therapist and client level main effects, since the interview number effect itself is very low.

5. There was a significant interaction between interview number and confrontation type, indicating that the frequency of resources confrontations was greater for Interview 1 than Interview 4, while the number of limitations confrontations was greater for Interview 4.

6. A significant second-order interaction was obtained for Therapist Level × Interview Number × Confrontation Type. For higher therapists in Interview 1, resources confrontations significantly exceeded limitations confrontations; in Interview 4,

TABLE 3–XIII

ANALYSIS OF VARIANCE OF DATA BASED ON CONFRONTATION TYPE AS DEPENDENT MEASURE

Source	df	MS	F
Therapist level (T)	1	.140	*ns*
Client level (C)	1	.390	5.00*
Interview number (I)	1	.015	*ns*
Confrontation type (V)	1	40.640	32.11***
T × C	1	.015	*ns*
T × I	1	.390	5.00*
C × T	1	.390	5.00*
T × V	1	1.265	*ns*
C × V	1	.140	*ns*
I × V	1	6.890	5.44*
S(T × C)	12	.078	
T × C × I	1	.015	*ns*
T × C × V	1	3.515	*ns*
T × I × V	1	17.015	13.44**
C × I × V	1	.140	*ns*

* $p \leq .05$.

** $p \leq .01$.

*** $p \leq .001$.

this situation was reversed. For low therapists, limitations confrontations exceeded resources confrontations in both interviews. These results are summarized in Table 3-XIII.

Discussion

Confrontation by high-functioning therapists was much more frequently associated with increased client DX than was confrontation by low therapists. Perhaps the high therapist, operating within the context of an empathic and accepting atmosphere, is more likely to be seen by the client as able and willing to help. Personality characteristics associated with high therapeutic functioning such as genuineness and DX would also indicate that these therapists might feel more at ease with confrontation behavior than would therapists who are less congruent; that is, since confrontation is more compatible with their everyday manner of DX, it is, for the high therapists, a more effective therapeutic tool. Since the client level main effect was not found to be significant, the change in DX following confrontation can be attributed mainly to therapist level.

The finding that more variability in DX level following confrontation occurred in the fourth interview, as compared with the first, probably indicates that a greater range of DX or emotional experiencing is characteristic of later interviews.

Also characteristic of later, as opposed to earlier, interviews was the increasing tendency for the therapist to focus confrontations toward client limitations, as seen by the finding that during the first interview most therapists directed their confrontations at client resources; while in the fourth session, most confrontations were directed at client limitations. This distinction between resources confrontations and limitations confrontations may be elaborated further: In the former type, the therapist's statement appears to be aimed at enhancing the client's self-image and at reducing the perceived discrepancy between the client's real situation and his ideal. Although it introduces an interpersonal discrepancy (between the therapist's view of a situation and the client's), it aims at reducing intrapersonal dissonance. In the limitations type of confrontation, both inter- and intrapersonal discrepancies are augmented. Here the therapist's remark tends to increase the perceived distance between the client's real behavior and his ideal. It also points out an area of discrepant perception between the therapist and the client. Thus, as the relationship progressed, for both levels of therapist and client, there was an increasing tendency to deal with discrepancies or conflicts and a decreasing tendency to focus on areas of consonance.

The significant second order interaction between therapist level, interview number, and confrontation type seems to indicate that for the high-functioning therapist, there is a much greater tendency to vary his type of confrontation behavior from one situation to another. The behavior of the low-functioning therapist was relatively more static, while the high therapist's behavior seemed to be more dependent upon the situation. This may be one of the factors which distinguishes the high- from the low-functioning therapist in general.

References

Anderson, S. C.: The effects of confrontations by high- and low-functioning therapists. *Journal of Counseling Psychology*, 15:411-416, 1968.

Carkhuff, R. R.: *Scale for Measurement of Client Depth of Self-Exploration.* University of Massachusetts, 1965.

Carkhuff, R. R., and Berenson, B. G.: *Beyond Counseling and Therapy.* New York, Holt, Rinehart and Winston, 1968.

SELF-ACTUALIZATION AND THE COMMUNICATION OF FACILITATIVE CONDITIONS DURING COUNSELING*

MELVIN L. FOULDS

The therapeutic relevance of the counselor-offered conditions or attitudinal qualities of empathic understanding, respect or positive regard, and facilitative genuineness has been verified by a substantial amount of research evidence (Carkhuff and Berenson, 1967; Rogers, Gendlin, Kiesler, and Truax, 1967; Truax and Carkhuff, 1967). There has been little research undertaken, however, to determine the relationship between particular personality characteristics of counselors and their ability to communicate

* Reprinted from the *Journal of Counseling Psychology,* 16:132-136, 1969, with permission of the American Psychological Association and the author.

these specific facilitative conditions to their clients. The need for such investigations has been advocated in recent publications (Berenson and Carkhuff, 1967; Bergin, 1966; Carkhuff, 1967; Carkhuff and Berenson, 1967; Truax and Carkhuff, 1967).

A review of the research literature revealed that this problem is almost completely unexplored. Unpublished papers by Bergin and Solomon (1963) and Truax, Silber, and Wargo (1966) represented initial efforts to investigate the personality correlates of ability to communicate the facilitative conditions within a counseling relationship, but both of these studies were based on small samples of counselors.

Theorists, researchers, and practitioners of counseling and psychotherapy have suggested a positive relationship between the ability of the counselor to facilitate constructive change or positive gain in his clients and his level of "wholeness" (Carkhuff and Berenson, 1967), personal adequacy (Combs, 1962), humanness (Dreyfuss, 1967), authenticity (Bugental, 1965; Jourard, 1964, 1966), self-actualization (Maslow, 1962, 1967), psychological openness (Allen, 1967; May, 1967), and fully functioning (Rogers, 1958, 1962, 1963). Thus a positive association may exist between psychological well-being and ability to communicate facilitative conditions during counseling. The demonstration of such a relationship would have important implications for the selection and/or education of counselors and psychotherapists.

The Personal Orientation Inventory (POI), a measure of self-actualization or positive mental health, has been developed by Shostrom (1964, 1966). This inventory attempts to identify the self-actualizing person who is more fully functioning than the average or below average individual, and findings of research conducted using the POI suggest that the inventory is a reasonably valid and reliable measure of psychological well-being, personal adjustment, freedom from neurotic symptoms, or self-actualization (Knapp, 1965; Shostrom, 1964, 1966; Shostrom and Knapp, 1966).

The present study was undertaken to investigate the relationship between self-actualization, as measured by the POI, and ability to communicate the facilitative conditions of empathic understanding, respect or positive regard, and facilitative genuineness during counseling. The purpose of the study was to determine particular personality characteristics of counselors which may be associated with their ability to provide these facilitative conditions for their clients during counseling.

Method

Subjects

The Ss of this study were 30 graduate students enrolled in a beginning supervised practicum experience in the counselor-education program at the University of Florida during the second trimester of the academic year 1966-1967. In this group were 14 men and 16 women ranging in age 21-44 years with a mean age of 27.7 years. Practicum settings included both on- and off-campus agencies.

Instruments

Assessment of levels of facilitative conditions communicated by the counselors in this study relied on three instruments developed by Carkhuff (1969). These scales, Empathic Understanding in Interpersonal Processes (E), Respect or Positive Regard in Interpersonal Processes (R), and Facilitative Genuineness in Interpersonal Processes (G), consist of five levels each, and they were derived from an earlier set of scales which have been validated in extensive counseling-outcome research (Truax and Carkhuff, 1967). The scales were designed for use with interaction samples excerpted from tape-recorded counseling sessions or from any other type of interpersonal encounter. Judges who are specifically trained in the use of each scale listen to a tape-recorded interaction sample and rate (using the appropriate five-level scale) the level at which the particular facilitative condition was provided by the counselor.

The POI was used to assess the personality characteristics associated with self-actualization. This scale was designed by Shostrom (1964, 1966)and attempts to provide a comprehensive measure of values and behavior believed to be of importance in the development of self-actualization, personal adjustment, fully functioning, or positive mental health, terms which Shostrom appears to use synonymously. The POI consists of 150 two-choice, paired-opposite statements of values, and scores are reported for 2 major scales and 10 secondary scales which purport to assess particular personality characteristics considered to be associated with self-actualization.

Procedure

Each S completed the POI 5 weeks prior to the close of the trimester and submitted one tape-recorded counseling session which he had conducted near the end of the counseling practicum experience. The taped session he submitted was to be one which he considered to be representative of one of his better counseling efforts at that particular stage of his development as a counselor. Three 3-minute interaction samples were selected at random from each tape, one from each one-third of the interview, with the restriction that both a counselor and a client verbalization be present in each sample. These segments ($N = 90$) were then recorded in random order on master tapes to be used in evaluating levels of facilitative conditions offered.

Three sets of two judges each, who were relatively sophisticated with respect to personality dynamics and psychotherapy theory and practice, were trained in the use of the research scales, and each set of judges rated one condition only. The following Pearson product-moment interjudge reliabilities were established at the end of the training program and prior to the rating of the data samples: .94 (E); .80 (R); and .88 (G). The 90 data samples were then independently rated by the six judges, and the interjudge reliabilities were: .57 (E); .48 (R); and .72 (G).

After all the data were obtained, all responses were totaled, and the data were tabulated and analyzed. Pearson product-moment coefficients of correlation were computed by the University of Florida Computing Center to determine the intercorrelations of all variables.

Results

Correlation coefficients of the relationships between each of the POI scales and each of the facilitative variables are presented in Table 3-XIV. The ability to communicate empathic understanding was significantly related to 6 of the 12 scales ($p < .05$), the ability to communicate facilitative genuineness was significantly related to 10 of the 12 scales of the POI ($p < .05$), and 6 POI scales were significantly related to total conditions offered ($p < .05$). No POI scales were significantly related to ability to communicate respect or positive regard.

The ability of counselors to communicate empathic understanding seems to be related to the following personality characteristics which the POI purports to assess: (*a*) the feelings or attitudes of personal freedom or independence and internal direction based upon inner motivations rather than upon external expectations and influences, thus, the opposite of behavioral compliance (I); (*b*) affirmation of the values associated with self-actualization and growth rather than conformity and "frozenness" (SAV); (*c*) flexibility in the application of values rather than compulsivity or dogmatism (Ex); (*d*) awareness of and sensitivity to one's own needs and feelings rather than estrangement from one's inner world of experience (Fr); (*e*) the ability to accept one's natural aggressiveness as opposed to defensiveness, denial, and repression of aggression (A); (*f*) the ability to develop intimate and meaningful relationships with other human beings which are unencumbered by expectations and obligations, to develop "I-Thou" relationships in the here and now, to contact the authentic "being" of another person, to invite intense involvement in human encounters, to enter in communion with another human being (C).

The ability of counselors to communicate facilitative genuineness appears to be related to the six personality variables described above *plus* the following characteristics which the POI purports to assess: (*a*) the ability to be open and disclosing, to express feelings in spontaneous action (S); (*b*) the ability to like one's self because of one's strength as a person as opposed to feelings of low self-worth (Sr); (*c*) acceptance of one's self in spite of one's weaknesses or deficiencies rather than inability to accept one's weaknesses (Sa); (*d*) the ability to be synergistic, to transcend dichotomies, to see opposites of life as meaningfully related (Sy).

Levels of facilitative conditions communicated to clients

TABLE 3–XIV
PRODUCT-MOMENT CORRELATIONS BETWEEN SCORES ON THE
PERSONAL ORIENTATION INVENTORY (POI) AND
FACILITATIVE CONDITIONS OFFERED

POI Scale	Empathic Under Standing	Respect, Positive Regard	Facili- tative Genuine- ness	Total Conditions
Time competence (Tc)	−.08	−.02	.27	.09
Inner direction (I)	.33*	.12	.49**	.42**
Self-actualizing values (SAV)	.32*	.20	.55**	.48**
Existentiality (Ex)	.31*	.10	.39*	.36*
Feeling reactivity (Fr)	.43**	.20	.46**	.48**
Spontaneity (S)	.17	.21	.40**	.35*
Self-regard (Sr)	−.03	.04	.33*	.16
Self-acceptance (Sa)	.24	−.10	.33*	.21
View of the nature of man (Nc)	.08	−.02	.26	.15
Synergy (Sy)	.17	−.11	.29*	.16
Acceptance of aggression (A)	.30*	−.03	.33*	.27
Capacity for intimate contact (C)	.32*	.04	.41**	.35*

* $p < .05.$
** $p < .01.$

ranged from Level 1 to Level 4 for each condition with mean ratings of 1.8 (E), 2.4 (R), and 2.5 (G).

Discussion

Findings of this study suggest that the ability to sensitively and accurately perceive the inner "being" or experiencing of another human being and to communicate this understanding to him, and the ability to be authentically real in a genuine encounter without defensive phoniness or without hiding behind the mask or facade of a professional role seems to be related to psychological well-being or self-actualization, as measured by the POI.

The ability to communicate respect or positive regard, however, was not significantly related to scores on the scales of the POI. One interpretation of this finding is that people who perceive themselves as "helping" persons and plan to enter a helping profession such as counseling generally value highly human life and the dignity and worth of human beings. Therefore, this self-selection process tends to result in a relatively homogeneous group with respect to the facilitative attitude of respect or positive regard for clients. There may be no relationship, however, between the attitude of respect for other persons and one's own level of genuineness or ability to communicate empathic understanding of others.

While a decrease in the reliability of the judges was anticipated in the ratings of the data samples, the extent of the decreases for E and R were unexpected. An inspection of the ratings revealed that the disagreement between judges could not be attributed to a bias on the part of any judge to rate samples consistently high or low. Mean ratings of judges for E were 1.7 and 1.9, and mean ratings for judges of R were 2.4 and 2.4. Thus the reduced reliabilities of the judges is the result of other unspecified factors such as inadequacies in the research scales and/or the training program or differences in accuracy of perception of inferred emotional meanings between the judges.

The present study did not investigate the relationship between the kinds of experiences provided in the counselor-education program and the measured attributes. Additional research is required to ascertain the effects of specific training experiences upon both the development of self-actualization and the ability to provide high levels of facilitative conditions during counseling.

Hypotheses presented by Bergin (1966), Carkhuff and Berenson (1967), Rogers (1958), and Truax and Carkhuff (1967) concerning the relationship between the psychological well-being of the counselor and his ability to provide facilitative conditions during counseling receive important research support from the present investigation. Perhaps, as suggested by Carkhuff and Berenson (1967), counseling is as effective as the counselor is living effectively. Additional research is required, however, to replicate this study for increased confidence in the findings, to determine if the personality characteristics are related to actual counseling outcome, and to ascertain if findings hold for experienced counselors as well as beginning counselors.

References

Allen, T. W.: Effectiveness of counselor trainees as a function of psychological openness. *Journal of Counseling Psychology, 14*:35-40, 1967.

Berenson, B. G., and Carkhuff, R. R. (Eds.): *Sources of Gain in Counseling and Psychotherapy.* New York, Holt, Rinehart and Winston, 1967.

Bergin, A. E.: Some implications of psychotherapy research for therapeutic practice. *Journal of Abnormal and Social Psychology, 71*:235-246, 1966.

Bergin, A. E., and Solomon, S.: *Personality and Performance Correlates of Empathic Understanding in Psychotherapy.* Paper presented at the meeting of the American Psychological Association, Philadelphia, September 1963.

Bugental, J. F. T.: *The Search for Authenticity.* New York, Holt, Rinehart and Winston, 1965.

Carkhuff, R. R.: Toward a comprehensive model of facilitative interpersonal processes. *Journal of Counseling Psychology, 14*:67-72, 1967.

Carkhuff, R. R. (Ed.): *The Counselor's Contribution to Facilitative Processes.* Urbana, Ill., Parkinson, 1969.

Carkhuff, R. R., and Berenson, B. G.: *Beyond Counseling and Therapy.* New York, Holt, Rinehart and Winston, 1967.

Combs, A. W.: A perceptual view of the adequate personality. In A. W. Combs (Ed.): *Perceiving, Behaving, Becoming.* Washington, D.C., Association for Supervision and Curriculum Development, 1962.

Dreyfus, E.: Humanness: a therapeutic variable. *Personnel and Guidance Journal, 45*:573-578, 1967.

Jourard, S. M.: *The Transparent Self.* Princeton, Van Nostrand, 1964.

Jourard, S. M.: Counseling for authenticity. In C. E. Beck (Ed.): *Guidelines for Guidance.* Dubuque, Iowa, W. C. Brown, 1966.

Knapp, R.: Relationship of a measure of self-actualization to neuroticism and extraversion. *Journal of Consulting Psychology, 29*:168-172, 1965.

Maslow, A. W.: *Toward a Psychology of Being.* Princeton, Van Nostrand, 1962.

Maslow, A. W.: Self-actualization and beyond. In J. F. T. Bugental (Ed.): *Challenges of Humanistic Psychology.* New York, McGraw-Hill, 1967.

May, R.: *Psychology and the Human Dilemma.* Princeton, Van Nostrand, 1967.

Rogers, C. R.: The characteristics of a helping relationship. *Personnel and Guidance Journal, 37*:6-15, 1958.

Rogers, C. R.: The interpersonal relationship: the core of guidance. *Harvard Educational Review, 32*:416-429, 1962.

Rogers, C. R.: The fully functioning person. *Psychotherapy: Theory, Research and Practice, 1*:17-26, 1963.

Rogers, C. R., Gendlin, E., Kiesler, D., and Truax, C. (Eds.) *The Therapeutic Relationship and its Impact: A Study of Psychotherapy with Schizophrenics.* New York, Harper and Row, 1967.

Shostrom, E.: A test for the measurement of self-actualization. *Educational and Psychological Measurement, 24*:207-218, 1964.

Shostrom, E.: *Manual, Personal Orientation Inventory.* San Diego, Educational and Industrial Testing Service, 1966.

Shostrom, E., and Knapp, R.: The relationship of a measure of self-actualization (POI) to a measure of pathology (MMPI) and to therapeutic growth. *American Journal of Psychotherapy, 20*:193-202, 1966.

Truax, C. B., and Carkhuff, R. R.: *Toward Effective Counseling and Psychotherapy.* Chicago, Aldine, 1967.

Truax, C. B., Silber, L., and Wargo, D.: *Personality Change and Achievement in Therapeutic Training.* Unpublished manuscript, Arkansas Rehabilitation Research and Training Center, University of Arkansas, 1966.

Chapter 4

STRATEGIES IN COUNSELOR EDUCATION AND SUPERVISION

Formal, systematic theories of counselor education and supervision are at best implicit; at worst nonexistent. *Strategies* related to the training of counselors do exist, however, and span the spectrum from experiential to cognitive with an amalgamation of the two extremes occupying an intermediate position. The task of selecting an approach or method for the would-be supervisor or counselor educator may resemble the challenge the novice counselor experiences as he embraces a theory of counseling. McGowan's (1956) plea that counselors adopt an orientation in harmony with their natural response style and personal ideology instead of the reverse would seem to be equally applicable to the counselor educator and supervisor.

Even though graduates from counseling programs will sooner or later be called upon to train others, little emphasis is placed on the acquisition of supervisory skills during the course of graduate training. To guard against inadequately trained trainers, Hansen and Stevic set forth a proposal ". . . for action toward more adequate preparation of practicum supervisors." Their contribution was selected as the lead article for this chapter because the authors suggest a framework within which supervisory strategies may be acquired.

Theories and strategies related to how we *should* teach, counsel, or supervise exist in reasonable abundance. Systematic investigations on how we actually *do* teach, counsel, or supervise are, however, quite limited. A number of investigations do exist, however, and a classic example is a study conducted by Walz and Roeber. These investigators discovered certain rather disturbing orientations and procedures utilized in the supervision of counselor trainees. In general, their findings suggest that the usual supervisory response seems to be cognitive and information-giving, with negative overtones. It should be noted that a later study by Johnston and Gysbers (additional reference list) contradicts the data gathered by Walz and Roeber. The studies differed methodologically, which may account for the different findings. Walz and Roeber's supervisors responded to transcripts of client comments. Johnston and Gysbers polled supervisors by mail, using a "critical incident" technique, in which respondents indicated their preferred mode of guiding counselor trainees. Another explanation may be that both studies did, in fact, reflect current orientations and that the later study suggests a trend away from the instructional mode. Other explanations may be as plausible. At any rate, the reader is urged to examine Johnston and Gysber's study for purposes of comparison and arrive at his own conclusions.

Anderson and Bown believe that maximum therapeutic trainee growth occurs within the context of free communication and that "free communication" means open, frank, and direct supervisory comments. In their article "Tape Recordings and Counselor-Trainee Understandings," the authors make only passing reference to a permissive, nonthreatening, nonevaluative supervisor-trainee relationship. In fact, they perceive the supervisory relationship as very directive, didactic and threatening to the novice counselor. Anderson and Bown illustrate their orientation by presenting case material from supervisory conferences based on tape-recorded client-trainee interviews.

Seemingly in accord with Anderson and Bown, Mazer and Engle ("Practicum Supervision: Good Guys and Bad Guys") are distressed at the derogatory comments often directed at the more instructionally oriented supervisor. They present some initial evidence suggesting that an instructional approach (impersonal, programmed) is as promising and, in some cases more promising, (as reflected on a number of therapist performance criteria) than the more relationship oriented supervisory practices.

Moving away from the position held by the authors of the two preceding papers, Patterson supports the view that the supervisory relationship should not reflect a didactic teaching approach nor should it be a nonevaluative, therapeutic relationship. Patterson's orientation, however, is nearer the latter than the former. In his article "Supervising Students in the Counseling Practicum," he elaborates on the central theme that "Supervision, while not therapy, should be, like all good human relationships, therapeutic."

Ruble and Gray discuss a student-centered approach to practicum supervision designed to promote the integration of self and counseling technique. Presumably, the effects of such an approach would translate into more effective client-counselor relationships. The authors' position that cognitive knowledge about counseling theory and technique may bear little relationship to performance in counseling situations merits serious consideration.

Lister contends that a counselor's awareness of his subjective experiencing can contribute to more mature and integrated counseling relationships. In his article "Counselor Experiencing: Its Implications for Supervision," Lister explores how the supervisor can assist the counselor trainee achieve increased awareness of his internal experiencing.

Integrating didactic and experiential training procedures, Truax ("An Approach to Counselor Education"), elaborates on a strategy applicable to professionals as well as nonprofessionals. The author spells out in concrete terms both selection and training procedures within the framework of an integrated didactic-experiential approach. Truax's orientation may be seen as occupying an intermediate position between the cognitive, instructional approach and the more relationship or therapeutically inclined strategies.

Hurst and Jensen argue that much "lip service" is paid to the importance of such counselor attributes as acceptance, warmth, and sensitivity. Opportunities, however, to develop these qualities in many graduate training programs are limited. The authors report on a well-designed study investigating the effectiveness of a personal growth approach to the training of counselors. This promising dimension in counselor education has been receiving increased attention in the past few years. The reader is encouraged to consider other articles (which include some initial research efforts) exploring the efficacy of incorporating personal growth experiences into existing counselor training programs.

In their paper, Hansen and Moore offer a thorough discussion of the off-campus practicum—a rather neglected issue. According to the authors, the nature of the field practicum makes it imperative that supervision be viewed in a broad context. Responsibility to the counselor candidate, the agency or institution, the university supervisor, as well as society and the client does, in fact, broaden the more limited training role suggested by counselor educators affiliated with academic institutions. If adequately implemented, the off-campus practicum provides a realistic training opportunity designed to integrate theory and practice, thus adding a much needed dimension in counselor training.

Lest we forget the complexities of any interpersonal encounter, Kadushin reminds us of the intricate supervisor-trainee relationship in his imaginative contribution "Games People Play in Supervision." A discussion of how games originate precedes descriptions of games initiated by supervisors and their charges.

In discussing the effects of social modeling in counselor education Jakubowski-Spector, Dustin, and George comment that

> What a counselor educator *does* may be more influential than what he *says*; our role as a model may be more important than our role as an instructor. If a counselor educator is trying to teach genuine communication, the educator's interpersonal dealings with his students should reflect or model the kind of behavior he endorses. Through our dealings with students, we show them what we are and what we expect from people. Too often, a counselor educator verbalizes the importance of genuineness and self disclosure while his students do not find these behaviors in their interaction with him as an advisor, practicum instructor, or professor. As models, counselor educators could more effectively facilitate learning through striving to consistently act out the behaviors they are trying to teach. This may lead to more consistent behaviors in counseling students [Jakubowski-Spector, Dustin, and George, 1971, pp. 248-49].

In his brief but provocative article "Alternative Strategies in Psychotherapy Supervision," Haigh concretely illustrates the double messages communicated when discrepancies occur between what the supervisor didactically teaches and what he experientially conveys to a trainee.

An approach that seems to hold some theoretical and empirical promise is explicated by Blocher in his paper "Counselor Education: Facilitating the Development of a Helping Person." Blocher sets forth a tentative theory of counselor education, which seeks to integrate the following response modes: immediate-intuitive, cognitive-theoretical, and empirical-pragmatic. His paper is a fitting close to this chapter in that he avoids the tendency to "go on faith" or resort to intuitively generated speculation to develop a testable theory of counselor education.

The papers in this chapter reflect attempts to look at the mentor-trainee relationship from a number of different perspectives. It seems unlikely that any one view or strategy will strike a responsive cord for all counselor educators or supervisors. An orientation, however, that proves compatible with one's natural response style (McGowan) and philosophical bent would in all probability be one's "position of choice."

References

Jakubowski-Spector, P., Dustin, R., and George, R. L.: Toward developing a behavioral counselor education model. *Counselor Education and Supervision, 10*:242-250, 1971.

McGowan, J. F.: Developing a natural response style. *Education, 4*:246-249, 1956.

Additional References

Apostal, R. A., and Muro, J. J.: Effects of group counseling on self-reports and on self-recognition abilities of counselors in training. *Counselor Education and Supervision, 10*:56-63, 1970.

Arbuckle, D. S.: Supervision: learning, not counseling. *Journal of Counseling Psychology, 12*:90-94, 1965.

Arnold, D. L.: Counselor education as responsible self development. *Counselor Education and Supervision, 1*:185-192, 1962.

Beier, E. G.: On supervision in psychotherapy. *Psychotherapy: Theory, Research and Practice, 1*:91-95, 1964.

Dreikurs, R., and Sonstegard, M.: A specific approach to practicum supervision. *Counselor Education and Supervision, 6*:18-26, 1966.

Gazda, G., and Ohlsen, M.: The effects of short-term group counseling on prospective counselors. *Personnel and Guidance Journal, 39*:634-638, 1961.

Hogan, R. A.: Issues and approaches in supervision. *Psychotherapy: Theory, Research and Practice, 1*:139-141, 1964.

Johnston, J. A., and Gysbers, N. C.: Practicum supervisory relationships: a majority report. *Counselor Education and Supervision, 6*:3-10, 1966.

Kell, B. L., and Mueller, W. J.: *Impact and Change: A Study of Counseling Relationships.* New York, Appleton-Century-Crofts, 1966, pp. 97-144.

Malcolm, D. D.: On becoming a counselor. *Personnel and Guidance Journal,* 46:673-676, 1968.

McClain, E. W.: A program for increasing counselor self understanding. *Counselor Education and Supervision,* 8:296-302, 1969.

McKinnon, D. W.: Group counseling with student counselors. *Counselor Education and Supervision,* 8:195-200, 1969.

Rogers, C. R.: Training individuals to engage in the therapeutic process. In C. R. Strother (Ed.): *Psychology and Mental Health.* Washington, D.C., American Psychological Association, 1957, pp. 76-92.

Van Atta, R. E.: Co-therapy as a supervisory process. *Psychotherapy: Theory, Research and Practice,* 6:137-139, 1969.

Woody, R. H.: Preparation in behavioral counseling. *Counselor Education and Supervision,* 8:357-362, 1968.

Woody, R. H.: Psychobehavioral therapy in the schools: implications for counselor education. *Counselor Education and Supervision,* 8:254-264, 1969.

PRACTICUM IN SUPERVISION: A PROPOSAL*

JAMES HANSEN and RICHARD STEVIC

Supervised practice in counseling is an accepted necessity in the professional preparation of counselors. Standards for programs of counselor education and state certification requirements emphasize this prerequisite. In many counselor preparation programs, the practicum is the culminating experience toward which previous didactic courses are directed. It should follow that the supervision of potential counselors would be considered crucial to counselor educators.

When a counselor educator is assigned practicum supervision as part of his instructional load, what preparation has he had for this job? Where did he learn to supervise counselors? Is there anything special to learn about supervision, or is being a good counselor sufficient training? Numerous other questions could be raised. The point to be made is that while the practicum occupies a central position in counselor preparation, there is relatively little emphasis placed on the supervisory process for potential counselor

* Reprinted from *Counselor Education and Supervision,* 7:205-206, 1967, with permission of the American Personnel and Guidance Association and the authors.

educators. This is true even though most of these persons will be expected to supervise.

Some counselor education programs provide a limited amount of supervisory experience for certain doctoral students. These people are assigned as supervisors for master's-level counselors. If the supervisory personnel are supervised by an experienced counselor educator, the experience should be a worthwhile one. However, without supervision there is some question concerning this practice. In a counseling practicum, the counselor can work with a client in a setting in which he can learn from the counseling, per se, and from the more experienced counselor, the supervisor. There is a need for a similar program for the learning of supervision.

Differences of opinion have been presented concerning the process of supervision. Sanderson (1954) considers the supervisory relationship a teaching and consulting process. Arbuckle (1958) states a point of view in which the counselor educator is more a counselor than a teacher. Patterson (1964) suggests that supervision is neither teaching nor counseling but falls somewhere between these two processes. Unless one accepts an Arbuckle approach to supervision, there is a more active teaching role for the supervisor. However, it is not the same teaching role as in a didactic course or even a seminar. There appears to be something unique about the process of individual supervision. This paper is a proposal for action toward more adequate preparation of practicum supervisors.

One approach in this direction would be a practicum and seminar focusing on supervision. The prospective counselor educator should actually supervise counselors. Lister (1966) suggests that the supervisory aspect of practicum can aid the counselor to become more open and more receptive to the client. The potential counselor educator needs to work through this process. Until he can interact with the counselor in an open manner, the supervisory session will prove relatively worthless. The outcome will usually be a picking out of negative or positive counselor statements rather than assisting the counselor to understand himself and the client in a way which will facilitate the growth of the client. The supervision could be observed and recorded in the same manner as a counseling practicum. An experienced supervisor would then work closely with the prospective counselor educator in improving his supervisory skills.

A seminar in conjunction with such a practicum would provide a place to learn and discuss the supervisory processes. Pierson (1965) found that practicum supervisors have unique behaviors and perform specific tasks. He suggests that the first job of the supervisor is one of helping counselors perceive the effects of their behavior on the client. Later, supervisors tend to concentrate more attention on the counselor-client relationship. Finally, attention should be focused on the counselor to help him use his own personality as an effective counseling instrument. Certain problems are apt to develop as the supervisor works through these steps with the counselor.

Ekstein and Wallerstein (1958) have noted several teaching and learning problems that arise in supervision. They state that there are always learning problems because of the different character make-ups and differing ways of learning and of teaching that each supervisor and counselor brings to the meeting. Some counselors come to the supervisor and deny all the supervisor suggests in an attempt to ward off the impact of the supervisor. Others try to learn by complete submission and will do just what the supervisor wants.

A program in supervision will help alleviate a continuing problem of insufficient supervisory time which affects many counselor education programs. In most cases, the counselor can expect an hour per week of individual supervision with an additional two or three hours in a seminar. By using potential counselor educators, the number of counselor contacts as well as the amount of supervisory time could be greatly increased. The end result would be better supervisors and counselors.

In summary, there is a need to prepare doctoral candidates for the supervisory aspect of counselor education. At present, this need is met in most programs on a chance basis. It is believed that a seminar for supervision is essential and that prospective counselor educators should have experience in supervising counselors. When done under the supervision of a practicum professor, the prospective counselor educator will be better able to perform in the supervisory capacity and may be more willing to undertake this as a primary activity of his professional position.

References

Arbuckle, Dugald S.: Five philosophical issues in counseling. *Journal of Counseling Psychology,* 5:211-15, 1958.

Ekstein, Rudolf, and Wallerstein, Robert S.: *The Teaching and Learning of Psychotherapy.* New York, Basic Books, 1958.

Lister, James L.: Counselor experiencing: its implications for supervision. *Counselor Education and Supervision,* 5:55-60, 1966.

Patterson, C. H.: Supervising students in the counseling practicum. *Journal of Counseling Psychology,* 11:47-53, 1964.

Pierson, George A.: *An Evaluation Counselor Education in Regular Session Institutes.* Washington, D.C., U.S. Government Printing Office, 1965.

Sanderson, Herbert: *Basic Concepts in Vocational Guidance.* New York, McGraw-Hill, 1954.

SUPERVISORS' REACTIONS TO A COUNSELING INTERVIEW*

GARRY R. WALZ and EDWARD C. ROEBER

Recent developments in counselor education have seen widespread support for the assignment of supervised counseling practice to a central position in counselor education. Both the APGA policy statement (1961) and the APA Division 17 statement (1952) on counselor education accord a major position to supervised practice. It is noteworthy that the APGA statement calls for supervised practice ". . . to consume approximately one-fourth of the entire counselor education program . . ." while an earlier APA statement on counselor training states that "The practicum is in some respects the most important phase of the whole process of training in counseling" (Rundquist, 1952, p. 183). Further support for supervised experience is provided by the Wrenn Report, the increased emphasis given to the supervised experience in recent NDEA Counseling and Guidance Institutes and the emphasis given it by recent writers.

Of particular interest is that the discussions and writings have not generally devoted attention to an important aspect of super-

* Reprinted from *Counselor Education and Supervision,* 2:2-7, 1962, with permission of the American Personnel and Guidance Association and the authors.

vised counseling practice, namely the supervisory process. The large majority of writings devoted to counselor supervision concern themselves with techniques and procedures useful in supervision rather than with the relationship between the supervisor and the counselor candidate, and the process by which the supervisor assists in the professional and personal development of the candidate. Sanderson (1954) is rare among textbook authors in devoting a chapter to the supervision of counselors; the usual practice is to make only passing references to supervision. The APGA statement skirts the topic by referring to conditions for the counseling practicum but ignoring the basic nature of the supervision other than to call it ". . . a tutorial form of instruction" (p. 8). This study was undertaken with the intention of revealing current orientations and procedures in the supervision of counselor trainees. By first defining existing supervision it was believed we would then be able to extend our research to relate supervisory practices to counselor behavior and, hopefully, to develop a model of supervision.

Experimental Procedures

Considerable thought was given to an appropriate means of sampling supervisory procedures. We especially wished to avoid a questionnaire study which would provide information on who did what, but probably provide little information on the attitudes and feelings which we regard as basic in the supervisory process. Any method selected necessarily had to be specific and concrete enough that it could be explained through written instructions and provide the same stimulus for supervisors in differing situations.

Our decision was to use a typescript of a counseling interview. Each participant was provided with the typescript and background data regarding the counselor and client. The interview was by a beginning practicum student and was notable for several shifts in counselor orientation and technique. It was our belief that the interview was likely to be provocative enough to evoke considerable supervisory response. We were proved to be right in this assumption!

Each participant was asked to respond to the typescript as if it had been given to him by a member of his practicum for his evaluation. The participant was instructed to make all of his comments in writing, either at the point in the interview where his reactions occurred or at the end.

It was apparent that supervisory responses on a typescript would not be a valid sample of the counseling supervision exercised by different supervisors. Some "dry-runs" of the technique did, however, reveal that this approach was remarkably sensitive to revealing the basic orientation and attitudes of the supervisor involved. Since our major concern was to identify such orientations and attitudes, it was felt to be an appropriate instrument for the purposes of this study.

All counselor education programs in the North Central Region which listed a counseling practicum in their program were contacted as to their interest in participating in a study on counseling supervision. Of the twenty-nine contacted, twenty-six affirmative replies were received. The analysis was made on twenty-two completed typescripts; four dropped out of the study because of "professional moves" or "heavy workloads." The idea was well received by those contacted, and the completed typescripts evidenced the expenditure of considerable time and thought.

The analysis of the typescripts involved two basic steps. The first step was to classify each counselor and client response on the interview typescript, sent to each participant, using Rundquist's revision of Snyder's Counselor and Client Response Categories. Two judges working together made the classifications. This classification enabled the experimenters to classify each counselor or client response that a supervisor chose to respond to. There were a total of 45 counselor and 44 client statements in the interview.

The second step involved the construction of a seven-category Supervisor Response Categories (SRC) classification system. Three judges working together classified the supervisory comments using the SRC. Multiple coding was adopted so that a given supervisory comment could appear in more than one classification. A total of 741 supervisory statements were classified using the SRC, 544 statements directed at the counselors' behavior and 197 statements directed at the clients' behavior.

Results

It is important to note that it was not our intention to evaluate or judge supervisory practices. Rather, we wished to identify current orientations and practices which could serve as a guide to further self-study by counseling supervisors. Time and space do not permit a listing of all the data obtained. Somewhat arbitrarily, therefore, the data which seemed most relevant to this discussion were selected for inclusion.

In responding to the interview, supervisors ranged in time from 30 minutes to 132 minutes with a median of 90 minutes. It is noteworthy that a fourth of the supervisors devoted 2 hours or more while another fourth devoted one hour or less. Though there are doubtless many variables present in this time differential it may well be indicative of a real difference regarding the time needed to adequately respond to a typescript.

The focus of supervisory attention would seem to be on the counselor rather than the client. The median number of supervisory comments concerned with the counselor was 25 per interview, while those concerned with the client averaged only 9. Clearly, the supervisors were more concerned with responding to what the counselor said than to what the client said. It should also be mentioned that the content of the supervisory statements rarely contained references to the relationship or the interaction between counselor and client.

Of particular interest in this interview was whether or not the supervisors responded equally throughout the interview or concentrated their responses in any one area. The data revealed there was a pronounced tendency to make fewer responses with each subsequent third of the interview. Though it may be hypothesized that this would be expected it should be noted that there was a major change in the interview dynamics in the last third of the interview, a change which does not seem to have been reflected in the frequency of supervisory response.

As previously stated, the supervisors focused primarily on counselor rather than client behavior. In focusing on the counselor, what was the nature of their comments? From Table 4-I it will be seen that 73 percent of the comments were either Ques-

TABLE 4–I

FREQUENCY OF SUPERVISORY COMMENTS CLASSIFIED IN EACH
OF THE SUPERVISOR RESPONSE CATEGORIES (SRC)

	N	% of Total
Questioning	144	26
Identifying error	27	5
Instruction	254	47
Suggesting alternatives	22	4
Interpretation	32	6
Support	62	11
Unclassifiable	3	1
Total	544	100

tioning or Instruction. Present in most of the aforementioned comments was the implication of counselor error. Supportive comments accounted for only 11 percent of the responses. The categories with the least responses were Suggesting Alternatives and Unclassifiable. Generally, it appeared that most of the comments had a strong informational slant to them.

The supervisory responses to the client were similar to the responses to the counselor in that Questioning and Instructional responses predominated, with 24 and 44 percent respectively. A difference was that Interpretation accounted for 24 percent of the responses to client statements while only 6 percent to counselor statements.

Of interest regarding the individual supervisor was the degree of consistency shown. An analysis of the responses suggests that supervisors in general were characterized by a relatively narrow response range; supervisors were identifiable as having one or two characteristic modes of response which they used throughout the interview. Thus over 50 percent of the responses in the Suggesting Alternatives category were contributed by one supervisor. Other supervisors also showed large predominances in one or two categories.

Perhaps a question of some importance is whether supervisors respond to the same parts of an interview. The answer to this question can be summarized by both a Yes and a No answer. The important variable in both frequency and agreement of response would seem to be "desirability." If the consensus of the supervisors is that a counselor statement is "undesirable," it is likely to evoke a large number of similarly classified supervisory responses. If a statement is regarded by some supervisors as a "desirable" response, it is likely to evoke fewer supervisory responses than the "undesirable" statement and to result in responses covering a variety of categories. Apparently, there is greater agreement on "incorrect" than "correct" counselor behavior and a greater inclination to indicate errors than to reinforce desirable behavior.

Conclusions and Implications

Let us summarize what we have found regarding supervisory behavior. It would seem to be focused on the counselor rather than the client and to be more concerned with the initial than closing stages of the interview. Supervisors responded to counselor candidate behavior primarily by instructional statements and to a lesser degree by raising questions, both frequently implying error. Supervisors showed consistency in response throughout the interview, generally using only one or two response categories. There was greater agreement and frequency of response among supervisors on counselor behavior evaluated as "undesirable" than behavior evaluated "desirable."

Like much research we have probably succeeded in raising many more questions than we have answered. At this stage of our investigation it may be that question raising is more palpable than question answering. Be that as it may, it would seem that we have emerged from this study with several questions that would have particular relevance for the supervisory process. They are herewith raised with the intention that they may serve as guides in the further study of the supervisory process.

1. As identified by this study, the usual supervisory response would seem to be cognitive and information-giving, with negative overtones. Essentially, they are rational and evaluative responses. This would suggest that we (supervisors) either feel that the relationship between supervisor and counselor is different than that between counselor and client or that we feel the rationale underlying counseling is inappropriate in this context. Is the relationship between supervisor and counselor more like that of the subject matter teacher and pupil, or like counselor and client? Operationally, we would seem to have defined it as more like the former than the latter.

2. It would seem that in our responses as supervisors we have been more concerned with what the counselor said than with what he did; more concerned with the content of a counselor statement than his relationship to a client. Is it possible we are reinforcing technique counseling by technique supervision? Would we assist the counselor more in acquiring greater self-understanding of his counseling behavior by focusing on the clients' needs rather than dealing with the specifics of counselor behavior?

3. It has been demonstrated that diagnosis often goes awry because of a diagnosis made too soon, on too little data. In our supervision are we too quick to classify and too insensitive to changes in the relationship? Is the most appropriate perspective for an interview that which includes all of the nuances of the relationship and interaction, rather than the impact of single counselor responses? It is perhaps germane to wonder if the supervisory position is leading us to make judgments and evaluations about a counselor rather than to assist the counselor to see the meaning of his behavior.

4. This study has identified a wide range of supervisory behavior. No two supervisors reacted to the same pattern of counselor/client statements or used similar wording and meaning in their statements. Nor did any one supervisor use even a fraction of the total variations in response used by the supervisors as a group. Realistically, differences should be expected. But how large should these differences be? Earlier we mentioned that counselor errors seemed to evoke the greatest supervisory agreement. Is this an indication that our major approach to supervision is a carry-over from when we were classroom teachers and checked papers to see how many errors had been committed?

Left unanswered by this study are the criteria used by supervisors in choosing to respond in the way they did. Further progress in supervision would seem to rest upon more sophisticated studies which would establish criteria usable by supervisors in their daily supervision.

In conclusion, it would seem important to consider standards, as we are doing, but it would also seem necessary to consider the supervisory process itself. The potentialities inherent in a counseling practicum are boundless. A practicum can become, however, a small class in techniques of counseling. There is decided merit in APGA's efforts to provide a realistic load for practicum supervisors. But it would surely seem a lost opportunity to do no more than spend additional time at what we are already doing.

The challenge is not just to acquire more time for supervision, but to make counseling supervision a vital process. Standards, Yes! Further study of the supervisory process, especially Yes! !

Earlier we set as our goal to describe, not to evaluate. Perhaps one evaluation is in order. We seem not to have an underlying rationale for how we supervise! If some of our products counsel from the seat of their pants, perhaps it is because we supervise from the top of our heads.

References

American Psychological Association Committee on Counselor Training, Division of Counseling and Guidance. *The Practicum Training of Counseling Psychologists. American Psychologist,* 7:182-187, 1952.

Rundquist, Richard M.: *A Comparison of the Analysis of Counseling Interviews by Topical Discussion Units and by the Total Case.* Unpublished Ed. D. dissertation, University of Missouri, 1952.

Sanderson, Herbert: *Basic Concepts in Vocational Guidance.* New York, McGraw-Hill, 1954.

Standards for the Preparation of School Counselors. A Policy Statement of the American Personnel and Guidance Association. Washington, D.C., APGA, 1961.

TAPE RECORDINGS AND COUNSELOR-TRAINEE UNDERSTANDINGS *

Robert P. Anderson and Oliver H. Bown

The present paper has two aims, to show one way in which interview recordings may be used in counselor training, and to describe the structure of the supervisory conference.

Background

Several methods of counselor training have been described in recent literature. As examples, Tennyson (1954) described one method of using interview recording wherein the trainees ex-

* Reprinted from the *Journal of Counseling Psychology,* 2:189-194, 1955, with permission of the American Psychological Association and the authors.

amined specific responses of the client-counselor interaction. The method of examining specific responses did not, however, meet our training requirements in that we considered it to be of fundamental importance to dispense with a technique-oriented approach. Schwebel (1953) in a provocative article listed the advantages of the role-playing method of training. Role-playing has been found to be effective during the early training experiences prior to the counselor's contact with clients and can be of supplementary value at later stages of training. Haigh and Kell (1950) related their experiences with the method of multiple counseling. In multiple counseling the supervisor can broaden his perception of the trainee's interview behavior. He can observe the interaction, and he can respond to the subtleties of trainee and client behavior. The vital learning that comes from multiple counseling is, of course, focused in the supervisor's sharing of his reactions about the interview situation.

Valuable as multiple counseling and role-playing may be, the time arrives in the course of every student's experience when he must be left alone with a client. He is placed in a position where no one is readily avilable to extricate him from a troublesome or anxiety-provoking counseling experience. Thus, a constant question which arose in our practicum and intern training program may be stated as follows: How can we most effectively and efficiently implement the reality approach to counseling with students who are having their first series of "solo" contacts with clients?

Like other training centers, we found that tape recordings of counseling sessions were an invaluable tool for working through the problems inherent in orienting a student to the counseling process. An objective picture of the communication process could be obtained when the counselor-in-training recorded the interaction between himself and his "live" clients. There is no doubt that recording sometimes poses a threat to the trainee, especially when the recording is being made for the purpose of supervision. However, the zeal with which trainees listened to and worked over their interview tapes outside the supervisory conference indicated the degree of their ego-involvement and showed the extent to which they were primed for significant new learning.

There was no intent in our intern and practicum programs of communicating to the counselors-in-training that supervision was carried out in a permissive, nonthreatening, nonevaluative atmosphere. On the contrary, we perceived the supervisory conference as being potentially very threatening to the trainee. It was a time when there would be very direct evaluation. We had a real investment in what went on between a trainee and his client, and in the training conference we felt the need to play an active role. Our concern was not to deny the realities of supervision but to face them openly. Thus, the training conference was oriented not only to the actual process of case supervision but to the way in which the trainee responded to the interaction with his supervisor.

We emphasized recording particularly during the early stages of training because of the objectivity afforded by the tape. While a counselor-in-training can report the content of his interviews to a supervisor, experience demonstrated that students tend to be selective in their perceptions when reporting a case. For example, not only may he omit relevant details of the interaction, but he has difficulty reproducing important variables of the counseling process such as the tone of his interview voice. Students do not consciously hold back material which may be relevant to the process of counseling. Rather, we operated on the assumption that counselors (or in this case counselor-trainees), like other people, are likely to deal only with those issues with which they have immediate conscious recognition. The tape recordings hold back no unconscious secrets. The interaction between the client and counselor is audible, and selective factors on the part of the trainee have little room to operate.

The Training Conference

The manner in which we implemented the basic philosophy of our approach will be demonstrated through the use of transcribed excerpts taken from a recorded training conference. The basic idea of this approach to counseling and counselor-training is that maximum therapeutic growth is possible for the client in a climate of free communication. The counselor, from our point of view, has a great deal of responsibility for facilitating or blocking the communication process. Since the counselor is a person and more than a mass of techniques and proper responses, his motives, fears, needs, and defenses are important variables in determining the direction and outcomes of the counseling process. Our specific aims within the conference were to be (a) honest, (b) direct, and (c) maximally open to the experience of the trainee-supervisor interaction.

The process of implementation has been broken down so that it will stand out with maximum clarity. Each general principle of action is illustrated with material from the recorded conference. Space limitations make it imposible to include all of the material from the conference. The case reported by the trainee started out as vocational guidance. After two interviews the client continued in a personal counseling relationship. The trainee was an intern at the Testing and Guidance Bureau of the University of Texas. His prior experience included a series of courses in counseling and a practicum experience in which he was gradually introduced to live case handling; the internship was the last stage of his formal training.

The Configuration

The first stage in case supervision was to obtain a picture of the configuration of the interview, or interviews, in question. We wanted to get a "feel" for the interaction. Frist, the counselor-in-training was asked how he perceived the case. Second, we tried to obtain a picture of the case through an objective interview recording. In listening to the case description, attention was focused on those factors in the relationship which tended to cause tension. There was an implicit assumption that the counselor's behavior is a function of the way in which he perceives himself within the context of the client-counselor interaction.

The Trainee's Perception

In this first excerpt, trainee Bill describes his client as he perceived him. First, he gave a global picture of the case.

> *Trainee:* Well, the thing that confuses me most about this relationship is that I really can't tell what goes on between us. He seemed to have a lot of real insight into the fact that he has had

trouble most of his life, and that he's the cause of it . . . and that he has some real responsibility in this . . . and that he really wants to do something about it. . . . I remember my first reaction to this guy, "Gee, he's a real expressive guy; he's easy to get along with; I feel comfortable with him." In fact, I've felt comfortable with him through all our interviews. We have had four or five now. . . . He's real easy to listen to and to talk to. Well, anyway . . . the second . . . after the first interview I've been kind of puzzled in that he'll talk about himself. And . . . I'm not sure just how much I mean to him or whether he's trying to affect me with his talk. He seems to be talking about the things that are of real concern to him; he talks about his pending divorce, about his difficulty with his former wife, about his job, and about his frustrations on his job. . . . And yet there is something about it that is very strange. Well, there seems to be something else that is interwoven in our interviews. There is a feeling on my part that he is looking for . . . he's looking for blame. And sometimes I have the feeling that I'm falling into this pattern and I'm beginning to point out things that he's done . . . responsibilities. And the things that I've pointed out seem to be true, that he seems to be falling into a pattern of his saying, "Yes, I'm a bad boy," something like that.

Bill's primary concern was that he felt caught in the trap of responding to the client in a way which, in the long run, would tend to reinforce the client's neurotic way of looking at himself. In a sense, Bill felt himself playing the client's game.

The second step, after the global description, was a brief summary of the interview played in the training conference. The question in the mind of the supervisor at this point was as follows: How does this interview illustrate the process of confused and inhibited communication? Trainee Bill continued the conference with a description of the interview he recorded. His description is, of course, limited and shortened.

Trainee: Well, for example, let me tell you a little bit about this interview. He started out by saying, "Gee, I just feel like getting away from everything, going off to the woods, being a lumberjack, getting away from my obligations . . . that my wife and I have built up." And I remember the feeling that was in me was, "that's bad; you shouldn't do this." That's what I was thinking. . . . An initial feeling of that's bad; and I want to tell him that he's a bad boy. And then almost getting hold of myself and kind of letting him own what he's saying and let's look at it together. Well, this is a typical interview. Why don't we listen to it.

The final stage in obtaining a perceptual configuration of the case was to listen to the recorded interview. The length of time devoted to listening was dependent upon the case itself. One may listen for five minutes or for half an hour. Here again, the focus is on obtaining a configuration of the interaction. What is the nature of the client-counselor interaction? How does the counselor block the interaction? What is the client communicating in the session that the counselor may be missing in his responses? The supervisor is not greatly concerned with specific counselor responses but with the meaning and understanding communicated in the totality of his responses.

Another general aim was to keep away from responding to the counselor's technique of interviewing. Whether a response is a reflection of feeling, an interpretation, or a direct question is of little consequence. The intent of trainee communication is, however, of much vital interest. Technique orientation is fostered, in our estimation, by the supervisor who reacts to the recording in terms of each and every counselor response, e.g. "You missed that feeling," or "That was too much of an interpretation."

The Interview

The following excerpt is taken from the recording brought into the training conference by trainee Bill. It is almost too brief for the reader to get a full picture of the client-counselor interaction, but it does show how Bill handles himself. It is well to point out that much of what transpires in the conference after the recording was heard is not based on the brief excerpt reported here. The supervisor listened for fifteen or twenty minutes before he made any comments.

> *Client:* . . . Well, I tell myself, I don't want to make a mistake again on this marriage proposition. And a lot of times when I get to thinking, it sure would be nice to be married again . . . when the right girl comes along or something like that.
> *Trainee:* Well, I think that the things you do like, like apparently this girl that you are talking about now. Apparently, when you first met her, there were a lot of things about her that you liked, that you wanted, and that you felt that (words lost). You got her to be acceptable, in other words, it is almost as if you forced her,

you tried to make her satisfy the things that you wanted and desired. In other words you were . . .

Supervisor: . . . time for a reaction, why don't you turn it off.
(Supervisor interrupted to turn off the tape machine.)

The Evaluation

The second stage in the process was termed the evaluation.
The supervisor attempts to share his reactions to the student with
honesty, directness, and lack of defensiveness; he does not deny
his own values. We find it is much more valuable to bring our
reactions out into the open than to set up a training situation
where the trainee is faced with implicit value judgments concerning his behavior. The key to the process is lack of defensiveness.
If the supervisor is defensive in his reactions, he can expect defense from the trainee. However, if he can communicate, "This
is what I see, but the responsibility for doing something about
it is up to you," the trainee has a frame of reference from which
he can begin to explore the interview interaction.

As an example of the evaluation process let us pick up the
training conference at the point where the supervisor asked to
have the recording turned off.

> *Supervisor:* Well, let me respond in terms of a couple of things
> that I felt about this thing. One, I think your responses indicated to
> me that you didn't know what you were talking about. You weren't
> sure yourself what you were saying because of the fact that you were
> using so many words. You were having to say what you had to say
> in so many different ways. And secondly, I felt that you were being
> defensive in the sense that you were covering up by using a lot of
> words.
>
> *Trainee:* That's very true. The feeling is, I don't have a clear
> understanding of . . . not what he says because I can get with the
> content of what he says but . . . I have very little understanding of
> what this means to him. I really didn't. It's almost as if I couldn't
> see that this was a real problem in the sense that this was something
> to work with to change. I just couldn't see the meaning of it.
>
> *Supervisor:* Well, there is only one thing that I see in this that
> he is expressing. He doesn't like people.
>
> *Trainee:* That makes a lot of sense to me. That feels like such
> a relief to me what you just said. But I was very far from that.
> I had no appreciation for that, absolutely none. I felt he was saying
> that he was trying to get people to do what he wants them to . . .

get people to . . . in a position where they'd be satisfying to him. You know, there is something about my use of words that is more than . . . because I don't understand what is going on. Well, that is a characteristic of mine being . . . almost a feeling of making sure that he understands the gem that floats from my mouth.

It is apparent that the supervisor's response had an emotional meaning to the trainee. In effect, the supervisor said, "You are defensive as indicated by your use of words," and, "There is one central theme in the client's communication." What next? The obvious approach would be to hearken back to the recording. A return to the tape at this point would be tantamount to stringing the trainee up on a high tree to dangle. In short, the vital *why* questions would be cut off. "Why can't I get with the client? Why am I defensive? Why do I want the client to understand me? What is my intent in this relationship?"

Understanding

There is a transition from the evaluation— this is what I have done—to the most vital stage of understanding—why have I done it. The therapist, or counselor, must understand the factors motivating his own behavior before he can hope to make even the simplest yet therapeutically effective modifications in his interview behavior.

The last few sentences spoken by Bill in the preceding excerpt characterize the stage of understanding. Bill approached attempts to understand himself by stating that there was more to his use of words than just the fact that he did not understand his client. He explored his reactions further:

Trainee: (excerpt picked up in the middle of a response) . . . what he says has no emotional meaning to me . . . whether an appropriate response would be not to respond . . . or an appropriate response would be, "I really can't get what you are saying" . . . or . . . what would be the thing for me to do? I hate to admit that I can't get with what he is saying . . . that bothers me.
Supervisor: Why?
Trainee: Because I feel inept. You got to be able to get with what he is saying.

At this point Bill's motivations become clear. His responses to the client are in part motivated by his desire to maintain prestige and status in the eyes of the client. Stated in another way, Bill said, "Counselors are supposed to understand people, and I can't let it be known that I lack understanding."

Whether or not we revert back to the recording now is irrelevant; it has served its purpose. That is, reality was brought out into the open. The main effort now is to seek understanding. Intellectual understanding? No, it is not enough. There must be emotional understanding of the same caliber that is expected of clients when modifications in their behavior are anticipated.

The reader may very well ask the question, "Does this mean that counselors must go through counseling before they can counsel others?" No. The trainee, like any client, cannot hope to have a successful therapetuic experience unless there is a real felt need. If the need is felt in the context of dealing with others, then he will go into it. If it is forced on him as a requirement, he will resist the process.

The process of understanding can be further illustrated by Bill's case conference. The conference is picked up at a point where the supervisor again makes a direct interpretive statement directed toward furthering Bill's understanding of the blocked communication.

> *Supervisor:* . . . I just wonder if he could by any chance be using people in the same way that you might be using people?
>
> *Trainee:* Well, my first reaction is to disagree with you. But then I reflect back on some of my thoughts about this guy and they are that . . . there's something about what he says that I feel a lot of kinship with. I really feel that I have the same problems that he does. When he begins to talk . . . I felt, I feel this . . . I feel in the back of my mind: How the heck am I going to help him when sometimes I have the very same trouble. There is another part . . . another similarity about myself that I see with this guy that might follow. And that is . . . I think what he's trying to do is to build up layers to compensate for feelings of emptiness. Well, I feel a lot of identification with that.
>
> *Supervisor:* Sort of a feeling of emptiness and you try to compensate for it to a certain degree by your relationship with people. That's the way I would put it.
>
> *Trainee:* . . . Well, this guy seems to be expressing the very same thing. I don't know what to do for him. I don't know . . . I guess

I could tell him how neutral I feel about him . . . this might. . . .

Supervisor: Why tell him how neutral you feel about him? You've been telling me here that you have some reactions toward him. You don't seem to want to bring those feelings out. It seems that talking about your neutrality toward him is a way of getting away from what you are expressing here that you feel about him.

Bill got into the heart of his explorations as follows:

Trainee: I guess I really feel kind of . . . I guess I don't right now, but I have felt in the interviews. I felt kind of impotent in the sense that, "How can I help you when I am just as concerned as you are about what you are talking about. But I haven't resolved anything that you are talking about . . . personally." What I try to do is to communicate to him my . . . my theoretical way of resolving these things for myself. (Pause) You know you can get . . . I can get so tied up in this mixture of theory and mixture of the way I feel . . . I mean I think the way I really feel sometimes is just withdrawing completely from people. I just don't have anything to do with them see . . . But a . . . my . . . all of my past experiences tells me that this is . . . all of my experience and everything else—reading books on mental hygiene—tells me that this is . . . this is not good, see. I mean that I've done this in the past, I mean I've completely withdrawn. I . . . I . . . (pause) I mean I get confused with whether I really want to do the opposite of withdrawing and be with people or whether I should do that. I . . . I . . . the two motivations are mixed up.

The conference progressed from a point where the trainee stated that the interviews with his client were causing a sense of uneasiness to a point where he was beginning to understand his uneasiness. With increased understanding and awareness of himself as a functioning individual within a relationship Bill was able to effect quantatively small but emotionally significant changes in his own awareness of himself, in his general behavior, and in his capacity as a counselor.

Summary

An approach to counselor training through the use of interview tape recording was demonstrated. The essential proposition is that maximum therapeutic growth occurs within the context of free communication. The counselor has a great deal of responsibility for facilitating or blocking the client-counselor communication process. An understanding of the counselor's needs, motives, fears, and defenses are imperative for meaningful and effective modifications in his behavior. There are three general stages in the process of case supervision. First, there is an *orientation to the problem*. The counselor presents the case from his viewpoint and then the recording is played. The latter provides a reality-bound record of the client-counselor interaction. Second, the supervisor *evaluates the recording* in terms of the facilitating or inhibiting factors in the communication. The characteristics of the evaluation are honesty, directness, and a lack of defensiveness. The third and final stage is that in which the supervisor works with the trainee toward the goal of *understanding the meaning and intent of the trainee's interview behavior*. The emotional understanding provides a framework for meaningful modification of trainee behavior.

References

Haigh, G., and Kell, B. L.: Multiple therapy as a method for training and research in psychotherapy. *J. Abnorm. Soc. Psychol.*, 45:659-666, 1950.
Schwebel, M.: Role-playing in counselor training. *Personnel Guid. J.*, 32: 196-201, 1953.
Tennyson, W.: Playback of interviews. *Personnel Guid. J.*, 32:279-281, 1954.

PRACTICUM SUPERVISION: GOOD GUYS AND BAD GUYS*

GILBERT E. MAZER and KENNETH B. ENGLE

Sometimes one wonders whether counselor educators (we humbly include ourselves) were exposed to too many movies during their tender years. We seem so inclined to portray "bad guys" of our profession and then with restrained grandiosity lay them low, only to find like Don Quixote, we are attacking illusions. During the past two decades to satisfy our need for heroics, we stirred our witches' brew and conjured up the demon "directive" counselor who, armed with a double-barrel SVIB, was allegedly impelling the Lighthouse Keeper's Daughter to become the only female telephone lineman in existence. By composing

* Reprinted from *Counselor Education and Supervision*, 8:147-149, 1968, with permission of the American Personnel and Guidance Association and the authors.

only a few million words we were able to rescue the fair damsel from this culprit, and with a magnanimous pat on her pretty little cranium sent her off into the hard, cold world free to "become whatever she wants to become." Ah, chivalry, thy name is counselor! What a disappointment to discover our culprit was an illusion.

The current adversary appears to be the autocratic practicum supervisor whose accouterments include a tape recorder and a report card. He is portrayed as warning the hapless student, "you do it my way or flunk!" Are we about to exhaust another decade striking down this illusion?

Although most counselor educators would undoubtedly readily dismiss this imagery as ludicrous, several of the influential papers on practicum supervision which have appeared during the past five years seem to have been addressed to it. Furthermore, one wonders to what extent such an illusion determined the recent retreat of practicum supervisors from a reported preference for an instructional role with students (Walz and Roeber, 1962) to one which is minimally structured (Johnson and Gysbers, 1966). Could it be an indication of how anxious we are to avoid being identified with this "bad guy"?

Several other widely solicited proposals concerning practicum supervision seem similarly founded on frail illusions of "good guys" and "bad guys." At the risk of sounding more than a little schizophrenic, and with appropriate trepidation, permit us to speculate about these additional popular notions which seem to be influenced by our underlying images and to propose their probable antitheses in reality:

Illusion I: Supervisors are good guys and somehow different from and superior to teachers. Therefore, supervision is *more than* or *different from* teaching.

Reality: Webster defines teaching as "imparting knowledge or skills and usually connotes some individual attention to the learner." The practicum supervisor is a teacher.

Objections to identifying the supervisor as a teacher are generated by our erroneous image of the teacher as another "bad guy"—an autocrat who places subject matter above student welfare. The modern teacher reads books like Moustakas' *The Au-*

thentic Teacher (1966) and is no less concerned about his relationships with students than we are as counselor educators. If we are able to establish productive and facilitating relationships with counselor candidates, we are not something other than teachers, merely very good ones who fortunately have time enough to offer much "individual attention to the learner." Good teaching should and often does provide opportunities for expression of feelings and for individual growth as well as for the acquisition of knowledge.

Students approach supervision anticipating assistance in acquiring the "knowledge and skills," attitudes, and personal variations appropriate to counseling. Should the supervisor refuse the teaching role, he is in effect denying the existence of standards of counselor performance and substantive content in counselor education (illusions)and the student's right of access to them.

It is unfortunate that Patterson and Arbuckle (Patterson, 1964; Arbuckle, 1963) have implied that providing information, i.e. instruction, is detrimental to the supervisor-student relationship. On the contrary, Snyder's (1961) finding that clients experience positive affect toward the therapist when he offers advice, and the results of numerous other studies (Delaney and Moore, 1966; Dreikurs and Sonstegard, 1966; Gysbers and Johnston, 1965; Miller and Oetting, 1966) support the reality that, especially in beginning practicum, students anticipate and welcome instruction, direction, and structure from the supervisor. Needless to say, informing and suggesting are not tantamount to criticizing.

Illusion II: Supervisors are "good guys" who offer students something unique and indispensible. Therefore, most personal supervision is better than none. Students cannot learn to counsel without it.

Reality: Considerable skill in conducting counseling and therapeutic interviews can be acquired by students in the complete *absence* of the supervisory relationship. In some cases, impersonal methods are superior to conventional approaches in educating counselors and therapists.

The results of some exploratory studies conducted by Palmer, Fosmire and their associates (Fosmire and Palmer, 1964; Palmer, *et al.*, 1963) which compare the relative efficacy of personal supervision and an impersonal "tape-and-commentary" method in the preparation of therapists give cause for dismay. Their findings suggest that the impersonal, programmed method was as successful or significantly more successful than personal supervision on a number of criteria of therapist performance, including ratings of the appropriateness of the students' responses. To explain the effectiveness of the "tape-and-commentary" method, the authors propose that "it minimizes those interpersonal reactions, so common in personal tutoring, that interfere with training" (Fosmire and Palmer, 1964). A harsh reality!

Illusion III: Supervisors are good counselors. Counseling is good. Trainees best learn how to counsel by being counseled.

Reality: Trainees "resist and resent the supervisor who approaches them as a therapist" (Miller and Oetting, 1966).

Supervising counselors by emphasizing interpersonal exploration may be rationalized on the assumption that underlying personality dynamics determine the students' responses in counseling, i.e. they are influenced more by what they need and feel than by what they know. The evidence fails to support such a contention (Campbell, 1962; Mazer, 1965).

Students who manipulate, evaluate, and direct while counseling, probably do so *not* because they are fulfilling psychological needs, but simply because these behaviors were rewarded in prior circumstances (such as classroom teaching) and are generalized to counseling. In most instances, students are simply ignorant.

On the positive side, the supervisor who functions as a therapist provides a model which the students may emulate in his efforts to counsel. However, the implications of being approached as a person needing therapy may evoke aversive feelings in students which vitiate the value of the modeling. By definition, such a situation is not therapeutic.

Students want counseling demonstrations (Delaney and Moore, 1966; Gysbers and Johnston, 1966) but with clients other than themselves. While good supervision, like good teaching, may be therapeutic, and should, as Carkhuff (1966) has suggested, provide therapeutic conditions, personal benefits to the student should be ends and not means.

Implications: If these, then, are realities, what are the implications for counselor education? Should supervisors receive courses in the methods, resources, and media of traditional pedagogy? Should supervisors become thoroughly familiar with the tenets of learning and reinforcement theory? Should counselor education include experiences in settings like a foreign language lab, complete with individual booths, earphones, and the piped-in voice and/or face of a client? If one accepts the tentative realities herein proposed, affirmative responses to these questions are in order.

It would appear that much of counselor preparation involves only cognitive learning and that a more systematic approach is therefore feasible. With imaginative instructional methods, more of the initial teaching which is presently the responsibility of supervisors could be accomplished in an impersonal context.

Emphasis on cognitive elements does not, in our minds, obviate the possibility of the supervisor-student relationship becoming a therapeutic one. On the contrary, relieved of much of his instructional and evaluative responsibilities, the supervisor would then be enabled to establish directly the kinds of personal and therapeutic relationships with students generally regarded as important to their preparation. It is perhaps toward these goals and not on our illusions of "bad guys" and "good guys" that our efforts should be directed.

References

Arbuckle, D. S.: The learning of counseling: process not product. *Journal of Counseling Psychology,* 10:163-68, 1963.

Campbell, R. E.: Counselor personality and background and his interview subrole behavior. *Journal of Counseling Psychology,* 9:329-34, 1962.

Carkhuff, R. R.: Training in counseling and therapeutic practices; requiem or reveille? *Journal of Counseling Psychology,* 13:360-67, 1966.

Delaney, D. J., and Moore, J. C.: Student expectations of the role of practicum supervisor, *Counselor Education and Supervision,* 6:11-17, 1966.

Dreikurs, R., and Sonstegard, M.: A specific approach to practicum supervision. *Counseling Education and Supervision,* 6:18-25, 1966.

Fosmire, F. R., and Palmer, B. E.: *A Comparison of a Method of Programmed Instruction and of Personal Supervision in Psychotherapy.* Mimeographed report, University of Oregon Psychological Clinic, 1964.

Gysbers, N. C., and Johnston, J. A.: Expectations of a practicum supervisor's role. *Counselor Education and Supervision,* 4:68-74, 1965.

Johnston, J. A., and Gysbers, N. C.: Practicum supervisory relationships: a majority report. *Counselor Education and Supervision*, 6:3-10, 1966.

Mazer, G. E., Severson, J. L., Axman, A. L., and Ludington, K. A.: The effects of teaching background on school counselor practices. *SPATE Journal*, 4:81-84, 1965.

Miller, C. D., and Oetting, E. R.: Students react to supervision. *Counselor Education and Supervision*, 6:73-74, 1966.

Moustakas, C.: *The Authentic Teacher: Sensitivity and Awareness in the Classroom*. Cambridge, Howard A. Doyle, 1966.

Palmer, B., Fosmire, R., Breger, L., Straughan, J. H. and Patterson, G. R.: *First Report of a Program of Research in Psychotherapy Training*. Mimeographed report, University of Oregon Psychological Clinic, 1963.

Patterson, C. H.: Supervising students in the counseling practicum. *Journal of Counseling Psychology*, 11:47-53, 1964.

Snyder, W. B., and Snyder, B. June: *The Psychotherapy Relationship*. New York, Macmillan, 1961.

Walz, G. R., and Roeber, E. C.: Supervisors' reactions to a counseling interview. *Counselor Education and Supervision*, 2:2-7, 1962.

SUPERVISING STUDENTS IN THE COUNSELING PRACTICUM*

C. H. PATTERSON

In contrast to the extensive literature on supervision in psychotherapy (e.g. Ekstein and Wallerstein, 1958), and in social casework (e.g. Robinson, 1936, 1949), there is almost nothing on the supervision of counseling. The articles by Cottle (1952, 1955), Korner and Brown (1952), Anderson and Bown (1955), and the study by Walz and Roeber (1962) practically exhaust the literature. The only text which deals with supervision is that of Sanderson (1954).

Since most counselor educators would agree that "the practicum is in some respects the most important phase of the whole process of training in counseling" (American Psychological Association, 1952), it would appear to be high time that we gave some consideration to the supervising process. The value of the practicum depends on two things: (a) the number and variety of clients with which the student works and the intensity or duration of his work with them, and (b) the supervision which he

---

* Reprinted from the *Journal of Counseling Psychology*, 11:47-53, 1964, with permission of the American Psychological Association and the author.

receives. The first is of little value, however, unless the amount and quality of supervision is adequate. My observation would indicate that most practicums are weak in both these areas. We are concerned here only with the latter, however.

That all is not well with supervision of counseling students is indicated by the study of Walz and Roeber (1962). They provided a typescript of a student interview to a group of counselor educators to be reacted to as in supervision. Forty-seven percent of the responses given were classified as instructional and twenty-six percent as questioning, both types being mainly concerned with defects in the student's performance. In addition another five percent of the responses simply identified errors. Six percent of the counselor educators' reactions were classified as interpretive, four percent as suggestions of alternative student responses, and eleven percent were classified as supportive. The concern was mainly with the student counselor rather than with the client, with few references to the relationship or interaction between the student and the client. The investigators conclude that supervision is cognitive and information-giving, with negative overtones.

If supervisors actually function as this study indicates, and there is no evidence to indicate that they do not, then supervision is woefully inadequate, and is perhaps more harmful than helpful to the student. It appears that counselor educators do not practice in their supervision what they (hopefully) teach in their classes. They are concerned with techniques rather than with attitudes, with content rather than with feelings, with specific responses rather than with the relationship. They are evaluative, diagnostically oriented, and judgmental rather than accepting, understanding and therapeutic. This is a serious indictment of supervision, yet it appears to be justified. The results of the study point to a number of questions or problems which must be raised and considered.

The Nature of Supervision

The first is the question as to what supervision is. Is the supervisor-student relationship a teacher-student relationship, or is it a therapist-client relationship? Most would agree that it is not, or should not be, a therapist-client relationship. Arbuckle (1963), however, feels that the supervisor should function primarily as a counselor rather than as an educator. Making the supervisory session a counseling or therapy session is to impose counseling on a captive client. The purpose of supervision is not counseling or psychotherapy with the student. Is it, then, or must it be a teacher-student relationship? Many would be ready to agree that supervision is or should be a learning situation. Is supervision the same kind of teacher-student relationship found in the usual classroom, but on an individual basis? This is apparently the concept accepted by counselor educators, if we can judge from the Walz and Roeber study. The emphasis is upon techniques of how to do it, resulting in directing, correcting, informing. It is a rational or intellectual process. But, as Sanderson (1954, p. 208) notes, such supervision is not likely to contribute to the student's personal and professional growth, even though it may enhance his knowledge. Supervision is, or should be, more than this, as has been recognized by those who have been concerned with supervision of psychotherapy.

Supervision, while not therapy, should be, like all good human relationships, therapeutic. Supervision is a relationship which is therapeutic and in which the student learns. But the learning is not the kind of learning which takes place in the usual classroom. It is more like the kind of learning which takes place in counseling and psychotherapy. It is concerned with the development of sensitivity in the student, of understanding and the ability to communicate that understanding, of therapeutic attitudes, rather than techniques, specific responses, diagnostic labeling, or even identifying or naming presumed personality dynamics in the client.

The supervisory session falls between teaching and counseling. It should not be an individual lecture to the student, nor a Socratic dialogue. It may be true that at times the student needs specific information, and, of course, this may be given as a part of supervision. But this is a minor aspect of supervision, as it usually is in counseling. On the other hand, it is true that students in a practicum, even when it comes after a full year of graduate work as it usually does at the University of Illinois, are far from completely prepared in terms of knowledge and background to handle all the problems which arise in counseling. They need information and knowledge of the kind obtained in didactic courses. But this is not the function of the individual supervisory process; moreover, it would be inefficient to include it. There are deficiencies which are present in all or most students, which are more efficiently, and effectively, dealt with in a regular class situation. My solution to this problem is to conduct regular class sessions for all practicum students. Problems arising in individual supervisory sessions can be brought up in the class since they often represent common problems.

The fact that the supervisor is the instructor in the group setting may appear to have some disadvantages. It would certainly militate against the supervisor counseling the student. But the advantages of the supervisor being the instructor include his being able to relate the class lectures and discussions to the current needs and problems of the students as they appear in supervision. It also allows him to keep the supervisory sessions from being lectures. A problem which may occur with some students involves their seeing the supervisor as an instructor and expecting a lecture or didactic relationship in supervision. But this is easily resolved with a little structuring to the student.

Supervision as an Influencing Process

If the supervisory situation is not therapy, and is not didactic teaching, then how is it conducted? We assume that it is directed to the development of behavior changes in the student—that it is an influencing situation. The supervisor who may claim, to himself as well as to students, that he has no biases, or point of view, or theoretical orientation, and disclaims any desire to influence the student's approach in counseling, is deceiving both himself and the student, since his supervision will show his biases or point of view. But not only is he deceiving the student, he is also confusing the student, who may not be aware of the source of his discomfort, although I have observed that often he is. It would appear to be better that the supervisor recognize and explicitly state his bias so the student will know where he stands and what is really expected of him. The supervisor, as the therapist, should be congruent, or real, in the supervisory relationship, and not attempt to play the role of being unbiased and objective with regard to various counseling points of view. This means, as I have pointed out elsewhere (Patterson, 1959, p. ix), that the practicum should be—and actually is—limited to one particular approach to counseling—that of the instructor and supervisor.

Direct Control of Student-Counselor Behavior

There is always an influencing process in supervision. The question, in addition to whether such influence is recognized and accepted, is the nature and goals of the influence. One approach is the direct control of the specific behavior of the student—his techniques, methods, and procedures. One example of this kind of influence is illustrated in the article by Korner and Brown (1952). They report the following interchange which was overheard over a sound system:

Client: My mother does some of the meanest things to me, but . . .

Counselor: You don't like your mother.
Client: Well, I . . . I . . . guess but I . . .
Counselor: She makes you very angry at her. Sometimes you are sure you hate her.
Client: Well, I . . . I . . . guess but I . . .
Counselor: And it makes you feel awful to hate her.

The supervisor was naturally disturbed by this, so he went to the counseling room, knocked on the door and said to the student counselor: "Look, your client is trying to tell you that she is ambivalent, that she also loves her mother. Now go back in there and help her to express it."

Parenthetically, it is interesting to speculate on what might have happened, or what the supervisor might have done, if the student (as he should have) had refused to come to the door. But the authors use this situation to illustrate the need for a method to communicate with the student during his counseling, and they did develop such a device, by which the supervisor could communicate with the counselor during the counseling session.

It might appear that this would be a desirable method of

supervision. But I would suggest that it is undesirable, and that it should be unnecessary. Any student who would function in this way is, in my opinion, not ready for a practicum, or should be prepared better for his first interview by the practicum supervisor or instructor. Perhaps these are the kinds of students with which the supervisor should use adhesive tape rather than recording tape—or in addition to recording tape. The remedy for such a situation is not a mechanical third ear, by which the supervisor can control the student, but better preparation of the student. It should be obvious, too, that the supervisor cannot monitor all the interviews of all his students.

The use of such a method of supervision raises a basic question about the nature of supervision. In my opinion this approach is undesirable because it takes the responsibility for the client away from the student and gives it to the supervisor. But the supervisor is not the counselor, and the student must be given responsibility for his clients. Only in this way can he develop independence and confidence in himself. If the student is adequately prepared it is rare that any irreparable damage can be done to the client in a single interview, before the supervisor can intervene if necessary. It is recognized that the supervisor does have a responsibility to the client, but his major responsibility is to the student and his growth and development as a responsible, independent counselor. The function of supervision is not for the supervisor to counsel the client through the student, or with the student as described by Cottle (1952, 1955).

Influencing by Creating an Atmosphere for Growth

There is another approach to supervision which fosters responsibility and independence in the student. This is an approach which avoids those methods or techniques which we know are not conducive to learning and which have thus been abandoned in the practice of counseling and psychotherapy—advising, correcting, pointing out errors, etc. These are not effective in supervision for the same reason that they are ineffective in counseling—they are threatening. Supervision, like counseling, must provide a nonthreatening, accepting, and understanding atmosphere.

But we now face an apparent dilemma. How can the supervisory session be nonthreatening, especially when the supervisor evaluates the student to give a grade and/or a recommendation as a counselor, and when the supervisor has a definite point of view or bias? These are reasons why the supervisory relationship is in some respects an even more difficult one than the counseling relationship.

To begin with it must be recognized that threat cannot be entirely removed in the supervisory relationship any more than it can be in any other situation. The playing of his tapes for someone else is threatening to the student. How many instructors play their own tapes to others, including their students? Pierson (1950) noted long ago that "insecure students may find it impossible to face recordings of their own interviews." This is perhaps not so much a problem at present, since recording of interviews is accepted by students as part of their training, and usually they have had some experience with doing this prior to the practicum.

But evaluation cannot be eliminated. The supervisor does evaluate, must evaluate, and should evaluate. No one is in a better position to evaluate the student-counselor than the practicum supervisor. This is part of his duty as an instructor. He cannot abdicate this to the student himself—this also is threatening to the student. Nor should the students be required to grade each other—this is more threatening than being graded by the instructor. I have seen classes of students so threatened by this requirement that they were unable to relax and open up in class discussion. Evaluation is also an obligation of the instructor to the profession and to potential future clients of the student-counselor. I see no way for the instructor to avoid evaluating his students. Arbuckle (1963) suggests having two supervisors, one who evaluates and one who only supervises. But this is not only impractical but probably would not remove evaluation from the supposedly non-evaluative supervisor. After all, the student will probably need or wish to use him for a reference, so that he is still an evaluator.

The necessity for evaluation must be faced with the students, and discussed with them. Students may be told that since they are advanced graduate students and have been selected for the practicum they should not worry about failure in the course. The use of grades S and U rather than the usual letter grades may help reduce the threat of grading by the instructor. After discussions I have found that the threat of grading is not a problem or an inhibiting factor, and that students enter into the course realizing that the emphasis is upon helping them develop as counselors.

But what about the contradiction between the instructor's teaching a point of view, and the freedom of the student to choose his own approach to counseling? This problem is similar to that occurring in counseling, when every counselor has a value system, goals for the counseling process, and a method or point of view.

It may be pointed out that as the client has his choice of therapists, so does the student have his choice of instructors. He may choose a college or university on the basis of its known point of view. Within the school he may—or should be able to—choose the instructor with whom he takes the practicum. The student in taking a course in effect enters into a contract. This is why it is important that the nature of the course and the point of view of the instructor be clear and recognized, so that the student knows what he is contracting for. And just as the supervisor, or any counselor or therapist, must be committed to a method or point of view if he is to function effectively, so must the student have a commitment to a point of view or approach if he wants to learn it (Ekstein and Wallerstein, 1958, p. 56). As Ekstein and Wallerstein (1958, pp. 63-64) point out, "the belief that a young psychotherapist ought to be schooled in a variety of methods, very different from one another, in order thus to acquire a broadminded research attitude and to avoid premature commitment to a particular point of view, sounds ideal but is actually unfeasible, and nihilistic in its effect. It stems, we believe, from ignorance about the nature and training for psychotherapeutic work."

There remains a problem here, nevertheless. I agree with Rogers (1961, p. 287) that one cannot impose one's feelings on one's students. But, as Rogers also recognizes, the instructor must be "the person that he is," and must express his attitudes, feelings, and beliefs. I do not feel that it is possible to be as unconcerned as Rogers appears to be (or to claim to be) about the outcomes of counselor training. If the instructor believes his approach is best—and if he doesn't he wouldn't have accepted or adopted it and continue to practice it—then he must be concerned about whether his students are able to accept and adopt it or not; and if he is concerned, this is going to influence his teaching and supervision.

In practice there is usually little difficulty, for several reasons. First, the emphasis is upon basic assumptions and attitudes, not upon specific methods or techniques. The student is not being forced to conform to a rigid system, but is helped to find his own style of counseling within the framework of the attitudes which are considered the necessary and sufficient conditions for therapeutic personality change (Rogers, 1957). Second, most students either have already essentially accepted the client-centered point of view and desire experience with it, or find that it is acceptable to them once they have acquired an understanding of it. Third, the student who has a commitment to another approach, or who has no commitment and is reluctant to identify himself with a "school" or a systematic approach, is not pressured or coerced, but is accepted and encouraged to discuss his attitudes and doubts, while being exposed to the instructor's point of view. There are limits to the student's freedom here as in all other human behavior. A student is not permitted to work with clients on a basis or with an approach which is inconsistent with the point of view of the course. Again, by the nature of previous preparation, selection (including self-selection) and entrance into a practicum with an explicit orientation, there has never been a situation where a student has (as he would be permitted to do) withdrawn from the course.

Supervision is a relationship. And as in any relationship, including the counseling relationship, there is an element of threat. In fact, it is more threatening than many other relationships. This is something that must be recognized, since we know that threat inhibits and restricts learning, that it leads to defensiveness and resistance. If then, we expect the student to change, to grow and develop, we must reduce threat to the minimum. This suggests that the methods or techniques of supervision are more similar to those of counseling and psychotherapy than they are to subject matter or didactic instruction.

Methods and Procedures in Supervision

In the first place, the supervisor listens, rather than lectures or talks. He listens to the student, when he talks about his perceptions of his client and of his perceptions of his own approach to and activities in the counseling session. He also listens to the student's tapes. He may listen for long periods of time, without comment, unles the student stops the tape and raises a question. I agree with Anderson and Bown (1955) who comment that "technique orientation is fostered . . . by the supervisor who reacts to the recording in terms of each and every counselor response, e.g. 'You missed that feeling,' or 'That was too much of an interpretation.'" I also would suggest that such an approach to supervision does two other things which are detrimental to the growth of the student. It creates a threat to the student, who becomes fearful of constant or continual criticism and the pointing out of errors. It also fosters dependence on the supervisor. The student does not develop the habit of self-observation and self-evaluation, but depends on the supervisor to evaluate his performance. In my supervision I stop the tape usually only when I feel the student has made a serious error, i.e. has missed completely what the client is saying or experiencing, when I do not understand what prompted the student's response, and when I feel the student has understood the client and communicated this understanding exceptionally well. The student controls the supervision, in terms of what tapes, or parts of tapes, he uses, and where the tape is stopped for discussion. I do, however, review at least briefly the status of each client with whom the counselor is working.

When the student does not feel threatened when he understands that the supervisor is not going to analyze his every response, and when the supervision is structured so that the student knows he is to evaluate himself and is expected to indicate his own questions or doubts about his performance, then the supervisory session becomes, like a counseling session, one in which the student takes the responsibility for himself and the session, and the supervisor, as does a counselor, follows the student in his self-analysis. Very often no comment is necessary by the supervisor, for the student will comment on his own performance. Often both the supervisor and the student may listen in silence for long periods. The student, listening to himself in the presence of another person (the supervisor), benefits as does the client, listening to himself in the presence of the counselor, often with little response except attention from the counselor. Students are encouraged to listen to their own tapes alone or with each other, but there is something about the supervisory relationship, as in the counseling relationship, which makes the situation different than listening to oneself, as counseling is different than talking to oneself. The student, if not interrupted, lectured to, criticized, with his mistakes being thrown in his face, will take the responsibility for analyzing and evaluating himself.

In this kind of supervisory situation I find no place for the kind of evaluation and analysis described by Anderson and Bown (1955). As in counseling, if the supervisor sets the stage, the student will conduct his own analysis and evaluation, and develop understanding of his counseling, without the probing and interpretations which Anderson and Bown utilize. It is interesting that these client-centered counselors do not feel they can be client-centered in their supervision. Why can't we have as much confidence in the ability of our students to develop understandings of their counseling behavior as we have in our clients to develop understanding of their behavior? This does not mean that the supervisor is not honest, direct, and open in his relationship with the student. As Rogers points out in his comment on the Anderson and Bown paper, there is a difference between evaluation and the expression of a personal feeling by the supervisor as his feeling. He suggests that the essence of the Anderson and Bown approach is that the supervisor understands the student's feelings and communicates this to the student. I would suggest that this can be done in a simpler, less threatening way than Anderson and Bown appear to do it.

What else is there to supervision? To me, there is nothing else.

The supervision creates an atmosphere or an environment, as free of threat as possible, which the student can use to grow in understanding and in skill in counseling. The focus is upon helping the student to understand the feelings and experiencing of the client at each moment of the interview, and to communicate this to the client. This is the essence of counseling, and this is what supervision should seek to develop in the student. The approach to supervision which I have outlined seems to achieve this goal.

Summary

Supervision is, then, not teaching, nor is it counseling or psychotherapy. It is, or should be, a learning situation. But the kind of learning is closer to that which occurs in counseling and psychotherapy than it is to classroom learning. Therefore, it follows that the supervisory situation and methods should be more like those of counseling and psychotherapy than didactic teaching. The conditions of supervision which appear to achieve the desired results in student growth appear to be those which are conducive for client growth in counseling. The supervisory relationship should be one in which the student is not threatened, but is accepted, respected, and understood, so that he may be free to analyze and explore his relationships with his clients and to modify and grow in such relationships. The problem of evaluation of the student by the instructor cannot be avoided, and thus must be faced with the student to reduce as much as possible the threat which it involves.

References

Anderson, R. P., and Bown, O. H.: Tape recordings and counselor-trainee understandings. *J. Counsel. Psychol.*, 2:189-195, 1955.

American Psychological Association, Division of Counseling and Guidance, Committee on Counselor Training. The practicum training of counseling psychologists. *Am. Psychol.*, 7:182-188, 1952.

Arbuckle, D. S.: The learning of counseling: process not product. *J. Counsel. Psychol.*, 10:163-168, 1963.

Cottle, W. C.: Supervising practicum courses in counseling. *Trans. Kans. Acad. Sci.*, 55:468-471, 1952.

Cottle, W. C.: The supervisor participates in training interviews. *Voc. Guid. Quart.*, 4:18-20, 1955.

Ekstein, R., and Wallerstein, R. S.: *The Teaching and Learning of Psychotherapy.* New York, Basic Books, 1958.

Korner, I. N., and Brown, W. H.: The mechanical third ear. *J. Consult. Psychol., 16*:81-84, 1952.

Patterson, C. H.: *Counseling and Psychotherapy: Theory and Practice.* New York; Harper & Row, 1959.

Pierson, G. A.: Utilizing internships in preparation of counselors. *Occup., 29*:92-94, 1950.

Robinson, Virginia P.: *Supervision in Social Casework.* Chapel Hill, University of North Carolina, 1936.

Robinson, Virginia P.: *The dynamics of Supervision Under Functional Controls.* Philadelphia, University of Pennsylvania, 1949.

Rogers, C. R.: The necessary and sufficient conditions of personality change. *J. Consult. Psychol., 21*:95-103, 1957.

Rogers, C. R.: *On Becoming a Person.* Boston, Houghton Mifflin, 1961.

Sanderson, H.: *Basic Concepts in Vocational Guidance.* New York, McGraw-Hill, 1954.

Walz, G., and Roeber, E.: Supervisors' reactions to a counseling interview. *Counselor Educ. Superv., 2*:2-7, 1962.

STUDENT-CENTERED APPROACHES TO PRACTICUM SUPERVISION *

Ronald A. Ruble and H. Dean Gray

One consistent problem in counselor education appears to be that of promoting the development, within the students, of a value system which will allow them to demonstrate a consistent self within the counseling situation. It is proposed that the practicum preparation of counselors should integrate learned counseling techniques with personality structure in a climate in which conditions established for learning are basically consistent with client-centered concepts.

Most students who enter the practicum are knowledgeable about various counseling techniques, but their behavior in a counseling situation does not usually demonstrate an integration of these techniques into a consistent internal congruence with their own personality and value systems. Carkhuff (1966) suggests, "there . . . [may be] no relationship between counselor knowledgeability of counseling and counseling competence" (p.

* Reprinted from *Counselor Education and Supervision,* 7:143-144, 1968, with permission of the American Personnel and Guidance Association and the authors.

468). If this is true, the goal of increasing student knowledge-ability may not be an adequate one.

If, on the other hand, the major goal of the practicum is that of integration of self and counseling techniques as a means of establishing meaningful relationships with clients, the developing counselor would be better served. The literature directed to this point is relatively limited (Rogers, 1961; Patterson, 1964; Clark, 1965; and Gysbers and Johnston, 1965). These authorities suggest that an approach to the practicum which is based upon client-centered concepts of empathy, self-consistency, and unconditional positive regard appears to be logical and consistent if one wishes to promote like attitudes in counselors in preparation.

If a goal of integration of self and counseling techniques can be accepted as a legitimate goal of the practicum, the question of supervisory techniques adequate to this goal may then be raised. It is suggested that the use of student-centered group techniques may allow the supervisor to provide a more meaningful experience for the students and to use time more efficiently and effectively.

To meet the needs of such groups, the practicum supervisor must conduct himself consistently within the group in the areas of self-congruence, empathy, and unconditional positive regard. He must strive to accept students and the problems that they have in learning new modes of behavior, and he must additionally help them to find realistic limitations for these behaviors. He must search out means of providing experiences and activities which will promote student growth and integrative experience, and he must establish, within the practicum, a climate wherein the students are free to explore the personal meanings of that experience. Finally, it seems likely that, for some students, the supervisor may serve as a role model for counseling behaviors.

In recorded interviews following a practicum which attempted to follow the attitudes and concepts expressed herein, the responses of the counselors in preparation were highly positive. Many of these counselors commented favorably about their feelings that the experience was a consistent and a unique one. Most perceived the focus of the practicum as one which compelled them to take responsibility for their own development as a consistent counselor, to explore the question, "as a counselor, how can I become more effective?"

The counselors expressed the feeling that, after initial hesitation, they were able to openly explore ideas and techniques that were congruent or in conflict with themselves as persons. The experience of coping with real problems of personal growth and integration as a developing counselor in a situation oriented to helping other people to cope with real and difficult problems should help the counselor in preparation to understand *directly* the dynamics which occur in a counseling situation. This hypothesis was supported by student responses that indicated the students *were aware* that change had taken place within them as they moved through the practicum. This awareness, it is thought, also pointed up the importance of being congruent with one's self-concept—both as a counselor and as a person. If the integration of values and technique is teachable and valuable in counselor education, and these responses appear to indicate that this is a possibility, then planning the direction and climate of the practicum should result in a more meaningful experience for the developing counselor.

In addition to the counselor's subjective responses to the practicum experience, the supervisors noted in some students definite changes in at least verbal attitude toward their role as counselors and toward the client's responsibility for internal change. The most dramatic case, in the estimation of the supervisors, was one student who early in the practicum professed doubt as to the ability of the client to help himself, and who, toward the end, made a pronouncement that it was entirely the responsibility of the client to direct any change. Whether this was an instance of basic expedient behavior would, of course, be open to some question, but the supervisors felt that the structure of the class would make this doubtful.

The supervisors' experience and the available literature seem to support some tentative conclusions: (a) a group-centered approach to supervision of the practicum gives both theoretical and practical experience to the counselors in terms of the dynamics of the counseling situation; and (b) a group-centered approach to supervision of the practicum increases the amount of counselor integration of techniques and attitudes.

In terms of openness to new experience and expression of affective reactions on the part of the practicum counselors, it appeared to the supervisors (based on this single, relatively intensive experience) that the process of group development in the practicum parallels the stages of client-centered therapy (Rogers, 1942). In terms of consistency of technique and approach to teaching, this approach seems logical, and it is held that it has high potential for exposing practicum students to more concentrated and varied experiences in a climate which is conducive to providing for a wider range of effective counseling behaviors.

References

Carkhuff, R. R.: Counseling research, theory and practice—1965. *Journal of Counseling Psychology, 13:*467-80, 1966.

Clark, C. M.: On process of counseling supervision. *Counselor Education and Supervision, 4:*64-67, 1965.

Gysbers, N. C., and Johnston, J. A.: Expectations of a practicum supervisor's role. *Counselor Education and Supervision, 4:*68-74, 1965.

Patterson, C. H.: Supervising students in the counseling practicum. *Journal of Counseling Psychology, 11:*47-53, 1964.

Rogers, C. R.: *Counseling and Psychotherapy.* Boston, Houghton Mifflin, 1942.

Rogers, C. R.: *On Becoming a Person.* Boston, Houghton Mifflin, 1961.

COUNSELOR EXPERIENCING: ITS IMPLICATIONS FOR SUPERVISION *

James L. Lister

Irrespective of the theoretical framework from which a counselor operates, his effectiveness is diminished when his communication with his client is in any way disrupted. In this article, the variable of counselor experiencing is examined as an avenue for maintaining and restoring counselor-client communication.

Experiencing is used here as Gendlin has defined it (1961, 1962). It refers to "an ongoing flow of events that occurs con-

* Reprinted from *Counselor Education and Supervision,* 5:55-60, 1966, with permission of the American Personnel and Guidance Association and the author.

tinuously in the individual" (1962, p. 234). Occurring as an organismic process in the immediate present, it can be referred to directly by the individual, and, while preconceptual, it can aid the individual in conceptualizing and articulating his meanings.

Counselors have focused on clients' experiencing as a guide to their behavior during an interview. Most counselors feel that they can function more effectively when they know what is "going on" within the other person. It seems that experiencing can also provide the counselor with a kind of "intrapersonal communication" which aids him in detecting and modifying within the immediate present subtle, moment-by-moment nuances of feelings within himself which disrupt his communication with his client. Although reference to counselor experiencing has come largely from client-centered theory (Rogers, 1961), to the extent that experiencing helps counselors maintain communication with their clients, it should be a useful variable to consider in several counseling approaches.

The anxiety a counselor experiences during an interview has external and internal concomitants. Each counselor comes to recognize external signs of anxiety which render him less effective in the immediate counseling relationship. Early in his development, the counselor often makes such discoveries "after the fact." In retrospect, he realizes that external evidence of his discomfort, present on the tape recording, was also accompanied by internal physical or emotional discomfort. He may later discover that his internal discomfort in fact preceded the impaired communication. When the counselor can associate the external signs of his discomfort with their internal concomitants, he can better anticipate and thereby modulate his counseling behavior.

Counselor Discomfort: External Evidence

External manifestations of counselor discomfort vary from counselor to counselor and from client to client for the same counselor; however, the following examples illustrate the general nature of such indicators. The counselor may miss an obvious "opening" for an interpretation or reflection. He may find it unusually difficult to formulate a response to his client's statements, or his response may be over-elaborated and argumentative as if driving home a certain point. The counselor's voice qualities and speech patterns also convey evidences of discomfort. Any marked changes in vocal tone, or speech patterns such as rate or volume, that occur within the interview are associated with an internal change in the state of the counselor. Additional evidence of internal discomfort is provided by the counselor's motor behavior, such as frequent shifts in posture, moving his chair, and readjusting the microphone or tape recorder. Significance of these external signs is usually determined "after the fact" when listening to the tape and discussing the interview during a supervisory conference. Sometimes they are glaringly apparent to the counselor when he views himself on video tape. At times, the counselor will recognize the significance of such factors while trying to piece together what went wrong in a particular interview.

External signs of counselor discomfort provide a basis for inferring their internal referents. A supervisor can readily *show* the counselor that he was uncomfortable during the interview. This is helpful insofar as it enables the counselor to take a first step toward the development of an "intrapersonal communication system" through which he can rectify his ineffective behavior. Until the counselor can *experience* directly the internal referents that precede his overt behavior, however, he cannot develop an intrapersonal language through which he can modulate his counseling behavior. The supervisor can only *infer* the counselor's internal state, he cannot experience it or tell the counselor how he felt at any given moment. His tentative inferences, however, can help to sensitize the counselor to his own inner experiencing.

Counselor Discomfort: Internal Evidence

As the counselor is able to "listen" to himself, he finds that his outward signs of discomfort or threat are often preceded and accompanied by some of the following internal states. The counselor may find that his throat feels tight and that this is causing a pinched, anxious tone in his voice. He may find that kicking or tapping of his foot accompanies immediate feelings of impatience or hostility. The counselor may become aware that certain voluntary muscles have been tense for several minutes and that during this time he has been fending off his client's request for direct answers to questions. Often, the counselor only senses that he is not completely "with" the client in the immediate present. He may be unable to follow his client's statements in an area that is familiar and not complex; he may grope for an appropriate response to a client statement; or, he may simply experience a vague internal prompting or "felt datum" (Gendlin, 1961, p. 235) which seems out of place in the immediate relationship but which, for the moment, is undifferentiated and inarticulate.

Utilizing "Experiencing"

When the counselor is simultaneously in touch with both internal and external aspects of his behavior during the counseling relationship, he is more congruent (Rogers, 1961), and his counseling "program" sustains less distortion. Parenthetically, an analogy can be drawn between a computer program and a counseling theory. Once developed, the computer program unerringly determines how all incoming data are classified and analyzed. Similarily, every counseling theory provides a framework for classifying and analyzing the "input" which the counselor receives during the interview. His response or "output" is a function of the input and program. Threat or anxiety which the counselor experiences impairs the efficiency of his program and results in "counselor errors."

As the counselor develops a language for his internal experiencing, he corrects certain "blind spots" that he had not identified before. He may also discover that more of his counseling behavior was based upon his "personal theory" (Lister, 1964) than upon his formal or textbook theory. In addition, the counselor's increased sensitivity to his experiencing enables him to immediately attend to any inward state that would reduce his operating efficiency. Gendlin (1962) has suggested that attending to the inward felt experience results in more clarity and more explicit meaning. Thus, the counselor who experiences a feeling of uneasiness may, by attending to his uneasiness, find that it is not uneasiness so much as anticipation that he feels. He may then recognize that the client's passing reference to a childhood event had caused him to wonder whether the client's present difficulties could stem from an early traumatic experience. At this point, the counselor may realize that while he was listening for evidence that would support this hypothesis, he missed the feeling underlying the client's statement. This counselor's client-centered program was temporarily impaired by his superimposing of a contradictory program, in this case, psychoanalytic.

With experience and maturity, most counselors and psychotherapists come to rely intuitively upon their inner experiencing as a means for operating more effectively during the counseling relationship (Reik, 1949; Rogers, 1961; Jourard, 1959). It is hypothesized that early, deliberate focus upon counselor experiencing would facilitate the counselor candidate's development of a mature, integrated counseling approach. In addition to enabling him to minimize the length of time his counseling "program" is impaired, sensitivity to experiencing would provide him with an additional resource for deepening the interpersonal counseling relationship, provided this would be compatible with his theoretical approach.

Sundland and Barker (1962) have shown that major approaches to psychotherapy can be ordered along a dimension ranging from "analytic" to "experiential." At the "analytic" end of the continuum, the counselor might utilize his internal experiencing exclusively as a means for maintaining his counseling "program." At the experiential end of the continuum, however, the counselor might share his experiencing with the client in order to present himself as an example of how other persons react to the client and to serve as a model to facilitate the client's further exploration of feelings during the interview. Through his own self-disclosure (Jourard, 1964), the counselor would thereby endorse this way of "being." Whether the counselor's experiencing is shared with his client depends on the counselor's theoretical orientation; however, it should aid counselors in maintaining the internal consistency with which they implement their various theoretical approaches.

Implementation in Supervision

In making counselor experiencing an explicit focus of counselor education, a variety of theoretical formulations can be employed.

It might be valuable for beginning counselors to consider their own experiencing from the vantage point of their own counseling theory. Thus, while counselors and supervisors implementing approaches based on learning theory (Gysbers, 1963), trait theory (Roeber, 1963), or self-theory (Walz, 1963) would describe experiencing in different terms, it might be equally useful within each framework.

In order for the variable of experiencing to make a contribution to the counselor candidate's development, opportunities should be provided that enable him to examine his subjective experience during the counseling interview. The cognitive, theoretical dimension of supervision is important, but it can, if made the exclusive focus, provide an intellectual buffer that prevents the candidate from developing lines of communication with himself.

The counseling supervisor plays a major role in helping beginning counselors become acquainted with their own experiencing. Through his behavior in the practicum seminar and in individual conferences, he can communicate to student counselors that the variable of experiencing is an integral part of counseling interaction, not something to be feared or repressed. He can make a valuable contribution by demonstrating how his own experiencing is used in his counseling. Through participation in role-playing or by playing tapes of his counseling interviews, the supervisor can point out external evidences of threat or discomfort, and he can describe their internal, subjective concomitants. By sharing his own set of "signs," the supervisor helps establish an atmosphere that enables his students to examine their experiencing with a minimum of defensiveness.

Many of the common techniques for increasing counseling skill, such as role-playing and reviewing audio and video tapes, can also be useful in helping students to grasp the relationship between their internal and external counseling behavior. When these activities are conducted in a group setting, counselors can obtain immediate feedback which helps them to discover some of the relationships between their feelings and their overt behavior.

Truax (1962) has developed a scale for measuring therapist self-congruence or genuineness which should be useful in an approach to the study of counselor experiencing. This scale attempts to measure the extent to which the counselor is himself during the relationship. As defined by the scale, a counselor is congruent when his feelings and attitudes are consistent with his verbalizations. By using this and similar instruments in monitoring his interviews (Truax, *et al.*, 1964), the beginning counselor can focus more directly upon those dimensions of his counseling behavior which enable him to understand and utilize his inner experience more efficiently.

References

Gendlin, Eugene T.: *Experiencing and the Creation of Meaning*. Glencoe, Illinois, Free Press, 1962.

Gendlin, Eugene T.: Experiencing: a variable in the process of therapeutic change. *American Journal of Psychotherapy, 15*:233-45, 1961.

Gysbers, Norman C.: *Practicum Supervision. 1. Theories, Learning Theory*. Mimeographed paper presented at the American Personnel and Guidance Association Convention, Boston, April 9, 1963.

Jourard, Sidney M.: I-thou relationship versus manipulation in counseling and psychotherapy. *Journal of Individual Psychology, 15*:174-79, 1959.

Jourard, Sidney M.: *The Transparent Self*. Princeton, New Jersey, D. Van Nostrand Company, 1964.

Lister, James L.: The counselor's personal theory. *Counselor Education and Supervision, 3*:207-13, 1964.

Reik, Theodore: *Listening With the Third Ear*. New York, Farrar, Straus and Company, 1949.

Roeber, Edward C.: *Practicum Supervision. 1. Theories, Trait Theory*. Mimeographed paper presented at the American Personnel and Guidance Association Convention, Boston, April 9, 1963.

Rogers, Carl R.: *On Becoming a Person*. Boston, Houghton Mifflin Company, 1961.

Sundland, Donald M., and Barker, Edwin N.: The orientations of psychotherapists. *Journal of Consulting Psychology, 26*:201-12, 1962.

Truax, Charles B.: A tentative scale for the measurement of therapist genuineness or self-congruence. *Discussion Papers,* Wisconsin Psychiatric Institute, University of Wisconsin, October, 1962.

Truax, Charles B., Carkhuff, Robert R., and Douds, John: Toward an integration of the didactic and experiential approaches to training in counseling and psychotherapy. *Journal of Counseling Psychology, 11*: 240-47, 1964.

Walz, Garry R.: *Practicum Supervision. 1. Theories, Self Theory*. Mimeographed paper presented at the American Personnel and Guidance Association Convention, Boston, April 9, 1963.

AN APPROACH TO COUNSELOR EDUCATION*

CHARLES B. TRUAX

Before considering the ideal counselor education program, we must first ask what a professional counselor is and how he got that way.

First, we must note that many of the leaders in the field did not receive doctoral degrees in counseling. It seems clear that competence and quality of performance are not *necessarily* products of university degrees. This prompts us to ask, "How did we become professional?" I, for one, did it through the "divine right" of a university doctoral degree. What in the four years of college and five years of post-graduate training actually prepared me to be of professional help to others? Almost certainly I know it was not the courses and seminars in chemistry, statistics, and physiology. It was not even the courses in the psychology of human and animal learning—I had already learned from my father early in life that praise and punishment alter behavior.

Most counselor educators—as well as educators in clinical psychology, psychiatry, and social work—point to the practicum and internship experience as the most important aspect of the educational process. With this I would strongly agree. What skills I have in counseling were acquired and sharpened mainly in practicum and internship contacts with real clients. As an educator, it is apparent to me that my students learn most from similar experiences rather than from even my best lectures. Note, however, that we university educators never refer to it as OJT (on-the-job training).

Since, unfortunately, we often teach different and even contradictory or opposing theories in substantive courses it is not unreasonable that OJT be one of the, if not *the* main, ingredients in professional counselor training.

It can be argued that the "professional," the holder of a master's or doctoral degree has two main advantages beyond his increased respectability when functioning as a counselor actually seeing clients: (a) he has been selected or screened for general

---

* Reprinted from *Counselor Education and Supervision*, 10:4-15, 1970, with permission of the American Personnel and Guidance Association and the author.

aptitude for specific interpersonal skills (hopefully), and for moral character; and (b) he has had intentionally structured OJT.

I believe that we can provide these two essential ingredients— selection and intentionally structured OJT—to people who don't have university degrees, or even high school diplomas. Moreover, I believe that if we use the best of our current knowledge in selecting them and in structuring their OJT we will wind up with a person who, under supervision, can excel as a rehabilitation counselor. I favor calling such a person a trained practical counselor.

Indeed, since there *are* more people willing to enter such OJT than there are people eligible to enter graduate studies in counseling, it is virtually certain that we could do a much better job of selecting trained practical counselors than professional counselors. Perhaps most importantly, we could probably also do a better job of weeding out those who do not excel during training and actual practice as well as older trained practical counselors who have soured in their jobs and become ineffective or damaging to their all-too-human clients. This latter point is no minor consideration since we are all quite aware of the difficulties involved in the weeding-out of ineffective professionals. Sanctified with a university doctorate, I myself can look forward to obtaining employment as a professional (unless the bottom falls out of the market) regardless of how ineffectual I become. It might be more in my self-interest however—and clearly more in the interest of my clients—if this were not the case.

Toward Selecting and Training Nonprofessionals

Given the above viewpoint and the prospect that, for better or for worse, the use of nonprofessional personnel is and will be a growing part of counseling in many settings, I would like to describe briefly an approach to selection and training that applies to both professional and nonprofessional counselor education.

First, let me review the research indicating the major ingredients of effective counseling. The most clear-cut and striking body of evidence available concerning basic ingredients in effective counseling deals with central interpersonal skills possessed by counselors. As the evidence accumulates, it becomes clear that the counselor's interpersonal skill in relating to clients has much to do with inducing positive client change. While specialized techniques and expert knowledge are believed important, it is already clear that they are secondary. The effective counselor is first and foremost an expert in interpersonal relations.

What is most striking in the research findings to date is that these same interpersonal skills are motivating, therapeutic, or change-inducing whether we measure delinquent behavior in delinquents, psychotic behavior in psychotics, arithmetic and reading achievement in the normal classroom, the degree of intimacy and self-disclosure in normal friendship relationships and parent-child relationships, socialization in preschool children, neurotic behavior in neurotics, vocational progress in the physically, emotionally, or mentally handicapped, or indeed the person's sense of adequacy, satisfaction in living, or ability to live constructively across the broad areas of human relationships and human problems (Truax and Carkhuff, 1967; Truax and Mitchell, 1970).

While the bulk of the research grew out of the rather narrow confines of group and individual psychotherapy and counseling, it became clear that accurate empathy, nonpossessive warmth, and genuineness existed along a continuum in all human relationships and, depending upon the degree they were present, these interpersonal skills or qualities led to the facilitation or inducement of a wide variety of socially and individually valued positive behavioral changes (Truax, 1963; Truax and Carkhuff, 1967; Truax and Wargo, 1966; Truax and Mitchell, 1968).

Solid research evidence suggests that the counseling process itself can be harmful if wrongly used. Further evidence suggests that while large numbers of counselors are indeed highly effective there are also sizable numbers of counselors who are ineffective and even damaging to clients. This tends to explain the puzzling mass of evidence (Truax and Carkhuff, 1967) suggesting that the therapetuic endeavor is, on the average, ineffective. Thus it appears that the demonstrable positive effects of competent counselors is offset by the negative effects of incompetent counselors.

An accurate and sensitive awareness of the other person's

feelings, aspirations, values, beliefs, and perceptions; a deep but unobtrusive concern for the other person's welfare; an open genuineness—all have long been recognized by philosophers, by novelists, and by theoreticians throughout the helping professions as beneficial in any human interaction.

In particular studies aimed at therapeutic strategy, we have discovered that the lowest and the mean levels of warmth and genuineness predict outcome quite well, but that the highest or altitude levels do not. Clinically, this suggests that the counselor should try not to offer seriously low levels of warmth and genuineness; otherwise the client will no longer trust the relationship. By contrast, it is the highest and the mean levels of accurate empathy, not the basal levels, that predict outcome. This suggests that we can be most therapeutic by attempting deep empathic responses even at the risk of being wrong, as long as our average is relatively high. The client can easily forgive the occasionally inept or unempathic response as long as he is generally understood and especially if at moments he is deeply understood.

One of the surprising findings in studying therapy with college populations has been the fact that higher levels of interpersonal skills are needed with underachievers than with more disturbed clients. Of course, just the opposite had been expected. This points to a need for more empathic, warm, and genuine counselors for the majority, that is the more normal, of the counseling cases. When difficult relationships are expected, as when white counselors interact with black clients, unusually high levels of therapeutic skills are required for client progress.

With these interpersonal skills in mind, let us now turn to the first stage of counselor education: the selection of trainees.

Selection

We are currently using a selection procedure both for professional counselors and nonprofessional trained practical counselors that is threefold.

First, the candidate must meet the agency's existing qualifications for employment. Primarily, these are the employer's judgments of the candidate's general abilities, dependability, sense of responsibility, ethics, appearance, and other such usual considerations for employment. These considerations are designed to ensure that the employee will be able to function where he is employed, and they will vary from setting to setting. Somewhat different standards, for example, might be used in the employment of so-called "indigenous" persons (a terrible word) in a ghetto setting than would be used in a middle class school.

The second aspect of selection involves drawing upon past research data (Truax, 1968) to the summary of research studies published since 1963 showing personality correlates of such interpersonal scales as Accurate Empathy. We have been using the Minnesota Multiphasic Personality Inventory (MMPI) and the Edwards Personal Preference Schedule (EPPS) as selection devices. Specifically, we look for candidates who on the MMPI (using K-converted raw scores) scored less than 27 on Pt, less than 20 on D, less than 30 on Mf, less than 21 on Si, less than 30 on the Welch Anxiety Index for the MMPI, and less than 0.92 on the Welch Generalization Ratio, and who scored higher than 19 on Ma and higher than 142 on the Constructive Personality Change Index of the MMPI. In using the EPPS for selection we look for candidates who scored less than 10 on N Deference, less than 8 on N Order, less than 21 on N Intraception, less than 7 on N Abasement, less than 11 on N Consistency, and who also scored higher than 14 on N Dominance, higher than 17 on N Change, and higher than 14 on N Autonomy. In an interpretive sense the research evidence suggests that we will get candidates with more natural therapeutic skill or interpersonal skill if we look for people low in anxiety, depression, and introversion who are at the same time striving, strong, dominant, active, and autonomous individuals. As one can tell from looking over the selection scores, we are looking for high, stable ego strength—"nice guys" who are strong rather than passive.

At the final and most critical stage of selection, candidates who passed the first two aspects of selection are asked to conduct one or more group interviews (or counseling, if you prefer) with real clients. They are told that their task is to get to know these particular clients—their feelings, their problems, their strengths, and their weaknesses. With these instructions they are placed in the role of a group leader and asked to conduct a session that is tape-recorded. So far, we have simply tried to present the candidate with a more or less randomly selected group of the kind of clients we would expect him to work with.

The tape recordings themselves, reflecting his adequacy in interpersonal skills, constitute the critical selection factor. These tapes are rated on the candidate's accurate empathy, nonpossessive warmth, and genuineness in interacting with real clients, and the degree of self-exploration he is able to elicit from the group. (These scales are available on request from the Arkansas Rehabilitation Research and Training Center, University of Arkansas.)

Candidates for trained practical counselors or for employment as professional counselors who averaged 4.0 or above on the nonpossessive warmth, 4.0 or above on the genuineness scale, and 5.0 or above on the accurate empathy scale were selected. In other words, we selected people who were unusually highly skilled in interpersonal relations and who could provide adequate levels of therapeutic conditions.

It is of considerable interest to note that post-internship and post-practicum students in clinical psychology and counseling psychology have been reported to score an average of 2.50 on the accurate empathy scale. In fact, it has been my experience over the past nine years that only a small percentage of professional counselors and psychotherapists achieve average scores of 5.0 or above. To give some indication of the degree of selection, in filling seven trained practical counselor positions only 7 of 34 individuals who passed stages one and two were able to achieve these minimally higher levels of interpersonal skills and were accepted.

It is probable that in some cases where the potential pool of candidates is quite large even more rigid selection procedures would be possible. Where such a potentially large pool exists, it might be useful and economical to first select people on the basis of relationship questionnaires filled out on candidates by clients after relatively brief interactions. (The relationship questionnaire, also available from the University of Arkansas, is a rough and inexpensive paper-and-pencil test measuring such interpersonal skills as accurate empathy, etc.)

In our continuing effort at selection, we are beginning to incorporate recent research findings which show that such additional counselor characteristics as degree of persuasive potency and type and extent of constructive confrontations with clients are also separate and significant contributions to client benefit. We than have candidates who, according to available research evidence, are "inherently helpful" people, the kind of people neighbors and friends seek out in time of need and distress: the kind of person we might wish were the only kind to enter graduate training in counseling. The question now becomes, "What can we do to make him more helpful and how can we best use his abilities?"

Training

The basic aspect of effective training, indeed the basis of the phenomenon of learning itself, is structured feedback, Feedback informs the counselor of his behavior and its consequences on the setting and personnel where he works and most centrally of the consequences to his client. This is the central aspect of training and indeed of continuous quality control throughout later employment, and the counselor who gets such feedback will continue to learn to become more effective.

It is perhaps the most glaring deficit in the helping professions that counselors, clinical psychologists, psychiatrists, social workers, and others rarely, if ever, are given any systematic feedback on their effects on clients. As I have said before, generally the professional in the helping relationship can conclude all of his training at a university, receive a doctorate, be employed, promoted, pass licensing examinations, and become a diplomate of a board of examiners in his profession *without any one, at any point, attempting to systematically evaluate the effects he has on his clients.*

In the normal process of on-the-job training the professional or nonprofessional will receive specific and concrete feedback about his performance in filling out forms, adhering to employer regulations and requirements, and his ability to follow standard operating procedures. He will also normally obtain quite specific feedback during OJT of any negative impact he has on other employees of the agency or facility. This is standard and predictable for any kind of employment in any kind of setting.

To insure that he will be able to provide maximum benefit for clients, however, he must also get relatively specific and systematic feedback in terms of: (a) the level of interpersonal skills he uses in relating to clients; and (b) how his clients benefit from counseling compared with clients seen by other professional or nonprofessional counselors. This is basic to any counselor education program at all interested in producing effective counselors.

The Arkansas Rehabilitation Research and Training Center has instituted short-term programs to train personnel to provide higher levels of interpersonal skills or therapeutic conditions in counseling situations.

An Approach to Effective Counselor Training

The majority of research studies assess the levels of empathy, warmth, and genuineness by the use of these research scales developed for use with tape recordings of actual counseling or psychotherapy. As was suggested some time ago (Truax, 1963), the rating scales themselves can be used didactically for training beginning therapists. An approach to training using the research scales in an integrated didactic and experiential program has been described by Truax, Carkhuff, and Douds (1964) and by Truax and Carkhuff (1967). This training program has been applied to several training groups, both at professional and nonprofessional personnel levels.

The three central elements in the training approach can be summarized as:

1. A therapeutic context in which the supervisor communicates high levels of accurate empathy, nonpossessive warmth, and genuineness to the trainees themselves.

2. A highly specific didactic training using the research scales for "shaping" the trainees' responses toward high levels of empathy, warmth, and genuineness.

3. A focused group therapy experience that allows the emergence of the trainee's own idiosyncratic therapeutic self through

self-exploration and consequent integration of his didactic training with his personal values, goals, and life style.

While a complete description of the training program is contained in a book developed specifically for use in training and
practice (Truax and Carkhuff, 1967), a few brief comments about
the use of the research scales should help to clarify the didactic
nature of the training. The scales are used to identify tape-
recorded samples of experienced therapists offering very high
levels of therapeutic conditions, thus providing models for imitation. It should be remembered that even the best recordings
of total sessions usually provide a number of examples of precisely what not to do. Secondly, the trainees are taught the use
of the scales so that they will learn to identify high and low
levels of empathy, warmth, and genuineness in their own therapy
and in that of others. Third, empathy training, warmth training,
or genuineness training is provided by playing a tape recording
of client interviews and then requiring trainees to make immediate therapeutic responses. These responses are immediately rated
on the research scales to provide prompt feedback. As the trainee
shapes his responses toward higher levels of empathy, warmth,
and genuineness, he begins role-playing which in turn is recorded, brought to class, and rated by a group of trainees on the
research scales. Thus, the trainees compete among themselves in
ability to communicate therapeutic conditions. Finally, they begin one-shot interviews with real clients which again are tape-
recorded and brought to class session for rating. *In all, the complete basic training program involves less than 100 hours of training.*

There now exist a number of studies (see Truax and Carkhuff,
1967) that indicate that trainees (both professional and nonprofessional) can be brought to a level of interpersonal skill that
is (a) nearly commensurate with that of highly experienced and
effective counselors; (b) significantly above that of post-practicum and post-internship trainees in counseling and psychotherapy at major universities involved in doctoral training; and
(c) effective in producing significant positive changes in mildly
and severely disturbed clients. Taken together, the available evi-

dence strongly suggests positive benefit for this approach to training.

More recently, our experience suggests that more lasting
effects on counselor behavior can be produced by periodic workshops or seminars for those who have completed a basic short-
term training program. These are intended to reinforce the habit
of effectively relating to clients and to discourage the counselor's
tendency to fall back on his old style of relating to others.

Recent research by Martin (1968) has demonstrated that
trainees in professional counseling show gains in accurate empathy, nonpossessive warmth, and genuineness by specific feedback from self-evaluations. It seems reasonable, and we are currently pursuing this in research, that minimally high levels of
counseling skill can be maintained and enhanced by simply having groups of counselors periodically tape-record their own
contacts with clients and obtain group feedback on their ability
to provide high levels of therapeutic conditions or interpersonal
skills.

Even more importantly, feedback from measurement of client
benefits is central to maintaining and enhancing the effective
qualities of counseling services. While no single criterion exists
(and probably never will) for measuring client benefits, it is the
clear and immediate responsibility of every counseling unit to
at least minimally state its goals for client benefits and then to
measure these benefits per client for professional and nonprofessional counselors. This gives the counseling unit quality control,
and provides information on what counselors should and should
not be doing and what does and does not lead to successful counseling outcomes. Also of value are evaluations of counseling units
in comparison with other units and evaluations of individual
counselors and supervisors. It hardly needs repeating that periodic feedback of client benefits should continue throughout the
counselor's tenure of employment.

Research on the effective use of support personnel at the Hot
Springs Rehabilitation Center (Truax, 1968) suggested that even
untrained nonprofessionals, selected on no special basis other
than the judgment of counseling personnel on the staff, could be
as effective or more effective in the role of counselor than mas-

ter's degree-level professional counselors. That same study also provided evidence that the nonprofessional counselors proved of greatest benefit to clients (in terms of a number of measures of vocational rehabilitation progress) when they were supervised informally on a one-to-one basis with professional counselors, yet handled their own caseload alone. Moreover, the research indicated that the poorest client benefits occurred when counselor aides were used as assistants to the professional counselor serving his own caseload. In fact, there was some evidence to suggest negative or deteriorative effects of a counselor and counselor aide working together on a single caseload. It should also be noted that under this informal one-to-one supervision no role conflicts occurred between the professional and the nonprofessional counselor. As a supervisor, the professional counselor wanted the nonprofessional with whom he was working to succeed—and if possible to be more successful than other nonprofessionals supervised by other professionals.

While that particular study is of considerable interest and perhaps has implications for many settings, it should be stressed that it was carried out over a period of several years in a large and reasonably stable comprehensive rehabilitation center. The Arkansas Rehabilitation Service, however, has authorized a number of positions for counselor aides in its field offices and other facilities. Judging from the experience of other agencies and institutions in rehabilitation and allied fields, we might expect that the trained practical counselor can do an effective job as a rehabilitation counselor in any setting where there are professional counselors available for supervision and for informal advice and guidance in handling individual clients. Indeed the findings fit very well with those of Poser (1967) in a Canadian mental hospital setting.

It can be strongly argued that the trained practical counselor can effectively provide counseling services to clients in almost any area currently being served by professional counselors. Additionally, he may be able to communicate more effectively and empathically with certain special groups of clients than can the middle class professional counselor. To be truly professional, to be confident of our efforts at effective counselor education, we must produce counselors who are demonstrably more effective with clients than are untrained nonprofessionals. At present we have not done this as a total field.

Present research findings strongly indicate that the selection and training procedures described here will produce professional counselors who obtain demonstrably greater client benefits than untrained nonprofessionals and the usual "control groups."

It is time that we seriously put our research knowledge to work in counselor education. If we do not, then we cannot with integrity call ourselves "professionals." Current evidence indicates that only one of three professional counselors have average positive effects on clients. The odds are, then, that you are either ineffective or harmful, but every counselor likes to believe he is in the upper third rather than the lower two-thirds. Only feedback such as I have suggested here will replace wishful thinking with evidence for your personal benefit and for your all-too-human clients' benefit.

Let us begin.

References

Aspy, D. N.: *A Study of Three Facilitative Conditions and Their Relationships to the Achievement of Third Grade Students.* Unpublished doctoral dissertation, University of Kentucky, 1965.

Aspy, D. N., and Hadlock, W.: *The Effect of Empathy, Warmth, and Genuineness on Elementary Students' Reading Achievements.* Unpublished thesis, University of Florida, 1966.

Baldwin, T., and Lee, J.: Evaluation of programmed instruction in human relations. *American Psychologist, 20:*489, 1965.

Bergin, A. E., and Solomon, S.: *Personality and Performance Correlates of Empathic Understanding in Psychotherapy.* Paper read at American Psychological Association Convention, Philadelphia, 1963.

Betz, B. J.: Bases of therapeutic leadership in psychotherapy with the schizophrenic patient. *American Journal of Psychotherapy, 17:*196-212, 1963.

Betz, B. J.: Differential success rates of psychotherapists with "process" and "nonprocess" schizophrenic patients. *American Journal of Psychiatry, 11:* 1090-1091, 1963.

Dickenson, W. A., and Traux, C. B.: Group counseling with college underachievers: comparisons with a control group and relationship to empathy, warmth and genuineness. *Personnel and Guidance Journal, 45:*245-248, 1966.

Fey, W. F.: Acceptance by others and its relationship to acceptance of self and others: a reevaluation. *Journal of Abnormal and Social Psychology*, 50:274-276, 1955.

Kanfer, F. H., and Marston, A. R.: Conditioning of self-reinforcement responses: an analogue to self-confidence training. *Psychological Reports*, 13:63-70, 1963.

Martin, D. B.: *A Method of Self-Evaluation for Counselor Education*. Washington, D.C., U.S. Department of Health, Education, and Welfare, Office of Education, Bureau of Research, 1968.

May, R.: Contribution of existential psychotherapy. In May, R., Angle, E., and Ellenburger, (Eds.): *Existence*. New York, Basic Books, 1958.

Melloh, R. A.: *Accurate Empathy and Counselor Effectiveness*. Unpublished doctoral dissertation, University of Florida, 1964.

Poser, E. G.: The effect of therapist training on group therapeutic outcome. *Journal of Consulting Psychology*, 30:283-289, 1966.

Raush, H. L., and Bordin, E. S.: Warmth in personality development and in psychotherapy. *Psychiatry*, 20:351-363, 1957.

Shapiro, J. G.: Relationships between expert and neophyte ratings of therapeutic conditions. *Journal of Consulting and Clinical Psychology*, 32: 87-89, 1968.

Strupp, H. H.: *Psychotherapists in Action*. New York, Grune and Stratton, 1960.

Truax, C. B.: A scale for the measurement of accurate empathy. *Psychiatric Institute Bulletin*, 1961, 1, Wisconsin Psychiatric Institute, University of Wisconsin.

Truax, C. B.: A tentative scale for the measurement of therapist genuineness or self-congruence. *Discussion Papers*, 1962, 35, Wisconsin Psychiatric Institute, University of Wisconsin.

Truax, C. B.: A tentative scale for the measurement of unconditional positive regard. *Psychiatric Institute Bulletin*, 1962, 2, Wisconsin Psychiatric Institute, University of Wisconsin.

Truax, C. B.: Effective ingredients in psychotherapy: an approach to unraveling the patient-therapist interaction. Symposium: The empirical emphasis in psychotherapy. *Journal of Counseling Psychology*, 10:256-263, 1963.

Truax, C. B.: *The Evolving Understanding of Counseling and Psychotherapy and the Use of Trained Practical Counselors or Therapists*. Paper presented at International Congress of Applied Psychology, Amsterdam, 1968. *Discussion Papers*, 1968, 1, Arkansas Rehabilitation Research and Training Center, University of Arkansas.

Truax, C. B., and Carkhuff, R. R.: *Toward Effective Counseling and Psychotherapy: Training and Practice*. Chicago, Aldine, 1967.

Truax, C. B., Carkhuff, R. R., and Douds, J.: Toward an integration of the didactic and experiential approaches to training in counseling and psychotherapy. *Journal of Counseling Psychology*, 11:240-247, 1964.

Truax, C. B., and Mitchell, K. M.: Research on certain therapeutic skills in relation to process and outcome. In Bergin, A., and Garfield, S. (Eds.): *Handbook of Psychotherapy and Behavior Change.* New York, Wiley, 1970.

Truax, C. B., Tunnel, B. T., Jr., and Glenn, A. W.: *Accurate Empathy, Warmth, and Genuineness and Patient Outcome in Silent and Verbal Outpatients.* Unpublished manuscript, Arkansas Rehabilitation Research and Training Center, University of Arkansas, 1966 (a).

Truax, C. B., Tunnel, B. T., Jr., and Glenn, A. W.: *Accurate Empathy, Non-possessive Warmth, and Genuineness of the Therapist and Patient Outcome in Most and Least Adjusted Patients.* Unpublished manuscript, Arkansas Rehabilitation Research and Training Center, University of Arkansas, 1966 (b).

Truax, C. B., and Wargo, D. G.: Antecedents to outcome in group psychotherapy with outpatients: effects of therapeutic conditions, alternate sessions, vicarious therapy pre-training and patient self-exploration. *Journal of Consulting and Clinical Psychology,* 1969 (a).

Truax, C. B., and Wargo, D. G.: *Effects of Therapeutic Conditions, Alternate Sessions, Vicarious Therapy Pre-training and Patient Self-exploration and Hospitalized Mental Patients During Group Therapy.* Unpublished manuscript. 1969 (b).

Truax, C. B., Wargo, D. G., Frank, J. D., Imber, S. D., Battle, C. C., Hoehn-Saric, R., Nash, E. H., and Stone, A. R.: Therapist empathy, genuineness, and warmth and patient therapeutic outcome. *Journal of Consulting Psychology,* 30:395-401, 1966.

Truax, C. B., Wargo, D. G., and Volksdorf, N.: *Antecedents to outcome in Group Psychotherapy with Juvenile Delinquents: Effects of Therapeutic Conditions, Alternate Sessions, Vicarious Therapy Pre-Training and Patient Self-exploration.* Unpublished manuscript, 1969.

Whitehorn, J. C.: Human factors in psychiatry. *Bulletin of New York Academy of Medicine,* 40:451-466, 1964.

Whitehorn, J. C., and Betz, B. J.: A study of psychotherapeutic relationships between physicians and schizophrenic patients. *American Journal of Psychiatry,* 3:321-331, 1954.

PERSONAL GROWTH: AN INGREDIENT IN COUNSELOR EDUCATION PROGRAMS*

James C. Hurst and Vern H. Jensen

Beginning at least as early as 1950 with Fiedler's (1950a, 1950b) classic studies and extending through Rogers (1957) and

---

* Reprinted from *Counselor Education and Supervision,* 8:12-17, 1968, with permission of the American Personnel and Guidance Association and the authors.

the present work of Truax, Carkhuff, and others (Truax, 1963; Truax and Carkhuff, 1965; Truax, Carkhuff, and Douds, 1964) research evidence has been accumulating suggesting that the crucial elements of a counselor's effectiveness are not his use of a given technique or his adoption of a particular theory. Rather, effective counseling relationships seem more dependent upon the nature of the helper's attitudes and his ways of perceiving himself, his client, and his goals. Among the most commonly identified attitudes and characteristics found necessary for a therapeutic relationship are self- and other-acceptance, empathic understanding, and interpersonal sensitivity. Continuing research provides evidence that counselees respond favorably to therapeutic relationships in which these factors are present and respond unfavorably in their absence.

In spite of the general acceptance of these attitudes and characteristics as crucial to effective counseling, they are almost universally ignored in the formal requirements of counselor education programs. Much is said to counselor candidates about the importance of developing acceptance, warmth, and sensitivity. Little, however, is done within formal programs to help students develop these qualities in their own personalities. Apparently, the development of these qualities is not considered important enough to warrant inclusion within formal preparation procedures, or it is thought (perhaps hoped) that they will develop concomitantly as the other program requirements are completed. More likely, however, their importance is recognized, but there are no tested and accepted procedures for bringing about their development. The present study was undertaken in an effort to evaluate just such a procedure and to assess its effectiveness when compared with the more traditionally didactic procedures.

Procedure

The twenty "house counselors" at the North Carolina Advancement School, a residential school for eighth-grade boys, were divided into three groups. None of these "counselors" had experienced a counselor education program. Beginning with the eleven-week school term, the first experimental group, designated the theory methodology group, started a program consisting of selected readings in theory and methods of counseling plus weekly seminars. This program was patterned after traditional approaches to counselor education in which knowledge of counseling theory and techniques is emphasized. The weekly seminar session consisted of didactic reviews of counseling theory, role playing, experiences, observing counseling sessions, and listening to tape recordings of counseling sessions conducted by Rogers, Seeman, Ellis, and other prominent therapists.

During this same period, the second experimental group, designated the personal growth group, experienced a program consisting of the Human Development Institute's Relationship Improvement Program plus weekly T-group sessions. The Relationship Improvement Program consists of a series of ten training sessions, which teach Rogerian principles by a programmed Skinnerian schedule. In these programs, two trainees sit side by side and take turns reading the step-by-step instructions aloud, answering questions, discussing items, or going through other special activities ranging from conversations to role-playing exercises. The general aims of these relationship programs are to (a) deepen one's ability to be more aware of his own feelings and the feelings of others; (b) to enhance one's appreciation of his own feelings and the feelings of others; (c) enhance one's appreciation of his own potential; and (d) develop the ability to apply these new behavior patterns to the real-life situation (Berlin and Wyckoff, 1964). The T Group sessions were designed to implement and enhance these goals within the group. They also provided opportunity for the generalization of what was learned in the training dyads.

The third group of "counselors" received no preparation of any kind during this period. They functioned just as other counselors in staff duties and student contact responsibilities. The only way their weekly work schedules differed from those of other counselors was in the absence of the training activities held during each week.

The effects of the differential procedures were assessed with a battery of three self-report inventories administered in a pre- and post-test arrangement before and after the eleven-week experimental session. The three tests were (a) the Berger Scales of Expressed Acceptance of Self and Others—1952 (Berger, 1952), (b) the Attitude Toward Self Scale (As) and Attitude Toward Others Scale (Ao) of the MMPI (Gibson, Snyder, and Ray, 1960), and (c) the Self-Acceptance and Other-Acceptance Scales, which utilized the statements of the Butler-Haigh Q-sort with a Likert-type scoring procedure (Butler and Haigh, 1954). Counselees seen by the subjects were also pre- and post-tested on measures of intellectual achievement, personal and social adjustment, and self-acceptance.

Results and Discussion

Analyses of variance, covariance, and t tests were used in a statistical analysis of the data. The first hypothesis predicted that the personal growth training procedure would produce greater changes in attitudes toward self in the direction of greater acceptance than would the theory-methodology training procedure and the absence of any training procedure. Data analyses showed no significant differences between pre- and post-test measurements on any of the three instruments for either training group I or group III. Group II, the personal growth group, however, demonstrated increases in self-acceptance on all of the measuring instruments with the increase of one scale (MMPI-As) being significant at the .01 level. Table 4-II the statistical comparisons of the three groups with each other, two at a time, reveal the

TABLE 4–II

SUMMARY OF MEANS, MEAN DIFFERENCES, AND t RATIOS FOR COMPARISON OF MEANS TWO AT A TIME FOLLOWING AN F TEST FOR THE As SCALE (MMPI)

Groups	Means		Differences	D.F.	t Ratio
	Pre-test	*Post-test*			
I	15.86	15.57	−0.29		
II	17.50	18.88	1.38	17	2.96*
II	17.50	18.88	1.38		
III	16.80	16.60	−0.20	17	2.54**
I	15.86	15.57	−0.29		
III	16.80	16.60	−0.20	17	0.135

* Significant beyond the .005 level in predicted direction. One-tailed test.
** Significant beyond the .02 level in predicted direction. One-tailed test.

superiority of group II, the personal growth group, over both groups I and III beyond the .005 level. There was no significant difference between groups I and III.

The second hypothesis predicted that the personal growth training procedure would produce greater changes in attitudes toward others in the direction of greater acceptance than would the theory-methodology training procedure and the absence of any training procedure. Data analyses show no significant differences for groups I or III between pre- and post-test measurements on any of the three instruments. Group II, the personal growth group, however, demonstrated increases in acceptance of others on all of the measuring instruments with the increase on one of the scales (MMPI-Ao) being significant at the .001 level. In Table 4-III the statistical comparisons of the three training groups with each other, two at a time, reveal the superiority of Group II, the personal growth group, over both groups I and III beyond the .005 level. There was once again no significant difference between groups I and III.

The third, fourth, and fifth hypotheses predicted that students counseled by the group II subjects, the personal growth group, would demonstrate greater intellectual achievement, personal and social adjustment, and a greater degree of self-acceptance than those counseled by counselors in the theory-methodology group and the control group. The Stanford Achievement Tests, Lorge-Thorndike Intellingence Tests, and California Test

TABLE 4-III

SUMMARY OF MEANS, MEAN DIFFERENCES, AND *t* RATIOS
FOR COMPARISON OF MEANS TWO AT A TIME FOLLOWING
AN F TEST FOR THE Ao SCALE (MMPI)

Groups	Means		Differences	D.F.	*t* Ratios
	Pre-test	*Post-test*			
I	15.57	15.43	−0.14		
II	14.38	17.25	2.88	17	5.84*
II	14.38	17.25	2.88		
III	15.80	15.40	−0.40	17	5.76*
I	15.57	15.43	−0.14		
III	15.80	15.40	−0.40	17	0.584

* Significant beyond the .005 level in predicted direction.   One-tailed test.

of Personality were used in the evaluation of these hypotheses. Although analyses of covariance on pre- and post-test scores failed to reveal significant differences in counselee intellectual achievement or personal and social adjustment, the counselees counseled by group II counselors showed consistent, albeit nonsignificant increases in self-acceptance greater than those in the other two groups. This should not be surprising in light of the finding by Truax and Carkhuff (1965) that the characteristics of self-acceptance in a counselor would lead to the development of the same characteristics in counselees. The two hypotheses relating to intellectual achievement and general personal and social adjustment in counselees seen by the subjects were not upheld by the data. Counselees seen by the personal growth subjects did show consistently greater acceptance of self that was short of statistical significance. Perhaps it is too much to ask that a group of counselor candidates assimilate a personal growth training procedure and pass the results of that assimilation on to their counselees, all in the relatively short space of eleven weeks. A follow-up study was in this case impossible.

Conclusions and Recommendations

The implications of this study for counselor education procedures and programs are as follows:

1. Evidence is provided that personal growth in terms of self- and other-acceptance will not occur in counselor candidates involved in programs that do not make a direct attempt to bring it about. That is, personal growth in counselor candidates cannot be expected to occur concomitantly as other traditional procedures are carried out. On the personal growth variables measured in this study there was no significant difference between a theory-methodology training procedure and no training at all.

2. Evidence is provided that a direct attempt to establish a preparation procedure designed to bring about personal growth in defined directions can be successful. This is not to say that the particular procedure used in this study is the only way, or is even the best way to bring about this change, but the evidence is here that it is one way.

3. Evidence is provided, although in this case it is tenuous, that an increase in the self- and other-acceptance of the counselors experiencing a personal growth preparation procedure tends to be followed by one in the counselees seen by them. Further research investigating this relationship is recommended.

4. The As and Ao scales of the MMPI appear to be uniquely sensitive to attitude changes in counselor candidates on the variables of self- and other-acceptance. Of the three instruments used in this study, the MMPI was clearly superior. This finding needs to be investigated further.

5. Finally, it is recognized that although most counselor education programs do not include within their formal requirements direct attempts to implement personal growth, many are making attempts to provide for it by bootlegging such activities as "voluntarily attended" workshops, seminars, and group activities that are therapeutically oriented. If, however, personal growth is desirable for counselor candidates, and research evidence indicates it is; and if direct attempts to bring it about are practical and successful and research evidence suggests they are; then perhaps it is time that formal programs adopt these requirements along with, or even in place of, some of their other requirements.

References

Berger, E. M.: The relation between expressed acceptance of self and expressed acceptance of others. *Journal of Abnormal and Social Psychology,* 47:778-82, 1952.

Berlin, J. I., and Wyckoff, L. B.: *Human Relations Training Through Dyadic Programmed Instruction.* Paper presented at the American Personnel and Guidance Association Convention, San Francisco, March, 1964.

Butler, J. M., and Haigh, G. V.: Changes in the relation between self-concepts and ideal concepts consequent upon client-centered counseling. In Rogers, C. R., and Dymond, Rosalind F. (Eds.): *Psychotherapy and Personality Change.* Chicago, University of Chicago Press, 1954.

Fiedler, F. E.: A comparison of therapeutic relationships in psychoanalytic nondirective, and Adlerian therapy. *Journal of Consulting Psychology,* 14:436-45, 1950 (a).

Fiedler, F. E.: The concept of an ideal therapeutic relationship. *Journal of Consulting Psychology,* 14:239-45, 1950 (b).

Gibson, R. L., Snyder, W. U., and Ray, W. S.: A factor analysis of measures of change following client-centered therapy. In Dahlstrom, W. G., and Welch, G. S. (Eds.): *An MMPI Handbook: A Guide to Use in Clinical Practice and Research.* Minnesota, University of Minnesota Press, 1960.

Rogers, C. R.: The necessary and sufficient conditions of therapeutic personality change. *Journal of Consulting Psychology, 21*:95-103, 1957.

Truax, C. B.: Effective ingredients in psychotherapy: an approach to unraveling the patient-therapist interaction. *Journal of Counseling Psychology, 10*:256-63, 1963.

Truax, C. B., and Carkhuff, R. R.: Client and therapist transparency in the psychotherapeutic encounter. *Journal of Counseling Psychology, 12*:3-9, 1965.

Truax, C. B., Carkhuff, R. R., and Douds, J.: Toward an integration of the didactic and experiential approaches to training in counseling and psychotherapy. *Journal of Counseling Psychology, 2*:240-47, 1964.

THE OFF-CAMPUS PRACTICUM*

James C. Hansen and Gilbert D. Moore

The importance of supervised counseling practice is seldom questioned. It has rapidly become accepted as an integral part of counselor education. Development of counseling practice has precipitated concomitant interest in the supervision of facilities for such practice. These new developments have resulted in some extremely imaginative and effective on-campus counseling laboratories. However, less attention has been paid to the most effective use of off-campus facilities. Likewise, most of the literature about supervision of counseling has ignored the task of supervising off-campus work.

Recently, there have been a few statements suggesting a wider perspective regarding practicum and supervision. Roeber (1962) has stated that a counseling practicum may be located in elementary or secondary schools and that part-time or on-the-job supervisors may be school counselors as a part of a training staff. McCully (1964) suggested that a teamwork approach could be developed by seeking participation of well-qualified school counselors in counselor education, particularly in connection with supervised practicum.

This paper suggests that an off-campus practicum program

* Reprinted from *Counselor Education and Supervision,* 6:32-39, 1966, with permission of the American Personnel and Guidance Association and the authors.

can be extremely fruitful if viewed in the perspective of the following three topics: potentialities in an off-campus practicum, a broader conceptualization of supervision, and differential roles for supervisors.

Potentialities in the Off-Campus Practicum

While trying to establish practicum practices, it was natural to use a laboratory situation which a counselor educator could supervise more directly. An on-campus facility has obvious advantages of proximity, control of counselee and observation possibilities, and ease of obtaining research data. There is no need to debate advantages. The following discussion is not designed to place one method against the other but only to suggest that a practicum experience need not be limited to one kind of environment. It is further suggested that for potential school counselors a school can provide a ready-made and available laboratory. As a laboratory, the school provides the following unique opportunities:

1. An off-campus practicum provides the beginning counselor with first-hand exposure to the work environment. True, many counselor candidates have had or are having teaching experience, but this does not necessarily mean an understanding of the counselor's work environment. Working in the counselor's office provides an overview of the school program not available in the classroom or on the college campus. There is excellent opportunity to view counseling behavior in relationship to other counselor behaviors. Most school counselors engage in a variety of activities other than counseling. The beginning counselor can observe the variety of skills and interpersonal relationships involved in the counselor's job. Importance of some of these other tasks need not be minimized but neither do they need to be called counseling.

2. In a good off-campus placement, the counselor candidate is exposed to a wide variety of counseling cases. The pool of counselees is far wider than that available on campus. However, care is taken to insure that the beginning counselor has an opportunity to see many counselees and is not asked to see just one

type of child or handle one kind of problem. When counseling a student in a school, the counselor in preparation has access to many forms of data. He has not only the usual standardized instruments but opportunity for direct observation as well as discussion with others who work with the counselee.

3. There is an excellent opportunity for the counselor candidate to see the relationship of theory and practice in wider perspective. He discovers that school children present a variety of problems ranging from simple choice conflict to severe anxiety. He is able to see that a child who needs information or a chance to discuss questions about several occupations need not necessarily react the same way to a particular theoretical approach as a child who has a fairly serious choice conflict. A student really has a chance to see the degree to which he is able to integrate counseling theory in a number of different situations.

4. The counselor in preparation can profit from more than one kind of supervisory relationship. A university supervisor has traditionally, and rightly so, concentrated on the specific counseling relationship in which the counselor candidate is engaged. He also is concerned with his own supervisory relationship with the candidate. With an off-campus practicum, all traditional relationships are retained, but there is added supervision which helps the beginning counselor on the job. The school counselor is able to help the counselor candidate understand how his work fits into the scheme of the school. He helps the candidate understand potential and real conflict between theory and practice.

When considering an off-campus practicum, it is obvious that supervision is a more complex phenomenon. Therefore, it is necessary to view supervision in a broader context.

A Broader Conceptualization of Supervision

Prevalent views about supervision are not consistent in their orientation. From their research, Walz and Roeber (1962) conclude that supervisors of high school counselors operate in a teacher-student relationship not unlike that found in a classroom. Supervision is largely an intellectual process involving directing, correcting, and informing. Arbuckle (1958), however, states that a supervisor should probably be more of a counselor with his student than a teacher. The student must go through actual experiences, and he must have someone who helps him understand what is happening. Arbuckle believes that only a small part of the education of counselors should be concerned with content; the major part should be concerned with process. Contrary to both of these approaches, Patterson (1964) believes supervision is neither teaching nor counseling, but falls in between. It is a learning situation in which the beginning counselor may be given specific information, but generally it is more concerned with the kind of self-learning that occurs in counseling.

Although the above views are diverse, they focus on the one-to-one relationship between the counselor candidate and supervisor. Moreover, the focus is on the role of the supervisor. Such a focus is understandable if major attention is given to on-campus counseling experiences. It is suggested, however, that such a focus provides a very limited concept of supervision.

Perhaps it is time to view responsibilities of supervision in a wider context, such as the supervisor's responsibilities to the institution in which he works and to society at large, as well as to counselor candidate and the counselee. In short, there are a variety of functional relationships involved in supervision. This view is thoroughly explored by Ekstein and Wallerstein (1958) in relation to teaching psychotherapy.

The following diagram shows different functional relationships involved in the off-campus practicum. The following paragraphs discuss more explicitly these relationships and responsibilities.

Figure 4.1. CC=Counselor Candidate; C=Counselee; US=University Supervisor; SC=School Counselor.

Responsibilities and Relationships to the Counselee. The traditional concern of counselor for counselee is not lost in this diagram. The counselor candidate is the one to carry basic responsibilty and relationship with the counselee. He has direct responsibilty for helping the counselee through the knowledge, understanding, and skill he possesses.

The school counselor has a direct responsibility to the counselee by virtue of the position he holds in the institution. Although he is willing to have the student counselor establish a counseling relationship with one of his counselees, he is not able to abrogate his institutional responsibility to the counselee. The community and institution expect the school counselor to bear ultimate responsibility involving work of a counselor in preparation. The school counselor also shares an ongoing relationship with the counselee. He continues to work with him after the student counselor has departed. At times, he may even assume or reassume a direct counseling relationship with him.

The university supervisor has a more remote responsibility for the counselee, but it is none the less important. The off-campus practicum continues only if counselor candidates perform in a satisfactory manner in schools. A university supervisor recognizes that exposing counselees to student counselors puts him in a position of responsibility for counselees' welfare. It is seldom, if ever, that he is directly involved in counseling the counselee.

Responsibilities and Relationships to the Counselor Candidate. The primary line of responsibility to the candidate is that of the university supervisor. He accepts the basic role of educating and helping the student counselor. It is in the supervisory relationship that the goals, purposes, skills, and understandings of the counselor candidate are brought into focus. A university supervisor transcends the formal teacher-student relationship and works with the candidate as a unique individual. In the process of supervision, acceptance, empathy, and congruence are as important as in the counseling process.

The school counselor has a secondary but direct responsibility and relationship to the student counselor. The school counselor has responsibility for providing experiences for a candidate that meet objectives of a practicum. He also has responsibility of being a model for the counselor candidate, illustrating the role of the school counselor. The school counselor's relationship to the candidate is one of colleague as well as supervisor. Hopefully, the school counselor's relationship with the candidate is empathic, warm, and helpful. It is also a relationship which facilitates the student counselor's performance of tasks and encourages exploration and questioning about tasks. It is not, however, focused on counseling per se and seldom, if ever, involves the same intensity as that of the university supervisor.

Responsibility and Relationship Between Supervisors. Although the university supervisor holds a higher staff-line position than the school counselor, a colleague relationship exists. A relationship is based on mutual respect and understanding of tasks and problems involved. There is a responsibility to jointly work out objectives of the program as well as activities which meet these objectives. The school counselor then has the responsibility to carry these out in a school, and the university supervisor adds support and assistance when needed.

Although not directly shown in the diagram, responsibilities to the institutions involved are a part of this relationship. The university supervisor's primary responsibility is to the university, to meet standards and expectations of the graduate program in which he is involved. Consequently, the university supervisor does not become so identified with the school portion of the practicum that he neglects his prime commitment to the university. Necessity for application of theory does not in any way relieve the university supervisor from responsibility for developing and interpreting theory. He continues to give primary allegiance to the basic orientation of the university, the creation, extension, and dissemination of knowledge.

In addition, he has responsibility to use only cooperating schools and school counselors that can provide the quality of experiences demanded in a practicum situation. After all, the quality of a guidance program and a school counselor are of paramount importance in an off-campus practicum. He also has a responsibility to a school, e.g. placing counselor candidates who can function effectively in the guidance program, both with students and other staff members. He likewise provides leadership and direction.

The school counselor's primary responsibility is to his school. He insures that services provided by the student counselor are not a liability to the guidance program of students. If a school counselor agrees to work with a counselor candidate, he has a responsibility to the university to give that candidate the best possible educational experience.

The above discussion of concepts reveals a need to clearly understand and appreciate specific functions of each person, particularly the two types of supervisors. Attention is now turned to specific behaviors of supervisors necessary for successful implementation of responsibilities and relationships.

Roles and Functions of Supervisors

The diagram suggests a number of different functions and activities for supervisors, including administration, teaching, evaluation, and coordination.

Administration. The primary administrative function of a university supervisor is organizing and overseeing the overall practicum program. One of the first steps is selecting local schools in which to place counselor candidates. He evaluates the nature and adequacy of counseling facilities, the interest and ability of the school counselor, and obtains the consent and cooperation of the school administrator. He also arranges for constant and meaningful dialogue between the school counselor and the university supervisor relating to the purpose of the practicum. The school counselor needs to be kept informed about the nature and scope of experiences which are desired for a candidate.

The school counselor arranges and coordinates school experiences suggested for a counselor candidate. He expands these experiences whenever possible. His primary responsibility is limited to one or more candidates in his school.

Typically, he sees that the candidate has adequate orientation to the school environment. Such orientation includes not only guidance and counseling facilities but the total physical environment of the school. In addition, some orientation to the school as a social institution in the community is provided. Later, the school counselor arranges experiences which lead the candidate to become a functioning member of the school staff.

Teaching and Supervising. The university supervisor conducts individual conferences with each counselor candidate and provides a small-group seminar. In his primary teaching role, he provides the theoretical understanding of the counseling process. Although candidates may have had a course in counseling theory, he continues to teach theory as necessary for understanding various counselees. He helps student counselors integrate knowledge from other didactic courses, such as testing and vocational development theory. As the counselor candidate brings questions and confusions to the university supervisor, they can discuss the theoretical nature and solution of the problem. The university supervisor helps the candidate put his problem into a theoretical framework from which a solution can follow. The school counselor aids the candidate in carrying out a solution on the job— examining the actual problem on the job.

The school counselor's teaching role is concerned with showing the counselor candidate the practical application of theory. The candidate's theory may be sound but not internalized or applicable. Because the school counselor's job involves more than counseling, he teaches how to operate in other aspects of the total guidance program and assists the candidate in developing skill based upon his knowledge. The candidate then can profit from two teaching situations: the theoretical understanding provided by the university supervisor and the practical application or "how-to-do" approach of the school counselor.

One significant aspect of supervision is that it goes beyond intellectualization. There is a need to include conative as well as cognitive learning. It is a self-learning process. Most educators consider counselor education a growth process which demands growth in self-understanding and self-acceptance—both personally and professionally. An individual conference with a university supervisor provides developmental opportunities for enhancing a counselor candidate's concept of himself. Effectiveness of supervision depends upon the atmosphere in which a supervisor works. It must be remembered that the supervisor is not a therapist for the candidate. However, as Patterson (1964) stated, supervision, while not therapy, is like all good human relationships, therapeutic. Most of this is done by the university supervisor in the supervisory conference; the candidate learns about his values, attitudes, and personality needs, particularly as these affect the counseling relationship.

At times, however, the counselor candidate approaches the school counselor with similar questions and problems. Although the school counselor helps, assistance typically concentrates on cognitive aspects of the candidate's confusion.

Evaluation. Evaluation which develops self-direction is another means of providing meaningful learning. A uniform and rigid form of evaluation is less applicable than a continuous individually determined, developmental process. Thus, the university supervisor and counselor candidate use joint evaluation as a part of the learning process. However, the university supervisor grades the candidate. He has an obligation to both the profession and future clients to evaluate the quality of the candidate's work. The university supervisor evaluates primarily the candidate's counseling skills. He depends upon the school counselor's comments for evaluating his conduct in other aspects of the guidance function. The school counselor has more opportunity to evaluate the candidate "operationally" than has a university supervisor. He sees a candidate from all dimensions and gives conference time to helping him see his strengths, limitations, growth, and potential.

Coordination. It is obvious from looking at preceding roles and functions of two supervisors that coordination between the two is necessary. In order that administrative detail runs smoothly, the university supervisor checks frequently with the school counselor. Each supervisor knows what the other is doing and what is occurring in the other setting. Teaching of theory and practice in two different settings demands that two supervisors plan certain activities and experiences for counselor candidates. Several two- or three-way conferences are held to evaluate candidates' work and various aspects of the program. When a particular candidate is having difficulty, supervisors work together—possibly including the candidate in a three-way conference—to help him through the problem.

Conclusion

The need for well-prepared counselors continues to grow in many more social settings. Counselor educators continually have to explore ways of effectively providing the necessary education.

Great strides have been made in providing important practicum and supervisory experiences. This paper suggests that off-campus practicum experiences have some merits not frequently explored. Development of such programs are not construed as an effort to replace on-campus programs but, rather, to supplement them.

References

Arbuckle, Dugald: Five philosophical issues in counseling. *Journal of Counseling Psychology,* 5:211-16, 1958.

Benson, Loren: Reaction—practicum and internship. In *Counselor Education—A Progress Report on Standards.* Washington. D.C., American Personnel and Guidance Association, 1962, pp. 31-34.

Ekstein, Rudolf, and Wallerstein, Robert: *The Teaching and Learning of Psychotherapy.* New York, Basic Books, 1958.

McCully, C. Harold: Making a troika work. *Counselor Education and Supervision,* 3:191-201, 1964.

Patterson, C. H.: Supervising students in the counseling practicum. *Journal of Counseling Psychology,* 11:47-53, 1964.

Roeber, Edward: Position paper—practicum and internship. In *Counselor Education—A Progress Report on Standards.* Washington, D.C., American Personnel and Guidance Association, 1962, pp. 24-31.

Walz, G., and Roeber, E.: Supervisors' reactions to a counseling interview. *Counselor Education and Supervision,* 2:2-7, 1962.

GAMES PEOPLE PLAY IN SUPERVISION*

ALFRED KADUSHIN

Gamesmanship has had a checkered career. Respectfully fathered by an eminent mathematician, Van Neumann, in his book *The Theory of Games and Economic Behavior* (1944), it became "The Art of Winning Games Without Actually Cheating" as detailed by Potter in *Theory and Practice of Gamesmanship* (1948). It was partly rescued recently for the behavioral sciences by the psychoanalyst Eric Berne in *Games People Play* (1964).

Berne defines a game as "an ongoing series of complementary ulterior transactions—superficially plausible, but with a concealed motivation" (p. 84). It is a scheme, or artfulness, utilized in the pursuit of some objective or purpose. A ploy is a segment of a game.

---

* Reprinted from *Social Work,* 13:23-32, 1968, with permission of the National Association of Social Workers and the author.

The purpose of engaging in the game, of using the maneuvers, snares, gimmicks, and ploys that are, in essence, the art of gamesmanship, lies in the payoff. One party to the game chooses a strategy to maximize his payoff and minimize his penalties. He wants to win rather than to lose, and he wants to win as much as he can at the lowest cost.

Games people play in supervision are concerned with the kinds of recurrent interactional incidents between supervisor and supervisee that have a payoff for one of the parties in the transaction. While both supervisor and supervisee may initiate a game, for the purposes of simplicity it may be desirable to discuss in greater detail games initiated by supervisees. This may also be the better part of valor.

Why Games Are Played

To understand why the supervisee should be interested in initiating a game, it is necessary to understand the possible losses that might be anticipated by him in the supervisory relationship. One needs to know what the supervisee is defending himself against and the losses he might incur if he eschewed gamesmanship or lost the game.

The supervisory situation generates a number of different kinds of anxieties for the supervisee. It is a situation in which he is asked to undergo some sort of change. Unlike the usual educational situation that is concerned with helping the student critically examine and hence possibly change his ideas, social work supervision is often directed toward a change in behavior and, perhaps, personality. Change creates anxiety. It requires giving up the familiar for the unfamiliar; it requires a period of discomfort during which one is uneasy about continuing to use old patterns of behavior but does not, as yet, feel fully comfortable with new behaviors.

The threat of change is greater for the adult student because it requires dissolution of patterns of thinking and believing to which he has become habituated. It also requires an act of disloyalty to previous identification models. The ideas and behavior that might need changing represent, in a measure, the introjection of previously encountered significant others—parents, teachers, highly valued peers—and giving them up implies some rejection of these people in the acceptance of other models. The act of infidelity creates anxiety.

The supervisory tutorial is a threat to the student's independence and autonomy. Learning requires some frank admission of dependence on the teacher; readiness to learn involves giving up some measure of autonomy in accepting direction from others, in submitting to the authority of the supervisor-teacher.

The supervisee also faces a threat to his sense of adequacy. The situation demands an admission of ignorance, however limited, in some areas. And in sharing one's ignorance one exposes one's vulnerability. One risks the possibility of criticism, of shame, and perhaps of rejection because of one's admitted inadequacy. In addition, the supervisee faces the hazard of not being adequate to the requirements of the learning situation. His performance may fall short of the supervisor's expectations, intensifying a sense of inadequacy and incurring the possibility of supervisory disapproval.

Since the parameters of the supervisory relationship are often ambiguous, there is a threat that devolves not only from the sensed inadequacies of one's work, but also from the perceived or suspected inadequacies of self. This threat is exaggerated in the social work supervisory relationship because so much of self is invested in and reflected by one's work and because of the tendency to attribute to the supervisor a diagnostic omniscience suggesting that he perceives all and knows all.

The supervisor-supervisee relationship is evocative of the parent-child relationship and as such may tend to reactivate some anxiety associated with this earlier relationship. The supervisor is in a position of authority and the supervisee is, in some measure, dependent on him. If the supervisor is a potential parent surrogate, fellow supervisees are potential siblings competing for the affectional responses of the parent. The situation is therefore one that threatens the reactivation not only of residual difficulties in the parent-child relationship but also in the sibling-sibling relationship.

The supervisor has the responsibility of evaluating the work of the supervisee and as such, controls access to important rewards and penalties. School grades, salary increases, and promotional possibilities are real and significant prizes dependent on a favorable evaluation. Unlike previously encountered evaluative situations, for instance working toward a grade in a course, this is a situation in which it is impossible to hide in a group. There is direct and sharply focused confrontation with the work done by the supervisee.

These threats, anxieties, and penalites are the losses that might be incurred in entering into the supervisory relationship. A desire to keep losses to a minimum and maximize the rewards that might derive from the encounter explains why the supervisee should want to play games in supervision, why he should feel a need to control the situation to his advantage.

Supervisees have over a period of time developed some well-established, identifiable games. An attempt will be made to group these games in terms of similar tactics. It might be important to note that not all supervisees play games and not all of the behavior supervisees engage in is indicative of an effort to play games. However, the best supervisee plays games some of the time; the poorest supervisee does not play games all of the time. What the author is trying to do is to identify a limited, albeit important, sector of supervisee behavior.

Manipulating Demand Levels

One series of games is designed to manipulate the level of demands made on the supervisee. One such game might be titled "Two Against the Agency" or "Seducing for Subversion." The game is generally played by intelligent, intuitively gifted supervisees who are impatient with routine agency procedures. Forms, reports, punctuality, and recording excite their contempt. The more sophisticated supervisee, in playing the game, introduces it by suggesting the conflict between the bureaucratic and professional orientation to the work of the agency. The bureaucratic orientation is one that is centered on what is needed to insure efficient operation of the agency; the professional orientation is focused on meeting the needs of the client. The supervisee points out that meeting client need is more important, that time spent in recording, filling out forms, and writing reports tends to rob time from direct work with the client, and further that it does not make any difference when he comes to work or goes home as long as no client suffers as a consequence. Would it not therefore be possible to permit him, a highly intuitive and gifted worker, to schedule and allocate his time to maximum client advantage and should not the supervisor, then, be less concerned about the necessity of his filling out forms, doing recording, completing reports, and so on?

For the student and recent graduate supervisee oriented toward the mortality of the hippie movement (and many students, especially in social work, are responsive to hippie ideology, often without being explicitly aware of this), professional autonomy is consonant with the idea of self-expression—"doing your thing." Bureaucratic controls, demands, and expectations are regarded as violations of genuine self-expression and are resented as such.

It takes two to play games. The supervisor is induced to play (a) because he identifies with the student's concern for meeting client needs, (b) because he himself has frequently resented bureaucratic demands and so is, initially, sympathetic to the supervisee's complaints, and (c) because he is hesitant to assert his authority in demanding firmly that these requirements be met. If the supervisor elects to play the game, he has enlisted in an alliance with the supervisee to subvert agency administrative procedures.

Another game designed to control and mitigate the level of demands made on the supervisee might be called "Be Nice to Me Because I am Nice to You." The principal ploy is seduction by flattery. The supervisee is full of praise: "You're the best supervisor I ever had." "You're so perceptive that after I've talked to you I almost know what the client will say next," "You're so consistently helpful," "I look forward in the future to being as good a social worker as you are," and so on. It is a game of emotional blackmail in which, having been paid in this kind of coin, the supervisor finds himself incapable of firmly holding the worker to legitimate demands.

The supervisor finds it difficult to resist engaging in the game because it is gratifying to be regarded as an omniscient source of wisdom; there is satisfaction in being perceived as helpful and in being selected as a pattern for identification and emulation. An invitation to play a game that tends to enhance a positive self-concept and feed one's narcissistic needs is likely to be accepted.

In general, the supervisor is vulnerable to an invitation to play this game. The supervisor needs the supervisee as much as the supervisee needs the supervisor. One of the principal sources of gratification for a worker is contact with the client. The supervisor is denied this source of gratification, at least directly. For the supervisor the principal source of gratification is helping the supervisee to grow and change. But this means that he has to look to the supervisee to validate his effectiveness. Objective criteria of such effectiveness are, at best, obscure and equivocal. However, to have the supervisee say explicitly, openly, and directly: "I have learned a lot from you," "You have been helpful," "I am a better worker because of you," is the kind of reassurance needed and often subtly solicited by the supervisor. The perceptive supervisee understands and exploits the supervisor's needs in initiating this game.

Redefining the Relationship

A second series of games is also designed to mitigate the level of demands made on the supervisee, but here the game depends on redefining the supervisory relationship. As Goffman (1959) points out, games permit one to control the conduct of others by influencing the definition of the situation. These games depend on ambiguity of the definition of the supervisory relationship. It is open to a variety of interpretations and resembles, in some crucial respects, analogous relationships.

Thus, one kind of redefinition suggests a shift from the relationship of supervisor-supervisee as teacher-learner in an administrative hierarchy to supervisor-supervisee as worker-client in the context of therapy. The game might be called "Protect the Sick and the Infirm" or "Treat Me, Don't Beat Me." The supervisee would rather expose himself than his work. And so he asks the supervisor for help in solving his personal problems. The sophisticated player relates these problems to his difficulties on the job. Nevertheless, he seeks to engage the supervisor actively in a concern with his problems. If the translation to worker-client is made, the nature of demands shifts as well. The kinds of demands one can legitimately impose on a client are clearly less onerous than the level of expectations imposed on a worker. And the supervisee has achieved a payoff in a softening of demands.

The supervisor is induced to play (a) because the game appeals to the social worker in him (since he was a social worker before he became a supervisor and is still interested in helping those who have personal problems), (b) because it appeals to the voyeur in him (many supervisors are fascinated by the opportunity to share in the intimate life of others), (c) because it is flattering to be selected as a therapist, and (d) because the supervisor is not clearly certain as to whether such a redefinition of the situation is not permissible. All the discussions about the equivocal boundaries between supervision and therapy feed into this uncertainty.

Another game of redefinition might be called "Evaluation Is Not for Friends." Here the supervisory relationship is redefined as a social relationship. The supervisee makes an effort to take coffee breaks with the supervisor, invite him to lunch, walk to and from the bus or the parking lot with him, and discuss some common interests during conferences. The social component tends to vitiate the professional component in the relationship. It requires increased determination and resolution on the part of any supervisor to hold the "friend" to the required level of performance.

Another and more contemporary redefinition is less obvious than either of the two kinds just discussed, which have been standard for a long time now. This is the game of "Maximum Feasible Participation." It involves a shift in roles from supervisor-supervisee to peer-peer. The supervisee suggests that the relationship will be most effective if it is established on the basis of democratic participation. Since he knows best what he needs and wants to learn, he should be granted equal responsibility for determining the agenda of conferences. So far so good. The game is a difficult one to play because in the hands of a determined supervisee, joint control of agenda can easily become supervisee control with consequent mitigation of expectations. The supervisor finds himself in a predicament in trying to decline the game.

For one, there is an element of validity in the claim that people learn best in a context that encourages democratic participation in the learning situation. Second, the current trend in working with the social agency client encourages maximum feasible participation with presently undefined limits. To decline the game is to suggest that one is old-fashioned, undemocratic, and against the rights of those on lower levels in the administrative hierarchy —not an enviable picture to project of oneself. The supervisor is forced to play but needs to be constantly alert in order to maintain some semblance of administrative authority and prevent all the shots being called by the supervisee-peer.

Reducing Power Disparity

A third series of games is designed to reduce anxiety by reducing the power disparity between supervisor and worker. One source of the supervisor's power is, of course, the consequence of his position in the administrative hierarchy vis-à-vis the supervisee. Another source of power, however, lies in his expertise, greater knowledge, and superior skill. It is the second source of power disparity that is vulnerable to this series of games. If the supervisee can establish the fact that the supervisor is not so smart after all, some of the power differential is mitigated and with it some need to feel anxious.

One such game, frequently played, might be called "If You Knew Dostoyevsky Like I Know Dostoyevsky." During the course of a conference the supervisee makes a casual allusion to the fact that the client's behavior reminds him of that of Raskolnikov in *Crime and Punishment*, which is, after all, somewhat different in etiology from the pathology that plagued Prince Myshkin in *The Idiot*. An effective ploy, used to score additional points, involves addressing the rhetorical question, "You remember, don't you?" to the supervisor. It is equally clear to both the supervisee and the supervisor that the latter does not remember— if, indeed, he ever knew what he cannot remember now. At this point the supervisee proceeds to instruct the supervisor. The roles of teacher-learner are reversed; power disparity and supervisee anxiety are simultanously reduced.

The supervisor acquiesces to the game because refusal requires an open confession of ignorance on his part. The supervisee in playing the game well cooperates in a conspiracy with the supervisor not to expose his ignorance openly. The discussion proceeds under the protection of the mutually accepted fiction that *both* know what they are talking about.

The content for the essential gambit in this game changes with each generation of supervisees. The author's impression is that currently the allusion is likely to be the work of the conditioning therapists—Eysenck, Wolpe, and Lazarus—rather than to literary figures. The effect on the supervisor, however, is the same: a feeling of depression and general malaise at having been found ignorant when his position requires that he know more than the supervisee. And it has the same payoff in reducing supervisee anxiety.

Another kind of game in this same genre exploits situational advantages to reduce power disparity and permit the supervisee the feeling that he, rather than the supervisor, is in control. This game is "So What Do You Know About It?" The supervisee with a long record of experience in public welfare makes reference to "those of us on the front lines who have struggled with the multiproblem client," exciting humility in the supervisor who has to try hard to remember when he last saw a live client. A married supervisee with children will allude to her marital experience and what it "really is like to be a mother" in discussing family therapy with an unmarried female supervisor. The older supervisee will talk about "life" from the vantage point of incipient senility to the supervisor fresh out of graduate school. The younger supervisee will hint at his greater understanding of the adolescent client since he has, after all, smoked some pot and has seriously considered LSD. The supervisor trying to tune in finds his older psyche is not with it. The supervisor younger than the older supervisee, older than the younger supervisee—never having raised a child or met a payroll—finds himself being instructed by those he is charged with instructing: roles are reversed and the payoff lies in the fact that the supervisor is a less threatening figure to the supervisee.

Another, more recently developed, procedure for "putting the supervisor down" is through the judicious use in the conference of strong four-letter words. This is "telling it like it is" and the supervisor who responds with discomfort and loss of composure has forfeited some amount of control to the supervisee who has exposed some measure of his bourgeois character and residual Puritanism.

Putting the supervisor down may revolve around a question of social work goals rather than content. The social action-oriented supervisee is concerned with fundamental changes in social relationships. He knows that obtaining a slight increase in the budget for his client, finding a job for a client, or helping a neglected mother relate more positively to her child are not of much use since they leave the basic pathology of society undisturbed and unchanged. He is impatient with the case-oriented supervisor who is interested in helping a specific family live a little less troubled, a little less unhappily, in a fundamentally disordered society. The game is "All or Nothing at All." It is designed to make the supervisor feel he has sold out, been co-opted by the Establishment, lost or abandoned his broader vision of the "good" society, becomes endlessly concerned with symptoms rather than with causes. It is effective because the supervisor recognizes that there is some element of truth in the accusation, since this is true for all who occupy positions of responsibility in the Establishment.

Controlling the Situation

All the games mentioned have, as part of their effect, a shift of control of the situation from supervisor to supervisee. Another series of games is designed to place control of the supervisory situation more explicitly and directly in the hands of the supervisee. Control of the situation by the supervisor is potentially threatening since he can then take the initiative of introducing for discussion those weaknesses and inadequacies in the supervisee's work that need fullest review. If the supervisee can control the conference, much that is unflattering to discuss may be adroitly avoided.

One game designed to control the discussion's content is called "I Have a Little List." The supervisee comes in with a series of questions about his work that he would very much like to discuss. The better player formulates the questions so that they have relevance to those problems in which the supervisor has greatest professional interest and about which he has done considerable reading. The supervisee is under no obligation to listen to the answer to his question. Question 1 having been asked, the supervisor is off on a short lecture during which time the supervisee is free to plan mentally the next weekend or review the last weekend, taking care merely to listen for signs that the supervisor is running down. When this happens, the supervisee introduces Question 2 with an appropriate transitional comment and the game is repeated. As the supervisee increases the supervisor's level of participation he is, by the same token, decreasing his own level of participation since only one person can be talking at once. Thus the supervisee controls both content and direction of conference interaction.

The supervisor is induced to play this game because there is narcissistic gratification in displaying one's knowledge and in meeting the dependency needs of those who appeal to one for answers to their questions, and because the supervisee's questions should be accepted, respected, and, if possible, answered.

Control of the initiative is also seized by the supervisee in the game of "Heading Them Off at the Pass." Here the supervisee knows that his poor work is likely to be analyzed critically. He therefore opens the conference by freely admitting his mistakes—he knows it was an inadequate interview, he knows that he should have, by now, learned to do better. There is no failing on the supervisor's agenda for discussion with him to which he does not freely confess in advance, flagellating himself to excess. The supervisor, faced with overwhelming self-derogation, has little option but to reassure the supervisee sympathetically. The tactic not only makes difficult an extended discussion of mistakes in the work at the supervisor's initiative, it elicits praise by the supervisor for whatever strengths the supervisee has manifested, however limited. The supervisor, once again, acts out of concern with the troubled, out of his predisposition to comfort the discomforted, out of pleasure in acting the good, forgiving parent.

There is also the game of control through fluttering dependency, of strength through weakness. It is the game of "Little

Old Me" or "Casework à Trois." The supervisee, in his ignorance and incompetence, looks to the knowledgeable competent supervisor for a detailed prescription of how to proceed: "What would you do next?" "Then what would you say?" The supervisee unloads responsibiltiy for the case onto the supervisor and the supervisor shares the caseload with the worker. The supervisor plays the game because, in reality, he does share responsibility for case management with the supervisee and has responsibility for seeing that the client is not harmed. Further, the supervisor often is interested in the gratification of carrying a caseload, however, vicariously, so that he is somewhat predisposed to take the case out of the hands of the supervisee. There are, further, the pleasures derived from acting the capable parent to the dependent child, and from the domination of others.

A variant of the game in the hands of a more hostile supervisee is "I Did Like You Told Me." Here the supervisee maneuvers the supervisor into offering specific prescriptions on case management and then applies the prescriptions in specific obedience and undisputed mimicry. The supervisee acts as though the supervisor were responsible for the case, he himself merely being the executor of supervisory directives. Invariably and inevitably, whatever has been suggested by the supervisor fails to accomplish what it was supposed to accomplish. "I Did Like You Told Me" is designed to make even a strong supervisor defensive.

"It's All So Confusing" attempts to reduce the authority of the supervisor by appeals to other authorities—a former supervisor, another supervisor in the same agency, or a faculty member at a local school of social work with whom the supervisee just happened to discuss the case. The supervisee casually indicates that in similar situations his former supervisor tended to take such and such an approach, one that is at variance with the approach the current supervisor regards as desirable. And "It's All So Confusing" when different "authorities" suggest such different approaches to the same situation. The supervisor is faced with "defending" his approach against some unnamed, unknown competitor. This is difficult, especially when few situations in social work permit an unequivocal answer in which the supervisor can have categorical confidence. Since the supervisor was somewhat shaky in his approach in the first place, he feels vulnerable against alternative suggestions from other "authorities" and his sense of authority vis-à-vis the supervisee is eroded.

A supervisee can control the degree of threat in the supervisory situation by distancing techniques. The game is "What You Don't Know Won't Hurt Me." The supervisor knows the work of the supervisee only indirectly, through what is shared in the recording and verbally in the conference. The supervisee can elect to share in a manner that is thin, inconsequential, without depth of affect. He can share selectively and can distort, consciously or unconsciously, in order to present a more favorable picture of his work. The supervisee can be passive and reticent or overwhelm the supervisor with endless trivia.

In whatever manner it is done, the supervisee increases distance between the work he actually does and the supervisor who is responsible for critically analyzing with him the work done. This not only reduces the threat to him of possible criticism of his work but also, as Fleming (1966) points out, prevents the supervisor from intruding into the privacy of the relationship between the worker and the client.*

Supervisors' Games

It would be doing both supervisor and supervisee an injustice to omit any reference to games initiated by supervisors—unjust to the supervisees in that such omission would imply that they alone play games in supervision and unjust to the supervisors in suggesting that they lack the imagination and capacity to devise their own counter-games. Supervisors play games out of felt threats to their position in the hierarchy, uncertainty about their authority, reluctance to use their authority, a desire to be liked, a need for the supervisees' approbation—and out of some hostility to supervisees that is inevitable in such a complex, intimate relationship.

One of the classic supervisory games is called "I Wonder Why You Really Said That?" This is the game of redefining honest

---

* *See* Norman Polansky, "On Duplicity in the Interview," *American Journal of Orthopsychiatry,* 37:568-579, 1967, for a review of similar kinds of games played by the client.

disagreement so that it appears to be psychological resistance. Honest disagreement requires that the supervisor defend his point of view, present the research evidence in support of his contention, be sufficiently acquainted with the literature so he can cite the knowledge that argues for the correctness of what he is saying. If honest disagreement is redefined as resistance, the burden is shifted to the supervisee. He has to examine his needs and motives that prompt him to question what the supervisor has said. The supervisor is thus relieved of the burden of validating what he has said and the onus for defense now rests with the supervisee.

Another classic supervisory game is "One Good Question Deserves Another." It was explicated some years ago by a new supervisor writing of her experience in an article called "Through Supervision with Gun and Camera":

> I learned that another part of a supervisor's skills, as far as the workers are concerned, is to know all the answers. I was able to get out of this very easily. I discovered that when a worker asks a question, the best thing to do is to immediately ask for what she thinks. While the worker is figuring out the answer to her own question (this is known as growth and development), the supervisor quickly tries to figure it out also. She may arrive at the answer the same time as the worker, but the worker somehow assumes that she knew it all along. This is very comfortable for the supervisor. In the event that neither the worker nor the supervisor succeeds in coming up with a useful thought on the question the worker has raised, the supervisor can look wise and suggest that they think about it and discuss it further next time. This gives the supervisor plenty of time to look up the subject and leaves the worker with the feeling that the supervisor is giving great weight to her question. In the event that the supervisor does not want to go to all the trouble, she can just tell the worker that she does not know the answer (this is known as helping the worker accept the limitations of the supervision) and tell her to look it up herself . . . [H.C.D., 1949].

In Response to Games

Before going on to discuss possible constructive responses to games played in the context of supervision, the author must express some uneasiness about having raised the subject in the first place, a dissatisfaction similar to the distaste felt toward

Berne's *Games People Play*. The book communicates a sense of disrespect for the complexities of life and human behavior. The simplistic game formulas are a cheapening caricature of people's struggle for a modicum of comfort in a difficult world. A perceptive psychiatrist said in a critical and saddening review of the book: "It makes today's bothersome 'problems' easily subject to a few home-spun models—particularly the cynical and concretely aphoristic kind that reduces all human experiences to a series of 'exchanges' involving gain and loss, deceit or betrayal and exposure, camouflage and discovery" (Coles, 1967). There are both a great deal more sensible sincerity and a great deal more devious complexity in multidetermined human interaction than is suggested by *Games People Play*.

However, the very fact that games are a caricature of life justifies discussing them. The caricature selects some aspect of human behavior and, extracting it for explicit examination, exaggerates and distorts its contours so that it is easier to perceive. The caricature thus makes possible increased understanding of the phenomenon—in this case the supervisory interaction. The insult to the phenomenon lies in forgetting that the caricature is just that—a caricature and not a truly accurate representation. A perceptive caricature, such as good satire, falsifies by distorting only elements that are actually present in the interaction in the first place. Supervisory games mirror, then, *some* selective, essentially truthful aspects of the supervisory relationship.

The simplest and most direct way of dealing with the problem of games introduced by the supervisee is to refuse to play. Yet one of the key difficulties in this has been implied by discussion of the gain for the supervisor in going along with the game. The supervisee can only successfully enlist the supervisor in a game if the supervisor wants to play for his own reasons. Collusion is not forced but is freely granted. Refusing to play requires the supervisor to be ready and able to forfeit self-advantages. For instance, in declining to go along with the supervisee's requests that he be permitted to ignore agency administrative requirements in playing "Two Against the Agency," the supervisor has to be comfortable in exercising his administrative authority, willing to risk and deal with supervisee hostility and rejection, willing to accept and handle the accusation that he is bureaucratically, rather than professionally, oriented. In declining other games, the supervisor denies himself the sweet fruits of flattery, the joys of omniscience, the pleasures of acting the therapist, the gratification of being liked. He has to incur the penalties of an open admission of ignorance and uncertainty and the loss of infallibility. Declining to play the games demands a supervisor who is aware of and comfortable in what he is doing and who is accepting of himself in all his "glorious strengths and human weaknesses." The less vulnerable the supervisor, the more impervious he is to gamesmanship—not an easy prescription to fill.

A second response lies in gradual interpretation or open confrontation. Goffman (1967) points out that in the usual social encounter each party accepts the line put out by the other party. There is a process of mutual face-saving in which what is said is accepted at its face value and "each participant is allowed to carry the role he has chosen for himself" unchallenged (p. 11). This is done out of self-protection since in not challenging another one is also insuring that the other will not, in turn, challenge one's own fiction. Confrontation implies a refusal to accept the game being proposed by seeking to expose and make explicit what the supervisee is doing. The supervisory situation, like the therapeutic situation, deliberately and consciously rejects the usual rules of social interaction in attempting to help the supervisee.

Confrontation is, of course, a procedure that needs to be used with some regard for the supervisee's ability to handle the embarrassment, discomfort, and self-threat it involves. It needs to be used with some understanding of the defensive significance of the game to the supervisee. It might be of importance to point out that naming the interactions that have been described as "games" does not imply that they are frivolous and without consequence. Unmasking games risks much that is of serious personal significance for the supervisee. Interpretation and confrontation here, as always, requires some compassionate caution, a sense of timing, and an understanding of dosage.

Perhaps another approach is to share honestly with the supervisee one's awareness of what he is attempting to do but to focus the discussion neither on the dynamics of his behavior nor on one's reaction to it, but on the disadvantages for him in playing games. These games have decided drawbacks for the supervisee in that they deny him the possibility of effectively fulfilling one of the essential, principal purposes of supervision—helping him to grow professionally. The games frustrate the achievement of this outcome. In playing games the supervisee loses by winning.

And if all else fails, supervisees' games may yield to supervisors' counter-games. For instance, "I Have a Little List" may be broken up by "I Wonder Why You Really Asked That?" After all, the supervisor should have more experience at gamesmanship than the supervisee.

References

Berne, Eric: *Games People Play*. New York, Grove Press, 1964.

Coles, Robert: *New York Times*, Book Review Section, October 8, 1967, p. 8.

Fleming, Joan, and Benedek, Therese: *Psychoanalytic Supervision*. New York, Grune and Stratton, 1966, p. 101.

Goffman, Erving: *The Presentation of Self in Everyday Life*. Garden City, N.Y., Doubleday, 1959, pp. 3-4.

Goffman, Erving: *Ritual Interaction*. Garden City, N.Y., Doubleday, 1967.

H.C.D.: Through supervision with gun and camera. *Social Work Journal*, 30:162, 1949.

Potter, Stephen: *Theory and Practice of Gamesmanship*. New York, Henry Holt & Co., 1948.

Von Neumann, John: *Theory of Games and Economic Behavior*. Princeton, N.J., Princeton University Press, 1944.

ALTERNATIVE STRATEGIES IN PSYCHOTHERAPY SUPERVISION *

GERARD V. HAIGH

Some dimensions that characterize the supervisory process are:

1. A shift in student attention from an exclusive concentration upon patient behavior to an inclusion of therapist behavior, too.

---

* Reprinted from *Psychotherapy: Theory, Research, and Practice*, 2:42-43, 1965, with permission of the journal and the author.

2. A shift in student attention from the patient's intra-psychic dynamics to the interaction between the patient and the therapist.

3. A shift from student preoccupation with specific techniques for responding to specific situations toward a widening understanding of the complexity of clinical interaction.

4. A broadening of the range of response alternatives available to the student therapist.

5. Increase in the student's awareness of an ability to use his own internal responses to the patient.

We observe these changes occurring in students during supervision. How can the supervisor contribute to maximize these changes? He may be confronted by a choice of two conflicting strategies, one didactic and the other experiential. Some difficulties of this choice are suggested by the following incident:

The student, "George," came to my office on other business. Having completed it, he told me he had just seen Mrs. R. in a therapy session. I had an intake interview with Mrs. R. a week before. George said that in their first interview yesterday they agreed on once-a-week appointments. But he also told Mrs. R. to drop in any time she felt overwhelmed. He thought she needed support now because she is separating from her husband. She had acted upon his invitation and had dropped in on him during the preceding hour.

Mrs. R. opened the emergency session by informing George that she had just moved out of the house she shared with her husband. George's response to this was, "Fine." He explained that she had to get away from her husband temporarily to re-establish the relationship on a reality basis. He described himself as an alter ego for his patient. The dialogue between us then proceeded somewhat as follows:

Supervisor: Why did you take a stand on whether or not she separates from her husband?

Student: I can't be non-directive and passive. I am interested in her and in her problems. There isn't a single doubt in my mind about what I am doing.

Supervisor: That bothers me. If you are bulling through without raising any questions about your own behavior, then you are closed off from learning, from growing as a therapist.

Student: Wait a minute. What are you telling me to do?

Supervisor: To let yourself be confused.

Student: About what?

Supervisor: Why do you let yourself get involved in the question of whether or not she should leave her husband?

Student: From the point of view of regression in the service of the ego. She needs to get away temporarily from the demand to be a wife and attempt to regroup her inner forces at a regressed level.

Supervisor: I hear you talking about *her* problem but not about *your* problem.

Student: What do you mean?

Supervisor: I'm asking you what are the implications of you taking a stand in regard to one of her reality problems? Is that what you are there for?

Student: What am I there for? I want to be her friend.

Supervisor: Fine. But as her friend and as her therapist your job is not to tell her what to do but to help her understand herself.

The reader may note with some irony the last statement of the supervisor. Here, while he is telling George not to tell the patient what to do, he is simultaneously telling George what to do. What the student may learn from the supervisor didactically (from the supervisor's words) is directly contradictory to what he may learn via identification with the supervisor.

The Strategies

One may define two alternative strategies for supervision as follows:

Strategy A

The supervisor defines for the student what his role should be.

The supervisor makes choices for the student.

This strategy focuses upon outcome in ensuring that the student learns the supervisor's point of view.

Learning occurs via the achievement of verbal consensus between student and supervisor.

Strategy B

The supervisor poses alternatives for the student to examine.

The student makes choices among the alternatives posed.

This strategy focuses upon process in ensuring that the student has experiences in making choices.

Learning may occur via identification as well as via verbal exchange.

In the cited incident there is a vacillation between these strategies. When the supervisor first asked George why he took a stand on the patient's reality problem, it was to focus on that response and then to consider possible alternatives. But the student's complacency defense provoked the supervisor into shifting to Strategy A. The third time he asked the "why" question, it was clearly not an invitation to reflect but rather an implicit injunction to stop taking a stand *re* the patient's non-therapy life. The supervisor then told the student what he *should* be doing.

The lesson the supervisor taught this student could have been taught in a classroom, thus freeing the supervisor from the "necessity" of using Strategy A.

One might relegate Strategy A to the classroom, or use the strategy in the early phases of supervision. This implies that the student therapist has two tasks: learning a theoretical structure and learning how to use his self. The theoretical structure is best learned didactically, via what Hogan has called "tuition." Learning the professional use of self best occurs in a different kind of process.

The central question I would like to raise is whether any therapy training, even theory, is best taught by tuition. Those who use this method are prompted by their responsibility to the student-therapist, the patient, and the institution. These responsibilities may lead the supervisor to insist that the theoretical context of the therapy be one which he finds defensible. In this case, "tuition" is probably the most effective method.

The danger of Strategy A is that it delays the student's discovery of his own authentic self. Consider the anxiety of the beginning therapist and his proclivity toward imitation. If the supervisor cooperates with the student's anxiety-ridden drive to imitate, he may conspire in a premature closure which impedes further growth.

210 *Counselor Education and Supervision*

Supervisors who do not consider their own theoretical orientation a close approximation to absolute truth (*e.g.* Albert Ellis and Carl Rogers) entertain the possibility of some students going beyond them in apprehending the reality of the psychotherapeutic process. Such a sense of tentativeness about our present theorizing might especially lead us to maximize the choice-making behavior of our students to precipitate them into discovering their own interpretations of experience. They may make discoveries that will enrich the whole field.

In summary, I find myself confronted by a dilemma: In response to my concerns for the patient and the institution and in acceding to the student's anxious urge to imitate, I am drawn toward using "tuition." In response to my concern for maximal growth in the student's authenticity and the enriching of the profession, I am drawn toward permitting decision-making by the student even in the elementary phases of training.

COUNSELOR EDUCATION: FACILITATING THE DEVELOPMENT OF A HELPING PERSON*

Donald H. Blocher

The past fifteen years have witnessed the evolution of a series of dramatic changes in the conceptualization of counseling and of psychotherapy. Formerly cherished notions of the counselor as a passive, shadowy acceptor and reflector of feelings and opinions have gradually given way to an image of the counselor as an active and dynamic agent of change in the lives of those with whom he engages in therapeutic encounter.

Concepts of congruence and confrontation, transparency and authenticity have replaced the older images of neutrality and objectivity as the *sine qua non* of helping relationships. Perhaps even that beloved and unfailingly innocuous "uh-huh" is no longer considered the modal response of the well-bred counselor. Instead, counselors have begun to admit and even to prize their abilities to influence values and to change behavior. The twenty-year orgy

* Reprinted from *Counseling Theories and Counselor Education*, Clyde A. Parker (Ed.), Houghton-Mifflin, 1968, 133-144, with permission of the publisher, editor, author, and the University of Minnesota.

of hand-wringing counselors over the presumed ethical dilemmas involved in the "directive" versus "non-directive" pseudo-issue has finally about run to extinction.

The transformation which is the culmination of those changes might well be called the defeminization of counseling. To rebut Farson's old phrase, the counselor is no longer a woman. This change in the Zeitgeist is readily apparent in the recent literature. Stieper and Wiener (1965), for example, talk unflinchingly of the "power factors" in therapy and of creating "bind" situations from which clients are forced to learn new ways of coping with interpersonal situations. Krumboltz, perhaps a bit ostentatiously, terms the impact of behavioral approaches the "Revolution in Counseling." Kell and Mueller (1967) summarize the new order of things when they say that "the process of counseling is a continual testing of the counselor's adequacy" (p. 15). They go on to point out that freedom from ambivalence, insecurity, and guilt about the relationship is essential for effective counselor behavior.

Unfortunately, if not unpredictably, this shift in conceptualization has left counselor education largely unprepared to meet the challenge. The essence of the change has been to offer counselor education the opportunity to put the emphasis back where it belongs, on education. If education at its best is liberating in intent and integrating in effect, then the challenge of preparing counselors today is truly an educational one.

The past two decades have seen an emphasis on "training" counselors rather than educating them. Counselors have been variously given a set of fixed techniques which they were instructed to apply in rigid ways, or taught to think solely within the confines of narrowly conceived theoretical approaches, or expected to dispense test results and other information in mechanical fashions justified by their so-called objectivity.

These kinds of counseling and counselor education approaches have sustained themselves on the most meager of intellectual diets. Although supposedly a psychologically based professional activity, counseling has not drawn much sustenance from psychological disciplines. Counselor educators themselves have hardly been a group distinguished by psychological sophistication or affiliation. A recent survey by the Association for Counselor Education and

Supervision (1967), for example, indicates that only half the counselor educators are affiliated with APA and only one-fourth hold their highest degree in some branch of psychology.

If any intellectual thread holds the counselor education enterprise together it is a philosophical rather than a psychological one. In many respects even the philosophical underpinnings of counselor education have been largely a rather sophomoric adherence to a creed of love and kindness which has been hard to dignify as especially unique or perspicacious, even with yeoman efforts to bring it under the mystical mantle of that most fashionable of philosophies, existentialism.

One reason for the failure of counselor education to build a firm foundation on the discipline of psychology has been its inability to look in the right places for support. For the past twenty or more years counselor education has pursued a very distant but hardly platonic infatuation with psychiatry. Personality theory, that romantic if ephemeral will-o'-the wisp, which has succeeded only in translating the speculations of philosophy into the jargon of psychology, has been viewed as the fountainhead of psychological wisdom.

Until quite recently counselor education has steadfastly ignored the only areas of psychological endeavor to make substantial progress in the past twenty years. I mean social psychology and the psychology of learning. These two branches of psychology, particularly as they merge into experimental social psychology, have finally begun to furnish some solid evidence about the most fundamental problems of concern to counseling and counselor education. We at last are beginning to be able to understand some of the dynamics involved in how people learn from each other as social beings engaged in interpersonal relationships —which, as it turns out, are neither mystical nor mysterious.

As this new evidence starts to penetrate the parochial insulation which counselor education has imposed upon itself, new approaches and methodologies are emerging. Largely as a result of new knowledge about group dynamics we have seen group counseling change from an expedient dictated by cost consciousness to a powerful and sophisticated tool designed to utilize the tremendously strong motivational factors inherent in group cohesiveness and public commitment.

A new technology for changing human behavior has issued from the explication of simple principles of learning, and counseling has finally begun to address itself to the task of harnessing and humanizing it. Studies of human perceptual and cognitive development and of the processes by which people organize and assign meanings to events have led to much more sophisticated approaches to the design of learning experiences.

Interpersonal Relationships

Not the least important of the new learnings is in the explication of the nature of those interpersonal relationships which facilitate personal and social learning. As social psychology continues to amass evidence that human behavior is very much a product of social interaction, the specific characteristics of the types of interaction which contribute to the development of effective human behavior become paramount. Again, social psychology presents ample evidence that at least two factors in social interaction are vital determinants of the behavior of participants: involvement and communication.

When people are actively and dynamically involved in an interpersonal situation, their behavior tends to change in response to that situation. This principle has become virtually a truism in social psychology. In counseling, conditions leading to involvement have been variously termed warmth, acceptance, caring, concern, or positive regard. The considerable evidence (Truax and Carkhuff, 1967) supporting the importance of this element in interpersonal relationships which lead to learning should hardly be surprising.

Similarly, behavior change in individuals operating in social systems has been shown to occur as a function of the communication patterns within the system. One basic characteristic of the behavior of higher organisms is that it is maintained or modified in accordance with feedback from the environment. In interpersonal situations that feedback is the product of communication process.

Several aspects of communication are of particular importance in counseling. One of them can be called perceptual sensitivity and applies to the counselor as a receiver of communication. Unless the receiver of communication has the sensitivity to pick up the signals emitted by others in the network, communication is limited, distorted, or lost entirely. Listening, or sensitivity, is central to counseling. A second aspect of receiving communication, however, also important, relates to the way communications are processed cognitively so that their meaning is understood. Unless counselors have cognitive structures which are open, tentative, and flexible, they may be unable to process information from clients in ways that allow real communication to occur. Taken together, perceptual sensitivity and cognitive flexibility help define the quality of empathy which has long been recognized as a major element in helping relationships.

Another aspect of communication concerns the counselor as a transmitter of communications. When people are able to convey clear, unambiguous communications to others, they can serve as sources of feedback which can modify behavior. Such feedback may be termed a reinforcer since it has the power to increase the probability of occurrence of responses to which it is linked by logic or contiguity. When signals are emitted that are ambiguous, conflicting, or confusing, the resulting feedback may be inadequate to modify behavior in any consistent or purposeful way.

The ability to emit consistent, unambiguous communications is closely related to what is now called in counseling congruence, authenticity, openness, or sometimes confrontiveness. Again theory and research support the relevance of this factor to learning in interpersonal relationships.

To summarize briefly, considerable support from social psychology, psychology of learning, and recent counseling theory and research exists for the position that interpersonal involvement, perceptual sensitivity, cognitive flexibility, and consistency of communication are important factors in interpersonal learning.

The above rationale has rather profound implications for counselor educators who are responsible for designing learning experiences which will shape desirable interpersonal behaviors for counselors. Counselors in preparation are essentially people who are attempting so to improve the quality of their interpersonal relationships that they will be able to facilitate the learning of others. In learning to become a counselor, an individual typically is introduced into a hierarchy of increasingly difficult interpersonal tasks which range from establishing a relaxed and secure atmosphere, to assisting toward greater self-exploration, possibly to intervening in a self-defeating pattern of social behavior. In coping with these essentially developmental tasks, he acquires new patterns of interpersonal behaviors, which are what counselor education programs are intended to produce.

As counselors in preparation approach new interpersonal situations, they are in a state of dissonance, which provides the motivation for new learning. The dissonance is reduced or heightened by the feedback or reinforcement the student receives in the social system represented by the counselor education program. The sources of feedback include the counselor education staff, other students, and clients.

In coping with new interpersonal tasks, the counselor in preparation draws upon any of several resources which could in a sense be termed response modes. The crucial purpose of the counselor education program is to shape behavior within these response modes in order to produce a counselor whose integrated pattern of interpersonal behavior will allow him to function as a helping person. It is the position of this paper that each response mode is best shaped through a particular kind of learning process.

Response Mode A: The Immediate-Intuitive

As they approach new interpersonal tasks or re-encounter old ones with new sets of expectations, counselors in preparation usually draw upon well-established patterns of social interactions which have been learned or overlearned to the point that they are at a rather low level of conscious awareness. The basis for behaving is an immediate and intuitive one; that is, it is what dimly *feels* right. If previous experience has taught the student to cope with particular kinds of situations and people according to specific patterns of behavior, these patterns will feel right and be the basis for similar behavior.

In the counselor education program several dissonance-producing situations occur to upset the equilibrium provided by a purely intuitive response mode. First efforts are directed toward making the student aware of his interpersonal behaviors and sensitizing him to feedback from others about the quality of his interpersonal relationships. A number of learning processes may impinge upon him in this regard, but the most useful type seems to be what will be called here the *experiential* process.

If a pattern of interpersonal behavior has been overlearned to the point that it is experienced as intuitively right, probably the process of learning that will reshape that pattern or replace it with another—which in turn will be experienced as intuitively right—must be very powerful in impact.

At the present state of knowledge about experiential learning some of the most powerful technologies available are those involved in sensitivity training—also called T-groups, or sometimes human resource groups. All of these approaches and their variations are based upon the principles of small-group dynamics. They especially stress the supportive functions of tight group cohesiveness combined with a degree of openness of communication which allows large doses of feedback, both positive and negative, to be exchanged by participants. In such situations previously learned patterns of behavior may be subjected to negative reaction and high levels of dissonance or anxiety aroused. When group cohesiveness is high, however, attempts at new methods of coping are given strong and immediate positive feedback or reinforcement, which tends both to maintain the new behavior and to reduce anxiety.

In effect the participant *experiences* acute sensitivity and awareness of his interpersonal behavior. In the presence of clear and immediate feedback from significant others in the group he begins to learn new behaviors, and as the group communicates approval and acceptance of them he begins to feel the new patterns as intuitively correct and to overlearn them until he is no longer self-conscious about them.

Within this framework the one vital kind of input in a successful counselor education program is an opportunity for experiential learning aimed at changing the immediate-intuitive response mode.

Response Mode B: The Cognitive-Theoretical

A second response mode available to the counselor in preparation can be termed cognitive-theoretical. The student approaches an interpersonal situation in terms of some set of cognitive structures through which he assigns meaning to his perceptions. In early stages of preparation these structures may be naïve and rudimentary. Typically, however, significant inputs in the counselor education program are aimed at upsetting these naïve constructs and replacing them with more psychologically sophisticated ones. This is usually accomplished through a *didactic* program of reading, lecture, and discussion aimed at developing a new theoretical-cognitive framework within which perceptions can be organized and meaning assigned to events.

Again, from what we know about learning it seems plain that the effectiveness of this kind of counselor education input will be determined by the degree of involvement in the process and the clarity of communication which is present. Use of small laboratory and discussion groups, programmed readings, programmed interpersonal relationships, and carefully planned audio-visual materials can probably increase considerably the impact of the didactic aspect of preparation.

Response Mode C: The Empirical-Pragmatic

A third response mode available to counselors in coping with interpersonal tasks can be termed empirical-pragmatic. This mode is based simply on what gives predictable results for the counselor. It involves a set of behaviors which in turn elicit a predictable set of responses from clients. For example, a counselor learns that "when I behave this way clients talk more about their feelings." If counselors in preparation have had almost no experience with the counseling type of interpersonal tasks, they will have a very limited repertory within this mode. As soon as they engage in actual counseling, however, a response repertory will begin to be built. The counselor education input in this mode is the practicum process.

The practicum process represents in many respects a reality testing function. For practicum to be effective, opportunities must be provided for real involvement with clients and for full and open communication between counselors in preparation and clients seeking help. The most important aspects of the practicum process is that feedback to the counselor comes from the client, not merely from fellow students or counselor education staff.

Often so-called practicum treatments are not really practicums at all because the only feedback to the counselor comes from fellow students or faculty. In such situations the treatment is merely a somewhat disguised form of either experiential or didactic work—a modified form of sensitivity training or a didactic instructional session dealing with theoretical constructs used to explain client or counselor behaviors. Such distortions of practicum often result from the limitations built into supervision conducted by tape recordings.

Several methods are available for ensuring that practicum treatments are really that. With one, the unit of practicum is viewed as the case, not the interview. Counselors in preparation should be helped to deal with clients on bases which permit sufficient contact for reasonable goals to be defined and attained so that outcomes can be evaluated. Another method uses multiple counseling as a form of supervision. That is, two counselors work with a client, both to help the client and to elicit feedback about each other. Still another method uses supervision to stimulate recall or feedback from the client in the presence of the counselor. This method can either involve direct confrontation or be carried out through a medium such as video tape.

The most important characteristic of practicum, in any case, is that the source of behavior-modifying feedback be real clients rather than peers or faculty. We need to prepare counselors who can help clients, not counselors who can merely please supervisors. If a repertory of behaviors in the empirical-pragmatic mode is to be established, the source of reinforcement must be the client.

The Problem of Integration of Response Modes

Three bases for counselor behavior have been discussed and some implications for counselor education relevant to each suggested. Probably the most significant problem in designing learning experiences for counselor education is the integration of these response modes into a natural, comfortable, and effective counseling style for each individual counselor.

Counselor education has generally failed to provide the kind of total educational experience that allows this integration to occur. Instead, counselors in preparation have often been given new theoretical constructs for viewing clients and had suggested to them new behaviors which have not been learned to the point that they are experienced as natural, genuine, or comfortable. They have not been helped to try out the new behaviors in ways which enable them to predict the responses of clients.

The products of this kind of partial and fragmented training are counselors with ambivalent, conflicting, and competing response tendencies. These counselors behave in inconsistent, confused ways, are guilt-ridden and ambivalent about their relationships, and are consequently threatened by any attempt to evaluate the results of their efforts.

It is the thesis of this paper that the effective or "fully functioning" counselor is able to integrate the three response modes into one genuine, consistent pattern of behavior which elicits predictable patterns of behavior from clients. Such counselors experience their counseling relationships with greater security and satisfaction, behave with greater consistency, take more risks within the relationship, and are more willing to evaluate the results of counseling.

Toward a Theory of Counselor Education

An examination of the foregoing discussion of counselor education reveals a number of elements which can be combined to form the rudiments of a theory of counselor education. Four constructs to conceptualize counselor behaviors which are the output variables in a counselor education process have been described: perceptual sensitivity, cognitive flexibility, consistency of communication, and interpersonal involvement.

Three response modes which form a basis for counselor behavior have been described: the immediate-intuitive, the cognitive-theoretical, and the empirical-pragmatic. Each mode has been linked to a learning process or treatment input method: experiential, didactic, and practical, respectively. From this theoretical frame of reference it is possible to draw some preliminary hypotheses of a testable nature.

1. In counselor education programs with high loadings of experiential inputs, counselors will tend to operate primarily in

the immediate-intuitive response mode, with resulting high degrees of perceptual sensitivity and consistency of communication.

2. In counselor education programs with high loadings of didactic input, counselors will tend to operate mainly in the theoretical-cognitive response mode, with resulting high degrees of cognitive flexibility.

3. In counselor education programs with high loadings of practicum input counselors will tend to operate in the empirical-pragmatic response mode, experiencing high degrees of interpersonal involvement.

4. In counselor education programs in which high inputs in experiential, didactic, and practical learning processes are maintained throughout the entire program, counselors will operate in a pattern integrating all three response modes and resulting in high degrees of all four output variables.

Research to test these and other hypotheses drawn from this theory of counselor education is now under way at the University of Minnesota. Instruments have been developed to measure the output variables described here, and learning experiences to maximize inputs on each of the treatment processes are being designed.

Further research will assess the relationships among selection and admission factors, counselor education treatments, counselor behavior outcomes, and various client behavior factors in counseling process and outcome.

Summary

An attempt has been made in this paper to move toward what might be—tentatively at least—termed a theory of counselor education. The position has been taken that it is possible to identify three distinct counseling response modes: immediate-intuitive, cognitive-theoretical, and empirical-pragmatic. Most significant in shaping these modes are three learning processes, termed experiential, didactic, and practical.

It was hypothesized that the crucial challenge facing counselor education is to design sets of learning experiences which will produce an integrated repertory of counselor behaviors that will be simultaneously experienced by the counselor as intuitively right, cognitively correct, and empirically self-validating. It was further suggested that the counselor who functions at this level of integration will be both more effective and more secure.

References

Association for Counselor Education and Supervision Research Committee Report, Minneapolis, Minn., 1967. Mimeographed.

Kell, W., and Mueller, W.: *Impact and Change.* New York, Appleton-Century-Crofts, 1967.

Stieper, D., and Wiener, D.: *Dimensions of Psychotherapy.* Chicago, Aldine, 1965.

Truax, C., and Carkhuff, R.: *Toward Effective Counseling and Psychotherapy.* Chicago, Aldine, 1967.

Chapter 5

THE OUTCOME AND EFFECTS OF COUNSELOR EDUCATION AND SUPERVISION

IN TODAY'S "SYSTEMS" ORIENTED WORLD, it becomes critical that any planned effort to accomplish a task specify clearly defined behavioral or operational objectives in advance of implementation. "A systems approach is designed to achieve explicitly stated performance objectives" (Thoreson, 1969, p. 6). The vital question for counselor education and supervision, not unlike that for counseling and psychotherapy, seems to be, what outcomes, what results are brought about? Does the counselor trainee reveal any significant change during or after his professional education? This is the question to which we address ourselves in this chapter.

The research literature seems to approach the problem with at least two different strategies. The first strategy is concerned with the immediate effects of certain supervisory practices upon the trainee. The second strategy is concerned with the broad, long-term effects of education and supervision.

Using a well-conceived experimental design, the first strategy is elegantly applied by Payne, Winter, and Bell in their article "Effects of Supervisor Style upon the Learning of Empathy in a Supervision Analogue." These investigators were concerned with the effects of various strategies of supervision. Contrary to what might be expected, trainees receiving cognitive "advice" and exemplary suggestions or models revealed a greater improvement in empathic understanding than trainees receiving "counseling type of supervision," patterned after the warm, understanding counseling relationship. The authors examine these surprising results in terms of the previous literature and novelty of their research design.

Blane ("Immediate Effect of Supervisory Experiences on Counselor Candidates") also examines the immediate effects of supervisory strategies upon counselor trainees. Very simply, three groups of trainees respectively received positive, negative, or no feedback from a supervisor after interviewing a coached client. Subsequent to supervision, a second interview with another client was conducted and any changes in level of empathy revealed by the trainee were assessed. Gain in empathic response was significant for trainees receiving positive supervisory feedback. Trainees receiving either negative feedback or no feedback at all from a supervisor did not show significant change in level of empathy revealed to their client.

Reddy ("The Qualitative Aspects of Feedback in Learning Empathy") refined this strategy even further by offering almost instantaneous feedback to trainees who empathically responded at selected points to a client's comments recorded on motion picture film in a counseling interview, and compared this feedback immediately after the trainee's response with a second group receiving supervisory feedback at the end of the film and a third control group receiving no feedback at all. Over a course of six successive filmed counseling interviews, the trainee's level of empathic response was monitored for each of the three supervisory groups and significant differences were found. Not only didactic and positive supervisory reaction but immediate feedback as well seems to be a significant ingredient to be considered in training.

Matarazzo, *et al.*, in their article "Learning the Art of Interviewing: A Study of What Beginning Students Do and Their Pattern of Change," approached the matter of training medical students to interview, using the second research strategy. Students received eight weeks of supervised experience counseling psychiatric inpatients. Subsequently, each student was evaluated again in a standard interview, to determine if there was a reduction in frequency of errors after eight weeks of supervised experience. The frequency and quality of errors made by student interviewers did show a significant change over the eight-week period, which the authors describe in detail. This study is notable for its well-planned experimental design and careful measurement.

Truax and Lister ("Effects of Short-Term Training upon Accurate Empathy and Non-possessive Warmth") offered an intensive forty-hour training program over a two-week period to experienced counselors with graduate degrees. The training program emphasized acquisition of empathy, warmth, and genuineness through such media as a therapeutic supervisory atmosphere, the use of research rating scales, and a quasi-group-therapy experience. Counselors as a whole showed significant gains in empathy from before to after this intensive training program. Again, carefully programmed supervision led to longer-term improvement in facilitative behavior, this time for well-seasoned counselors, and these changes took place within a two-week period.

Carkhuff's review of the literature ("Critical Variables in Effective Counselor Training") suggests that a critical determinant of whether supervision and education will lead to longer-term changes in trainee behavior is the level of facilitation offered by the supervisor or trainer. He concluded that level of empathic understanding offered by the trainee tended to converge with the level offered by his trainer or supervisor. Trainees seemed to gain the most with high-empathy trainers and deteriorate in counseling skill with low-empathy trainers. The most effective training programs employed supervisors who were very sensitive, empathic, understanding people, especially with their students. The dynamics of the trainer-student relationship are further examined by the author.

Pierce and Schauble (1970) report essentially the same findings. Within one graduate program, students receiving a high level of empathy, positive regard, and genuineness from their supervisors improved significantly on these dimensions with their clients. Students receiving supervision which was less empathic, positive in regard, and genuine did not reveal significant improvement in the level of these dimensions offered to their clients. In a follow-up study of these students, reprinted in this chapter, the investigators found that no significant changes had taken place in level of facilitative dimensions developed by students, nine months after supervision had terminated.

Demos and Zuwaylif ("Counselor Attitudes in Relation to the Theoretical Positions of their Supervisors") considered a serious by-product of supervision. Does the trainee ultimately emulate the methods and theoretical preference of his mentor? These investigators compared the outcome of trainees supervised by a client-centered, an eclectically oriented, or a directively oriented staff member. While all trainees did show significant improvement in facilitative behavior, it was also found that the manner of change depended upon the theoretical preference of the supervisor. The study opens up some important questions which further research may clarify.

Can the counselor trainee also benefit from feedback other than that from a supervisor or trainer? With so many recent advances in instrumentation, it becomes natural to ask if mechanical or electronic sources of feedback may also produce positive change within the trainee.

Yenawine and Arbuckle, in their article "Study of the Use of Videotape and Audiotape as Techniques in Counselor Education," compare the effects of audiotape and videotape feedback upon trainee behavior in the counseling practicum. Rather interesting changes took place in trainee attitudes as the practicum progressed. It seemed as if the playback of videotaped counseling interviews in the presence of supervisor and peers resulted in characteristic differences in trainee response and the reaction of others to the trainee's recorded behavior when compared to audiotaped interviews.

The evidence is somewhat conflicting, however, as Markey, *et al.* in their article "Influence of Playback Techniques on Counselor Performance," report no significant differences in student counselor's performance after receiving various combinations of audio and video recorded feedback. One critical difference, however, was the absence of any supervision while such feedback was received. Markey, *et al.*, further suggest that the effect of videotape playback may arouse negative emotional responses initially, but continued video feedback of interview behavior may lead to a "cooling off" period as students become less threatened and more objective. It is beginning to appear, however, that mechanical feedback without supervision may be of limited value to the student counselor.

Another question which may be asked is whether mechanical feedback augments the effects of supervision. The answer appears to be affirmative. Martin and Gazda ("A Method of Self-Evaluation for Counselor Education Utilizing the Measurement of Facilitative Conditions") compare two groups of student counselors. The first group of trainees, in addition to receiving supervision, self-evaluated their tape-recorded interviews. The second group received supervision without the opportunity for self-evaluation. Self-evaluation of tape-recorded interviews did appear to augment the effects of supervision. Again, mechanical feedback may be a helpful adjunct to the supervisory process.

Looking at the research collectively, it would appear that individual or group supervision leads both to short-term specific gains and long-term general growth for the counseling trainee. Such gains are further augmented by mechanical feedback. But we are left with the tentative conclusion that counselor training is no better nor no worse than the professional skills and characteristics of the counselor educator or supervisor who offers it.

References

Pierce, R. M., and Schauble, P. G.: Graduate training of facilitative counselors: the effects of individual supervision. *Journal of Counseling Psychology, 17*:210-215, 1970.

Thoresen, C. E.: The systems approach and counselor education: basic features and implications. *Counselor Education and Supervision, 9*:3-17, 1969.

Additional References

Delaney, D. J., Long, T. J., Masucci, M. J., and Moses, H. A.: Skill acquisition and perception change of counselor candidates during practicum, *Counselor Education and Supervision, 8*:273-282, 1969.

Hansen, J. C., and Barker, E. N.: Experiencing and the supervisory relationship. *Journal of Counseling Psychology, 11*:107-111, 1964.

Kassera, W. J., and Sease, W. A.: Personal change as a concomitant of counselor education. *Counselor Education and Supervision, 9*:208-211, 1970.

Martin, J. C., and Carkhuff, R. R.: Changes in personality and interpersonal functioning of counselors-in-training. *Journal of Clinical Psychology, 24*:109-110, 1968.

McKinnon, D. W.: Group counseling with student counselors. *Counselor Education and Supervision, 8*:195-200, 1969.

Patterson, C. H.: Effects of counselor education on personality. *Journal of Counseling Psychology, 14*:444-448, 1967.

Payne, P. A., and Gralinski, D. M.: Effects of supervisor style and empathy upon counselor learning. *Journal of Counseling Psychology,* 15:517-521, 1968.

Peters, H. J., and Thompson, C. L.: School superintendents view counselor preparation. *Counselor Education and Supervision,* 8:379-386, 1968.

Pierce, R., Carkhuff, R. R., and Berenson, B. G.: The differential effects of high and low functioning counselors upon counselors-in-training. *Journal of Clinical Psychology,* 23:212-215, 1967.

Reddy, W. B.: Sensitivity training as an integral phase of counselor education. *Counselor Education and Supervision,* 9:110-115, 1970.

Roark, A. E.: The influence of training on counselor responses in actual and role-playing interviews. *Counselor Education and Supervision,* 8:289-295, 1969.

EFFECTS OF SUPERVISOR STYLE UPON THE LEARNING OF EMPATHY IN A SUPERVISION ANALOGUE*

PAUL A. PAYNE, DONNA E. WINTER, and GLENN E. BELL

Evidence of a positive relationship between therapist characteristics (such as empathy, positive regard, and congruence) and various indices of client improvement (Truax and Carkhuff, 1967; Carkhuff and Berenson, 1967) has led to systematic efforts to teach such therapeutic characteristics to trainees. Appreciable improvement in therapeutic conditions offered have been reported for relatively brief training efforts representing a variety of trainee levels of sophistication, training tasks, and instructional methods (Fosmire and Palmer, 1964; Ivey, Normington, Miller, Morrill, and Haase, 1968; Miller, 1969; Pierce and Drasgow, 1969; Reddy, 1969; Truax and Carkhuff, 1967). Most of these studies have represented a combination of training procedures, and although some comparisons are made with control groups, such research has not ordinarily assessed the relative effectiveness of different approaches to supervision or training. Since much training time traditionally involves individual supervision, it would seem to be especially useful to know more about the effects of individual supervision and in particular, the effects of different types or styles of supervision.

In their review of the literature on supervision, Truax, Cark-

---

* Reprinted from *Counselor Education and Supervision,* in press, with permission of the American Personnel and Guidance Association and the authors.

huff, and Douds (1964) classify major approaches as either didactic or experiential. Didactic supervisors (e.g. Krasner, 1962; and Krumboltz, 1967) see their job as that of providing feedback and reinforcement in order to shape the behaviors a counselor needs for successful work. Experiential supervisors (e.g. Ekstein and Wallerstein, 1958; Rogers, 1957; Patterson, 1964), on the other hand, see the didactic approach as mechanistic and impersonal, and emphasize the trainee's need for security and the opportunity to learn from his own experience. In an effort to test the effects of these two basic approaches, Payne and Gralinski (1968) compared a techniques-oriented supervision (didactic) with a counseling-oriented supervision (experiential) in a supervision analogue on the criterion of empathy. In that study trainees receiving the techniques-type supervision showed significant improvement, whereas those receiving the counseling-type supervision declined in level of empathy.

It was the purpose of the present study to provide an extension of the Payne and Gralinski (1968) work again comparing techniques, counseling, and control groups on empathy learning in a supervision analogue. In the effort to make a more thorough test of treatment effects, supervisors with more experience were utilized, and the number of counseling and supervisory sessions per trainee were increased. Additional experimental and control groups were also employed. Against the possibility that placebo effects influence trainee behavior (Paul, 1967), a placebo-type supervision was offered in which supervisors followed neither the counseling nor techniques approaches, but rather gave brief lectures on the psychodynamics of the simulated client.

The other factor considered as possibly influencing counselor behavior was suggested by the rather dramatic improvement of the control group in the Payne and Gralinski study. From these results, as well as from the work of Claus (1968), it was hypothesized that control group improvement might be attributable to the initial audio modeling of empathic counselor behaviors and the commentary which they received. Thus, in the present study, control and placebo conditions were offered with as well as without this initial orientation. By way of summary, the six treatment groups were as follows: techniques, counseling, placebo-modeling, placebo-no modeling, control-modeling, and control-no modeling (c.f. Table 5-I).

TABLE 5–I

SUMMARY OF TREATMENT STEPS

Treatment Group	Audio Modeling With Cues (30 min)	Trial 1 (10 min)	First Super-vision Session (15 min)	Trial 2 (10 min)	Second Super-vision Session (15 min)	Trial 3 (10 min)
Techniques	X	X	X	X	X	X
Counseling	X	X	X	X	X	X
Placebo-Modeling	X	X	X	X	X	X
Placebo-No Modeling	O	X	X	X	X	X
Control-Modeling	X	X	O	X	O	X
Control-No Modeling	O	X	O	X	O	X

X = condition administered
O = condition not administered

Method

Subjects

Supervisors were one senior staff member at the University of Cincinnati Counseling Service (male), one fourth-year graduate student in counseling psychology (male) and one third-year graduate student in clinical psychology (female). Trainees were 54 male and 54 female undergraduates in introductory psychology whose participation met their research requirement for the course.

Procedure

Supervisees were divided into six groups of eighteen each—four experimental and two control. Four of the groups (techniques, counseling, one placebo group and one control group) were initially given a 30-minute group orientation (audio modeling with cues) on the meaning of empathy. In this recorded orientation, empathy was described and examples from two interviews, one high and one low in counselor empathy, were presented. On the tape a commentator provided cues by pointing out the differences in the performances of the two counselors, and the interview segments were then repeated. In order to control for set, counselors not receiving the above orientation (one placebo group and one control group) heard the introductory section of the above tape on which empathy was briefly defined and its importance in counseling was stressed. However, no interview examples were included.

Following the modeling or non-modeling conditions described above, each trainee in the experimental groups was assigned a supervisor and training sessions were held. The first tape of an experimental interview consisting of a recorded series of six client statements was then played. Thirty-second pauses followed each client statement during which each trainee responded on his dictation equipment as if he were counseling the client. After the first and again after the second tape of client statements, each trainee in the experimental groups was given a 15-minute supervision interview. The supervisory methods were either (a) supervision-counseling type, (b) supervision-techniques type, or (c) supervision-placebo type. Each supervisor had three male and three female supervisees in each of the four experimental groups.

Controls followed the same procedures except that no supervisors were present during their performance and they proceeded directly through the three tapes of client statements with only brief pauses between tapes 1 and 2 and tapes 2 and 3. A summary of the above treatment steps is given in Table 5-I.

Empathy Scale

A 7-point rating scale based upon Truax (1961) and Barrett-Lennard (1962) was utilized for the making of all ratings of empathy. On this scale empathy was defined as "the tendency of a person to perceive another's feelings, thoughts, and behavior as similar to his own. When another has empathy toward you, he understands exactly how you feel and what you mean. At a low level of empathy the person indicates he is not interested or is interested but unable to be aware of your feelings. At a high level of empathy the message 'I am with you' is clear. The person's remarks fit in just right with what you are feeling at the moment."

Experimental Interview

The experimental interview presented a tape recording of a college student discussing a variety of typical problems—grades, dating, roommate, parents, professors, loneliness, etc. This recording was divided into three sets of client statements and these three sets were randomized in the form of a Latin square with each of the three orders being given an equal number of times to each sex in each treatment group.

Supervisory Conditions

Under *supervision, counseling type,* supervision was patterned after a nondirective counseling relationship. Of primary importance was the establishment of an empathic relationship with the supervisee. In this way it was hoped that the supervisor would provide an effective model of empathic behavior. Supervisors focused on the trainee's frame of reference and responded to his feelings about the experimental task, his reactions toward the "client," "counselor" assessment of his own performance, etc. However, supervisors avoided any negative evaluation of supervisee performance and the giving of any direct suggestions for improvement.

Under *supervision, techniques type,* supervisors again worked for a positive interpersonal relationship. However, in this supervisory condition, the trainee's effectiveness in offering empathy and a discussion of his techniques in counseling were introduced. Supervisors further gave specific examples of responses which would have been more empathic than the ones given by the supervisee.

Under *supervision, placebo type,* supervisors attempted to offer warmth and interest in the supervisee but did not model empathy by responding to the trainee's feelings, did not express approval or disapproval of his performance, and made no suggestions for improvements. Supervisors rather gave brief descriptions of the psychodynamics of the "client."

Scoring of Empathy

Following the collection of data, each set of six trainee responses were randomized and rated directly from the tape by two independent judges utilizing the 7-point empathy scale. Each set of six trainee statements was given a single rating by each judge, and the two judges' ratings were averaged for each trainee. Because of randomization procedures for the sequence in which the supervisees responded to the stimulus tapes 1, 2, or 3, judges had no way of knowing which trial of a given trainee was being rated. Thus each trainee in the study had three ratings, one for each set of six client statements to which he responded. The average inter-judge agreement on a 25% sample of supervisee responses to each of the three stimulus tapes was r = .88.

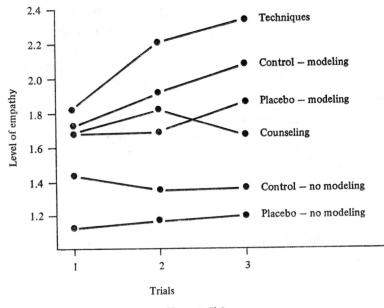

Figure 5.1.

Results

Average empathy scores for each treatment group by trials are shown in Figure 5.I. It will be seen that appreciable differences in initial scores as well as in subsequent trials are indicated among the various groups. A two-way analysis of variance for repeated measures (Table 5-II) indicated that the main effects from both treatments and trials were significant beyond the .01

TABLE 5–II

ANALYSIS OF VARIANCE FOR TREATMENTS BY TRIALS ON THE
CRITERION OF EMPATHY

N = 108

Source of Variation	Sums of Squares	df	Mean Square	F
Treatments	33.00	5	6.600	9.98*
Error (a)	67.36	102	.660	
Trials	1.49	2	.745	11.29*
Treatments × trials	2.92	10	.292	4.42*
Error (b)	13.48	204	.066	
Total	118.25	323		

* $p < .01$

level. Because the treatments by trials interaction ($p < .01$) showed that learning curves across trials were not the same for different treatment groups, a separate analysis for each treatment group across trials was then performed (analysis of simple main effects, Winer, 1962). Significant changes across trials were found for the techniques ($F = 19.62$; $p < .01$) and for the control modeling groups ($F = 8.11$; $p < .01$). As may be seen from Figure 5.I, these changes are in the direction of increased empathy. Thus, the techniques and control-modeling groups show improvement with experience, while no significant improvement is noted for the other groups.

In order to test for the initial effects of audio modeling, an analysis of variance for trial 1 (before any supervision had been given) was conducted ($F = 4.43$; $p < .01$) and an orthogonal comparison was made between the four groups receiving the audio modeling and the two groups which did not (Edwards, 1960). Results indicated that the groups receiving modeling were significantly higher ($F = 13.12$; $p < .01$) than those without it. A measure of the residual effects of the initial audio modeling beyond the first trial was provided in the control-modeling group, referred to above, which did not receive any supervision. The significant improvement made by this group supports the assumption that modeling not only influences the initial performance by counselors, but also creates a potential for future additional improvement which is evidenced in subsequent trials.

Discussion

Within the limits of a rather brief training analogue, these results give additional support to the conclusions of Payne and Gralinski (1968) concerning the superiority of a techniques orientation to the more widely advocated counseling type of supervision on the criterion of empathy.

Although an initial impression might be that "feedback" involved in the techniques supervision was superior to the "modeling" approach of the counseling type, this would over-simplify the comparison. Both types can be thought of as involving modeling. In the techniques supervision, the supervisor models specific examples of high empathy responses to "client" statements within a context very close in time and task similarity to that which is required of the trainee. In the counseling supervision, on the other hand, the supervisor models empathic responses to trainee statements rather than to those of the "client." It is probably less clear in the latter case that the supervisor is trying to function as a model and a greater degree of transfer is needed to move from a realization of "here's how the supervisor is responding to me" to "here's how I should be responding to the 'client.'" In addition, response acquisition in the techniques group is apparently facilitated by the selective reinforcement of supervisee responses and by the training in cue discrimination given when the supervisor contrasts his own examples to those given by the trainee.

Although the techniques group showed the greatest degree of improvement, it was not significantly higher than the control group receiving the audio modeling alone. Inasmuch as the techniques group received the additional modeling, selective feedback, and training in cue discrimination previously noted, it is somewhat surprising that the difference was so small. It may be that the trainee who has heard the audio model already has close to the maximal amount of information that he can process at this stage of training. It may also be, as Fosmire and Palmer (1964) suggest, that face-to-face supervision to some extent interferes with early skill acquisition.

Although any type of live supervision may involve some interference, the evidence for the interference hypothesis seems especially strong in the case of the counseling type of supervision. Unlike the control-modeling group, those receiving the counseling supervision following the initial audio modeling, failed to show any improvement. Two possibilities might be considered. It has been shown by Delaney and Moore (1966), and Gysbers and Johnston (1965) that beginning counselors expect evaluation and suggestions, and their absence may have been disruptive. A second possibility was raised by the occasional observation of supervisors that the counseling-type supervision seemed to lower trainee inhibitions. In these cases, if the supervisee tended to have rejecting feelings toward the "client," he was more likely to express them in subsequent trials. Thus, supervisor empathy may have the effect of raising congruence rather than empathy.

In terms of practical applications, the brevity of the training makes it relatively safer to generalize these results to the initial stages of training or to pre-practicum work. However, for the early stages of training at least, these results support the use of recorded models and a supervisor style which deals specifically with techniques as effective means of improving empathic skills. Presumably, other counselor skills could also be improved through these procedures.

References

Barrett-Lennard, G. T.: Dimensions of therapist response as causal factors in therapeutic change. *Psychological Monographs*, 76 (43 Whole No. 562), 1962.

Carkhuff, R. R., and Berenson, B. G.: *Beyond Counseling and Therapy.* New York, Holt, Rinehart and Winston, 1967.

Claus, K. E.: *Effects of Cueing During Modeling and Feedback Sessions on Learning a Teaching Skill.* Paper presented at the meeting of the American Psychological Association, San Francisco, August, 1968.

Delaney, D. J., and Moore, J. C.: Student expectations of the role of the practicum supervisor. *Counselor Education and Supervision*, 6:11-17, 1966.

Edwards, A. L.: *Experimental Design in Pychological Research.* New York, Holt, Rinehart and Winston, 1960.

Ekstein, R., and Wallerstein, R. S.: *The Teaching and Learning of Psychotherapy.* New York, Basic Books, 1958.

Fosmire, F. R., and Palmer, B. E.: *A Comparison of a Method of Programmed Instruction and of Personal Supervision in Psychotherapy.* Paper presented at the meeting of the National Society for Programmed Instruction, Trinity University, San Antonio, April, 1964.

Gysbers, N. C., and Johnston, J. A.: Expectations of a practicum supervisor's role. *Counselor Education and Supervision,* 4:68-74, 1965.

Ivey, A. E., Normington, C. J., Miller, C. D., Morrill, W. H., and Haase, R. F.: Microcounseling and attending behavior: an approach to prepracticum counselor training. *Journal of Counseling Psychology, 15* (Monogr. Suppl.), 1968.

Krasner, L.: The therapist as a social reinforcement machine. In Strupp, H. H., and Lubrosky, L. (Eds.): *Research in Psychotherapy.* Washington, D. C., American Psychological Association, 1962, vol. 2.

Krumboltz, J. D.: Changing the behavior of behavior changers. *Counselor Education and Supervision,* 6:222-229, 1967.

Miller, B.: Acquisition of a specified verbal response set amongst counselor trainees. *Journal of Counseling Psychology, 16*:314-316, 1969.

Patterson, C. H.: Supervising students in the counseling practicum. *Journal of Counseling Psychology, 11*:47-53, 1964.

Paul, G. L.: Strategy of outcome research in psychotherapy. *Journal of Consulting Psychology,* 31:109-118, 1967.

Payne, P. A., and Gralinski, D. M.: Effects of supervisor style and empathy upon counselor learning. *Journal of Counseling Psychology,* 15:517-521, 1968.

Pierce, R. M., and Drasgow, J.: Teaching facilitative interpersonal functioning to psychiatric inpatients. *Journal of Counseling Psychology, 16*: 295-298, 1969.

Reddy, W. B.: The effects of immediate and delayed feedback on the learning of empathy. *Journal of Counseling Psychology,* 16:59-62, 1969.

Rogers, C. R.: Training individuals to engage in the therapeutic process. In Strother, C. R. (Ed.): *Psychology and Mental Health.* Washington, D.C., American Psychological Association, 1957.

Truax, C. B.: A scale for the measurement of accurate empathy. *Psychiatric Institute Bulletin.* Wisconsin Psychiatric Institute, University of Wisconsin, 1961, vol. 1, p. 12.

Truax, C. B., and Carkhuff, R. R.: *Toward Effective Counseling and Psychotherapy: Training and Practice.* Chicago, Aldine, 1967.

Truax, C. B., Carkhuff, R. R., and Douds, V.: Toward an integration of the didactic and experiential approaches to training in counseling and psychotherapy. *Journal of Counseling Psychology,* 11:240-247, 1964.

Winer, B. J.: *Statistical Principles in Experimental Design.* New York, McGraw-Hill, 1962.

IMMEDIATE EFFECT OF SUPERVISORY EXPERIENCES ON COUNSELOR CANDIDATES*

STEPHEN M. BLANE

Most counselor educators seem to agree that supervision is a major part of any counselor education program (Walz and Roeber, 1962; Munger and Cash, 1963; Peters and Hansen, 1963). Gone are the days when supervision was viewed as only an adjunct to the program. However, in spite of this there still appears to be a dearth of empirical research in this vital area. Hansen and Barker (1964) appropriately summarize the feelings of most counselor educators: "The real task ahead for research is to specify further the separate types of supervisor behavior and evaluate their relevance to counselor education." While a few studies such as Davidson and Emmer's (1966) and Miller and Oetting's (1966) have been conducted in the area of supervision, Cash and Munger (1966), after reviewing the literature on counselor preparation, reported that "The scarcity of investigations in the area [supervision] indicates the need for study in this important area of the counselor education program." Recently, in an entire issue of *Counselor Education and Supervision* devoted to supervised experiences in counselor education, Lister (1966) succinctly called for rigorous evaluative research in counselor education, particularly in the area of supervision.

What does supervision do for counselor candidates? What happens to supervisees during and after supervision? These among other important questions concerning supervision need to be answered.

This study was designed to investigate one aspect of the supervisory process: the immediate effect of positive, negative, or no supervisory experiences on the measured empathic understanding of counselor candidates.

Procedure

Thirty members of the 1966-67 NDEA Counseling and Guidance Institute conducted at the University of Florida participated

---

* Reprinted from *Counselor Education and Supervision*, 8:39-44, 1968, with permission of the American Personnel and Guidance Association and the author.

as subjects. At the time of the study, each institute member was nearing the completion of his master's-level counselor preparation. Each of the subjects had participated in a one-and-a-half-month practicum experience prior to experimentation.

The 30 counselors were assigned by age and sex to three 10-person groups. The treatments (positive, negative, or no supervision) were then randomly assigned to the groups. During the experiment, each counselor conducted a 30-minute tape-recorded interview with a client. Two female undergraduate students were paid an hourly wage to participate as clients. They were only aware that the researcher was investigating counselor behavior and knew nothing of the design of the study. Each client's problem was her own and was very real to her. The clients were instructed to be as natural as possible during their interaction with the different counselors. The counselors were unaware that each was seeing the same clients. One girl (client) was always the first client interviewed by the counselor while the other girl (client) was always the second client. Following the first client interview, the counselor was given either a 15-minute positive or negative supervisory experience or received no supervisory experience.

Twenty positive and 20 negative statements (compiled from a pilot study in which three expert judges rated 50 items as to whether the statements represented strong, mild, or weak positive or negative supervisory statements) were used by the supervisor (the experimenter) in the supervisory sessions. The statements were used in a natural, counselor-supervisor interaction throughout the entire supervisory session and were always related to the particular counselor's specific interview content. All treatment experiences were directed at interview content rather than toward the personality of the subject counselor. All 20 negative statements were used with all subjects undergoing the negative supervisory experience, and the 20 positive statements were used with all subjects experiencing positive supervision.

In the positive supervision session, the supervisor concentrated on the strong aspects of the supervisee's counseling behavior, e.g. "There was excellent rapport established." "You really were 'with' your client." "You certainly understood your client's feelings very well." The supervisor concentrated on weak aspects of the supervisee's counseling behavior in the negative supervisory situation, e.g. "You did not establish even a minimum of rapport." "You seemed very unaware of your client's feelings." "You made gross mistakes." The no supervision group received no supervisory experience.

Immediately after the supervisory treatment all subjects conducted a second tape-recorded, 30-minute interview with a second client. The middle four-minute segment (minutes 13½ through 16½) was selected from each of the pre- and post-treatment interviews for each subject. These data samples were recorded in random order on a master tape.

Three judges, trained in the use of Carkhuff's (1966) Empathic Understanding in Interpersonal Processes II scale, independently rated the data samples. The three judges' ratings were totaled for each of the 60 data samples on the master tape. Each of the 30 counselors received two composite empathic understanding ratings, a pre-treatment and a post-treatment composite empathic understanding score. An interjudge reliability coefficient of .66 (Ebel, 1951) was found for the 60 data samples.

Results

Table 5-III presents each group's mean score and standard deviation for pre- and post-supervision measures of empathic understanding.

The t tests performed between the different groups on the pre-supervision measures of empathic understanding found that no significant differences among groups existed at the .05 level. The groups were therefore shown to be comparable in empathic

TABLE 5–III

PRE- AND POST-SUPERVISION GROUP MEANS AND STANDARD DEVIATIONS FOR MEASURES OF EMPATHIC UNDERSTANDING

| | Empathic Understanding Scores | | | |
| | Pre-Supervision | | Post-Supervision | |
Group	Mean	SD	Mean	SD
Positive supervision	4.90	1.370	6.80	1.398
Negative supervision	5.60	1.776	6.50	1.581
No supervision	5.20	1.229	5.80	1.398

understanding before the supervisory treatments were administered.

An analysis of variance test was performed using difference scores from pre- to post-supervision empathic understanding to determine significant differences between subjects and within groups. Only the factor of empathy measurements (pre- to post-supervision) was significant at the .01 level (F = 16.19 with 1 degree of freedom). Differences between the groups were not significant (F = .50 with 2 degrees of freedom). However, it should be mentioned that in follow-up *t* test comparisons using difference scores, only the difference between the positive and no supervision groups approached the .05 level.

A graph was plotted to depict the magnitude and direction of change in all groups between pre- and post-supervision mean empathic understanding scores. Figure 5.2 clearly illustrates that all groups changed in a positive direction. However, the control group (no supervision) changed the least. While the negative supervision group also changed in a positive direction, the group which showed the most change was the positive supervision group.

A series of *t* tests for use with repeated measures on the same subject were performed on each group, utilizing the pre- and post-supervision empathic understanding scores.

As shown in Table 5-IV, only within the positive supervision group was there a significant change between pre- and post-

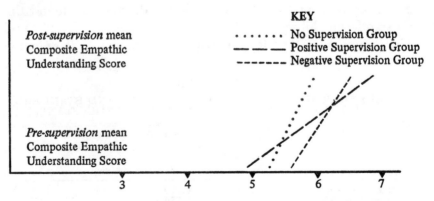

Figure 5.2. Group changes between pre- and post-supervision mean empathic understanding scores.

TABLE 5–IV

t TESTS OF THE DIFFERENCES BETWEEN PRE-SUPERVISION
AND POST-SUPERVISION EMPATHIC UNDERSTANDING
SCORES FOR TREATMENT GROUPS

Supervision Group	Empathic Understanding		Amount of Change D	df	t
	Pre-Super-vision Mean	Post-Super-vision Mean			
Positive	4.9	6.8	+1.9	9	4.38*
Negative	5.6	6.5	+0.9	9	1.65
No supervision	5.2	5.8	+0.6	9	1.26

* $p < .01$

supervision empathic understanding scores with the post-supervision empathic understanding scores significantly higher than the pre-supervision scores.

Conclusions

From the above results, it would appear that the following conclusions are warranted:

1. A positive supervisory experience significantly increases the level of empathic understanding a counselor is able to offer to his client.

2. The level of empathic understanding does not change without supervision during the time interval investigated here.

3. Receiving a negative supervisory experience does not significantly increase a counselor's level of empathic understanding.

Discussion

It must be clearly stated that this experiment was an attempt to study the immediate effect of supervisory experiences on counselor candidates. It cannot, therefore, be concluded that any long-range effects would yield precisely the same results. It would be important to experimentally utilize the three supervisory experiences of this study over a number of weeks or months to determine whether repeated supervisory contacts would accentuate the results found in the present research. Further experimentation is needed to explore the effect of a supervisory session composed of a combination of positive and negative experiences.

Another area for research which would be meaningful to counselors already in the field indirectly arises from this study as a result of the effect of the different supervisory experiences.

Most counselors in the field no longer receive supervision or even feedback about their counseling ability from their colleagues. The results of the present study indicate that not receiving a supervisory experience produced almost no change in a counselor's empathic understanding. Therefore, it seems important to determine if practicing counselors remain the same, grow or regress in empathic understanding when no longer receiving feedback about their counseling.

References

Carkhuff, R. R.: Empathic understanding in interpersonal processes II. Unpublished materials, 1966.

Cash, W. L., and Munger, P. F.: Counselors and their preparation. *Review of Educational Research, 36*:256-63, 1966.

Davidson, T. N., and Emmer, E. T.: Immediate effect of supportive and nonsupportive behavior on counselor candidates' focus of concern. *Counselor Education and Supervision, 6*:27-31, 1966.

Ebel, R.: Estimation of the reliability of ratings. *Psychometrika, 16*:407-24, 1951.

Hansen, J., and Barker, E.: Experiencing and the supervisory relationship. *Journal of Counseling Psychology, 11*:107-11, 1964.

Lister, J. L.: Supervised counseling experiences: some comments. *Counselor Education and Supervision, 6*:69-72, 1966.

Miller, C. D., and Oetting, E. R.: Students react to supervision. *Counselor Education and Supervision, 6*:73-74, 1966.

Munger, P. F., and Cash, W. L.: Supervised counseling practice in the first semester of graduate training. *Counselor Education and Supervision, 2*:197-200, 1963.

Peters, H. J., and Hansen, J. C.: Counseling practicum: bases for supervision. *Counselor Education and Supervision, 2*:82-85, 1963.

Walz, G. R., and Roeber, E. C.: Supervisors' reactions to a counseling interview. *Counselor Education and Supervision, 2*:2-7, 1962.

THE QUALITATIVE ASPECTS OF FEEDBACK IN LEARNING EMPATHY*

W. Brendan Reddy

Carkhuff (1967) and Truax and Carkhuff (1964) have shown that effective psychotherapy is contingent, at least in part, on

---

* Reprinted from *Counselor Education and Supervision*, 8:176-181, 1969, with permission of the American Personnel and Guidance Association and the author.

the patient's perception of the therapist as empathic, congruent, and having nonpossessive warmth. Truax, Carkhuff, and Douds (1964) have presented evidence that these behaviors are teachable to both professional and nonprofessional persons. Based upon the assumptions of knowledge of results research (Annett, 1964) and "the mechanical third ear" of Korner and Brown (1952), Reddy (1969) trained subjects to be significantly more empathic by presenting them with immediate feedback as to their performance rather than delaying the feedback. The latter technique is typical of most counselor education programs.

While the major findings of the study focused on the superiority of the immediate feedback technique, both immediate and delayed feedback groups showed significant pre- to post-training gains in accurate empathy. The present study examined what factors contributed to the superiority of the immediate feedback technique.

Method

While the complete methodology may be found in the original study (Reddy, 1969), the following briefly outlines the procedure.

Thirty-six male volunteer students were placed randomly into one of three groups, 12 students to a group. Subjects were shown six simulated psychotherapy films in a Latin square design and asked to respond to appropriate film stops as empathically as they would if they were the therapists. When subjects of the immediate feedback group responded to the training films, their statements were immediately followed by the experimenter's numerical rating on an empathy scale and a predetermined response which served as an example of a highly rated comment to that film sequence. The Ss of the immediate feedback group were able to hear these ratings and examples via a small ear-plug controlled by the experimenter. A second group followed the same procedure but received results in delayed fashion at the completion of each training film. A third control group received no feedback. All responses were recorded. Responses of the first and sixth film presentations were rated independently and served as pre- and post-measures of empathy, respectively. There were no significant differences among subjects or between groups on the pre-measure of accurate empathy.

In the present study, the pre accurate empathy (AE) responses, and the post AE responses were further analyzed. In order to examine more closely what kinds of learning took place, subject's pre- and post-responses were analyzed into the median number of words used per response and the total number of affect words used per group. Responses were also categorized and analyzed by content. Individual open-ended interviews were conducted in order to determine subjects' subjective reactions in the films and techniques of feedback.

Results

The subjects in the immediate feedback group were reported to have responded more completely than the delayed feedback groups or the control group. It was contended that analyzing the number of words used in the empathic responses would in part answer this question. As Table 5-V shows, at the end of training the median number of words per response used by the immediate feedback group had increased by one-third. The delayed feedback group gained a few words per response, and the no feedback group remained the same.

Since high empathy was defined in terms of a subject's responding to a client's full range of feelings in their exact intensity (Truax, 1961), it seemed consistent to examine subjects' use of affect words before and after training. Any word whose dictionary meaning denoted affect was counted, e.g. angry, frightened, happy, etc. Table 5-VI shows little pre-and post-changes in the control group but a large pre- to post-difference in both the immediate and delayed feedback groups.

In a modification of Danskin's (1955) Checklist of Roles used by counselors, all responses of the three groups were analyzed

TABLE 5–V

MEDIAN NUMBER OF WORDS PER RESPONSE

Group	Pre-training	Post-training
Immediate feedback	17.4	24.1
Delayed feedback	17.9	19.4
No feedback	15.1	15.4

TABLE 5–VI

TOTAL NUMBER OF AFFECT WORDS USED PER GROUP

Group	Pre-training	Post-training
Immediate feedback (N = 12)	16	90
Delayed feedback (N = 12)	22	97
No feedback (N = 12)	22	27

in terms of their content. Three judges independently agreed beyond chance ($p < .001$) in labeling the content of the responses. Those responses which were not consistent were labeled Unclassifiable. Table 5-VII shows the heavy increase in reflective type responses in both the immediate and delayed feedback groups. While the control group showed gains, it was below the level attained by the two experimental groups. Also noteworthy was that supporting and advice-giving statements were extinguished in both the experimental groups when measured at the time of post-test.

In selecting counselor education procedures, motivational or attitudinal factors are at least important as considerations of method of effectiveness. Therefore, in order to examine some subjective aspects of each group's experience, and especially to seek out any commonalities of response, subjects were given a brief open-ended questionnaire. No attempt was made to quantify the obtained data. The summaries which follow are descriptive and impressionistic.

Immediate Feedback Group. The immediate feedback group quickly adjusted to the earplug and to hearing the experimenter's

TABLE 5–VII

CONTENT ANALYSIS OF PRE- AND POST-TRAINING RESPONSES
IN TOTAL NUMBER PER GROUP

Category	Immediate Feedback Pre	Immediate Feedback Post	Delayed Feedback Pre	Delayed Feedback Post	No Feedback Pre	No Feedback Post
Reflecting	10	62	10	63	10	21
Describing	17	12	14	6	9	14
Advice giving	15	0	22	0	16	10
Supporting	12	0	17	0	12	5
Questioning	12	7	15	12	21	18
Interpreting	7	8	10	6	8	7
Information gathering	11	1	10	6	5	5
Unclassifiable	6	0	7	2	9	10

ratings and pre-planned examples. The majority of subjects stated
they "didn't notice" the earplug after the first session. Being rated
immediately, however, put the subjects "under pressure." Most
felt they had to do well and were disappointed or annoyed when
they did not. As a consequence, they reported trying to listen
more intently to the films and trying out new responses until they
received verification of accurate ones. A common reaction was,
"Knowing what you wanted made it easier." However, some subjects reported they felt they knew what the experimenter was
looking for, but when this was not confirmed and they received
a low rating, they felt frustrated. Three subjects stated they
wanted to quit the experiment at that point. This was in the early
training sessions. Many thought the technique was novel and a
good way to learn in that it was challenging and kept their interest and motivation high. The films themselves were seen as
realistic by all but one of the subjects, who stated that the films
were "corny." The group was split as to whether they would go
through the experience again. Most maintained they did not
know much about the concept of empathy but did feel they
could better respond to people who came to them with problems. As one subject put it, "I got the message pretty quick that
you shouldn't give advice!"

Delayed Feedback Group. Of the three feedback groups, the
delayed feedback group seemed to have the least intense experience. While members of that group claimed they did their best,
they also indicated experiencing minimal pressure to give accurate responses. Feedback was seen as "helpful" rather than motivating. A number of subjects indicated boredom or lack of
interest when they listened to their responses and to the experimenter's ratings during the feedback sessions. This was particularly true after the last two training films. It seems at least a portion of this attitude was related to spending another 15 minutes
of listening after the film was over. All subjects thought the films
to be realistic. As in the immediate feedback group, subjects in
the delayed feedback group did not feel they knew any more
about the concept of empathy, but they had learned how *not* to
respond.

No Feedback Group. The experience of the no feedback
group was one of frustration in knowing they were being rated

but were receiving no results as to their performance. The consensus seemed to be that after the second or third film responses became routine and new ways of responding abandoned. As might be expected, the technique was not seen as a good means of learning, and most subjects would not care to repeat the experiment on a volunteer basis. Interestingly, one-fourth of the subjects in this group felt the films were lacking in realism.

Discussion

The results of the present study show that by giving feedback to subjects they learned the verbal tools of making empathic statements. In the original study, both immediate and delayed feedback groups made significant increases in their level of empathy. Further analysis showed that both groups increased in total affect words and reflective statements. Yet the immediate feedback group showed a significantly higher level of empathy than the delayed feedback group. The immediate feedback group learned to respond more fully, and the empathic quality of their responses was of a higher level. The subjects' level of motivation and concentration seems to be the important factor in the immediate feedback group. Truax and Carkhuff (1967) maintain that one of the keys to the successful use of accurate empathy may well be in the counselor's concentration upon the client. They suggest that such intense concentration on receiving a client's communication automatically achieves several counselor goals. For example, the counselor consciously thinks how the client's conduct, norms, etc., relate to his own value system. Therefore, the counselor is less likely to give evaluative statements to the client. In the present study, both experimental groups greatly reduced the percentage of evaluative statements in their responses. Anecdotal evidence derived from the post-experimental interview lend support to this contention. Subjects in the immediate feedback group reported they felt they had to listen to the film carefully and be alert to the feedback, and they felt pressured to respond accurately because they could hear the experimenter rating them as soon as they commented. The delayed feedback group, while reporting they felt they wanted to do well each time, did not indicate any felt pressure while in the experimental room. The control group which received no feedback indicated frustration in not knowing how well they were progressing, yet being aware they were being rated by the experimenter.

It appears that when subjects are in a position to hear immediate commentary on how well they are performing the task of responding empathically, they are more intent on giving a good performance and maintain an optimal level of anxiety. Consistent with this, Smith (1966) maintains that the more training requires students to attend to people, the more effective they will be in their judgments. Knower (1945) found a correlation of .55 between the ability to perceive feelings and to accurately express those feelings.

Using this technique in an integrated program would assure that subjects trained by the immediate feedback method learn not just cognitive empathic responses but would be able to introject empathic learning. That is, the criticism may be made that subjects learn only verbal responses "parrot fashion" and might not be perceived by "real" clients as being empathic. A multiphased study by Buchheimer, *et al.* (1965) does throw light on this question. These writers found that the hypothesized differences between conceptual and functional empathy were not confirmed. They concluded that this distinction may be artificial or nonexistent.

Another question is posed as to whether the kind of empathic responses taught with the present technique might be more appropriate for one counseling orientation than another. It would seem, for example, that the type of empathic-reflective statements learned are more consistent with a relationship approach rather than a directive or behavior approach. However, if one accepts the well supported contention that the major facilitative variable of successful counseling is empathy, no matter what the therapeutic orientation, then the technique is apropos to any training program. Further empirical research is needed in both this area and in the "live" situation.

The technique of presenting immediate feedback to subjects is an important parameter in empathy training programs. As the present analysis has shown, subjects learn specific as well as general empathic skills. This model of training also permits investigators to explore more specifically other facilitative variables of psychotherapy.

References

Annett, J.: The role of knowledge of results in learning: a survey. In De-Cecco, J. P. (Ed.): *Educational Technology: Reading in Programmed Instruction.* New York, Holt, 1964.

Buchheimer, A., et al.: *Videotapes and Kinescopic Recordings as Situational Test and Laboratory Exercises in Empathy for the Training of Counselors.* Technical report to the U.S. Office of Education, NDEA, Title VII, Research Project No. 7-42-0550-1670. New York, Hunter College, 1965.

Carkhuff, R. R. (Ed.): *The Counselor's Contribution to the Facilitative Processes.* Urbana, Ill., Parkinson, 1967.

Danskin, D. G.: Roles played by counselors in their interviews. *Journal of Counseling Psychology,* 2:22-27, 1955.

Knower, F. H.: Studies in the symbolism of voice and action. V. The use of behavioral tonal symbols as tests of speaking achievement, *Journal of Applied Psychology,* 29:229-235, 1945.

Korner, I. N., and Brown, W. H.: The mechanical third ear, *Journal of Consulting Psychology,* 16:81-84, 1952.

Reddy, W. B.: The effects of immediate and delayed feedback on the learning of empathy. *Journal of Counseling Psychology,* 16:59-62, 1969.

Smith, H. C.: *Sensitivity to People.* New York, McGraw-Hill, 1966.

Truax, C. B.: A scale for the measurement of accurate empathy. *Psychiatric Institute Bulletin.* Wisconsin Psychiatric Institute, University of Wisconsin, 1961, vol. *1*, p. 12.

Truax, C. B., and Carkhuff, R. R.: *Toward Effective Counseling and Psychotherapy: Training and Practice.* Chicago, Aldine, 1967.

Truax, C. B., and Carkhuff, R. R.: Significant developments in psychotherapy research. In Abt, L. E., and Reiss, B. F. (Eds.): *Progress in Clinical Psychology.* New York, Grune & Stratton, 1964.

Truax, C. B., Carkhuff, R. R., and Douds, J.: Toward an integration of the didactic and experiential approaches to training in counseling and psychotherapy. *Journal of Counseling Psychology,* 11:240-47, 1964.

LEARNING THE ART OF INTERVIEWING: A STUDY OF WHAT BEGINNING STUDENTS DO AND THEIR PATTERNS OF CHANGE*

RUTH G. MATARAZZO, JEANNE S. PHILLIPS, ARTHUR N. WIENS, and GEORGE SASLOW

In regard to the teaching of psychotherapy, Rogers (1942) was one of the first writers to publish specific rules for conduct-

* Reprinted in abridged form from *Psychotherapy: Theory, Research and Practice,* 2:49-60, 1965, with permission of the Journal and the authors.

ing an interview, and to categorize the kind of utterances to be used by the therapist (reflection, clarification, etc.). Porter (1950) also provided the student with guidelines for specific kinds of responses to patients. He devised a pre -and post-training questionnaire for evaluating modifications in counselor "attitudes" as revealed in the specific categories of response, utilized by the learner. Wolberg (1954), in his comprehensive volume on psychotherapy, recommends some specific do's and don'ts for the therapist. Ekstein and Wallerstein (1958) have published detailed descriptions of the novice's "problems in learning" (his neurotic defenses which impede learning). Heine, Aldrich, Draper, Meuser, Tippett, and Trosman (1962) described a general program for teaching psychotherapy to senior medical students and attempted to evaluate student learning through the students' self-report on a questionnaire.

Few studies, however, present specific observational measures of the novice interviewer's behavior (rather than his retrospective self-report), or objective measures of how and at what rate his behavior changes with experience and supervision. The present study is the first of a series in which we have been observing and attempting to measure actual novice behaviors, their patterns of change, and the relative effectiveness of different kinds of supervision. This paper presents some measures of directly observed novice interviewer behavior before and after eight weeks of instruction.

Procedure

Six sophomore medical students taking an elective summer clerkship in psychiatry in 1960 were observed before and after their summer's supervised introductory experience in interviewing psychiatric patients. None had previous interviewing experience; all had taken a required two-term (six months) psychiatry course which included lectures and demonstrations of general interviewing methods.

In order to assess their baseline interview behavior prior to being assigned any patients, each of the six students was observed while interviewing the same six patients, in counterbalanced order. These were six patients who had been hospitalized previously on our inpatient psychiatric service (an "open" ward), who earlier had been discharged as having received maximal benefit from treatment, who were judged by two staff members (RGM, JSP) as likely to undergo little change in the ten-week summer clerkship period, and who agreed to take part in the study. These six patients were test patients for pre- and post-instructional measurement of student interviewing behavior and they received no psychotherapy during the ten-week summer clerkship period. They were selected to provide a sample varying in patients' verbal fluency, sex, and type of emotional problem. The students were given no information about the patients other than what they obtained in their own pre- and post-interviews. Written instructions given to each student prior to the interview were: "You are to conduct an interview with the patient, lasting about 35 minutes, in which you should try to get to know the patient and understand his (her) present problem. Do not conduct a review or medical questionnaire, but concentrate largely on the patient's emotional or behavioral problems." The students had no contact with the six patients outside of the experimental interviews.

Each student was then assigned two newly admitted psychiatric inpatients for eight weeks of intensive psychotherapy (psychotherapy patients). The students attended group therapy and all of the administrative and therapeutic conferences of the psychiatric ward which is run as a "therapeutic community" (Saslow and J. D. Matarazzo, 1962). Two psychiatrists each supervised three of the six students, meeting with them as a group two times a week. During these supervisory sessions, each student described his psychotherapy interviews and received suggestions for the tactic and strategy of therapy. Readings in Rogers (1942), Wolberg (1954), and other texts were suggested to the students. In order not to contaminate the research observations, the supervisors were requested not to observe the pre-clerkship "test" interviews, or any student therapy interviews during the course of the summer. They also were not acquainted with the research ratings being made by the investigators. Neither were the students given any feedback regarding their interview behavior by the research observers (RGM, JSP) who continued to observe them while interviewing their assigned psychotherapy patients twice a week over the course of eight weeks. (The data obtained during the observations of the interim, psychotherapy interviews are not included in this paper.)

Subsequently each student again interviewed, in counterbalanced order, the initial six test patients (with whom he had had no contact in the interim. Because of incapacitating non-psychiatric illness (brain tumor), one of these patients had to be replaced with a new patient.

The experimental interviews, both pre- and post-training, were rated on a check list by RGM (and by both RGM and FHK in order to establish reliability). In addition the number of speech units and their duration, interruptions, silence, etc., were recorded by the Chapple Interaction Chronograph (J. D. Matarazzo, Saslow, and R. G. Matarazzo, 1956). For both check list and interaction chronograph a response unit was defined as the total verbal (and gestural) contribution in any one thought unit by either the interviewer or patient. This response unit could be a single word (e.g. "Yes"), or it could be a verbal response containing 20 sentences and requiring five minutes to complete.

The Check List of Therapist "Error" Behavior * involves, first, a rating of the general quality of each therapist as *good, fair,* or *poor.* If the quality rating of a single response unit was either *fair* or *poor,* the rater checked as many of the specific errors as were embodied in the unit. Each therapist response unit was given only one of the three quality ratings (*good, fair,* or *poor*). However, depending upon its length and/or the degree of skill exhibited in it, this same unit, if scored either *fair* or *poor,* could receive one or more errors of focus, one or more errors of role definition, one or more errors of faulty facilitation, and one or more other errors. In practice, however, the typical "fair" or "poor" therapist response unit contained a total of only 1 to 3 errors. The errors seemed to fall into three broad types: I. Errors of Focus; II. Faulty Role Definition—authoritarian or social; III. Faulty Facilitation of Communication; IV. Other errors (two residual

---

* The list of potential errors was developed (by RGM) from books by Rogers (1942) and Wolberg (1954) with the addition of other errors which it was found, empirically, were descriptive of the six students' verbal behavior.

errors which seemed not to fit into any of these categories). Errors of Focus involved such items as pointless questions about physical symptoms or inaccurate reflections. Faulty Role Definition included, for example, the interviewer's giving the patient direct advice, or telling the patient about himself (the student). Faulty Facilitation of Communication included "yes-no" type questions, interruptions, prolonged silence, etc.

In order to obtain a preliminary estimate of the reliability of the check list, two judges (RGM, FHK) independently rated some student interviews for practice and then rated six test interviews while observing through a one-way vision mirror. They compared their ratings for each type of student error at the end of each practice interview, and gradually increased their inter-rater reliability through discussion and agreement on guidelines. After several practice interviews they undertook the six "test" reliability interviews. Their degree of agreement on "test" interviews reached a satisfactory level (i.e. percentage agreements were as follows: errors of focus, 84%; errors of role definition, 93%; errors in facilitation of communication, 88%; and other errors, 96%). That they obtained this measure of agreement is not surprising, since, by this process, the two judges had achieved considerable consensus.

Although psychotherapists will not always agree on what is a "correct" or "incorrect" student response to a patient statement, we believe that the check list presents such common and basic therapist "error" behaviors that most supervisors would be in general agreement as to their poor quality. A primary rule in the use of this check list is that an interviewer statement is always rated *good* unless the rater clearly sees a specific student error to which the patient ordinarily could be expected to respond with relatively unproductive behavior. That is, a *good* statement (a) facilitates further communication from the patient; (b) is focused upon a significant topic; and (c) reflects an appropriately professional and empathic attitude. A *fair* statement (a) may be ineffective in regard to facilitating exploration; (b) may not be focused most effectively but is not entirely therapeutically irrelevant; and (c) nevertheless reflects an appropriate therapist attitude. A statement is scored *poor* only when it would be expected to produce a serious block to communication. In our experiences such poor responses are typically associated with an inappropriate attitude or role definition (social or authoritarian).

Results

Quantity of "Errors"

The *mean* number of errors (sum of types I through IV) made by each student per interview in Series 1 (before instruction and experience) was markedly decreased in Series 2 (after 8 weeks of experience and instruction). The decrease was from a group mean of 56.2 to 25.6 errors. The F-value of this difference is 4.53, significant at the .01 level of confidence. While the students varied greatly among themselves in their initial skill (sigma of 27.9), they were much more homogeneous in their error behavior after eight weeks of experience and training (sigma of 15.2). This, it should be remembered, is despite the fact that there were two different supervisors and that neither of them was aware of the content of the "error" scale. It appears, then, that a certain amount of learning or indoctrination had taken place; that the students had adopted much of the behavior wanted by the supervisors and had tended to abandon their idiosyncratic, initially preferred modes of interaction. Despite the fact that they had become more alike, however, the students tended to retain their relative position in regard to total numbers of errors per student. The Pearson r was .54 for total number of errors made by each student in Series 1 and Series 2 in the 60 interviews during which the patients were constant.

Kind of "Errors"

The type of errors made in Series 1 was markedly different from the type of errors made in Series 2. In Series 1 errors were predominantly in the Facilitation of Communication category (52% were of type III and 32% of type I), whereas in Series 2 they were Errors of Focus (59% were of type I and 26% of type III). In Series 1 the students apparently tended to prevent the patients from communicating freely. In Series 2 they had learned to be better listeners, but still had not learned to focus effectively on significant material as a result of the relatively short eight-week training period. Although many supervisors will not be surprised at this, such demonstrations are conspicuous by their absence in the research literature as shown in a recent review by R. G. Matarazzo, Wiens, and Saslow (1965).

In addition to measurement of individual differences among the students, it is of interest to examine what the individual patients contributed to the interview interaction. In Table 5-VIII it can be seen that there was a tendency for certain patients to elicit consistently more therapist errors than did others ($F = 4.74$, p of .01 for Series 1 and $F = 2.99$, p of .05 for Series 2). Apparently the most difficult (to interview) patient was Ma, a hostile and dominating middle-aged woman diagnosed as an hysteric. While she remained one of the most difficult patients, in terms of number of errors elicited, the students improved considerably in their ability to interview her in Series 2 (mean number of errors decreased from 85 to 31). Inspection of Table 5-VIII indicates that there is a general consistency in patients' ranking on number of errors elicited, although the students improved greatly in their interviews with each of them.

Inspection of the specific items within the four gross categories of errors indicated that during Series 1, the five most common specific student-therapist errors were: interruptions (category III); asking brief-answer questions (III); focusing on irrelevant, nonproductive material (I)—often on medical symptoms in particular (I); and awkwardness, consisting of long speeches, abruptness, long unplanned silences, etc. (III).

Thus, one of the first things a student interviewer must learn

TABLE 5–VIII

NUMBER OF THERAPIST ERRORS ELICITED BY EACH PATIENT

	Patients					F test	P
	Ba	Hu	Ma	Ro	Sch		
Series 1							
Mean	41.2	45.5	85.3	47.5	61.7	4.74	.01
Sigma	26.6	17.8	37.2	18.4	16.1		
Series 2							
Mean	27.7	11.7	31.2	22.8	34.5	2.99	.05
Sigma	13.5	7.5	20.1	15.2	10.5		

is to keep his own impulses in check so that he can listen to the patient. Before training, interruptions, accounted for 19 percent (the largest single category) of errors, but were of rare occurrence in Series 2. Interruptions and asking "yes-no" type questions accounted for 34 percent of all errors in Series 1 and, together with "awkwardness," were the only major errors under "Facilitation of Communication." Focusing on medical symptoms and on generally irrelevant material were the other errors of major importance prior to instruction. After eight weeks, they asked considerably fewer "yes-no" type questions (decrease from 15% to 4% of their error behavior) but tended to substitute an equally poor therapeutic technique, i.e. stating a conclusion or inference and asking the patient if it were correct (increase to 10%).

After weeks of instruction the student had not yet learned to focus on significant material, shown by their relatively great (increase from 11 to 21 percent) tendency to focus on a trivial aspect of a significant topic so that its impact was largely lost (i.e. focus on a significant marital problem but skip superficially over a number of situations in which the partners disagreed rather than extracting from them some of the underlying or recurrent issues; focus on irrelevant aspects of the partner's history or appearance, etc.). The students had, however, ceased to focus excessively on medical complaints. After instruction they increased the percentage (to 8%) of non-contributory statements or questions that neither particularly aided nor impeded the progress of psychotherapy. By Series 2, then, the students had learned a few simple rules about what *not* to do but they had substituted some other poor behaviors, and still often did not know what to listen *for* or what to *do* in regard to responding sensitively to significant cues. It will be remembered that the experimenters had requested the supervisors not to observe any student's interviews (in actuality, for all six students, a total of two intervening psychotherapy interviews was observed). We then realized that the supervisor's only source of information was the students' reporting of their interviews which was necessarily incomplete. Our own subsequent research (R. G. Matarazzo, Wiens, and Saslow, 1965)also suggests that other teaching programs can, indeed, be more effective in improving interviewing skill.

References

Ekstein, R., and Wallerstein, R. S.: *The Teaching and Learning of Psychotherapy*. New York, Basic Books, 1958.

Goldman-Eisler, Frieda: A study of individual differences and of interaction in the behavior of some aspects of language in interviews. *J. Ment. Sci., 100*:177-197, 1952.

Heine, R. W., Aldrich, C. K., Draper, E., Meuser, Mary, Tippett, Jean, and Trosman, H.: *The Student Physician as Psychotherapist*. Chicago, University of Chicago Press, 1962.

Kanfer, F. H.: *Determinants of Social Initiation (Mands) in Dyads*. Paper read at Wisconsin Conference on Exper. Anal. of Soc. Interaction, August, 1963.

Matarazzo, J. D., Saslow, G., and Matarazzo, Ruth G.: The interaction chronograph as an instrument for objective measurement of interaction patterns during interviews. *J. Psychol., 41*:347-367, 1956.

Matarazzo, J. D., Saslow, G., Wiens, A. N., Weitman, M., and Allen, Bernadene V.: Interviewer head nodding and interviewee speech durations. *Psychother., 1*:54-63, 1964.

Matarazzo, J. D., Weitman, M., Saslow, G., and Wiens, A. N.: Interviewer influence on durations of interviewee speech. *J. Verb. Learn and Verb. Behav., 1*:451-458, 1963.

Matarazzo, J. D., Wiens, A. N., and Saslow, G.: Studies of interview speech behavior. In Krasner, L., and Ullman, L. P. (Eds.): *Research in Behavior Modification: New Developments and Their Clinical Implications*. New York, Holt, Rinehart and Winston, 1965.

Matarazzo, J. D., Wiens, A. N., Saslow, G., Allen, Bernadene V., and Weitman, M.: Interviewer mm-hmm and interviewee speech durations. *Psychother., 1*:109-114, 1964.

Matarazzo, Ruth G., Matarazzo, J. D., Saslow, G., and Phillips, Jeanne S.: Psychological test and organismic correlates of interview interaction behavior. *J. Abnorm. Soc. Psychol., 56*:329-338, 1958.

Matarazzo, Ruth G., Wiens, A. N., and Saslow, G.: Experimentation in the teaching and learning of psychotherapy skills. In Gottschalk, L. A., and Auerbach, A. (Eds.): *Methods of Research in Psychotherapy*. New York, Appleton-Century-Crofts, 1965.

Porter, E. H., Jr.: *An Introduction to Therapeutic Counseling*. Boston, Houghton Mifflin, 1950.

Rogers, C. R.: *Counseling and Psychotherapy*. Boston, Houghton-Mifflin, 1942.

Saslow, G., and Matarazzo, J. D.: A technique for studying changes in interview behavior. In Rubinstein, E. A., and Parloff, M. B. (Eds.): *Re-*

search in Psychotherapy. Washington, D.C., American Psychol. Assn., 1939, pp. 124-159.

Saslow, G., and Matarazzo, J. D.: A psychiatric service in a general hospital: a setting for social learning. *Int. J. Soc. Psychiat.*, 8:5-18, 1962.

van der Veen, F.: *The effects of the therapist and the patient on each other's therapeutic behavior early in therapy: a study of the beginning interviews of three patients with each of five therapists.* Paper read at Amer. Psychol. Assn., Philadelphia, August, 1963.

Whitehorn, J. D., and Betz, Barbara J.: Further studies of the doctor as a crucial variable in the outcome of treatment with schizophrenic patients. *Amer. J. Psychiat.*, 117:215-223, 1960.

Wiens, A. N., Saslow, G., and Matarazzo, J. D.: *Interruption Behavior During Interviews.* Submitted for publication.

Wolberg, L. R.: *The Technique of Psychotherapy.* New York, Grune & Stratton, 1954.

EFFECTS OF SHORT-TERM TRAINING UPON ACCURATE EMPATHY AND NON-POSSESSIVE WARMTH*

Charles B. Truax and James L. Lister

During recent years it has become increasingly clear that effective interpersonal skills such as the communication of accurate empathy and nonpossessive warmth lie at the heart of therapeutic endeavors aimed at the changing of people for the better (Truax and Carkhuff, 1967; Truax and Mitchell, 1969). Available research evidence strongly suggests that existing professional personnel in counseling and psychotherapy are inadequately prepared in the interpersonal skills that have been demonstrated to markedly enhance therapeutic effectiveness (Bergin and Solomon, 1963; Carkhuff, 1968; Lister, 1970). Moreover, prior evidence has shown that it is possible to improve significantly the levels of empathy and warmth in students through an experiential-didactic training approach (Truax, Carkhuff, and Douds, 1964). The effectiveness of this approach has been demonstrated in concentrated 100-hour programs with beginning trainees (Carkhuff and Truax, 1965).

The present study was an attempt to determine whether

* Reprinted from *Counselor Education and Supervision*, 10:120-125, 1971, with permission of the American Personnel and Guidance Association and the authors.

significant improvement in accurate empathy and non-possessive warmth for *experienced counselors* could be effected over a 40-hour training period. Specifically, it was hypothesized that counselors already functioning in the field would have the background and experience to enable them to make rapid improvement in the levels of empathy and warmth provided to clients. In addition, it was hypothesized that counselors initially highest on measures of empathy and warmth would change most through training, and that counselors initially lowest on empathy and warmth would show least change.

Procedures

Twelve counselors with at least two years of counseling experience met for a total of approximately 40 hours of training over a two-week period. The counselors included 11 males and 1 female with a median age of 34. Ten counselors held the master's degree, one the Ed.D., and one the Ph.D. Each had completed at least one supervised practicum in counseling.

The training procedures employed have been described in detail in earlier publications (Truax, Carkhuff, and Douds, 1964; Truax and Carkhuff, 1967). The central elements in the training approach can be summarized as (a) a therapeutic context in which the supervisor communicates high levels of empathy, warmth, and genuineness to trainees; (b) a didactic use of research scales for the measurement of empathy, warmth, and genuineness for "shaping" trainees' responses; and (c) a quasi-group-therapy experience designed to aid trainees to achieve an integration of the didactic training with their personal values, goals, and life-styles.

Role-playing interviews with a standard client were made prior to training, during the training and at the end of training. Three 4-minute recorded samples of counselor-client interaction were taken from the middle two-thirds of five interviews across the two-week period. These recorded samples were then coded and rated for levels of empathy and warmth. Judges were trained to apply scales for the ratings of accurate empathy and non-possessive warmth (Truax and Carkhuff, 1967). The rationale and procedures for training judges have been described by Lawlis (1968). Minimum inter- and intra-judge reliabilities of .50 are required for all data analyses, and substantially higher levels of agreement are obtained in most instances, generally averaging above .70 for Ebel (1951) intraclass reliability coefficients (Truax and Carkhuff, 1967, p. 45).

Findings

Analysis of variance for linear and quadratic components of the trends across time were performed on the data. The group as a whole showed significant gains in empathy, and these gains were approximately equivalent for counselors initially high in empathy and those initially low. However, those counselors initially low in accurate empathy ($N = 6$) remained lower than the "highs" at the conclusion of training and at all points throughout the training.

From Tables 5-IX and 5-X it is clear that substantial and statistically significant gains occurred on accurate empathy but that there was no systematic change for levels of warmth across all counselors. Among those initially lowest on warmth ($N = 6$),

TABLE 5–IX

MEAN VALUES FOR ACCURATE EMPATHY AND NON-POSSESSIVE WARMTH ACROSS TWO WEEKS OF TRAINING

	Accurate Empathy			Non-possessive Warmth		
Rating Occasion	*High*	*Low*	*Total*	*High*	*Low*	*Total*
1	3.9	3.4	3.7	3.5	3.0	3.2
2	4.4	3.5	4.0	3.5	3.0	3.2
3	5.2	4.5	4.9	3.0	3.7	3.4
4	5.7	4.4	5.0	3.3	3.2	3.3
5	4.7	4.3	4.5	3.1	3.0	3.0

TABLE 5–X

ANALYSIS OF VARIANCE FOR TREND CHANGES IN LEVELS OF ACCURATE EMPATHY AND NON-POSSESSIVE WARMTH

		Accurate Empathy			Non-possessive Warmth		
Source of Variance	*df*	*High*	*Low*	*Total*	*High*	*Low*	*Total*
Linear change	1	50.40*	74.67*	119.00†	3.69	—	—
Quadratic change	1	3.20	12.50	9.20	—	67.00*	2.09

* $p < .05$.

† $p < .01$.

there was a tendency first to improve but then to decline across time in training. The general decline in warmth observed in those initially highest is more disturbing.

Discussion

The results of this study support the effectiveness of the short-term training program for accurate empathy but not for non-possessive warmth. The mean accurate empathy rating for the combined group ($N = 12$) over the last three points in training is 4.8. This compares favorably with the levels achieved by lay counselors (4.58) and graduate students in clinical and counseling psychology (5.14) at the end of a 100-hour training program (Carkhuff and Truax, 1965) comparable to the abbreviated program studied here. The gains in accurate empathy across the 40 hours of training were significant for the combined group and approximately equal for counselors initially high ($N = 6$) and initially low ($N = 6$) in accurate empathy. This suggests that many practicing counselors, while increasing their levels of accurate empathy through short-term programs, may require an extended training experience to bring them to levels commensurate with those achieved by the initially higher level counselors.

The findings for nonpossessive warmth suggest that the 40-hour training program was ineffective in increasing the levels at which experienced counselors were functioning. While the combined group maintained approximately the same level across the training, those initially high in warmth decreased from a rating of 3.5 to 3.1. Those initially low began at a level of 3.0, rose to 3.7 at the midpoint of training, and dropped again to 3.0 at the completion of training. It could be expected that warmth would respond to training more slowly than empathy. Truax and Carkhuff (1967, p. 316) have observed that "the communication of warmth can be greatly enhanced by training, but to be effective it must be a distinctly human communication completely congruent with the personality of the therapist." It is possible that these counselors' focus on accurate empathy, on which the most rapid gains are possible and hence from which comes the most reinforcement during training, may have detracted somewhat from their spontaneous communication of respect and caring for clients during the training experience. Longitudinal research is necessary to study this question further.

The initial levels of accurate empathy and non-possessive warmth manifested by the experienced counselors in this study provided the opportunity to examine Carkhuff's (1968) hypothesis that traditional graduate training in the helping professions actually reduces the counselor's capacity to provide growth-producing conditions to clients and that there is an increase in this capacity during the years after training. Before training these experienced counselors were functioning at 3.7 and 3.2 on empathy and warmth, respectively. These levels are considerably above those end-of-training levels reported from studies involving "traditional" counselor education programs. Bergin and Solomon (1963) reported a mean accurate empathy rating of approximately 2.5 for the 18 post-internship students in clinical psychology; Melloh (1964) found an average empathy level of 2.46 for 28 NDEA counseling institute enrollees at the completion of their first counseling practicum; and Antenen and Lister (1968) found a mean empathy level of 2.53 for 58 master's degree students at the end of their counseling practicum. These studies used the 9-point Truax (Truax and Carkhuff, 1967), scale for the measurement of accurate empathy. Foulds (1967) studied the end-of-training levels of empathy and warmth of 30 master's-level counselors near the end of their counseling practicum. His study employed the Carkhuff (1969) rating scales. The Carkhuff scale for empathic understanding is a 5-point scale. The Truax scale for the measurement of warmth (designated as "respect" in the Carkhuff scale) involves a 5-point scale. The obtained empathy rating of 1.8 on the 5-point scale converts to approximately 2.4 on the Truax scale. On warmth, the mean rating was also 2.4.

The four studies reviewed above involved students from training programs in which no specific, systematic training was provided in the communication of empathy and respect as employed in this and similar programs (Carkhuff and Truax, 1965; Truax, Carkhuff, and Douds, 1964). Martin (1968) reported research in which training focused more specifically on these conditions. Supervisor ratings made during the last one-third of practicum for 22 experienced and 22 nonexperienced counselors (counselors with less than one-half year of counseling experience) were as follows: experienced counselors—empathy 4.85, warmth 3.33; nonexperienced counselors—empathy 4.89, warmth 3.57. For the purpose of these comparisons, empathy and warmth ratings from Martin's study (1968) were combined for the two experimental groups of experienced (p. 64) and nonexperienced (p. 66) counselors. Martin's results are consistent with those of numerous studies (Truax and Carkhuff, 1967), indicating that higher levels of empathy and warmth are achieved in those programs that make them an explicit focus during training. The levels of empathy and warmth at which the counselors in the present research functioned at the end of their graduate training in counselor training is, of course, not known. The comparison data, however, suggest that they may well have made substantial gains after training and that these gains were accelerated during the short-term training program described here.

References

Antenen, W. W., and Lister, J. L.: *Personality Correlates of Accurate Empathy.* Unpublished manuscript, University of Florida, 1968.

Bergin, A. E., and Solomon, S.: *Personality and Performance Correlates of Empathic Understanding in Psychotherapy.* Paper read at American Psychological Association, Philadelphia, September, 1963.

Carkhuff, R. R.: *Helping and Human Relations: A Primer for Lay and Professional Helpers. Volume II: Research and Practice.* New York, Holt, Rinehart and Winston, 1969.

Carkhuff, R. R.: A "non-traditional" assessment of graduate education in the helping professions. *Counselor Education and Supervision,* 7:252-61, 1968.

Carkhuff, R. R., and Truax, C. B.: Training in counseling and psychotherapy: an evaluation of an integrated didactic and experential approach. *Journal of Consulting Psychology,* 29:333-36, 1965.

Ebel, R. L.: Estimation of reliability ratings. *Psychometrika,* 16:407-24, 1951.

Foulds, M. L.: *An Investigation of the Relationship Between Therapeutic Conditions Offered and a Measure of Self-Actualization.* Unpublished doctoral dissertation, University of Florida, 1967.

Lawlis, G. F.: Current practices in training tape-raters at the Arkansas Rehabilitation Research and Training Center. *Discussion Papers,* University of Arkansas, 1968, vol. 2 (1).

Lister, J. L.: School counseling: for better or for worse? *Canadian Counselor,* 4:33-39, 1970.

Martin, D. G.: *A method of Self-Evaluation for Counselor Education.* U.S.

Department of Health, Education, and Welfare, Office of Education, Bureau of Research, 1968.

Melloh, R. A.: *Accurate Empathy and Counselor Effectiveness.* Unpublished doctoral dissertation, University of Florida, 1964.

Truax, C. B., and Carkhuff, R. R.: *Toward Effective Counseling and Psychotherapy.* Chicago, Aldine, 1967.

Truax, C. B., Carkhuff, R. R., and Douds, J.: Toward an integration of the didactic and experiential approaches to training in counseling and psychotherapy. *Journal of Counseling Psychology,* 11:240-47, 1964.

Truax, C. B., and Mitchell, K. M.: Research on certain therapist interpersonal skills in relation to process and outcome. In Bergin, A. E., and Garfield, S. L. (Eds.): *Handbook of Psychotherapy and Behavior Change: An Empirical Analysis.* New York, John Wiley & Sons, 1969.

CRITICAL VARIABLES IN EFFECTIVE COUNSELOR TRAINING*

ROBERT R. CARKHUFF

From the vast amount of literature on the training of counselors and psychotherapists, three factors, alone and in their various interactions, emerge as critical variables: (*a*) the trainer's level of functioning on interpersonal dimensions related to constructive helpee change; (*b*) the trainee's level of functioning on the relevant dimensions; (*c*) the type of training programs operationalized (Carkhuff, 1968).

Level of Trainer Functioning

Perhaps the most critical variable in effective counselor training is the level at which the counselor-trainer is functioning on those dimensions related to constructive helpee change. In relation to helpee change, research has led to the discernment of what is termed both facilitative and action-oriented interpersonal dimensions (empathy, respect, concreteness, genuineness, self-disclosure, confrontation, immediacy) as the critical ingredients of effective interpersonal processes (Carkhuff, 1968; Carkhuff and Berenson, 1967a). Hopefully, the trainer is not only functioning at high levels of these dimensions but also attempting to impart learnings concerning these dimensions in a systematic manner,

* Reprinted from the *Journal of Counseling Psychology,* 16:238-245, 1969, with permission of the American Psychological Association and the author.

for only then will he integrate the critical sources of learning, the didactic, the experiential, and the modeling. In this regard, it simply makes good sense that, whatever the task, whether it be research or counseling, science or art, the implementer of any training program should fulfill at least the following key conditions: (*a*) he should have demonstrated a level of expertise or excellence in the relevant area; (*b*) he should be experienced in the relevant area.

A number of research projects assessing the effects of training have addressed themselves directly to these questions. While there are many more such projects, they do not provide for systematic assessments which can be employed for comparative purposes. Table 1 summarizes the levels of overall functioning of trainers at the beginning and trainees at the beginning and the end of training when cast in the helping role with adults, and thus establishes the overall effect of training. It should be emphasized that, independent of duration of training, only those programs or those aspects of programs that have made full discharge of all relevant aspects of training as seen by their promulgators are included for consideration. In addition, while changes in trainee level of functioning are noted, only the initial level of trainer functioning is available and similar differentials are not recorded for the trainer. Indeed, it is quite likely that just as in counseling (Kratochvil, Aspy, and Carkhuff, 1967), the direction of change in trainer functioning may be just as critical or more critical than absolute level of functioning.

As can be seen, in all cases where the data are available the trainees move in the direction of their trainers. In one instance, it may be noted, the trainees beginning at an extraordinary low level progress over the course of training to the point where they are even functioning at a level slightly (although not significantly) above their relatively low-functioning trainers (Program V). As can also be seen, in general, the higher functioning trainers tend to invest themselves in the more innovating, shorter term, "lower level" training programs while the lower functioning trainers become involved in longer term, professional graduate programs. Overall, subprofessional and helpee-trainees tend to gain more in their level of functioning over the course of brief

TABLE 5-XI

MEAN LEVELS OF OVERALL FUNCTIONING OF BEGINNING AND ADVANCED TRAINEES AND THEIR TRAINERS

Levels of Professionalization of Program

Levels of functioning	Professional				Intermediate			
	I Clin. (PhD)	II Clin. (PhD)	III Clin. (PhD)	IV Couns. (PhD)	V Rehab. (MA)	VI Guid. (MA)	VII Teacher-counselor (MA)	VIII Beginning psych. (MA)
Beginning of training	2.1 (N = 8)	2.1 (N = 14)		2.1 (N = 10)	1.4 (N = 8)	1.9 (N = 14)	1.7 (N = 8)	1.8 (N = 10)
Advanced state (noted)	2.0 (N = 8) 4th yr.	1.8 (N = 8) 2nd yr.	3.0 (N = 12) 100 hr.	3.0 (N = 10) 3rd yr.	1.8 (N = 8) 2nd yr.	2.8 (N = 14) 50 hr.	2.6 (N = 8) 50 hr.	2.3 (N = 10) 30 hr.
Trainer level	1.9 (N = 9)	1.7 (N = 3)	3.3 (N = 2)	3.6 (N = 3)	1.6 (N = 7)	3.5 (N = 1)	4.0 (N = 1)	3.0 (N = 2)
Trainees' net change	−.1	−.3		.9	.4	.9	.9	.5

Levels of functioning	Subprofessional					Helpee			
	IX Nurs. (nondegree)	X Dorm counsel (nondegree)	XI Commun. volunteer (nondegree) A	B	XII Hosp. attend. (nondegree)	XIII Parent-teacher (racial relations)	XIV Child psychiatric parents (treatment)	XV inpatients (treatment)	XVI inpatients (treatment)
Beginning of training	1.7 (N = 10)	1.8 (N = 12)	1.6 (N = 9,8)	1.5		1.4 (N = 25)	1.5 (N = 10)	1.2 (N = 7)	1.2 (N = 12)
Advanced state (noted)	2.3 (N = 10) 20 hr.	2.7 (N = 12) 20 hr.	2.4 (N = 9,8) 20 hr.	1.9	2.8 (N = 5) 100 hr.	2.6 (N = 25) 20 hr.	2.9 (N = 10) 25 hr.	2.4 (N = 7) 25 hr.	2.6 (N = 12) 30 hr.
Trainer level	3.0 (N = 1)	3.0 (N = 1)	3.1 (N = 1,1)	2.0	3.3 (N = 2)	4.0 (N = 2)	4.5 (N = 1)	3.5 (N = 2)	3.8 (N = 1)
Trainees' net change	.6	.9	.8	.4		1.2	1.4	1.2	1.4

Note: All scores reflect communication level between adults only   Studies from which data were taken are: I: Carkhuff, Kratochvil, and Friel, 1968; II: Carkhuff, Kratochvil, and Friel, 1968; III: Carkhuff and Truax, 1965; IV: Carkhuff and Berenson,
1967b; V: Anthony, 1968; VI: Martin and Carkhuff, 1968; VII: Carkhuff, 1968b; VIII: Carkhuff, Friel, and Kratochvil, 1968;
IX: Kratochvil 1968; X: Berenson, Carkhuff, and Myrus, 1967; XI: Pierce, Carkhuff, and Berenson, 1967; XII: Carkhuff and
1965; VIII; Carkhuff and Banks 1968; XIV: Carkhuff and Bierman, 1968; XVI: Vitalo,

training than professional trainees do over years of training. However, this again is not unqualified. For example, while two of the professional programs assessed demonstrate low final levels of trainee functioning (Programs I and II),* within the professional programs trainees of high level trainers demonstrate highly positive results (Programs III and IV).

The contrasting findings of studies of intermediate, subprofessional, and helpee programs demonstrating significantly positive changes with high-level-functioning counselor-trainers may be summarized as follows: In general, those trainees whose trainers are functioning (a) above minimally facilitative levels (Level 3) and (b) approximately one level above the trainees, demonstrate the most positive changes. In this regard, the fact that the trainers in many of these projects were functioning well above the norms of their membership groups is relevant. In addition to the results of the rehabilitation counselor program (Program V), the fact that one of the trainers in Program XI who was functioning above his trainees but not at minimally facilitative levels elicited some constructive change from his trainees suggests that a trainer who approaches meeting one of these conditions may make a contribution, albeit a limited one, to the growth of his trainees. On the other hand, those trainers who are functioning neither at minimally facilitative levels nor significantly above their trainees have nothing to offer their trainees while those who are functioning at levels lower than their trainees can only promise their trainees no change or deteriorative change.

Overall, the results can be summarized in tabular form in terms of the trainers' levels of functioning, independent of all other considerations, that is, number of trainers or trainees, level of trainees, type and duration of program, etc. As can be seen in Table 5-XII, whether or not the estimates for Programs IV and XII derived from Table 5-XI are employed, there is a very high

---

* The results of assessments of other professional programs are consistent. For example, the transformations of the data of Bergin and Soloman (1963) indicate that the trainees' final level of functioning on only one dimension, empathic understanding, was 1.7. While the necessary data are unavailable, if it could be assumed that the trainees began at 2.1, the modal level of beginning professional trainees, two inferences might be made: (a) that the net change of the trainees would be —.4; (b) that the trainers were functioning at level 1.7 or less.

TABLE 5–XII

MEAN LEVEL OF TRAINER FUNCTIONING AND MEAN LEVEL
OF TRAINEE GAIN

Program	Mean Level of Trainer Functioning	Mean Level of Net Trainee Gain
XIV	4.5	1.4
VII	4.0	.9
XIII	4.0	1.2
XVI	3.8	1.4
X	3.7	.9
IV	3.6	.9
XV	3.5	1.2
VI	3.5	.9
XII	3.3	1.0*
III	3.3	.9*
XI A	3.1	.8
VIII	3.0	.7
IX	3.0	.6
XI B	2.0	.4
I	1.9	−.1
II	1.7	−.3
V	1.6	.4

* Estimated from Table 5–XI.

relationship between trainer's level of functioning and the mean gain in level of functioning of the trainee. Thus, the level of the counselor-trainer's functioning would appear to be the single most critical aspect of effective training.

Some insights into the dynamics of interpersonal functioning may be obtained by viewing the data on the discrimination of counselor functioning by trainers and trainees. Whereas, initially, trainees enter training deviating approximately one level or more from the ratings of experts, just as with communication, the trainees demonstrate movement in the direction of their trainers' levels of discrimination over the course of training. Indeed, a high or accurate level of discrimination (approximately one-half level deviation from experts) by the trainers in the rehabilitation counselor-training program (Anthony, 1968) may account in part for the fact that the trainees were able to go beyond their trainers in level of interpersonal functioning, that is, the trainers can make accurate discriminations concerning the trainees even if they cannot establish as accurate experiential and modeling base for training. Obviously, what is most puzzling is that the trainers function at fairly high levels of discrimination and low levels of communication, a finding that is consistent with those results establishing the independence of discrimination and communication among low-level communicators (Carkhuff, Kratochvil, and Friel, 1968). It appears that many people see but do not act upon what they see with perhaps a socially conditioned dynamic base in not believing what they see or being afraid to act upon what they see. Since the problem is not unlike the insight-action conflict of therapeutic processes the relevant questions might be whether systematic training or psychotherapy or both are the answers for these trainers. At a minimum it must be concluded that those persons functioning at the highest levels behaviorally are not conducting the professional training programs.

Level of Trainee Functioning

The level of trainer functioning cannot be considered independently of level of trainee functioning. The results of Table 1, which are consistent with base-rate data in the field (Carkhuff, 1968, 1969a; Carkhuff and Berenson, 1967a), indicate that, in general, trainees functioning relatively at the highest levels are selected by themselves or the professional programs, whether inadvertently or not. The intermediate-level-program trainees are essentially unselected from those persons in the general public with interests in helping, with at least one program (V) apparently receiving those trainees who are functioning at unusually low levels perhaps reflecting a "left over" nature of this sample, that is, those applicants who are unable to get into the doctoral clinical and counseling programs.

Unfortunately, the results also indicate that, in general, those trainees functioning relatively at the highest levels initially tend to deteriorate over the course of training. With the professional-subprofessional dimension confounded with trainer level of functioning, it can also be seen that the highest level trainees are most often interacting with the lowest level trainers; thus a deterioration effect is to be anticipated. The follow-up studies of Programs I and II provide relevant data. In the longitudinal study of Program I, there were 6 drop-outs by the second year from among the 14 original first-year students. The two highest level functioning students and four of the six functioning above Level 2 terminated or were terminated. Overall, the initial level of functioning of those who ultimately dropped out was approximately 2.2 to approximately 2.0 for those who were to continue in the programs (Carkhuff, Kratochvil, and Friel, 1968). Further, a tentative hypothesis that the best and the worst trainees might be eliminated from traditional programs received no additional support from the results of a follow-up of Program I. From the eight first-year clinical and eight first-year nonclinical trainees, five had dropped out voluntarily by the first semester of the second year; the five drop-outs were five of the six trainees who were functioning above Level 2; overall their comparative mean levels of functioning were approximately 2.3 to approximately 1.9 for those who remained. Another interesting follow-up process study by Holder (1968) revealed that, in addition to level of facilitative functioning, those dropping out tended to be functioning in the more action-oriented direction (masculine), that is, they were trying to *do* something about their clients' problems, while those who remained functioned in a more passively acceptant manner (feminine), a finding consistent with interpretations of Patterson's (1967) review of selection literature. Thus, it appears that the only consistent finding is that the trainees functioning at the highest levels of both facilitative and action-oriented dimensions will be eliminated from traditional programs.

Needless to elaborate, Programs III and IV in which relatively high-level trainees interact with high-level trainers provide a vivid contrast to the results of the other programs. In addition, those trainees in the intermediate, subprofessional, and helpee programs who were functioning initially at low levels tend to demonstrate positive gains over the course of training. Again, in general, these trainees have had the benefit of interacting with high-level trainers. The positive results of the one program (Program V) with trainers functioning at low levels can be accounted for in part by the extraordinarily low initial trainee level of functioning. In effect, these trainees stood to gain by getting back to the average level of functioning of the population at large.

While at first glance, then, initial level of trainee functioning bears no relationship with trainee gain; when it is considered in interaction with trainer level of functioning, a number of critical trends emerge. Perhaps the most significant of these is the intensity of the discrepancy between trainer and trainee level of functioning. In general, where the differential is greatest between trainer and trainee level of functioning the greatest positive or negative change can be expected. A gross summary of a prediction equation for change indicates that, independent of all other variables (including, in particular, duration of training) over the course of training, the amount of trainee change is approximately one-half of the discrepancy between initial trainer and trainee level of functioning. This may be checked by calculations from Table 5-XI.

These findings, of course, have implications for selection. That is, knowing the level of trainer functioning, differential predictions according to level of trainee functioning can be generated. In predictive validity studies (Carkhuff, 1969b; Carkhuff and Banks, 1968; Carkhuff and Bierman, 1968) an index of communication has been found to be the best predictor of future functioning in the helping role: In interaction with a high-level-functioning trainer, trainees functioning initially at relatively high beginning levels (in general around Level 2) (*a*) functioned at the highest final levels and (*b*) gained the most, while those functioning initially at relatively low levels functioned at lower final levels and gained the least. In regard to discrimination there was no relationship between discrimination indexes and functioning in the helping role. Again, in general, trainees move in the direction of their trainers on discrimination. In those instances where the trainers are discriminating at relatively high levels and communicating at low levels, then, this means that the trainees improve in discrimination while not improving in communication.

Type of Training Program

Trainer and trainee levels of functioning, in turn cannot be considered independently of the type of program implemented. Again, the apparent effects of type and duration of program are confounded by the level of functioning of the trainers promulgating these programs. Thus, the professional programs conducted by low-level-functioning counselors are also characterized by the curious blend of psychoanalytic and behavioristic approaches that dominate many academic training centers today. Similarly, Program V, the rehabilitation counselor training program, is dominated by another curious blend of nondirective and trait-and-factor orientations. In each instance it may be said that the programs involved focus upon what might be called secondary dimensions or potential preferred modes of treatment rather than systematically upon those core dimensions for which the greatest support has been received. Similarly, these programs tend to focus exclusively upon the didactic source of learning, even in the case of the client-centered training where, interestingly enough, the emphasis appears to be upon teaching and "shaping" rather than the experiential base of the trainee. All too often, these experiences leave the trainees in a "double-bind" situation where, for example, the effects of modeling counteract those of the trainer's teaching. Finally, concerning the duration of the program, while the negative relationship with trainee change is confounded, the best that can be said is that these programs are wasteful in the time allotted to effect trainee functioning in the helping role.

By contrast, the remaining programs for which there is positive evidence may be considered eclectic programs focusing (*a*) upon core conditions shared by all interview-oriented processes for which there is research support complemented by a consideration of the unique contributions of the various potential preferred models of treatment and (*b*) integrating the different critical sources of learning. The model that has been employed (Carkhuff, 1968; Carkhuff and Berenson, 1967a) means that the counselor-trainer not only offers high levels of facilitative and action-oriented dimensions (thus providing the trainee with the same experiential base as the helpee is to be offered) but also establishes himself as a model for a person who can sensitively share experiences with another as well as act upon these experiences, both within and without the pertinent interpersonal process. In addition, the training process is that much more effective when the trainer is also systematically focusing in his didactic teaching and "shaping" upon the conditions which he is employing in interaction with the trainees. These programs have produced changes on not only the objective measures assessing level of functioning in the helping role but also on expert and self-ratings, the ratings of clients and significant others, and on indexes of the constructive personality change of the trainee. These programs have produced changes significantly greater than training control groups of traditional programs (Berenson, Carkhuff, and Myrus, 1966; Carkhuff, Collingwood, and Renz, 1969; Martin and Carkhuff, 1968) as well as the usual control groups.

Concerning what is taught, there is evidence to indicate that concentration upon the didactic teaching of discrimination results in changes in discrimination only (Carkhuff, Collingwood, and Renz, 1969; Carkhuff, Kratochvil, and Friel, 1968). The direct implication that people functioning at low levels by and large learn only what they are taught, making no generalizations, is further buttressed by the differential findings of Anthony (1968) where he found changes in attitudes toward the physically handicapped in a program emphasizing such changes and Kratochvil (1969) who did not find changes in values in a program placing no stress upon such. The fact that discrimination does not translate itself readily into functioning in the helping role in conjunction with the fact that there is no evidence to relate discrimination to client or patient benefits in any way has implications for a behavioristic approach to training.

While there is empirical as well as experiential evidence to indicate that high-level-functioning people can generalize from one learning experience to another (e.g. from discrimination to communication), the inability of low-level persons to do likewise has implications for training both high- as well as low-functioning persons to do what one wants them to do. If one wants trainees to function effectively in the helping role then they must be given plenty of practice in the helping role. If one wants the trainees to learn to communicate effectively they must be given practice in communication. In particular, in relation to the low-functioning trainees, if one does not do so, they will be functioning at levels commensurate with the clients and patients whom they are treating and thus will have nothing to offer (Pagell, Carkhuff, and Berenson, 1967). Those behaviors which are in fact helpful and those which are not must be reinforced differentially. One must explicitly and systematically teach that which one wishes for them to learn. Again, particularly in relation to the low-functioning trainee, nothing must be left implicit and no indirect effects must be expected in other spheres of the trainee's life or upon other individuals in the trainee's life (Donofrio, 1968). Gradations of practice must be worked up in "shaping" effective behavior. Upon conclusion of training, those changes which have been effected must be further supported. Again, in relation to the low-level trainee, generalization to other behaviors and other situations cannot be expected. The environment and the systems of reinforcements within the environment to which they return must be controlled in order to maintain lasting effects. In particular, for the low-level-functioning trainee the immediate effects of one learning experience will be neutralized by the effects of succeeding experiences (Kratochvil, 1968). Simply stated, while the hope for low-level-functioning trainees is to enable them to function at higher levels; in general, they function in a given role in a manner in which they are trained to function via all of the sources of learning under the control of the trainer. They change only if they are trained to change. Obviously, it is an advantage to begin with higher level functioning trainees but even they can benefit from explicit and systematic programs offered in the context of a facilitative atmosphere.

One alternative, then, is to select relatively high-level-functioning trainees. However, the necessity for high-level-functioning trainers in these instances is imperative. Indeed, under the present professional system and trainers which dominate, trainee losses would be minimized by selecting low-level trainees. Concerning selection, the evidence indicates that the best index of a future criteria is a previous index of that criteria. Thus, in order to predict future functioning in the helping role, one must obtain an index of present functioning in the helping role. In this regard, again, there is no evidence to indicate that discrimination gives an index of anything other than discrimination and unless persons are being trained to discriminate at high levels, as for example, research raters, there is no value to such extended efforts. Even here, however, there is clear-cut evidence to indicate that those persons who are (*a*) functioning at the highest levels interpersonally and (*b*) are most experienced in the relevant interpersonal relations, as for example, counseling and psychotherapy, are the most accurate discriminators or raters (Cannon and Carkhuff, 1969).

In summary, it is apparent that dependent upon the level of functioning of (a) trainers and (b) trainees and (c) the types of programs implemented in training, the effects may run the gamut from severe loss in trainee functioning over years of training to significant gains within months. In this regard, in addition to assessment of facilitative and action-oriented dimensions, means are necessary for assessing the effectiveness with which helpers implement the techniques of potential preferred modes of treatment, as, for example, assessments of how effectively a helper implements a counter-conditioning process or employs and interprets a Strong Vocational Interest Blank (Carkhuff and Berenson, 1967a). Accordingly, programs of both high- and low-level-functioning trainers may focus explicitly upon relevant or extraneous learnings. For example, many, if not most, programs emphasize trainee "statements of positive attitudes toward patients," and indeed eliminate those candidates who do not conform to meeting this expectation, yet the dimension emphasized remains unrelated to indexes of client change or gain. In the same vein, many of the trainees' learnings, whether from high- or low-level-functioning trainers, have been inadvertent. That is, for example, a high-level-functioning trainer may effect constructive trainee changes on dimensions related to helpee change even while emphasizing extraneous learnings; similarly, a low-level trainer may effect deteriorative trainee change while focusing upon very relevant dimensions. The direct implication, then, is that those programs in which high-level-functioning trainers focus explicitly upon dimensions relevant to helpee gains and make systematic employment of all significant sources of learning, including, in particular, modeling, are most effective.

The results have implications not only for the selection of trainers and trainees and the conduct of their training programs but also for treatment. One may, for example, be able to employ the same relevant indexes for assessing the level of functioning of clients. In addition, within treatment the same behavioristic principles that apply to low-level-functioning trainees will apply to low-level-functioning clients. In this regard, explicit teaching and systematic "shaping" and programming through differential reinforcement schedules and control of the environment at least to the point where one can anticipate and similarly program otherwise difficult conditions, particularly those involving people in the environment to which the helpee returns, may constitute a preferred mode of treatment.

References

Anthony, W.: *The Effects of Rehabilitation Counselor Training upon Discrimination, Communication, and Helping Attitudes.* Unpublished doctoral dissertation. State University of New York at Buffalo, 1968.

Berenson, B. G., Carkhuff, R. R., and Myrus. P.: The interpersonal functioning and training of college students. *Journal of Counseling Psychology, 13*:441-446, 1966.

Bergin, A., and Soloman, S.: Personality and performance correlates of empathic understanding in psychotherapy. *American Psychologist, 18*: 393, 1963.

Cannon, J., and Carkhuff, R. R.: *The Effects of Level of Functioning and Experience on Accuracy of Discrimination.* Unpublished manuscript, American International College, 1969.

Carkhuff, R. R.: *Helping and Human Relations: A Primer for Lay and Professional helpers.* New York, Holt, Rinehart and Winston, 1968.

Carkhuff, R. R.: Helper communication as a function of helpee affect and content. *Journal of Counseling Psychology, 16*:126-131, 1969 (a).

Carkhuff, R. R.: The prediction of the effects of teacher-counselor training: the development of communication and discrimination selection indexes. *Counselor Education and Supervision,* 1969 (b).

Carkhuff, R. R., and Banks, G.: *Effects of Human Relations Training on Negro Parents and White Teachers.* Unpublished manuscript, American International College, 1968.

Carkhuff, R. R., and Berenson, B. G.: *Beyond Counseling and Therapy.* New York, Holt, Rinehart and Winston, 1967 (a).

Carkhuff, R. R., and Berenson, B. G.: *Effects or Systematic Training.* Unpublished manuscript, State University of New York at Buffalo, 1967 (b).

Carkhuff, R. R., and Bierman, R.: *Effects of Human Relations Training upon Child Psychiatric Parents in Treatment.* Unpublished manuscript, American International College, 1968.

Carkhuff, R. R., Collingwood, T., and Renz, L.: The prediction of the effects of didactic training in discrimination. *Journal of Clinical Psychology,* 1969.

Carkhuff, R. R., Kratochvil, D., and Friel, T.: The effects of professional training: the communication and discrimination of facilitative conditions. *Journal of Counseling Psychology, 15*:68-74, 1968.

Carkhuff, R. R., and Truax, C. B.: Training in counseling and psycho-therapy: an evaluation of an integrated didactic and experiential approach. *Journal of Consulting Psychology, 29*:333-336, 1965.

Donofrio, D.: *The Effects of Therapist-Offered Conditions upon Parents in Group Therapy and Their Children.* Unpublished doctoral dissertation, State University of New York at Buffalo, 1968.

Holder, B. T.: *A Follow-up Study of the Activity-Passivity and Facilitative Non-Facilitative Dimensions of Continuing and Terminated Graduate Trainees.* Unpublished manuscript, State University of New York at Buffalo, 1968.

Kratochvil, D.: *The Cumulative Effects of Facilitative Conditions upon the Physical, Emotional and Intellectual Functioning of Grammar School Students.* Unpublished doctoral dissertation, State University of New York at Buffalo, 1968.

Kratochvil, D.: Changes in values and interpersonal functioning of nurses in training. *Counselor Education and Supervision,* 1969.

Kratochvil, D., Aspy, D., and Carkhuff, R. R.: The differential effects of absolute level and direction of growth in counselor functioning upon client functioning. *Journal of Clinical Psychology, 23*:216-218, 1967.

Martin J., and Carkhuff, R. R.: The effects of training upon changes in trainee personality and behavior. *Journal of Clinical Psychology, 24*: 109-110, 1968.

Pagell, W., Carkhuff, R. R., and Berenson, B. G.: The predicted differential effects of the level of counselor functioning upon the level of functioning of outpatients. *Journal of Clinical Psychology, 23*:510-512, 1967.

Patterson, C. H.: *The Selection of Counselors.* Paper presented at the Conference on Research Problems in Counseling, Washington University, St. Louis, Missouri, 1967.

Pierce, R., Carkhuff, R. R., and Berenson, B. G.: The differential effects of high and low functioning counselors upon counselors-in-training. *Journal of Clinical Psychology, 23*:212-215, 1967.

Vitalo, R.: Effects of training in interpersonal skills upon psychiatric inpatients. Veterans Administration Hospital, Buffalo, N.Y., and Buffalo State Hospital, 1968.

FOLLOW-UP STUDY ON THE EFFECTS OF INDIVIDUAL SUPERVISION IN GRADUATE SCHOOL TRAINING*

RICHARD M. PIERCE and PAUL G. SCHAUBLE

An earlier study (Pierce and Schauble, 1970) concerning the effects of individual supervision in the graduate school training of counselors found the following results: (*a*) supervisees who

* Reprinted from the *Journal of Counseling Psychology, 18*:186-187, 1971, with permission of the American Psychological Association and the authors.

received supervision from supervisors who themselves were functioning at high levels on the facilitative core dimensions of empathy, positive regard, genuineness, and concreteness grew significantly on these dimensions, (b) supervisees who had supervisors functioning at low levels on these dimensions did not gain, (c) supervisees of the high-level supervisors were functioning significantly better on the core dimensions than the supervisees of the low-level supervisors at the end of the supervision period.

The purpose of the present study was to follow up these results to see if there have been any within group changes and to see if the between group differences were still significant.

The subjects were 14 of the 15 subjects who participated in the earlier research. These original subjects were 13 interns and two advanced practicum students working at a large college counseling center. They were recontacted 9 months after the termination of the previous study and asked to submit a tape of their counseling. Of the 14 who complied 6 were from the high-supervision group and 8 from the low. Nine of these subjects held regular jobs in which counseling constituted a major part of the work, 4 had become advanced interns at the same counseling center, and 1 was unemployed. Arrangements were made for this last subject to see a coached client in a 1 hour counseling interview.

The tapes were then rated by two experienced investigators not connected with the previous study and who did not know the earlier outcomes in regard to specific individuals. They sampled a 3-minute excerpt from the beginning, middle, and end of each counseling tape. Using a Pearson r, their interrater reliabilities were as follows: empathy (.92), positive regard (.89), genuineness (.85), and concreteness (.87).

A Wilcoxan matched-pairs signed-ranks test indicated no significant changes on any of the dimensions involved for the high-supervision group during the 9-month period. In the low-supervision group there were no significant changes on the dimensions of empathy, positive regard, and genuineness, but there was significant positive improvement on the concreteness dimension ($T = 2.5, p < .02$. A Mann-Whitney U was used to analyze the between-group data. The data indicated that the high-supervision group was superior to the low-supervision group on the dimensions of empathy ($U = 10, p < .05$), positive regard ($U = 6, p < .01$), genuineness ($U = 7, p < .02$), and concreteness ($U = 8, p < .02$).

With the exception of concreteness, then, the results indicate that both the high-supervision group and the low-supervision group remained unchanged during the 9-month follow-up period. The results also show that the high-supervision group retained its superiority on all dimensions of the core variables. Why the low group should have gained on the concreteness dimension is difficult to explain. We have no knowledge of the experiences they encountered and the result has no theoretical base. To the extent we can generalize to other populations, however, we can conclude that the higher functioning trainees tend to remain high while the lows tend to remain low.

References

Pierce, R. M., and Schauble, P. G.: Graduate training of facilitative counselors: The effects of individual supervision. *Journal of Counseling Psychology, 17*:210-215, 1970.

COUNSELOR ATTITUDES IN RELATION TO THE THEORETICAL POSITIONS OF THEIR SUPERVISORS *

George D. Demos and Fadil Zuwaylif

A provocative question for counselor educators to ponder deals with the effect that their theoretical positions may have on their counselor trainees. Thus, this investigation attempted to ascertain (*a*) what significant changes in counselor attitudes resulted from an intensive six-week program in counselor training and (*b*) whether the differences, if any were related to the theoretical positions of the counselor supervisors. It has been the feeling of the investigators from considerable personal experience in supervising field workers that it would be extremely difficult for one to take such a completely objective position in supervising

* Reprinted from *Counselor Education and Supervision*, 2:8-13, 1962, with permission of the American Personnel and Guidance Association and the authors.

counselors that his own personal biases would not come through to some degree—even if at an unconscious level (à la Greenspoon effect).

Many supervisors suggest the impossibility of expressing varying positions along the counseling continuum objectively and fairly and, therefore, openly admit a position bias to their trainees and deliberately teach and supervise in this light, sometimes parenthetically stating, "This is where I stand, but it does not necessarily mean that it is the right or best or only position for *you*, but this happens to be my bias, therefore, view my critiques from this frame of reference."

Other supervisors attempt to conceal their own theoretical or philosophical positions so as not to unduly influence the trainee to the point where he is likely to mimic or imitate the counseling procedures or techniques of the supervisor. Supervisors who propound this point of view point out that if one does not do so, he is likely to reinforce *one* approach, namely *his*, to such a degree that the counselors utilize techniques not in line with their personality, background, affinities, etc. Some may suggest, however, that this is not necessarily undesirable, in that a counselor must come to grips with this position sooner or later and it provides him with a frame of reference in which to evaluate new knowledge. He may also reject his supervisor's position at a later date; prime examples being the former students of Carl Rogers who later altered their positions—notably, Bixler, Combs, Haigh, and Porter, to name a few.

All of the supervisors in this study took the former positions. They openly avowed certain theoretical positions, since all believed it impossible to conceal it in dealing with trainees in a close supervisory relationship. It was also felt by the supervisors in this study that the most influential period during the six-week training period would probably take place during the practicum phase rather than the didactic phase of the institute.

In reviewing the literature, considerable research has been accumulated with regard to the "halo-effect" in myriad situations which appear related to this topic; i.e. a counselor is likely to continue or discontinue various counseling leads depending upon the reinforcement given by his supervisor. There have also been several studies dealing with the changes that take place in counselors as a result of a counseling experience such as in the NDEA Counseling Institutes. Giblette (1960), Munger and Johnson (1960), Demos and Zuwaylif (1962), Runkel and Damrin (1962), and Runkel, Hastings and Damrin (1961), to mention only a few, indicate that significant differences do accrue as a result of participation in counselor training institutes. However, there has been little, if any, published research with regard to the specific question regarding the counselor supervisor's theoretical position and its relationship to counselor change.

Method

The NDEA Counseling and Guidance Training Institute took place in the summer of 1960 at the University of Southern California. A relatively homogenous group of 40 secondary school counselors participated in the institute. The institute staff was comprised of five full-time members, three of whom were directly involved in supervisory practicum experiences. The dominant phase of the institute appeared to be the extensive supervised counseling done with secondary school students.

The supervisory staff represented three diverse theoretical positions along the counseling continuum, namely (a) client centered, (b) eclectic, and (c) a more directive clinical point of view. All three of these supervisors were devoted to their positions and had considerable experiences in teaching and supervising counselors prior to the institute. The Porter pre- and post-tests were utilized in measuring counselor movement.

The tests of significance were accomplished by means of analysis of variance. The data for each category were classified by type of response and by supervisor. Total variation between individual scores in each category was broken down into four components: (a) variation between column means, (b) row means, (c) interaction between column and row means, and (d) variation within cells (residual). The estimated variance of the interaction was not significant in relation to the variance within cells. Therefore, the denominator of the F ratio used in testing the significance of the difference between column means and between row means was obtained by pooling the variation of interaction and within cell groups (Croxton and Cowden, 1955).

Results

Significant differences were found for all five categories of the Porter Test on the pre- and post-test administrations. The counselors, as a result of this six-week training program, became significantly less evaluative, less supportive, more understanding, and significantly more interpretive * and less probing. In analyzing the data by type of supervisor, namely client-centered, eclectic, and directive, it was found that the most significant areas of difference were found in the understanding and probing categories (see Table 5-XIV). In these cases the counselors of the client-centered supervisor made the greatest movement in both of these areas. That is, they gave significantly more understanding responses and fewer probing responses at the end of the six-week period than did the counselors of both the eclectic and directive supervisors. The other three scales of the Porter test did not show any significant differences between counselor responses and the theoretical position of the supervisor; however, a trend does seem indicated in all three groups.

TABLE 5-XIII

MEANS OF PRE- AND POST-TESTS OF COUNSELORS FOR FIVE
CATEGORIES OF THE PORTER TEST OF COUNSELOR ATTITUDES
IN RELATION TO TYPE OF SUPERVISOR

Supervisors	Evaluative Pre - Post		Interpretive Pre - Post		Supportive Pre - Post		Probing Pre - Post		Under- standing Pre - Post	
Client-centered N = 17	2.18	.29	.71	1.29	2.29	.71	3.06	1.71	1.76	6.00
Eclectic N = 10	1.50	.40	.50	1.00	2.00	.80	1.80	2.10	4.20	5.70
Directive N = 9	1.56	.00	.33	1.33	2.00	1.22	4.11	2.44	2.00	5.00
Total N = 36[1]		***		**		***		*		***
	1.83	.25	.56	1.22	2.14	.86	2.97	2.00	2.50	5.67

*** Significant at .001 level of confidence.
** Significant at .01 level of confidence.
* Significant at .05 level of confidence.
[1] Forty enrollees participated in the institute, but complete data were compiled on only 36.

* It should be pointed out, however, that many of the responses labeled as "interpretative" by Porter could also be characterized as "reflecting" or "clarification" remarks—counseling leads characteristic of the client-centered counselor. In fact, the term "interpretative" may be more accurately described in many cases as "reflection of feelings,"—at least in terms of the examples given in the Porter tests.

TABLE 5–XIV

F RATIOS FOR VARIANCES BETWEEN COLUMN MEANS AND
ROW MEANS OF COUNSELORS FOR PRE- AND POST-TESTS
OF THE PORTER TEST OF ATTITUDES IN RELATION
TO THE TYPE OF SUPERVISOR

N = 36	Evaluative	Interpretive	Supportive	Probing	Under-standing
Column Means (Pre- and post-tests)	38.68***	8.47**	26.24***	4.63*	41.84***
Row Means (Type of supervisor)	1.23	.46	.19	2.37*	2.55*

*** Significant at .001 level of confidence.
** Significant at .01 level of confidence.
* Significant at .05 level of confidence.

Discussion

The question of whether counselor supervisors influence their trainees in a manner coinciding with their theoretical position seems indicated by these findings. The kinds of responses that the client-centered counselor values to a great degree would undoubtedly fall within the understanding category and the kind of responses that the client-centered counselor would be least likely to positively reinforce would fall within the probing and evaluative areas. In the case of probing, the findings seem to verify this hypothesis. However, it is also noteworthy that the counselors of the so-called directive and eclectic supervisors also move significantly in the same direction as did the counselors of the client-centered supervisor, but not to the same degree.

It would appear then, that the influence of one's supervisor, regardless of his theoretical position, seems to affect the trainees *similarly*—but not to the same degree. It would also appear that the often heard charge that the so-called "directivist" is not really concerned with understanding the client's remarks, but only probes, evaluates, and interprets, would not be a valid statement in view of these findings. We sometimes look at our colleagues who happen to be of a more "directive bent" in counseling to be lacking in warmth, permissiveness, and understanding, and that they view counseling as being essentially advising, teaching, or telling the client—apparently is not warranted. An opportunity to meet counselor educators like Williamson, Rothney, and others also poignantly shows this not to be the case.

Summary

An intensive six-week counseling institute was found to make significant attitudinal changes in counselors. Significant differences were noted on the Porter Attitude Tests. As a group, the counselors moved in the direction of being less evaluative, less supportive, less probing, and more understanding and interpretive. However, when counselor responses were analyzed in terms of the theoretical position of their supervisors, two scales were found to be significant. The counselors of the client-centered supervisor were found to be significantly more understanding in their responses than were both the counselors of the eclectic and directive supervisors. Contrariwise, the counselors of the client-centered supervisor gave significantly fewer probing responses to the test than did the counselors of both the eclectic and directive supervisors. However, the movement made by all of the counselors, despite the theoretical position of the supervisors, was essentially in the same direction. These findings may have special meaning to those counselor educators concerned with the question of indoctrination of their students with their own personal biases. The differences, on the whole, appeared minimal in comparison with the similarities found in the counselor attitudes.

References

Croxton, F. E., and Cowden, D. J.: *Applied General Statistics.* New York, Prentice Hall, 1955, 714-720.

Demos, G. D., and Zuwaylif, F. H.: *Counselor Movement as a Result of an Intensive Six Week Training Program in Counseling.* Unpublished manuscript, San Fernando Valley State College, 1962.

Giblette, J. D.: *Differences Among Above Average, Average and Below Average Secondary School Counselors.* Ph.D. dissertation, Univ. of Penn., 1960. *Diss. Abstracts, 21*:812, 1960.

Munger, P. F., and Johnson, C. H.: Changes in attitudes associated with an NDEA Counseling and Guidance Institute. *Personnel and Guid. J.,* 751-53, 1960.

Porter, E. H.: *An Introduction to Therapeutic Counseling.* Boston, Houghton Mifflin, 1950.

Runkel, P. J., and Damrin, Dora E.: *Summer Guidance Institute Follow-up*

Study, Preliminary Report No. 1 to Participants. Unpublished manuscript, Bureau of Educational Research, College of Education, University of Illinois, Spring, 1960.

Runkel, P. J., Hastings, J. Y., and Damrin, Dora E.: *Changes in Schools Which Do and Do Not Send Staff Members to Training Institutes in Counseling.* Cooperative Research Project No. 939. Urbana, Illinois, Bureau of Educational Research, College of Education, University of Illinois, 1961.

STUDY OF THE USE OF VIDEOTAPE AND AUDIOTAPE AS TECHNIQUES IN COUNSELOR EDUCATION*

GARDNER YENAWINE and DUGALD S. ARBUCKLE

A number of reports, such as Schmidt and Pepinsky (1965), Kagan, Krathwohl, and Miller (1963), Kagan, Krathwohl, Goldberg, Campbell, Schankle, Greenberg, Danish, Resnickoff, Bowes, and Bandy (1967), Ivey, Normington, Miller, Morrill, and Haase (1968), and Poling (1968a, 1968b), have suggested uses for videotape in the education of counselors, the assessment of client-counselor interaction, counselor effectiveness, recall, the acceleration of client progress in counseling, and the study of nonverbal communication. All have been implicitly predicted on the assumption that videotape has a unique advantage for the recording and playback of counseling interviews.

Videotape is not an unfamiliar recording medium in the process of counselor training. Considering the emphasis in counselor education on the study of human behavior, interpersonal relations, group process, and self-appraisal, assumptions regarding important uses of videotape in such training programs have been both natural and compelling. Often counselor educators, the authors included, have used the medium without any attempt to determine the appropriateness or the legitimacy of such assumptions.

This exploratory investigation sought to examine the appropriateness of these assumptions and focused on the uses of audiotape and videotape within the context of the counseling practicum. Proceeding with the desire to clarify advantages and limitations of videotape recording techniques in contrast to audiotape record-

* Reprinted from the *Journal of Counseling Psychology, 18*:1-6, 1971, with permission of the American Psychological Association and the authors.

ing techniques for the purposes of playback and analysis of counseling sessions within the practicum, we specifically asked, What,
if any, distinctions can be made between the *experiences* of two
groups of student counselors in their respective counseling practicums, where, in one practicum, student participants regularly
play back audio reproductions of their counseling interviews for
analysis, while in the other, audiovisual reproductions are utilized? Contrasts were based on the personal reactions, feelings,
and impressions of student counselors to their practicum experiences as reported in writing to the principle investigator immediately following weekly practicum meetings.

Method

Subjects

From the master's degree candidates entering their second
practicum experience in the spring term of academic year 1967-68
at Boston University's Department of Counselor Education, 14
individuals were randomly assigned to two practicum groups. All
students received field work assignments in higher educational
settings. Biographic data on the study sample indicated that the
composition of both groups varied little in relation to medium
age, sex, marital status, mean date of college graduation, undergraduate degree, and previous professional experience. The supervisor in both groups was a postdoctoral student enrolled in a
seminar concerned with the supervision of student counselors.
Although familiar with the medium of videotape as a device for
recording counseling interviews, she had little personal experience
with the medium and only vague knowledge of the authors' specific interests. Two "senior" supervisors, one assigned to each
group, were drawn from the full-time faculty in the Department
of Counselor Education to serve as her consultants. The senior
supervisors occasionally attended practicum meetings throughout
the semester.

Instruments

Our desire to gain insight into the nature and personal meaning of the practicum experience led to the decision to directly

question all participants, including the supervisor. A practicum critique form entitled "Counselor Log" was developed which (*a*) provided a common framework within which all respondents might react to their experience, (*b*) allowed considerable freedom for self-expression (*c*) was suitable for use immediately following the experience itself, and (*d*) was found when used with pilot groups to elicit spontaneous reactions directly or indirectly related to the use of audiotape and videotape without drawing attention to either medium per se. The log underwent three revisions in the process of its development. The final form of the log consisted of the following seven questions:

1. As I reflect on today's meeting, what seemed to be the prevailing issues, ideas, and concerns? How might I describe *my* feelings and reactions to them?

2. From my perspective what seemed to be the feelings and reactions of the *other* individuals in the group toward them?

3. To what extent did our discussions tend to be critical and/or evaluative? How might I describe *my* attitudes, feelings, or reactions to these aspects of our discussion?

4. How might I describe the attitudes, feelings, or reactions of the *other* individuals to these aspects of our discussions?

5. What strikes me as notable about *my* involvement with and relationship to the other individuals in the group?

6. What about *their* involvement with and relationship to me?

7. In retrospect how might I summarize the meaning of today's practicum for me?

Students were requested to complete independently and return a log as soon as possible subsequent to each weekly practicum meeting.

Procedures

Excepting one meeting in which audiotape was used, the students in one group used videotape recordings of their counseling sessions for playback and analysis in their practicum, while the students in the other exclusively used audiotape recordings for the same purpose. In addition, 15-minute segments, early, middle, and late in the second and twelfth meetings of the videotape group were videotaped. A similar procedure was followed on the second and thirteenth meetings of the audiotape group. These videotapes provided an audiovisual record of practicum meetings in progress early and late in the life of both groups. We assumed, and found it to be true, that during their last meetings of the semester, group members found it beneficial to listen to and see themselves interacting at these two points in their experience together. We indeed felt some obligation to provide at least one opportunity for the audiotape group to view themselves on videotape presuming that some members of the group were aware that another group of students with the same supervisor was using the medium regularly. We assumed and found it informative to note the logged reactions of the audiotape group to this isolated experience with the medium of videotape. Although the regular use of videotape recordings in counseling practicum represented an obvious departure from traditional practice, student awareness of existing facilities and equipment made it possible to present the idea in a "matter of fact" manner. Most students in both groups were familiar with the idea of a log or diary report from experiences in other courses in the counselor education program. Student awareness of the videotape facility and the log concept made it possible to implement the study without detailed discussion of its purpose.

At the first meeting of each group, the supervisor was asked and consented to have each student participant choose a partner, decide on a "client" and "counselor" role, and depending on the group, either videotape or audiotape brief role-play situations. These recordings were evaluated during the groups' second meeting. No effort was made beyond that to control events in either group. Our intention in this single case was to immediately expose all participants to the problems, technique, and experience of taping on the assumption that there existed relative degrees of anxiety about this aspect of the practicum experience, and that in light of the requirement, the sooner the issue was dealt with the better.

Subsequent to the experimental period, a detailed examination of the content of all logs was undertaken. Once satisfied with our basic understanding of the data, a variety of comparisons and contrasts were made. From these comparisons the following data categories were established: (*a*) attitudes of practicum participants toward tape-recording their counseling interviews; (*b*) how tape recordings were used by participants in their counseling practicums; (*c*) supervisor observations related to group process during the evaluation of tape-recorded counseling interviews; (*d*) attitudes of practicum participants toward criticism and evaluation of previously recorded counseling interviews.

Results

The requirement to videotape one's counseling interviews was initially perceived as more threatening than the requirement to audiotape. Yet after recording and evaluating role-played interviews in the first two meetings of each group, anxiety about taping among student counselors using videotape fell below the level of anxiety existing among students using audiotape. Following this procedure, but prior to experiencing their first contacts with actual clients, student counselors using videotape reflected in their comments a greater awareness of what a counseling relationship is than did their counterparts using audiotape.

At the beginning of their practicum experience, all participants appeared to share the desire not to "hurt" each other in the process of evaluating each other's tapes. Each group had spokesmen who openly expressed this desire. Even after role-playing together and subsequently evaluating these mock interviews, related fears, that is, of criticizing or being criticized, persisted in the audiotape group. A similar experience in the videotape group reduced these fears beyond recognition. At this point in the semester, the supervisor observed a persisting pattern of "defensiveness" in the interaction among audiotape group members. Conversely she observed a pattern of increasing "openness" in the videotape group which she tentatively related to the confrontations with videotape recordings.

Consistent with this beginning, members of the videotape group began presenting tapes of their own earlier in the semester and presented considerably more tapes than members of the audiotape group. All members of the videotape group presented one tape, two members presented two each, and one member presented three tapes. Contrary to our expectation, counselors in the videotape group who asked permission of clients to videotape made no reference to client resistance. On the other hand, only one member of the audiotape group presented a second tape and two members of the group chose, in contradiction to practicum requirements, not to present any tapes. Throughout the semester, members of the videotape group were openly and frankly critical of themselves and one another, and each consistently perceived this criticism to be constructive. The opposite was found to be true in the audiotape group. Members of the videotape group frequently referred to the "objectivity" they experienced in relationship to the critical analysis of taped interviews, whereas members of the audiotape group did not.

Critical discussion among the audiotape group participants in conjunction with tape listening centered on the dynamics and diagnosis of client problems. Among the videotape group participants, discussion centered on the counselor's role and functioning, with the counselor himself typically assuming a leading role in the discussion. Students in this group reflected in their discussion more awareness of the subtleties or nuances of human interaction and behavior than did students in the audiotape group. In their discussion of critical issues they depended less on the leadership of the supervisor, a finding confirmed by the supervisor herself. Similarly, members of the videotape group found it easier than their counterparts in the audiotape group to grasp the concept that the real "self" of the counselor may be more essential to a productive counseling relationship than the specific techniques a counselor might employ from time to time.

Supervisor and student reactions were found to complement one another on the issue of self-disclosure and self-examination in conjunction with critiques of recorded interviews in the practicum. Beginning with the videotape group's second meeting and continuing throughout the semester, the supervisor observed that the group member presenting a tape on any occasion openly and honestly evaluated his or her performance. The reactions of student participants indicated agreement. She did not observe a similar willingness in members of the audiotape group. She also observed in the videotape group, but not in the audiotape group, the tendency of other group members to respond actively to another individual's self-evaluation. Members of the videotape group were found to anticipate the leadership of the individual presenting a tape, viewing it as the keystone of group process and discussion. In contrast, self-evaluation in the audiotape group was found to be an insignificant aspect of the group's experience.

On the other hand, the supervisor reported that viewing videotapes of counseling interviews week after week in the practicum can become, like television viewing generally, a very passive and uninvolving experience. Again support for this finding was evident in the written reactions of student participants. Group members observed each other as becoming noticeably less interested in the process of tape evaluation when individuals began presenting second tapes for criticism. Having viewed and evaluated what they considered to be a sufficient number of videotapes, group members expressed concern about the difficulty of sustaining interest over a prolonged period in experiences they could not easily identify with at an emotional level. Because considerably fewer audiotapes were presented in the audiotape group, a meaningful between-groups comparison of reactions to tape listening over similar periods could not be made. Based on reactions to tape listening in the audiotape group, and a comparison of reactions following the critique of an audiotape in the videotape group's third meeting and a videotape in their fourth, most participants felt it easier to become emotionally involved in counseling interviews recorded on audiotape.

Reflecting on the final meetings of both groups in which videotaped segments of earlier meetings were reviewed and evaluated, the supervisor expressed the view that such recordings serve as excellent vehicles through which students can re-experience their own group process. Members of the audiotape group were perceived by the supervisor on this occasion as "sharing" an experience for the first time together. In contrast, in the videotape group she viewed the experience more as a culminating one than a beginning, and indicated that group members reflected in their critique an awareness of changes as individuals and as a group from early to late in the semester. She concluded that members of this group had moved faster and farther in their professional growth than their fellow student counselors in the audiotape group.

In this regard, reactions of student participants explicitly indicated strong agreement. Extremely positive reactions resulted from the opportunity to review and evaluate videotaped segments of the two previous meetings. Many participants communicated that it would have been helpful to have had a similar opportunity earlier in the semester. These reactions clearly indicated that all participants perceived their participation in group process as vital to their professional and personal growth. Particularly in the audiotape group, this single exposure to videotape recordings provoked unprecedented openness and honesty, both of which were characteristic in the weekly discussions of the videotape group. On this, more than any other occasion, members of the audiotape group perceived each other as responding positively to critical and evaluative comments.

Conclusions

Before stating our conclusions, it seems appropriate to stress their tentativeness. Although students were randomly assigned to the audiotape group and the videotape group, only 13 were involved, a number not great enough to insure that the sample was representative of the local population. Both the sample size and design features render impossible the assumption of identical composition between groups on basic personality characteristics. Although field work placements of all subjects were in higher educational settings, work requirements and the availability of live clients varied from setting to setting. Thus some subjects found it necessary to record role-playing situations for the purposes of playback and analysis in the practicum setting. Finally, the practicum experiences, and as a consequence, the findings and conclusions of this study, are limited by the personality and professional orientation of the one supervisor who worked consistently with both groups of student counselors.

1. Fear related to self-exposure, having to deal with one's own inadequacies, and being criticized by others provokes resistance among student counselors to the idea of being required

to tape-record their counseling interviews for subsequent playback in the counseling practicum. Due to this reaction and a sense that others share it, student counselors are initially reluctant to criticize the functioning of a fellow counselor.

2. In advance of any experience, anxiety and resistance to taping rises as the known degree of self-exposure inherent in a recording rises. As a result, the idea of videotaping counseling interviews is more threatening than the idea of audiotaping. Poling (1968a) came to a similar conclusion but did not discuss specifically "why" the counselors in his study reacted with more anxiety to the idea of videotaping.

3. In relation to the use of videotape only, once confronted with the procedure through the process of role-playing, anxiety about taping among student counselors yields to enthusiastic acceptance.

4. After the potential for growth is experienced, arising from a critical analysis of one's recorded counseling interviews by self and others in a counseling practicum, motivation to record and present tapes increases. Because this potential is realized more quickly when videotape is used, student counselors using it tend to produce and present recordings with more interest and less delay than do students recording with audiotape.

5. The preceding conclusions imply that due to the relative completeness of the recordings, videotape provides a more objective basis for the evaluation of counselor interviews than audiotape. Consequently, a greater degree of objectivity is achieved in the evaluation of videotaped interviews. Objectivity and relevancy of reactions are positively related to criticism perceived as constructive.

6. Open criticism of one's own counseling or the work of others is basically difficult. In addition, because the "naïve" student counselor tends, perhaps with justification, to doubt the accuracy of his perceptions of the dynamics of a client-counselor relationship, it is safer and more comfortable when evaluating tapes to focus on the missing party, the client, than the counselor who is present and often quite anxious.

However, this avoidance tendency is arrested and reversed the more completely or totally an original interview is recreated. The more clearly perceived the counselor's role becomes, the more that role occupies the interest and concern of practicum members. Similarly, a student counselor's critical response to *his own* performance is influenced positively by the degree to which he is able to relive the original experience. This conclusion is shared by counselor educators in many fields and was a principle assumption underlying the recently completed research program in the use of videotape in counselor education at Michigan State University (Kagan, *et al.*, 1967). Introducing videotape as a substitute or alternate for audiotape for the purposes of recording and playback increases the likelihood that a counselor-centered focus as opposed to a client-centered focus will be maintained in the review and evaluation process. It also increases the likelihood that the student counselor whose tape is being evaluated will assume a leading role in this process. Student counselors who are willing and proceed to take an active role in evaluating their own performance elicit more constructive commentary from their peers.

7. When compared with audiotape, videotape recordings produce on replay more relevant material for review, for example, physical appearances, gesticulations, nonverbal expressions, and environmental conditions. Because these aspects of the total situation are highlighted by the medium itself, practicum groups using videotape are less dependent on the insight and leadership of a supervisor for spotting and examining them. A supervisor working with students who are recording and evaluating videotapes enjoys more flexibility in the way he functions in the practicum.

8. Again because of the relative completeness of the recording, student counselors using videotape are inclined to sense and discuss more quickly the significance of the concept that the counselor's total personality as it manifests itself in relationship with the client is the most essential ingredient in a productive counseling relationship. Expanded discussion of *personal* needs, motives, and values results from this awareness. In contrast, the tendency to limit discussion to theoretical issues, relatively insignificant segments of verbal interaction, client problems, and counselor techniques for dealing with these problems persists

among students evaluating audiotape recordings. This conclusion supports the observations of Demos (1964).

9. Our findings suggest, however, that the relative vividness and completeness of videotape recording does create a problem for student counselors. Because of the completeness of videotape recordings and the resulting specificity of focus, students find it more difficult to become emotionally involved in or identified with the performance of a fellow counselor recorded on videotape. Based on the findings of this investigation we conclude that student counselors at the beginning stages of their professional training identify more easily and completely with counselor roles recorded on audiotape than similar roles recorded on videotape.

To clarify, the problem involves the ability of the counselor to literally project himself emotionally as well as intellectually into the role of the counselor whose tape is being evaluated as distinct from a relatively detached and more purely intellectual involvement. When a recorded interview is being evaluated in a counseling practicum, the difficulty for those not directly involved seems to stem from the ease with which a counselor can personally dissociate himself from events or experiences as these more specifically and totally focus on another. The relative lack of definition in strictly audio reproductions of counseling interviews makes the distinction between self and other less likely.

10. A primary goal of any counselor education program is to improve the student counselor's effectiveness in interpersonal relations. This goal is reflected in the design and nature of any practicum experience with an emphasis on group interaction. Student counselors share this goal and are themselves concerned about the nature and quality of their interaction in the practicum. Our findings indicate that feedback via videotape recordings of practicum meetings is a very appropriate and meaningful springboard to a critical analysis of relationships and interaction.

References

Demos, G. D.: Suggested uses of tape recordings in counseling supervision. *Personnel and Guidance Journal,* 42:704-705, 1964.

Ivey, A. E., Normington, C. J., Miller, C. D., Morrill, W. H., and Haase,

R. F.: Microcounseling and attending behavior: an approach to pre-practicum counselor training. *Journal of Counseling Psychology, 15*(5, Pt. 2), 1968.

Kagan, N., Krathwohl, D. R., and Miller, R.: Stimulated recall in therapy using video tape—A case study. *Journal of Counseling Psychology, 10*: 237-243, 1963.

Kagan, N., Krathwohl, D., Goldberg, A., Campbell, R. J., Schankle, P. G., Greenberg, B. S., Danish, S. J., Resnickoff, A, Bowes, J., and Bandy, S. B.: *Studies in Human Interaction: Interpersonal Process Recall Stimulated by Videotape.* Ann Arbor, Michigan State University, Educational Publication Services, College of Education, 1967.

Poling, E. G.: Video tape recordings in counseling practicum: I. Environmental considerations. *Counselor Education and Supervision,* 7:348-356, 1968 (a).

Poling, E. G.: Video tape recordings in counseling practicum: II. Critique considerations. *Counselor Education and Supervision,* 8:33-38, 1968 (b).

Schmidt, L. D., and Pepinsky, H. B.: Counseling research in 1963. *Journal of Counseling Psychology,* 12:418-428, 1965.

INFLUENCE OF PLAYBACK TECHNIQUES ON COUNSELOR PERFORMANCE*

MARTIN J. MARKEY, RONALD H. FREDRICKSON, RICHARD W. JOHNSON, and MARY ALICE JULIUS

As television playback equipment becomes less expensive and more adaptable to various situations, it is expected that its use as a device for educating counselors will increase. However novel and appealing audio-video playback seems to be, its value in influencing counselor performance needs to be studied.

Audio playback has been widely used for at least 20 years. While audio-video playback is currently gaining increased usage in the education of counselors, little work of an experimental nature has been conducted concerning the relative differences of various playback techniques on counselor performance.

The work of Walz and Johnson (1963), Boyd and Sesnay (1967), and Ivey *et al.* (1968) suggests that audio-video feedback is beneficial for individual assessment, while the research described by Kagan (1967) and Logue, Zenner, and Gohnam (1968) suggests that an initial encounter with audio-video feedback is not always helpful in individual assessment.

---

* Reprinted from *Counselor Education and Supervision,* 9:178-182, 1970, with permission of the American Personnel and Guidance Association and the authors.

Despite these somewhat contradictory and incomplete findings on television recording, the trend is currently in the direction of increased use of audio-video playback techniques in the education of student counselors. It is generally assumed that audio-video playback is an improvement over audio playback in that the former captures nonverbal as well as verbal behavior (Shapiro, 1966).

The purpose of this study was to investigate the relative effectiveness of different methods of playback upon student counselor performance.

Procedure

Thirty-two undergraduate females were assigned to one of four following conditions:

1. *Audio-Video Playback.* Student counselors in this condition received audio-video playback of their initial interviewing performance by means of videotape.

2. *Audio Playback.* Student counselors in this condition received only audio playback of their initial interviewing performance by means of videotape in which the visual material was not presented.

3. *Video Playback.* Student counselors in this condition received only visual feedback of their initial counseling performance by means of videotape in which the audio material of the tape was not played.

4. *No Playback.* Student counselors in this condition received no recorded playback of any nature of their initial interviewing performance.

Following the random assignment of student counselors to the playback conditions, all subjects interviewed a trained client for 20 minutes. Following the initial interviewing session, all student counselors were given a written checklist which described the characteristics of good interviews and characteristics of preferred counselors (Bingham, Moore, and Gustav, 1959; McQuary, 1964). Student counselors were instructed to self-evaluate their interviewing performance according to this checklist. Some of the items on the checklist included:

1. Were you friendly to the client (i.e. smile, gesture, posture, voice)?

2. Did you express an interest in the client or client's problem?

3. Did you express an attitude of respect toward the client?

4. Did you indicate to the client that you were listening to him by posture, gesture, verbal statement?

As the student counselors studied the checklist, the subjects were presented with the playback of their initial interviewing session according to their assigned experimental conditions. Subjects were instructed to observe or listen to the playback of their interviewing behavior and evaluate their behavior according to the checklist. In the condition of no playback, subjects were only instructed to study the checklist and review their interviewing behavior according to the checklist.

Following the experimental conditions, each student counselor immediately participated in a second 20-minute interview with a different trained client. The pre- and post-playback interviews were recorded on audio-video tapes for later evaluation. Eight-minute segments of the 20-minute interviews were selected for evaluation. Three advanced graduate students in counselor education were trained to rate the performance of the student counselors on the following three rating scales: the Nonverbal Behavior Scale developed by the authors based on the findings of Dittman (1962), Dittman, Parloff, and Boomer (1965), Ekman (1964, 1965), and Fretz (1966); Griffen's (1968) Audio-Visual Counseling Scale, and a modified version of the Counselor Evaluation Inventory (Linden, Stone, and Shertzer, 1965).

Results

The analysis of the mean scores on the rating scales did not reveal a main or interaction effect ($p < .05$) depending upon type of playback conditions that each student counselor received. Two-way analysis of variance (client x playback) technique was used. Student counselor performance was not influenced by any difference among the four trained clients. Inter-judge agreement was significant ($p < .01$) on all the rating scales. Kendall's coefficient of concordance, W, was used to determine degree of inter-judge agreement (Siegel, 1956).

Discussion

There are several relevant questions related to apparent lack of playback effect. Even though both verbal and nonverbal scales were used, the instruments were probably too global in structure to identify specific skills for remodeling. The work of Ivey, Normington, Miller, Morrill, and Haase (1968) also supports this contention.

One-time playback may not provide sufficient opportunity for self-observation and behavioral modification. The trained clients appeared to become progressively more at ease as the numbers of interviews progressed.

Initially the student counselors may have been apprehensive. In such cases they may not have lowered their defenses enough to see or hear their playback objectively. In other instances, they may have over-reacted to the audio tapes or, particularly, the videotapes. A number of negative statements such as "I didn't know I looked like *that*," or "My voice is too high pitched," indicated that few students were pleased with their performances. Additional experience with the playback techniques may have reduced such fears and anxieties. Poling (1968) reported similar observations.

Future research might seek to determine the optimal position of the playback in relation to the first interview. Immediate playback seems to permit recapturing of the emotional cues, but perhaps a "cooling off" period is necessary to allow the viewers to see their performance more objectively.

Without supervision, the student counselors may have missed the specific behaviors requiring modification. Experienced supervisors or, possibly, constructive comments by peers may have significantly enhanced the effect of the playback period. The work of McDonald, Allen, and Orme (1966) suggests that audio-video playback has limited value without supervision. In addition, more research is needed to verify these findings with a more representative population of graduate students in counselor education programs.

Although it is reasonable to believe that audio-video review with a supervisor is one of the best methods available for counselor supervision, it is also one of the most expensive and time consuming. Until further research establishes the advantages of audio-video playback over other techniques for various populations, it is premature to consider it to be a panacea for counselor education. This technique would seem to have advantages, but counselor educators planning to use audio-video playback for the education of counselors should be aware of the questions raised in this study.

References

Bingham, W. V. Moore, B. V., and Gustav, H. J.: *How to Interview*, 4th ed. New York, Harper, 1959.

Boyd, H. S., and Sesnay, V. V.: Immediate self-image confrontation and changes in the self-concept. *Journal of Consulting Psychology, 31*:291-94, 1967.

Dittman, A. T.: The relationship between body movement and moods in interviews. *Journal of Consulting Psychology, 26*:480, 1962.

Dittman, A. T., Parloff, M. B., and Boomer, D. S.: Facial and bodily expression: a study in the receptivity of emotional cues. *Psychiatry, 28*: 239-44, 1965.

Ekman, P.: Body position, facial expression and verbal behavior during interviews. *Journal of Abnormal and Social Psychology, 68*:295-01, 1964.

Ekman, P.: Differential communication of affect by head and body cues. *Journal of Personality and Social Psychology, 2*:726-35, 1965.

Fretz, B. R.: Postural movements in a counseling dyad. *Journal of Counseling Psychology, 13*:335-43, 1966.

Griffin, G. G.: Audio-visual counseling scale. *Personnel and Guidance Journal, 46*:690-93, 1968.

Ivey, A., Normington, C. Miller, D., Morrill, W., and Haase, R.: Microcounseling and attending behavior: an approach to prepracticum counselor training. *Journal of Counseling Psychology, Monograph Supplement, 15*:1-12, 1968.

Kagan, N., and Krathwohl, D. R.: *Studies in Human Interaction: Interpersonal Process Recall Stimulated by Videotape.* East Lansing, Michigan, Educational Publishing Services, 1967.

Linden, J. D., Stone, S. C., and Shertzer, B.: Development and evaluation of an inventory for rating counselors. *Personnel and Guidance Journal, 44*:267-76, 1965.

Logue, P. E., Zenner, M., and Gohman, G.: Video-tape role playing in the job interview. *Journal of Counseling Psychology, 15*:436-38, 1968.

McDonald, F. J., Allen, D. W., and Orme, M. E.: *Effect of Self-Evaluation and Social Reinforcement on the Acquisition of a Teaching Behavior.* Paper presented at the American Educational Research Association Convention, February, 1966.

McQuary, J. P.: Preferred counselor characteristics. *Counselor Education and Supervision,* 3:145-48, 1964.

Poling, E. G.: Video tape recordings in counseling practicum: I. Environmental considerations. *Counselor Education and Supervision,* 7:348-56, 1968.

Poling, E. G.: Video tape recordings in counseling practicum: II. Critique considerations. *Counselor Education and Supervision,* 8:33-38, 1968.

Shapiro, J. G.: Agreement between channels of communication in interviews. *Journal of Consulting Psychology,* 30:232-36, 1966.

Siegel, S.: *Non-parametric Statistics.* New York, McGraw-Hill, 1956.

Walz, G. R., and Johnston, J. A.: Counselors look at themselves on videotape. *Journal of Counseling Psychology,* 10:232-36, 1963.

A METHOD OF SELF-EVALUATION FOR COUNSELOR EDUCATION UTILIZING THE MEASUREMENT OF FACILITATIVE CONDITIONS *

DONALD G. MARTIN and GEORGE M. GAZDA

Leaders in the field of counselor education have stressed two main points of concern: (a) the counselor should develop the ability to examine, criticize, and improve upon his own counseling performance; and (b) the counselor should receive immediate and concrete feedback on his performance in order to improve upon it (Boy and Pine, 1966; Carkhuff and Truax, 1965; Dreikurs and Sonstegard, 1966; Hansen, 1965; Hansen and Moore, 1966; Miller and Oetting, 1966; Patterson, 1964; Peters, 1963; Truax, 1965; Truax, Carkhuff, and Douds, 1964).

The need for a method of counselor self-evaluation extends beyond the training program. Customarily, the in-service supervision of counselors is conducted through staff meetings, review of audio- or videotape-recorded counseling sessions and consultation with available counselor educators. There are many instances, however, when counselor supervision is impractical or impossible. In some college and university counseling centers,

* Reprinted from *Counselor Education and Supervision,* 9:87-91, 1970, with permission of the American Personnel and Guidance Association and the authors.

for example, the staff size and counseling load limit supervision, and some elementary and secondary schools, vocational rehabilitation centers, and employment offices are too isolated for consultation and supervision. Thus, self-evaluation is needed to enable counselors to evaluate their own efforts, and such a system should facilitate personal and professional growth.

The present study represents an attempt to answer three questions: (a) can counselors make valid self-evaluations of their counseling performance by means of four selected scales measuring psychotherapeutic interaction between counselor and client?; (b) is self-evaluation by this method a valuable counselor education device?; and (c) do gross personality orientations such as self-concept strength and defensiveness affect a counselor's ability to evaluate his own counseling performance on these scales?

Subjects

A 44-person sample was selected from three counseling practicum classes at the University of Georgia. One subject withdrew, leaving 43 subjects for final analysis. The sample was then divided into two groups: Group I, which used the self-evaluation method: and Group II, which did not. Each member of Group I was matched with a member of Group II on the basis of age, sex, marital status, teaching experience, counseling experience, noneducational experiences, level of training in counseling, and professional affiliation with school counseling or rehabilitation counseling.

Instruments

Four psychotherapeutic interaction scales were employed for evaluation and self-evaluation of counseling performance: nonpossessive warmth (NPW) (Truax, 1962a); accurate empathy (AE) (Truax, 1961); intensity and intimacy of interpersonal contact (IIC) (Truax, 1962); and therapist genuineness or self congruence (GEN) (Truax, 1962c).

Each subject was pretested with the Tennessee Self Concept Scale (TSCS) in order to gain a measure of the subject's self-concept strength and degree of defensiveness.

Procedure

Eight counseling practicum supervisors were given instruction on the nature and use of the scales. The supervisors then proceeded to evaluate an audio training tape consisting of 16 segments drawn from four counseling sessions with both professional and sub-professional counselors. The average reliabilities of these evaluations were computed using the method proposed by Ebel (1951) and were as follows: AE: .88; NPW: .89; GEN: .86; IIC: .90.

In order to facilitate honest responses, each member of the 44-person sample was assigned a code number to be used for identification purposes on all tests and evaluation forms. The subjects were then pretested with the TSCS. Next, the entire sample was given five hours of instruction on the nature and use of the scales. The entire sample was given training sessions in order to minimize the effects of differential treatment between experimental and control subjects.

The subjects were then divided into two groups. Twenty-two subjects were randomly placed in the experimental group (Group I), with the corresponding matched subjects being placed in the control group (Group II).

The counselors of Group I were instructed to evaluate their own counseling immediately after each live counseling session utilizing the four scales. They were instructed to consider the live session as a whole in retrospect.

During the course of the weekly individual supervision meeting, the supervisor evaluated four segments of the tape, each of which was at least four minutes in length. These tape segments were chosen by the supervisor consecutively from beginning to end of the tape and were irregularly spaced. Each of the tape segments was evaluated with each of the four scales (NPW, AE, IIC, and GEN), giving each tape four evaluations per scale or a total of 16 evaluations per tape.

The members of Group II did not self-evaluate their counseling sessions. During the practicum supervision meeting, the supervisors evaluated the Group II tapes according to the procedure used with Group I. The actual tape evaluations were not discussed by the supervisor and the student counselor in either group, and practicum supervision proceeded in the manner normally used by each supervisor. The average number of clients seen was 7.6 for Group I and 7.8 for Group II.

Results

To test the concurrent validity of counselors' self-evaluations on the scales of live counseling sessions, the self-evaluations were compared with supervisors' evaluations of tape recordings of the counseling sessions. The extent of relationship between the two set of evaluations was determined by constructing a contingency table and computing corrected coefficients of Contingency Cc. Results are shown in Table 5-XV.

TABLE 5–XV

CONCURRENT VALIDITY OF SELF-EVALUATIONS/EVALUATIONS
OF THERAPEUTIC INTERACTION

Scale	X^2	df	C_c
NPW	57.67*	4	.620
AE	55.66*	4	.615
IIC	41.68*	1	.628
GEN	100.28*	4	.751

* $p < .001$

To test for the significance of the improvement in offered psychotherapeutic conditions as measured by the scales, a one-tailed Sign Test was employed. The significance of the differences in the amount of gain between Groups I and II was examined by means of the Kolmogorov-Smirnov Two-Sample Test ($K-S^2$). Results are shown in Table 5-XVI.

TABLE 5–XVI

IMPROVEMENT IN EVALUATIONS OF OFFERED
THERAPEUTIC CONDITIONS

	Significance of Improvement in Offered Therapeutic Conditions:* Sign Test		Significance of Difference in Amount of Improvement Between Groups: $K-S^2$ Test		
Scale	Group I	Group II	D	$\bar{X}^2$	df
NPW	.001	.018	.1602	1.09	2
AE	.001	.315	.6298	17.05**	2
IIC	.001	.291	.2102	1.87	2
GEN	.001	.006	.1216	0.63	2

* Obtained directly from a table of probabilities associated with the binomial test·
** $p < .01$

As a sub-hypothesis, the question was raised as to whether the amount of counseling experience on the part of the subject was related to the amount of improvement in ability to offer therapeutic conditions as measured by the scales. For purposes of analysis, Groups I and II were subdivided into two groups each. The experienced counselor groups were composed of subjects with one-half year or more of counseling experience, while the nonexperienced counselor groups were composed of subjects who had no counseling experience beyond practicum. The results were not statistically significant with but one exception. Nonexperienced counselors who self-evaluated their performance on the scales showed significantly ($p < .05$) greater improvement on the Empathy Scale than did nonexperienced counselors who did not self-evaluate.

The relationship between counselor self-concept strength (TSCS: total P subscale), defensiveness (Defensive Position subscale), and self-criticism (SC subscale) and ability to self-evaluate counseling performance was investigated by means of the W-S^2 test. No significant relationship was indicated between these TSCS subscales and accuracy of self-evaluation except on the SC subscale. Counselors who scored high on self-criticism achieved significantly higher ($p < .001$) levels of intensity and intimacy of interpersonal contact with their clients than did low-scoring counselors.

Discussion

The results of this study indicated that counselor self-evaluation of live counseling sessions on the scales had highly significant concurrent validity when compared with supervisor evaluations of the tape-recorded sessions. This would seem to indicate that self-evaluation by this method might be of value not only in counselor education programs but also for counselors who could not obtain field supervision. The effect of the absence of the counselor-supervisor relationship is, of course, not known.

One of the prime objectives of this study was to investigate the value of a counselor education procedure utilizing four psychotherapeutic interaction scales. Results indicate that while the counselors in this study who used these scales for self-evaluation

did make significant gains in their ability to offer high therapeutic conditions, their gains were significantly greater on only
one of the four scales when compared with the counselors who
received traditional counseling practicum training. Counselors
who used the scales for self-evaluation made a significantly
greater gain in their ability to offer higher levels of empathy
(AE) than did counselors who did not self-evaluate.

Attempts to correlate gross personality orientations such as
self-concept strength and defensiveness with accuracy of self-
evaluation were, on the whole, unproductive. Results did indicate, however, that persons who tended to be more self-critical
(self criticism subscale on the TSCS) were significantly more
able to achieve higher levels of intensity and intimacy of interpersonal contact (IIC) with their clients. This would seem understandable in that persons who score high on the SC subscale
tend to more freely admit to test items of a mildly derogatory
nature. A willingness on the part of the counselor to admit such
faults might create a model which would encourage many clients
to talk more freely of their own shortcomings.

References

Boy, A. V., and Pine. G. J.: Strengthening the off-campus practicum. *Counselor Education and Supervision,* 6:40-43, 1966.

Carkhuff, R. R., and Truax, C. B.: Training in counseling and psychotherapy: an evaluation of an integrated didactic and experiential approach. *Journal of Consulting Psychology,* 29:333-36, 1965.

Dreikurs, R., and Sonstegard, M.: A specific approach to practicum supervision. *Counselor Education and Supervision,* 6:18-26, 1966.

Ebel, R. L.: Estimation of the reliability of ratings. *Psychometrica,* 16:407-
24, 1951.

Miller, C. D., and Oetting, E. R.: Students react to supervision. *Counselor
Education and Supervision,* 6:73-74, 1966.

Patterson, C. H.: Supervising students in the counseling practicum. *Journal
of Counseling Psychology,* 11:47-53, 1964.

Peters, H. J., and Hansen, J. C.: Counseling practicum: bases for supervision. *Counselor Education and Supervision,* 2:82-85, 1963.

Truax, C. B.: Therapeutic conditions. *Discussion Papers,* Wisconsin Psychiatric Institute, University of Wisconsin, No. 13, 1961.

Truax, C. B: Intensity and intimacy of interpersonal contact: relationship
between the level of intensity and intimacy offered by the therapist and
the level of patient intrapersonal exploration throughout the course of

psychotherapy. *Research Report No. 56,* Wisconsin Psychiatric Institute, University of Wisconsin, 1962(a).

Truax, C. B.: Intimacy and intensity of interpersonal contact: relationship between intensity and intimacy offered by the therapist and patient-stratifying variables of age, sex, socioeconomic status and degree of chronicity. *Research Report No. 61,* Wisconsin Psychiatric Institute, University of Wisconsin, 1962(b).

Truax, C. B.: A tentative approach to the conceptualization and measurement of intensity and intimacy of interpersonal contact as a variable in psychotherapy. *Discussion Papers,* Wisconsin Psychiatric Institute, University of Wisconsin, No. 25, 1962(c).

Truax, C. B.: *An Approach Toward Training for the Aide-Therapist: Research and Implications.* Address: Symposium on Non-traditional Preparation for Helping Relationships. American Psychological Association Convention, Chicago, September 5, 1965.

Truax, C. B., Carkhuff, R. R., and Douds, J.: Toward an integration of the didactic and experiential approaches to training in counseling and psychotherapy. *Journal of Counseling Psychology, 11:*240-47, 1964.

Chapter 6

INNOVATIVE PROCEDURES IN COUNSELOR
EDUCATION AND SUPERVISION

THE GROWTH OF A particular field may be gauged by the presence or absence of "new thinking." Contributors to the field of counselor education and supervision have not been delinquent in this respect, as they have responded to the need for developing new and modifying old methods of training.

Based on the microteaching approach, Ivey ("Attending Behavior: The Basis of Counseling") discusses the emergence of a promising training strategy, microcounseling. The author's exposition of the technique is focused on one of its constituent parts, attending behavior.

Hardly a recent innovative procedure, role-playing has, nonetheless, enjoyed widespread application in counseling and in the training of counselors for at least a few decades. Because of the popularity of the role-playing strategy, Schwebel's article, "Role-Playing in Counselor Training," is included for the reader's consideration. The author explores the purposes, use, and theoretical basis for role-playing.

Believing that the application rather than the accumulation of knowledge is a more meaningful training objective, Winborn, Hinds, and Stewart ("Instructional Objectives for the Professional Preparation of Counselors") discuss their innovative approach as it relates to counselor training. Although the setting of instructional objectives is not in itself new (Mager, 1962), its application to counselor development represents an innovative conceptualization of the outcome problem; that is, how a counselor educator or supervisor can adequately determine whether a trainee has, in fact, acquired certain skills or accomplished specified training objectives.

Although a step or two removed from actual client contact,

Delaney ("Simulation Techniques in Counselor Education: Proposal of a Unique Approach") explores and justifies the use of simulation techniques in counselor training. The author spells out the underlying objectives and purposes of such an approach and offers a concrete training program utilizing the simulated environment.

The effectiveness and ineffectiveness of counseling has been well documented. The issue of what the counselor *specifically* does to effect certain outcomes has not until recently received proper attention. Wittmer ("An Objective Scale for Content-Analysis of the Counselor's Interview Behavior") describes a content-analysis scale (the Counselor Activity Profile) that can be used to objectively and systematically quantify and profile a counselor's interview behavior. The author defines the scales' 16 categories; indicates how the instrument may be used; and suggests some possibilities for future research endeavors.

As evidenced by the articles in this chapter, traditional approaches to supervision (e.g. supervisor "going over" trainee's tape of a counseling session) have been supplemented by new strategies stimulated by clinical experience and research activity. A major thrust seems to be toward the development of concrete, measurable and readily applied approaches that can be acquired within a relatively short period of time. The readings presented in this chapter by no means exhaust current innovative practices, but do reflect a few of the more promising and potentially far-reaching possibilities.

References

Mager, R. F.: *Preparing Instructional Objectives.* Palo Alto, Fearon, 1962.

Additional References

Chenault, J.: The diary report in counselor education. *Counselor Education and Supervision, 1*:193-198, 1962.

Dilley, J. S.: Rating scale statements: a useful approach to counselor evaluation. *Counselor Education and Supervision, 5*:40-43. 1965.

Dunlop, R. S.: Pre-practicum counselor education: use of simulation program. *Counselor Education and Supervision, 7*:145-146, 1968.

Eisenberg, S., and Delaney, D. J.: Using video simulation of counseling for training counselors. *Journal of Counseling Psychology, 17*:15-19, 1970.

Foreman, M. E.: T-Groups: their implications for counselor supervision and preparation. *Counselor Education and Supervision,* 7:48-53, 1967.

Fraleigh, P. W., and Bucheimer, A.: The use of peer groups in practicum supervision. *Counselor Education and Supervision,* 8:284-288, 1969.

Gysbers, N. C., and Moore, E. J.: Using simulation techniques in the counseling practicum. *Counselor Education and Supervision,* 9:277-284, 1970.

Haase, R. F., and DiMattia, D. J.: The application of the microcounseling paradigm to the training of support personnel in counseling. *Counselor Education and Supervision,* 10:16-22, 1970.

Haseley, L. L., and Peters, H. J.: Practicum: on-campus and off-campus. *Counselor Education and Supervision,* 5:141-147, 1966.

Kagan, N.: Television in counselor supervision—educational tool or toy? In Berger, M. M. (Ed.): *Videotape Techniques in Psychiatric Training and Treatment.* New York, Brunner/Mazel, 1970, pp. 83-92.

Lewis, M. D., and Lewis, J. A.: Counselor education: training for a new alternative. *Personnel and Guidance Journal,* 49:754-758, 1971.

Loughary, J. W., Friesen, D., and Hurse, R.: Autocoun: a computer-based automated counseling simulation system. *Personnel and Guidance Journal,* 45:6-15, 1966.

Mankin, V.: Art in the counseling practicum. *Counselor Education and Supervision,* 10:91-92, 1970.

McLain, E. W.: A program for increasing counselor self understanding. *Counselor Education and Supervision,* 8:296-302, 1969.

Meek, C. R., and Parker, A. W.: Introductory counseling course: use of practicum students. *Counselor Education and Supervision,* 5:154-158, 1966.

Miller, C. D., Morrill, W. H., and Uhlemann, M. R.: Microcounseling: experimental study of prepracticum training in communicating test results. *Counselor Education and Supervision,* 9:171-177, 1970.

Mills, D. H.: The use of fantasy and imagery in the training of counselors: the cognitive trap in graduate education. *Counselor Education and Supervision,* 10:188-191, 1971.

Mitchell, D. W.: *Interactional Analysis and the Counseling Interview.* Western Kentucky University, 1971.

Perrone, P. A., and Sanborn, M. P.: Early observation: an apprenticeship approach to counselor education. *Counselor Education and Supervision,* 6:63-68, 1966.

Reddy, W. B.: Sensitivity training as an integral phase of counselor education. *Counselor Education and Supervision,* 9:110-115, 1970.

Rogers, C. R.: A revolutionary program for graduate education. In Rogers, C. R.: *Freedom to Learn.* Columbus, Ohio, Merrill, 1969.

Seligman, M.: *The Use of the Critical Incident Technique in Counselor*

Education and Supervision. Unpublished manuscript, University of Pittsburgh, 1971.

Sorenson, G.: Laboratory experiences: counseling classes. *Counselor Education and Supervision, 5*:148-153, 1966.

Thoresen, C. E.: The systems approach and counselor education: basic features and implications. *Counselor Education and Supervision, 9*:3-17, 1969.

Turner, J. A., and Lair, C. V.: The use of video tape in teaching and evaluating training of individual testing. *Journal of Clinical Psychology, 25*: 218-221, 1969.

ATTENDING BEHAVIOR: THE BASIS OF COUNSELING *

ALLEN E. IVEY

How does one person have an impact upon another? This is the question with which we began in our search to identify the developmental skills of counseling. In initial exploratory work, videotapes were made of experienced counselors as they talked with students. In looking at these tapes, we sought to discover common elements of counselor behavior. What characteristics seemed to be present in the behavior of a number of experienced counselors?

Counselor Attentiveness

We found a number of characteristics representing a "good" counselor. For example, experienced counselors appeared to be relaxed physically, with natural movements and gestures. Experienced counselors maintained an appropriate amount of eye contact with the students. Experienced counselors "followed" what the student was saying, in that they tended to stay with topics introduced by the student, rather than jumping from subject to subject. In short, the experienced counselors were attentive to the subject with whom they were talking. This attentiveness on the part of the counselor was helping the counselor to learn about the student and was also communicating an attitude of interest to the student. Attending behavior, as we labeled this complex of behaviors, appeared to be a powerful tool, having the poten-

* Reprinted from *The School Counselor, 18*:117-120, 1970, with permission of the American Personnel and Guidance Association and the author.

tial for both contributing to the self-respect and security of the student and serving as a reinforcer and facilitator of communication.

B. F. Skinner, in *Science and Human Behavior* (1953), has discussed concepts of attention: "The attention of people is reinforcing because it is a necessary condition for other reinforcements from them. In general, only people who are attending to us reinforce our behavior. The attention of someone who is particularly likely to supply reinforcement—a parent, a teacher, or a loved one—is an especially good generalized reinforcer and sets up especially strong attention-getting behavior" (p. 78).

Teaching Attending Behavior

We wanted to know if we could "teach" attending behavior to another person, and so we called our office secretary, Mary, to where we were working, and asked her to interview a volunteer student. Their session was videotaped, and then Mary was given verbal instructions on how to attend to another person. She was requested to (a) find a comfortable, relaxed posture, in order to be more free to listen to the other person; (b) use eye contact, focus upon the other person, and communicate attentiveness; and (c) to "follow" what the other person was saying, by taking cues from the other person, and staying with the topics that were introduced. After receiving these instructions, viewing a videotape of an experienced counselor, and reviewing her initial tape, Mary again talked with the volunteer student, and the change in her behavior in the desired direction was dramatic. Further, this change in behavior generalized to other interpersonal situations. Mary came in following the weekend and indicated, full of enthusiasm, that attending behavior had been useful in many social situations as well. She said, "I went home and paid attention to my husband and he paid more attention to me, and I paid more attention to him. . . ."

We felt that the teaching of attending behavior might indeed be feasible, and we began work on the following: (a) the development of a set of video "modeling" tapes illustrating both high and low degrees of counselor attending; (b) writing a manual describing attending behavior; (c) rating scales for the measurement of attending behavior; and (d) semantic differential forms for student evaluation of counselors. After preliminary work with these materials, a research study was designed and carried out, in which residence hall counselors were trained in attending behavior (Ivey, Normington, Miller, Morrill, and Haase, 1968).

Microcounseling

Before describing the results of the research, it may be helpful to point out the method of teaching attending behavior. We used "microcounseling" which is a video method of training counselors in the basic skills of counseling in a short period of time. Modeled after the microteaching research of Dwight Allen (1967) of the University of Massachusetts, microcounseling is a scaled-down sample of counseling in which beginning counselors talk with volunteer "clients" during brief five-minute sessions that are video recorded. Microcounseling provides an opportunity for practice of counseling without endangering clients.

Research Results

Data from this study were analyzed and showed that (a) attending behavior can be taught via the use of the materials and procedures that have been developed; and (b) students rated counselors trained in attending behavior more positively than they rated counselors who did not receive such training.

Students who went through attending behavior training were enthusiastic about their experience and felt considerably more comfortable about their counseling competence. It seems clear that the relatively simple concept of attending is an important precursor to training counselors in more complex skills of interpersonal interaction.

Discussion

We feel we have focused upon what is a basic dimension of counselor behavior, relevant to all areas of counseling, whether it be test interpretation, vocational planning, consideration of personal problems, etc. We see attending behavior on the part of the counselor as being essential to any counselor-client interaction and, indeed, as having far broader application also.

For instance, attending behavior is vital to student-teacher interaction. A faculty member talked to a group of students who had been trained in attending behavior. The faculty member was not aware that the students had been instructed to be inattentive initially, and then to begin to attend and cease to attend on cue. There was a dramatic improvement in quality of teaching during the period of student attentiveness. It seems that by attending, students can markedly influence the quality of instruction being provided to them! Here, then, is one way attending behavior can be applied outside the counseling setting.

We have considered the dimension of attending behavior in a number of frameworks. For example, reflection of feeling is considered a case in which the counselor *selectively attends* to a certain emotional dimension of client interaction. In reflection the counselor attends to feeling aspects of the interview, rather than to objective content. Nondirective summarization falls in this same category, and our research suggests that teaching counselors to attend to important dimensions when they summarize client statements is vital. More recent research has explored interpretation of tests (Miller, Morrill, and Uhlemann, in press) and dimensions of teaching two people how to talk to one another more effectively (Higgins, Ivey, and Uhlemann, in press).

Although still an innovation, microcounseling has been well implemented in a variety of practical settings. These methods have been tried and found useful not only in counselor training, but also in instructing teachers basics in counseling skills, businessmen in interviewing skills, and medical students in diagnostic methods.

Some practical applications for the school counselor include using the methods and concepts of microcounseling and attending behavior for in-service training, consultation with teachers who want to improve their relationship skills with students, and even direct training of students in listening skills. These ideas and extensions into new dimensions have proven to be useful adjuncts to the role of the school counselor and provide him with a method through which counseling skills and concepts can be employed more fully in the schools.

This brief paper has been an effort to describe our recent work in the use of videotape to teach counselors more rapidly and effectively. We like to think the method of teaching attending behavior that we term "microcounseling" is a useful technique in itself. It is hoped that this brief description of some of the thinking underlying our research will stimulate further inquiry and innovative use of television equipment.

References

Allen, D. W. (Ed.): *Microteaching: A Description.* Stanford, California, Stanford Teacher Education Program, 1967.

Higgins, W. H., Ivey, A. E., and Uhlemann, M. R.: Media therapy: a programmed approach to teaching behavioral skills. *Journal of Counseling Psychology,* in press.

Ivey, A. E., Normington, C. J. Miller, C. D., Morrill, W. H., and Haase, R. F.: Microcounseling and attending behavior: an approach to prepracticum counselor training. *Journal of Counseling Psychology,* 15 (Pt. 2): 1-12, 1968.

Miller, C. D., Morrill, W. H., and Uhlemann, M. R.: Microcounseling: an experimental study of pre-practicum training in communicating test results. *Counselor Education and Supervision,* in press.

Skinner, B. F.: *Science and Human Behavior.* New York, Macmillan, 1953.

ROLE-PLAYING IN COUNSELOR TRAINING*

MILTON SCHWEBEL

The lecture was over. The class was dismissed. Students started leaving the room, their loose-leaf books thick with notes on the laws of learning. One bright young lad came up to the instructor. "Say, Prof," he asked, "if the laws of learning are so good, why don't *you* practice them?"

Maybe this is the way it began; maybe not. No matter how it started, many teachers are now reexamining their methods, and some are testing them out experimentally. One product of this reexamination is the use of role-playing in counselor-training.

Role-playing is the process of acting the part of a real or imagined person. The role-player identifies with the person, assuming his attitudes and characteristic modes of behavior. This paper discusses role-playing in the interview relationship; hence the roles are those of counselor and of client.

* Reprinted from *Personnel and Guidance Journal,* 32:196-201, 1953, with permission of the American Personnel and Guidance Association and the author.

Role-playing has almost the same allure for students as the motion picture, although the two serve some very different purposes. It, too, evokes "oohs" and "aahs." But its interest-inciting value for the learning process is secondary to its other purposes, which are discussed below.

1. Role-playing gives the student counselor an opportunity to come face to face with a client early in his training. In fact, he can start this process in the early weeks of his first course in guidance. Operating in the protected environment of the classroom he can afford to make mistakes; for here he is counseling a student client who is relatively invulnerable to damage from inept counseling, and he is under constant supervision by the instructor and the other students. Thus, the student counselor can start from the first days of his professional training the lengthy process of learning to be comfortable and non-defensive in his relationship with a client.

A high percentage of students in the guidance field are in teaching, which for many of them has become synonymous with the dissemination of information. Even after much book-learning about counseling, even after discussion and observation, they tend to revert to traditional teaching methods—lecturing, preaching, dominating—when they face a client. With utmost sincerity, some want so much to help their client that they feel compelled to provide answers to all problems. They have equated "helping" with giving answers. The utilization of role-playing even in their first courses enables the supervised period of relearning to extend through their entire training period.

Role-playing is used even in the first or second meeting of a first course in guidance and counseling. For example, in an early discussion on student problems and the need for guidance services, a student will refer to "incorrigible pupils" who are intent upon making life difficult for teachers. Others in class will take issue with this assertion. The instructor offers to role-play the "incorrigible pupil" and asks the class member to role-play himself in conference with the pupil. The interview proceeds:

Pupil: You told me to see you this period. Well, here I am.
Counselor: I want to help you.
Pupil: What kind of help?

Counselor: I want to get you to change the way you're behaving in class.

Pupil: What's wrong with the way I'm behaving?

Counselor: You're making it hard for the teachers.

Pupil: They make it hard for me. They don't care about me.

Counselor: Your attitude won't help you. For your own good you'd better change.

The instructor will terminate the role-playing and will ask for reactions. There is general agreement that the student-counselor may be role-playing a policeman, but not a counselor, and that his attitude has been conducive to the reinforcement of "incorrigibility."

2. Role-playing gives the student the experience of being a client. The psychoanalyst experiences a personal analysis as part of his training. We have not reached the point of including the undergoing of counseling as part of the experience of the counselor-trainee. Playing the client's role is an inadequate substitute for analysis, psychotherapy, or counseling, but the simulated experience seems to be more productive than other learning devices in achieving a sense of the client's position. Some students have reported learning more from enacting this role than from acting as the counselor. One said, "What a contrast! I felt my Irish worked up by the first counselor who seemed to be trying to force me to say that my trouble was that I didn't study enough; and then with the second counselor I felt free to look at myself. I didn't feel put on a spot." For this person, this experience was more convincing evidence of the effect of pressuring a client, than the words of an "expert" or even the report of other students in discussion.

3. Role-playing offers the student experience in developing a critical eye for the counseling relationship, especially for the feelings of the client. By focusing on feelings, he learns to analyze *his* impact on the client. Role-playing helps to develop early in the student counselor's training the habit of self-criticism, of self-appraisal, one of the marks of the professional worker in human relations. Thus, when an interview fails, he does not necessarily attribute it to the client's lack of motivation, or unreadiness for counseling, or rigidity of personality. He may see that his own

defensiveness against implied criticism by the client, or his own subtle insistence on injecting his own values doomed the relationship.

4. Role-playing compels students to face reality. They cannot hide behind a façade of intellectualization. For example, they are discussing how you help an individual accept negative information, such as "Your boy's IQ is low, and his average is 'C' even if you do want him to study medicine." There is a clash of ideas, and people begin to defend their position. The instructor suggests, "Let's try out your differing points of view. Let's role-play them and observe how the client reacts. Make your judgments not on how you think the clients *should* react, but on how they actually *do* react." All agree that the realities of the situation must be faced and that the counselor's responsibility is to present these realities to the parent who wants her scholastically mediocre son to become a physician. "Lay the cards on the table whether they like it or not, that's your duty," says one student insistently. When he attempts to role-play the counselor, the role-playing parent becomes defensive and fights back. Class members ask the student counselor, "What were you angry about? Why was it so important to *you* to harp on the boy's negative qualities?" The insistence of this student counselor who might have gone on *ad nauseam* became rather thoroughly dissipated during the discussion.

Issues in counseling become clouded by generalizations. To say that Rogers says this and Williamson that about a problem in counseling is not so helpful to the counselor trainee as to see theory concretized in a counseling situation. The student who adheres dogmatically to a counseling doctrine, refusing even to examine another, becomes more humble when compelled in the free marketplace of ideas to test out his theory with a concrete problem in counseling.

5. Role-playing is a useful device for the teaching of psychodynamics. The phenomenon of unconscious motivation—or at least of motivation at a low level of awareness—can be observed in the behavior of both counselor and client. To illustrate, a 14-year-old boy tells his school counselor of his job as usher in a movie theater where he works until midnight. Believing that the

boy was just applying for the job, the counselor tells him he would not be able to get it because of his age. The boy says he has been working two weeks. The counselor responds that she will have to phone the boy's parents. A verbal duel ensues in which the boy tries to protect himself, the employer, and his parents, and the counselor attempts to stand for "law and order." During discussion the student counselor claims that he did this to protect the boy. Then he agrees that he was "trying to protect my own neck." Finally, under the pressure of class discussion and a played-back recording, he admits that he was angry and was striking back. Here was the underlying motive.

Two adaptations of role-playing are helpful in stressing dynamics. First is the "asides" or "strange interlude" interview in which both counselor and client speak of their inner nonverbalized feelings and thoughts after their regular responses are made. The usual role-playing interview reveals the thoughts and feelings that the client is prepared to express and those that are implicit in his behavior; it reveals even less about the role-playing counselor. The "asides" method, however, taps those feelings whose expression is inhibited by the counseling situation itself (fear of expressing socially disapproved behavior) and especially those that are generated by the inept counselor (hostility toward the counselor).

One student counselor who was genuinely interested in developing good rapport advocated a deliberate delay in starting an interview as a means of preparing and relaxing the client. The role-playing proceeded as follows:

Client (aside, as he knocks hesitantly on open door of counselor's office): Am I supposed to knock or just walk in?

Counselor: Please come in.

Counselor (aside): He looks nervous—doesn't know what to do.

Client: I have an appointment for now.

Client (aside): I don't know what I'm supposed to say to him. Don't even know if he's the kind of guy I can talk to about this.

Counselor: Have a seat and make yourself comfortable. I'll be with you in a minute.

Counselor (aside): Maybe this will relax him and make him ripe for counseling.

Client: Thank you.

Client (aside as counselor examines papers on desk): Maybe he's too busy to see me . . . What's he looking through . . . I'll bet it's about me . . . How did he get wind about it? . . . What'll I tell him (as another minute passes) maybe nothing . . . What does he think I am, keeping me waiting all the time. I'd like to tell him off.

Counselor: How can I be of help to you?

Counselor (aside): That's a good opening. Let's see where he picks up.

Client: I don't know.

Client (aside): Let him sweat—I wouldn't tell him anything.

Counselor (aside): What's eating him, I wonder.

The class concluded that in some instances, at least, a deliberate delay like this causes frustration and undermines rapport. Perhaps more important, students commented on a new awareness of the force of unexpressed feelings in the interview relationship.

A second adaptation of role-playing is the content-free interview (Thompson and Bradway, 1950) in which numbers only are used as statements to develop the counselors sensitivity to feeling in the intonation of voice and facial expression and bodily reaction. The student counselor receives the client by some combination of numbers, e.g. 4–6–8–10 (perhaps, "won't you come in?"); the client might respond "94," (perhaps, "thank you"). This role-playing demonstrates dramatically that the content of responses is usually no more important and frequently much less significant, than the feeling tone associated with the response, that, for instance, two counselors can use the same words in informing parents that their child is mentally retarded, one of them arousing the antagonism of the parents, the other the cooperation.

These two kinds of role-playing, like others, have value for the student observer-supervisors as well as for the participants.

Use of Role-Playing

These are the purposes for role-playing. Now for some methods of introducing and using it. These methods are used in a variety of graduate courses in guidance and counseling, learner-centered courses in which no formal lecture is given. The primary techniques are case discussions, role-playing demonstrations and evaluations of the role-playing. Frequently the case discussions are prompted by discussion of psychological tests, school problems, social problems, etc. The instructor leads discussion, raises questions, provides information, clarifies feelings, and interprets behavior.

Role-playing excites the class, but it also threatens. For who will do the interviewing? Is it early in the semester; the class has not yet achieved that sense of groupness and common purpose that comes in time. Who will allow himself to become a target? This dilemma is avoided by engaging in group role-playing. The class is discussing an issue in a case: a young man who has impregnated his girlfriend comes to his counselor perplexed. The class is perplexed; many suggestions are made. The instructor says, "Look, let's try these ideas. I'll be the young man. You all be the counselor." Within a few minutes almost everyone is participating. Counselor statements are made, followed by client statements. After a time the class stops to take note of what the counselor statements have evoked from the client in the way of feeling and verbalization, in the way of rapport.

In this way the habit of role-playing begins. After several ventures of this kind, students freely volunteer to play a single counselor or client.

Another technique for reducing threat and for widening participation is by dividing the class into groups of four or five. The groups engage in interviewing and evaluating, usually on a role-rotating basis. These groups bring reactions and questions when the full class reconvenes, and sometimes they contribute a role-playing interview to the class. Still another plan for lending security to the students is to have two persons playing the counselor's role simultaneously (Haigh and Kell, 1950).

The instructor uses his judgment as to when to interrupt an interview. If it is going well, he will allow it to be concluded by the role-players. If the counselor is stalled, the class will come to his aid, determining the reason for his difficulty. Then the counselor will be encouraged to continue.

While the criticism is not easy to handle, the role-playing counselors are helped by the attitude of the class that the players represent them in a joint venture, and by the instructor's care in offering support when needed. He will interpret their fear of criticism and of not showing up well, especially before the person who will turn in a grade for them at the semester's end. He will

assure them that inexpert counseling is the norm and is anticipated in a course designed to improve counseling.

Role-playing has its flaws. Some students are so guarded
about themselves (perhaps so unimaginative about the feelings
of others) as to make poor clients; a few others allow themselves
to be carried into anxiety-provoking areas in their own life history. The instructor needs to be alert for this, although it seems
not to be a great hazard, for those who reveal themselves appear
to find satisfaction in the process. McClelland (1951) has devised a scale to measure role-playing ability. The results of his
study are "suggestive" of the scale's validity.

Some of the flaws attributed to role-playing have been exaggerated. Surely role-playing before a class does make one nervous and fearful. But counselors are sometimes tense, nervous, and
fearful in real life counseling, and here the students have a chance
to see the effects of their nervousness and fear both on *their* own
behavior and on the *client*. Another criticism is that the role-
playing client is not predictable; but, alas! that is true of the real-
life client, too. Still another criticism is that the role-playing
client cannot behave and respond exactly as the person whose
case he is playing. True, but we can forget the case and evaluate
the counseling as performed with the live role-playing client.
Students will rationalize their blunders (which they are expected
to make) by claiming that the client in the case would react
differently. They are hastily returned to the reality of their relationship with the role-playing client.

The "reality" of a role-playing interview has been clearly
stated by Thompson and Bradway (1950) in an article on the
content-free interview: "The most telling criticism of the method
is that it is play-acting rather than real. To this one can say only
that it has been our experience and the experience of the un-
believers who have tried it, that when in a content-free interview, one takes the role of therapist, he *feels* like a therapist.
When he takes a patient role, he feels like a patient."

Theoretical Basis for Role-Playing

There is no research evidence to support nor dispute the
judgment that role-playing is a valuable technique in counselor

training. In the absence of such evidence a rationale for it may be found in learning theory.

Cameron (1947) indicates the function of role-play in the learning process of the child: "Play's most significant contribution is not so much rehearsal in the role as practice in role-taking, in acting in concert with others and sharing or opposing their aims, in acquiring skill in reciprocal relations. Perhaps most important of all, is the skill play allows one to acquire in the techniques of making a shift from one role to another, when the need arises for gaining an impartial view of one's own behavior or understanding the point of view of someone else." While the child may live out as an adult very few of the roles he has played, he is developing a skill important to adult adjustment: "If, for example, a man is able to predict the reactions of others, by putting himself in their place and gaining momentarily their points of view, he thereby immediately wins a strategic position from which he can predict and prepare for their behavior from its inception." Role-play experiences, in Cameron's view, develop empathic abilities and contribute to the individual's effectiveness in interpersonal relations.

The counselor-trainer seeks to help a group of persons who wish to improve their effectiveness in the interpersonal relationships of counseling. Presumably they have come for help because their responses to the stimulus for client statement and client behavior are inappropriate or inadequate. They have come for help because their ineffectiveness in the counseling relationship provokes dissatisfaction.

The responses of the student counselor are inappropriate because they grow out of his life-experiences. He has been son, brother, friend, employee, husband, father, teacher. None of these roles has provided the response that is characteristically that of the expert in human relations, specifically the "expert" counselor or therapist (Fiedler, 1950). In addition, he has responded in terms of the stereotyped concept of counselor as a person who finds the answers for people, a process that for many is satisfying in itself, and is akin to the traditional teacher role.

The counselor-trainer wants to provide the student with experience in a new role. In classes which rely upon lecture and demonstration, it is possible for the student to accept intellectually and to verbalize "approved" relationships with the client, without altering his perception of counselor role or his reaction to client statement stimulus. The counselor-trainer seeks to provide the setting wherein the student's typical counseling responses are produced so that their inadequacy may be made apparent and understood. To achieve this, he must create the psychological climate wherein the fear of criticism does not inhibit exposure of attitudes and behavior.

Next he needs to begin the process of counter-conditioning whereby to the stimulus of client statement and client behavior the student counselor responds now not as teacher or friend, father or brother, but as "counselor," that is, as one who can be concerned with the values and feelings of the client to the exclusion of his own. Through this process the student counselor establishes a new connection (or a reorganized perceptual field), namely that between client-statement and "counselor-type," appropriate, adequate response. With continued experience the student becomes adept at reponding as counselor and at evaluating his response in terms of adequacy and appropriateness. He becomes adept at recognizing when the stimulus of client statement sets off a chain reaction in himself wherein these personal reactions (values, guilt, anxiety) rather than the client statement determines the response of the counseling student.

Supervised role-playing in a permissive atmosphere supplies a practical instrument for the improvement of counseling. Used in the classroom, or for in-service training in schools or agencies, it promotes learning and relearning.

References

Cameron, N.: *The Psychology of Behavior Disorders.* N.Y., Houghton-Mifflin, 1947.

Fiedler, F. E.: A comparison of therapeutic relationships in psychoanalytic, nondirective and Adlerian therapy. *J. Consult. Psychol.,* 14:436-445, 1950.

Haigh, G., and Kell, B. L.: Multiple therapy as a method for training and research in psychotherapy. *J. Abnorm. Soc. Psychol.,* 45:659-666, 1950.

McClelland, Wm.: A preliminary test of role-playing ability. *J. Consult. Psychol.,* 15:102-107, 1951.

Thompson, C. W., and Bradway, K.: The teaching of psychotherapy through content-free interviews. *J. Consult. Psychol.,* 14:321-323, 1950.

INSTRUCTIONAL OBJECTIVES FOR THE PROFESSIONAL PREPARATION OF COUNSELORS*

Bob B. Winborn, William C. Hinds, and Norman R. Stewart

Recent developments in educational technology hold great promise for the improvement of instructional programs in schools and institutions of higher education. The application of principles of learning psychology and electromechanical technology to instruction has generated new models for conceptualizing the instructional process. These models, in turn, have caused increased attention to be focused on the creation of new instructional procedures, materials, and evaluation criteria. More specifically, innovative teachers at all instructional levels are experimenting with the use of instructional systems, programmed learning, computer assisted instruction, simulation techniques, and instructional media.

The new educational technology has had a modest impact on counselor education. Landsman and Lane (1963), Walz and Johnston (1963), Kagan and Krathwohl (1967), Dunlop (1968), Poling (1968), and Ivey, Normington, Miller, Morrill, and Haase (1968) have used some of the new media and techniques. Most of this experimentation, however, has been restricted to the use of videotape recordings in training counselors and counseling psychologists. Counselor educators, as yet, have not made widespread use of the various instructional designs, programs, and materials that have been developed by educational technologists. In brief, the technologist is well ahead of the professor.

In this paper we shall call attention to one of the keystones of the new educational technology—instructional objectives—and demonstrate their use in designing programs and courses for training counselors.

A Breakthrough in Educational Technology

Flanagan (1967) has pointed out that the factors that have prevented the use of modern decision-making and operating

---

* Reprinted from *Counselor Education and Supervision,* *10*:133-137, 1971, with permission of the American Personnel and Guidance Association and the authors.

procedures in education are lack of well-defined instructional objectives and inadequate measuring procedures for determining whether students attain objectives. It was, therefore, a major breakthrough for educational technology when specifications for writing instructional objectives were developed. The development of specific requirements for writing objectives gave psychologists and educators a tool with which to "identify the end products of instruction in terms of observable human accomplishment" (DeCecco, 1968) and paved the way for such innovations in instruction as the application of the systems approach to instructional design. As evidence of the acceptance and use of behavioral objectives in instruction, a depository bank has been opened by UCLA's Center for the Study of Evaluation from which can be drawn both explicit behavioral objectives and the means for evaluating learning outcomes.

Criteria for Writing Instructional Objectives

Several books and manuals provide specific requirements and instructions for writing instructional objectives that specify behavioral outcomes as the end products of instruction (Banathy, 1968; DeCecco, 1968; Gagne, 1965; Mager, 1962; Smith, 1964). All are quite similar in content. They stress the importance of defining the outcomes of instruction in terms of observable human performance. Each indicates that the specific circumstances for the performance of the learner must be stated. They point out the necessity for including a criterion of success for evaluating the performance of the learner. Mager (1962), for example, writes that a statement of instructional objectives is a collection of words or symbols that describe an educational *intent*. The statement describes (a) what the learner will be *doing* (terminal behavior) when demonstrating his achievement, (b) the important conditions under which the terminal behavior is to occur, and (c) a criterion of acceptable performance or standard that indicates when the learner has successfully demonstrated his achievement. The following demonstrates the use of such specifications in writing an instructional objective for a counseling practicum.

Objective: Upon completion of counseling practicum, the trainee must have established counseling objectives with a minimum of

10 clients. To be considered adequate, the objectives must meet the specifications for preparing counseling objectives as stated in the Michigan State University (MSU) *Counseling Practicum Manual* (Winborn, Hinds, and Stewart, 1968) and must be exemplified in audio or video recordings of the trainee's interviews.

The objective identifies the terminal behavior of the trainee —the trainee must establish counseling objectives with clients. It states the conditions for the terminal behavior: (a) completion of counseling practicum and (b) exemplification of objectives in audio or video recordings. The objective specifies a standard for successful performance: (a) establishment of objectives with a minimum of 10 clients and (b) attainment of standard specifications.

Other Examples of Instructional Objectives

Instructional objectives that meet the above specifications are currently being used in the design of a master's level school counselor training program at Michigan State University. Four examples of instructional purposes and objectives used in the beginning course of this program are:

1. Purpose: To teach trainees to listen to clients with the purpose of recalling data.

Objective: After viewing a video tape of a three-minute client monologue, the counseling trainee must be able to list at least 8 of 10 autobiographic items that appear on the videotape. The trainee will be given one minute to list the items on a video recall exercise form, and they must be stated exactly as given in the monologue. He may not use any aids for this exercise.

2. Purpose: To teach trainees how to communicate their functions to three different publics.

Objective: Given situations with staff members role-playing the parts of a superintendent of schools, a teacher, and a parent, the counseling trainee must state orally the appropriate functions of a counselor in response to 10 questions for each of the 3 situations. He cannot refer to training materials. The appropriate functions of the counselor are defined as those appearing in the American School Counselor Association's Statement of Policy for Secondary School Counselors, the Guidelines for Implementation of the ASCA Statement of Policy, and the MSU supplement to these documents.

3. Purpose: To teach trainees the skills involved in receiving nonverbal communications.

Objective: Given a dyad of counseling trainees, one trainee is given five minutes to communicate nonverbally five items of personal data such an anger, happiness, despair, interest, boredom, and confusion. The second trainee may nonverbally react, question, and check out the data received from the first trainee. At the end of five minutes, the second trainee must be able to state correctly four of the five items of personal data.

4. Purpose: To teach trainees the ethical and legal codes that guide the conduct and decision-making processes of the counselor.

Objective: Given 10 written incidents, such as those involving confidentiality, referrals, or discipline that portray situations faced by counselors that require decisions based on ethical and legal codes, the counseling trainee must verbally state the section of the APGA Ethical Standards that provides the basis for making decisions as they apply to each of the 10 incidents. No training aids may be used.

Advantages for Counselor Preparation Programs

Behavioral objectives provide a foundation for systematically planning for instruction. Once objectives are defined clearly in behavioral terms, the instructor may create or select the optimal combination of media, equipment, methods, and other instructional components that will assist the trainee in meeting the established performance standard. Objectives provide a basis for selecting optimum conditions for teaching the skills and tasks a trainee must learn in order to perform the functions of a counselor.

Objectives that meet the specifications cited in this article provide the means for measuring and evaluating the outcomes of instruction in observable behaivor terms. Both the instructor and trainee easily can identify what is required for successful performance in a course or a program. Measurement of learning outcomes can be focused on criteria for individual performance rather than a normative measure of learning. The trainee can direct his attention to the attainment of an established standard rather than to competition with fellow students for grades based upon the performance of an entire group.

Programs and courses for preparing counselors and counseling psychologists that are based on performance objectives
would bring about a major shift of emphasis away from the traditional lecture-recite orientation of training programs. Gagne
(1968) has stressed that instruction must be directed toward the
application, rather than the accumulation of knowledge. His statement would seem to be especially vital to the counseling profession. Performance, after all, is the counselor's raison d'etre.

References

Banathy, B. H.: *Instructional systems.* Palo Alto, Fearon Publishers, 1968.

DeCecco, J. P.: *The Psychology of Learning and Instruction: Educational Psychology.* Englewood Cliffs, Prentice-Hall, 1968.

Dunlop, R. S.: Pre-practicum education: use of simulation program. *Counselor Education and Supervision,* 7:145-146, 1968.

Flanagan, J. C.: Functional education for the seventies. *Phi Delta Kappan,* 48:27-32, 1967.

Gagne, R. M.: *The Conditions of Learning.* New York, Holt, Rinehart and Winston, 1965.

Gagne, R. M.: Educational technology as technique. *Educational Technology,* 8:5-13, 1968.

Ivey, A. E., Normington, C. J., Miller, C. D., Morrill, W. H., and Haase, R. F.: Microcounseling and attending behavior: an approach to pre-practicum counselor training. *Journal of Counseling Psychology, 15* (Part II):1-12, 1968.

Kagan, N., and Krathwohl, D. R.: *Interpersonal Process Recall Stimulated by Videotape.* Final Report, Project No. 5-0800, Grant No. OE 7-32-0410-270, Office of Education, U.S. Department of Health, Education, and Welfare, 1967.

Landsman, T., and Lane, D.: AV media, yes; depersonalization, no. *Audio Visual Instructor,* 8:24-28, 1963.

Mager, R. F.: *Preparing Instructional Objectives.* Palo Alto, Fearon Publishers, 1962.

Poling, E. G.: Video tape recordings in counseling practicum: I. Environmental considerations. *Conuselor Education and Supervision,* 7:348-356, 1968.

Smith, R. G., Jr.: *The Development of Training Objectives.* Alexandria, Virginia, George Washington University, Human Resources Research Office, 1964.

Walz, G. R., and Johnston, J. A.: Counselors look at themselves on video tape. *Journal of Counseling Psychology,* 10:232-236, 1963.

Winborn, B. B., Hinds, W. C., and Stewart, N. L.: *Counseling Practicum Manual.* Unpublished manuscript, Department of Counseling and Educational Psychology, Michigan State University, 1968.

SIMULATION TECHNIQUES IN COUNSELOR EDUCATION: PROPOSAL OF A UNIQUE APPROACH*

Daniel J. Delaney

In advanced courses in counselor education and in practica in counselor-education programs, many hours are spent in analyzing verbal behavior of counselor candidates as an aid to developing adequate response leads for effective counseling. Such need not be the case. Certain response leads can be taught by more effective means. This paper describes an approach to developing effective repertoires of counseling response leads.

This paper presents a procedure for the use of simulation techniques in counselor education. Such techniques will provide counselors with opportunities to develop appropriate behaviors in selected areas, either prior to enrolling in practicum or internship, while in counseling practicum, or as on-the-job upgrading of their professional competencies. Such instructional programs will enable counselors to attain a high degree of competence in working in select areas in a safe, nonthreatening atmosphere through which they can develop at individual rates without the possibility of harming clients while learning.

Existing procedures require the counselor candidate to interact with a "live" client. In this situation, there can be no control over such "live" client behavior as presenting problems other than the one specified by him for counselor assistance, the manner by which he engages in verbal and nonverbal aspects of communication, etc. The traditional counseling practicum is a "hit-and-miss" affair, with the supervisor hoping the counselor candidate has "hit" all of the experiences with clients necessary to help him develop the behaviors for good counseling, and hoping the student has "missed" clients he could actually harm through incompetence.

Simulation, on the other hand, will bring maximum control of the counseling student-client interaction for desired objectives. No longer will practicum experience be a hit-and-miss affair, since a counselor education program will be enabled to shape

---

* Reprinted from *Counselor Education and Supervision*, 8:183-188, 1969, with permission of the American Personnel and Guidance Association and the author.

certain counselor behavior while preventing harmful effects to the client.

Simulation

By definition, simulation is to assume the appearance of without really being. Utsey, Wallen, and Beldin (1966) have indicated that the results of their simulation techniques to prepare reading teachers were "quite good." Their instructional package (Informal Reading Inventory Instructional Process) has aided reading teachers in preparation "in correctly assessing each child's functional level and placing him in a text of appropriate difficulty" (p. 574).

Wallen (1966) states that "instructional simulation is a powerful tool for developing the referential resources of reading teachers. By showing student teachers examples of the specific behaviors of children which characterize different reading levels and different work-attack skills in a setting which exaggerates these characteristics and makes them more obvious, student teachers can develop referential categories for the different behaviors."

Kersh (1961) used multiple projection techniques to present realistic problems to student teachers and asked them to react as if in a real situation. In using an image size comparable to a 17-inch television monitor for stimulus presentation, Kersh (1964) concluded that the smaller, less realistic projection may be most effective in instruction. Adams (1962) and Twelker (1966b) support the contention that realism is not a primary consideration in transfer of training. It appears also that simulation affects actual performance (Ulcek, 1964; Kersh, 1965) and that simulation techniques provide for more economy of time (Kersh, 1965). In another study in classroom simulation, Twelker (1966a) stated that the results indicate "that giving prompts that guided students' subsequent response made learning more efficient in terms of number of sessions required for learning, number of trials required to meet criterion, and adequacy of student teachers' first response in training on each problem" as compared with not giving the same prompts.

Using twenty-eight counseling practicum students, Beaird

and Standish (1964) constructed a simulated environment to train counselors to discriminate between cognitive and affective client responses and to use counselor response leads to facilitate more affective client responses. Their study, using audio stimuli, yielded the following results: (a) the experimental group demonstrated a significant performance gain over the control group; and (b) there was significant difference between experimental and control groups in post-training interview performance.

In summary, research supports the following conclusions:

1. Simulation is effective as an instructional technique.

2. The use of a television monitor for stimulus presentation is appropriate.

3. Realism is not a primary requirement for transfer of training.

4. Simulation positively affects actual performance.

5. Simulation provides economy of time and reduces long-term expense.

6. The application of simulation techniques to counselor education has shown to be feasible and effective.

7. The use of prompts or cues is desirable as part of the simulation makeup program.

Objectives and Purposes

The goal of this suggested program would be to develop and test materials which can be used in the education of school counselors. Such material will consist of prepackaged videotape programs to assist the counselor candidate to develop basic competencies in verbal and nonverbal behavior patterns and counselor response leads. These video-taped programmed instructional packages will aid the future counselor in learning repertoires of behaviors in working with various types of clients, at various levels of counseling, and at various stages in the counseling process. The four selected areas for developing instruction materials to strengthen basic simple skills might be, for example, as follows: (a) to aid in the development of a counselor's repertoire of verbal behaviors in working with a nontalkative client in the early stages of counseling; that is, to help the counselor to know what to do and what to say to facilitate a client to "open up" and verbalize in counseling; (b) to aid in the development of a counselor's skills in working with a client who is interested in test-reinforcing support for some decision; that is, to aid the counselor to help the client become more aware of just why he desires to take a test, and whether test-taking will help him reach his goal; (c) to increase the counselor's awareness in determining and interpreting nonverbal communications of the emotions of anger, despair, fear, and happiness; that is, to train the counselor to pick up nonverbal cues of the client and to be able to "read" them correctly as has been shown feasible in earlier studies (Delaney, 1965; Delaney and Heimann, 1966); and (d) to instruct the counselor in methods of shaping the verbal responses of the client toward such goals as communication of more affect or feeling-level responses and preventing nontherapeutically induced catharsis.

Using a learning theory model as applied to programmed instruction, the program would attempt to bring counselor behavior under the control of a learned discriminative repertoire of behavior and bring counselor behavior under control of the stimuli comprising the instructional situation.

Suggested Procedure

Following a branching programmed instructional model, materials could be broadcast taped at a television studio. These materials would include the following for each of the selected areas (the nontalking client; client seeking test support; interpreting nonverbal client cues; and shaping client responses for more affect as well as controlling client responses in preventing nontherapeutically induced catharsis):

1. A main program consisting of 30 two-minute client response leads. These responses would serve as the stimulus to the counselor candidate and would elicit his response leads back to the client.

2. A subprogram for positive reinforcement of counselor responses consisting of 60 one-minute responses. This subprogram would contain client behavior material to allow the student counselor to realize that he's "on the right track" in the manner he is responding to the stimulus material in the main program.

3. A subprogram for no reinforcement of counselor responses consisting of 60 one-minute client responses. This material would allow the student counselor to realize that his response lead to the stimulus presented in the main program was not appropriate.

It is obvious that the possible range of counselor responses is limited in the counseling situation. To further limit the possible range of these responses, advanced drama students could be used as client subjects for the development of the videotape material. This approach has shown to be quite feasible in portraying emotions (Delaney and Heimann, 1966) in that drama students can be coached and directed so that what is captured on film appears real and spontaneous. Beaird and Standish (1964) found that the problem in constructing possible counselor response leads was "more conceptual than real."

The broadcast tape would then be dubbed to Ampex® tape for efficiency and economy of time and equipment use. The program on Ampex tape would then be used for further development and revision of the program. By using the program with many students at various levels of counselor education, the researchers, with the comments of the students, supervisors, and observers would be better able to make revision. The behaviors to be learned are specific (how to get a nontalker to talk), and the programmed responses would be general enough to have wide applicability, and at the same time client responses would construct possible counselor response leads.

The completed, revised program on Ampex tape would be used to edit and revise accordingly the broadcast tape. At that time, supervisor prompts or cues used in the programmed instruction unit would be included in the final development of the instructional materials. It has been shown that such cues make learning more effective (Twelker, 1966a). It would also appear that pre-practicum students expect such help from their practicum supervisors (Delaney and Moore, 1966).

Suggested Training Procedure

While seated in the counseling room (simulated environment) the following procedures will take place:

1. S is presented with audio-video stimulus on television monitor.

2. S responds (verbally, nonverbally) to the stimulus.

3. Supervisor gives S some cue or prompt concerning the client response.

4. S is presented once again with the audio-video stimulus.

5. S responds to the stimulus.

6. If the supervisor determines (from present acceptable response range) that S's response is satisfactory or appropriate, he presents S with a stimulus from the subprogram that, in effect, allows S to realize that his response lead was effective, and he verbally reinforces the student ("nice job," etc.) The next main program stimulus is then presented.

7. If the supervisor determines that S's response is not appropriate or satisfactory, he presents S with a stimulus from the second subprogram that, in effect, allows S to realize that his response lead was ineffective (client silence, for example).

The procedures 1 through 7 are then repeated until S is positively reinforced. These procedures would apply for all programs developed. The counselor would be provided with a "stop" button enabling him to stop the main program stimulus when he is ready to respond. This would make for a more real situation as well as enabling the researchers to determine if response latency (time between the onset of the stimulus and pushing the stop button) may be an additional criterion measure.

These programs would run at the student's own rate, therefore enabling him to complete the task sequences for all programs as quickly as he can without sacrificing his efficiency and effectiveness.

As a result, programmed instruction techniques will have been wed to audio-video simulation in an attempt to educate counselors. The materials developed for specific behaviors would be available for further research. This approach will also enable others to become involved in education in more complex counselor behaviors.

The successful completion of such a program would enable counselor education programs to use their resources—faculty, time, space—more efficiently, economically, and with more effectiveness. There are also powerful implications for using these techniques to shape desired client behavior by simply reversing the instructional procedures of using programmed counselor responses to shape certain client behavior.

References

Adams, J. A.: Some considerations in the design and use of dynamic flight simulators. In Guetzkow, H. (Ed.): *Simulation in Social Science: Readings*. New Jersey, Prentice-Hall, 1962.

Beaird, J. H., and Standish, J. T.: *Audiosimulation in Counselor Training*. Final Report, NDEA Title VII No. 1245, Oregon System of Higher Education, Monmouth, Oregon, 1964.

Delaney, D. J.: *A Study of the Effectiveness of Sensitivity Training on the Perception of Nonverbal Communications in Counselor Education*. Unpublished doctoral dissertation, Arizona State University, 1965.

Delaney, D. J., and Heimann, R. A.: Effectiveness of sensitivity training on the perception of nonverbal communications. *Journal of Counseling Psychology, 13*:436-440, 1966.

Delaney, D. J., and Moore, J. C.: Student expectations of the role of practicum supervisor. *Counselor Education and Supervision, 6*:3-10, 1966.

Kersh, B. Y.: *Classroom Simulation: Further Studies on Dimensions on Realism*. Teaching Research Division, Title VII, NDEA, Project No. 5-0848, 1965.

Kersh, B. Y.: *Fidelity in Classroom Simulation: the Effect of Variations in the Visual Display on Learning Rate and Laboratory Performance Ratings*. Paper read at American Educational Research Association Convention, Chicago, Illinois, February, 1964.

Kersh, B. Y.: The classroom simulator: an audiovisual environment for practice teaching. *Audiovisual Instruction*, 447-48, 1961.

Twelker, P. A.: *Prompting as an Instructional Variable in Classroom Simulation*. Paper read at American Educational Research Association Convention, Chicago, Illinois, February, 1966(a).

Twelker, P. A.: *Simulation Applications in Teacher Education*. Presented at American Educational Research Association Convention, Chicago, Illinois, February, 1966(b).

Ulcek, C. W.: *Assessing the Effect and Transfer Value of a Classroom Simulation Technique*. NDEA Title VII, No. 7-32-0410-264, Michigan State University, 1965.

Utsey, J., Wallen, C., and Beldin, H. O.: Simulation: a breakthrough in the education of reading teachers. *Phi Delta Kappan, 47*:572-74, 1966.

Wallen, C. J.: *Developing Referential Categories with Instructional Simulation*. Paper read at American Educational Research Association Convention, Chicago, Illinois, February, 1966.

AN OBJECTIVE SCALE FOR CONTENT-ANALYSIS
OF THE COUNSELOR'S INTERVIEW
BEHAVIOR*

JOE WITTMER

Attempts to identify and evaluate the interview behavior of the effective counselor have absorbed the time and energy of many researchers. Much of this research has resulted in the development of scales used to analyze the counselor-client interaction (Amidon, 1965; Dipboye, 1954; Porter, 1943). For the most part, the emphasis in counseling content-analysis research has been aimed toward distinguishing the levels of counselor interview behavior such as empathy, warmth, and genuineness (Truax, 1961).

These content-analysis scales have provided a useful method for global ratings of process or constructs and have provided means for evaluating a counselor's effectiveness. However, the highly subjective nature of many of these scales has been a hindrance to scientific research as the inter-rater reliability coefficients are often low.

As counseling acquires the status of a scientific discipline, more objective research should be done in regard to the actual contributions of the counselor to the interview. For example, the literature abounds with research studies that yield the statistical evidence of the effectiveness or noneffectiveness of counseling; however, few if any of these studies indicate how the experimental counselor utilizes his time. If counseling is to approach a scientific discipline, research on the effects of counseling should include investigation of the methods used by the counselor. That is, an actual interpretation of the counselor's time utilization should accompany research that is addressed to determining the effectiveness of counseling. This type of content-analysis would provide for a more accurate replication of research.

The counseling interaction process is often subjective behavior; however, it is possible to objectively quantify subjective

* Reprinted from *Counselor Education and Supervision*, *10*:283-290, 1971, with permission of the American Personnel and Guidance Association and the author.

counseling responses. It is clear that the counselor sets the climate of the helping relationship and equally clear is the need for increased attention to the techniques and procedures utilized by the counselor in setting this climate.

This article's purpose is to describe a content-analysis scale that can be used to objectively and systematically quantify and profile a counselor's interview behavior according to the amount of interview time devoted to various discrete counseling responses. The scale is known as the Counselor Activity Profile (CAP).

The Counselor Activity Profile

The Counselor Activity Profile (CAP) was developed as an effort to improve the quality of counseling practicum supervision. Truax, Carkhuff and Douds (1964) indicated that (a) the threat of supervisory evaluation would be lessened, and (b) communication between the counselor candidate and his supervisor would be improved through the use of measuring scales. Lister (1966) suggested that measuring scales would help the student counselor to focus more directly upon the dimensions of counseling behavior that would enable him to understand and utilize his inner experiences more effectively.

Utilizing the Counselor Activity Profile, the rater focuses directly on the counselor's responses and indirectly on the client's interview activity. This is not to say that a client's behavior is unimportant and that in all likelihood it could vary with the CAP; however, the author at this time will focus only on an accurate portrayal of the counselor's interview activity. The charted profile of the counselor candidate's interview behavior can be effectively utilized by the supervisor and the student counselor to reconstruct the interview. Reconstruction of the counseling session allows for an examination of the effectiveness of techniques utilized and permits a consideration of possible alternatives for the next interview. Aside from the insight gained into their method of counseling, counselor candidates profit from learning the number of minutes they have spent using various techniques during a counseling interview. The completed profile also yields the number and length of certain discrete counselor responses. As previously mentioned, a rater focuses directly on the counselor's activity; however, contrary to what one might imagine, the CAP sharpens the supervisor's perception of the counselor-client interaction rather than interfering with it.

The CAP was developed with the anticipation that it would provide data for subsequent analysis in counseling research, and it was constructed to lend itself to efficient computer control. As many as five analyzed profiles of a particular counselor's interview behavior with the same or with five different clients can be efficiently recorded on one IBM card for future reference or research purposes.

Inter-rater reliability coefficients were obtained for the CAP by having five graduate counselor trainees, trained in the use of CAP, chart one-half hour segments for each of three counseling tapes. The five students did the rating simultaneously without inter-rater communication. Kendall's Coefficient of Concordance W was utilized to determine the relationships among the chartings of the five raters for each tape. The three counseling tapes charted were of counselors from the following three theoretical approaches to counseling: nondirective, directive, and rational-emotive. Kendall's W's were .94, .84, and .76, respectively. The problems of observer reliability do not appear to be complex with the CAP, as rater error is generally small in most of the categories. To be optimally effective, a potential rater should have counseling experience. Training subjects to use the CAP generally requires two or three hours.

Definitions of the CAP Categories

First, it should be acknowledged that the CAP was not meant to be used in the evaluation of counseling techniques or procedures. Therefore, although some of the writer's biases may show, the descriptions of the counselor response categories are not ordered from effective (good) to ineffective (harmful). Since much of the case for the CAP is built on its research potential, an attempt has been made to give unbiased behavioral descriptions of the various counselor activities. The 16 CAP categories are presumed to be totally inclusive of all the counselor communication acts that could possibly occur in a given counseling situation. The CAP has not been factor analyzed and it is assumed that some overlap exists among categories; however, a rater must decide to place a response in one category only. If a rater is doubtful as to the appropriate category in which to record a particular response, it can be recorded in the miscellaneous category to await further scrutiny.

In order to become effective, a rater must familiarize himself with the definitions of the 16 behavioral categories. This does not necessarily require memorization, as one can stop the recorder and further screen a response. The CAP categories are defined as follows:

1. *Rapport/Structure.* Counselor makes statements in an attempt to create an atmosphere of mutual trust (such as a discussion of common interests, etc.). Also counselor statements relating the goals of the counseling process, those indicating the role of the client, those reducing the ambiguity and early anxiety, setting time limits, and other aspects of structure are also charted within this response category.

2. *Informative.* Counselor responds to the questioning of the client by stating different courses of action and/or alternatives. Also lectures, readings, demonstrations, and other types of voluntary information belong here. A rater should be especially careful not to confuse this category with *Leading* (No. 7), as voluntary proposals or alternatives posited by the counselor are often leading statements.

3. *Content Reflection.* Counselor is "parroting" or simply restating the client's words.

4. *Feeling Reflection.* Counselor expresses in fresh words essential attitudes and feelings previously expressed by the client (e.g. "You seem to be saying you don't like her, but yet you don't dislike her either, sort of ambivalent like).

5. *Reassurance/Reinforcement.* Counselor conveys his support and reinforces the client's words or actions. Also, counselor statements are directly stated to reduce the client's personal anxiety by using a personal example (e.g. "Actually, I once had the same problem and I worked through it and so will you"). The counselor's personal example statements may sometimes fall within the *Informative* (No. 2) category.

6. *Questioning.* Counselor asks client to clarify, restate or express feelings (e.g. "How do you feel about that?"). Open-ended counselor questions also belong here.

7. *Leading.* Statements indicating that the counselor is ahead of the client's thinking and is pulling or directing his thinking (e.g. "Perhaps you should give some thought to attending a junior college").

8. *Understanding.* Counselor statements that convey the feeling of understanding or acceptance of the client's words or action (e.g. "I understand your feelings"). These statements should not be confused with *Reassurance/Reinforcement* (No. 5) statements.

9. *Diagnosing.* Statements indicating that the counselor has formulated a judgment or hypothesis concerning the client's problem.

10. *Probing.* Searching inquiry or penetrating cross-examination by the counselor.

11. *Evaluative.* Counselor responds to the client by an expression of his own morals and values (imposing his own values). Includes stating personal, judgmental, and objective opinions.

12. *Silence.* More than just a pause—complete silence for at least five seconds by both the counselor and the client.

13. *Rejection.* Counselor deflates client's ego, is sarcastic, antagonistic, defensive, cynical—more than mild disagreement with the client and disciplinary-type statements.

14. *Termination.* Statements are aimed toward the termination of the session—recapping the session's theme, assignments for next time, etc.

15. *Miscellaneous.* Nonverbal responses may be tallied here along with counselor statements that the rater feels have no apparent focus or purpose except to consume time. Also, statements awaiting further screening can be temporarily recorded here.

16. *Listening.* Complete silence while client is responding. (Intermittent counselor utterances such as "umm," etc., fit this category unless they indicate otherwise.)

Directions for Using the Counselor Activity Profile

When the counselor is responding, continuous tallying is employed at a constant rate so that the relative proportion of activity in each category can be adequately determined. The rater must pay special attention to the passing minutes, therefore a watch with a second hand is a necessity.

The amount of time spent in *Listening* (No. 16) is never charted in actuality, but it is subsequently obtained by subtracting the time spent in other categories from the total length of the session charted. That is, if the total amount of counselor responses is 10 minutes over all the categories, and the session charted was 30 minutes in length, the amount of time spent listening is obviously 20 minutes minus the amount of *Silence* (No. 12) recorded. The following are specific directions for using the CAP:

1. Jot down the time of day and subsequent three-minute intervals in the appropriate spaces (e.g. 10:43, 10:46, 10:49, etc.). (See Figure 6.1.) This serves as a baseline for the rate, and, with a glance at his watch, will enable him to chart the counselor's response in the correct moment of time following a long client statement, silence, or whatever.

2. The rater should glance at the watch's second hand the instant a counselor's response begins, wait for its completion, and then record its length within the appropriate CAP category. If the counselor's response is more than one word and is five seconds or less in length, a dot (·) is recorded in the correct category within that particular moment of time. If the response continues for more than five seconds, the rater merely extends the dot into a line designating the total length of this response. It can be seen from Figure 6-1 that the smallest unit of the CAP is one-half minute segments. Therefore, if a counselor's response is 15 seconds in length, a line taking up half of the segment would be drawn, a 10-second response taking up one-third of the segment, etc. Of course, if the counselor's response continues for a minute or more, the line is continuously drawn until the response terminates. (It has been found that after two or three charting experiences, a rater finds it relatively simple to distinguish between the different lengths of responses and is able to chart accordingly. However, he should glance at the second hand the instant a counselor's response begins).

One-word counselor responses such as "yes" or "uh-uh" are counted as being one second in length and are recorded in the appropriate category by utilizing the first letter of the particular word. That is, if the counselor says the word "yes" in an understanding manner the letter "y" is recorded in the *Understanding* (No. 8) category within that particular moment of time. (The CAP provides for a tally of particular type responses regardless of length.) Except for the described method of recording one-word responses as being one second in length, no attempt should be made to differentiate the length of a counselor's response within 5-second time limits and the nearest interval of five should be recorded for the length of a response; that is, if a counselor's statement appears to be 8 seconds in length, a 10-second line should be recorded and the same rule applies if the statement appears to be around 12 seconds in length. Admittedly, this makes the CAP less than accurate; however, it is totally confusing to attempt a differentiation of the length of particular responses with more finesse than five-second intervals.

3. Figure 6-1 reveals that the CAP has a minute and percentage

summary for each category. This summary should be completed immediately after the charting, and subtractions to obtain the amount of time spent listening should also be done immediately. However, if the CAP is being utilized for research purposes and is being recorded on IBM cards, the summary can be left to the computer.

A researcher using the CAP may wish to further analyze the type of statement within a particular response category. That is, a counselor may ask a question that would automatically be charted in the *Questioning* (No. 6) category; however, subscripts could be used by the rater to further break down the type of question that was asked. In other words, if a response fell within the Questioning category and it was a question seeking clarification, the rater could classify this by marking the response with a "c" while a question seeking feeling might be subscripted by an "f", etc.

The notes for discussion at the bottom of CAP can be utilized by the observer to describe any unusual movement of the profile or as a method of remembering a point to be discussed with the counselor candidate. It can be observed from Figure 6-1 that each three-minute segment of time is identifiable by a letter. These letters allow the rater to key a point that he wishes to remember to this particular three-minute interval. This will provide a more accurate method of reconstructing the experience following the rating (see Figure 6-1).

The profile analysis of the counselor candidate's counseling session is not meaningful unless it is utilized effectively by supervisors. The author has found counselor candidates to be extremely interested in their profile and also that providing candidates with a carbon copy of the profile, along with the CAP criteria, is an effective method of helping the candidate gain insight into his counseling techniques and procedures. Also, counselor candidates can learn to accurately analyze and profile their own taped interviews preceding supervisory sessions. A practicum supervisor often asks his practicum student to listen to his taped interview before bringing it to the supervisory session. Thus, this self-profiling permits the counselor candidate to analyze and scrutinize his techniques and procedures and profit more from the supervisory discussion because of his ability to ask intelligent questions about his interview behavior. The CAP (see Figure 6-1) allows for only 21 minutes of charting; however, the profile can be continued on a second CAP if more than 21 minutes of an analysis of a particular counseling session is desired.

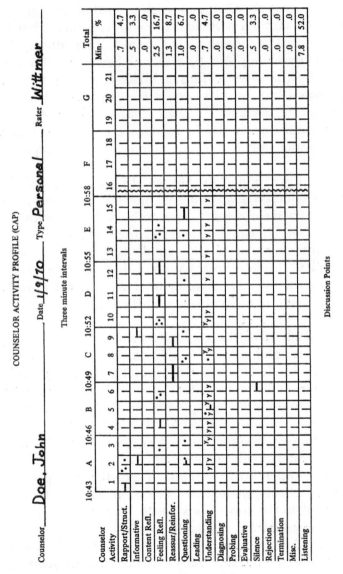

Figure 6.1.

Research Possibilities of the CAP

As previously indicated, the CAP can be efficiently utilized in counseling research. Over 100 hours of counseling interview time has been charted and several research studies are in progress. The CAP can be effectively used in the comparison of the time utilization of counselors with different theoretical orientations with the same client or otherwise. A research study in progress is comparing counselors with and without teaching experience on their interview behavior. One recent study (Wittmer and Lister, in press) used the CAP to investigate the use of the school counselor's interview behavior as compared to vocational rehabilitation counselors with the same coached client. A significant difference was found between the two groups with five of the CAP categories. Another recent investigation (Wittmer and Ferendin, 1969) used the CAP to profile the experimental counselor's interview behavior over 12 group counseling sessions with black delinquents. Definite shifts occurred in the profile over the 12 sessions.

References

Amidon, E. A.: A technique for analyzing counselor-counselee interaction. In Adams, J. F. (Ed.): *Counseling and Guidance: A Summary View.* New York, Macmillan, 1965.

Dipboye, W. J.: Analysis of counselor style by discussion units. *Journal of Counseling Psychology,* 1:21-26, 1954.

Lister, J. L.: Counselor experience: its implications for supervision. *Counselor Education and Supervision,* 5:55-60, 1966.

Porter, E. H., Jr.: The development and evaluation of a measure of counseling interview procedures. *Educational and Psychological Measurement,* 3:105-126, 1943.

Truax, C. B.: A scale for the measurement of accurate empathy. *Discussion Papers,* Wisconsin Psychiatric Institute, University of Wisconsin, September 26, 1961, No. 20.

Truax, C. B., Carkhuff, R. R., and Douds, J.: Toward an integration of didactic and experiential approach to training in counseling and psychotherapy. *Journal of Counseling Psychology,* 11:240-47, 1964.

Wittmer, J., and Lister, J. L.: Rehabilitation and non-rehabilitation counselors: a comparison of personality and interview behavior. *Counselor Education and Supervision,* in press.

Wittmer, J., and Ferendin, F.: The effects of group counseling on the GPA and attitude of underachieving Negro delinquents with a profile of the counselor's interview behavior. *Journal of Comparative Groups Studies,* in press.

Chapter 7

THE TRAINING OF THE GROUP COUNSELOR

In their book *Group Psychotherapy*, Mullan and Rosenbaum contend that "Because of the differences, training in individual psychotherapy . . . does not properly prepare one for the practice of group psychotherapy. Indeed, specific training is indicated because of the complexity, uniqueness and power of the group method" (Mullan and Rosenbaum, 1962, p. 300).

It seems appropriate to apply Mullan and Rosenbaum's observation to the training of group counselors as well. Experienced group practitioners generally agree that the development of a group worker requires academic and training inputs that differ from those suggested for the development of trainees engaged in individual counseling. This notion is supported by all of the contributing authors in this chapter.

The issue of training in group work has received some attention from clinical psychologists and psychiatrists. Counselor educators, however, have been rather unresponsive to this issue. This is particularly curious in light of the present-day emphasis on group procedures. It seems as if counselor educators and supervisors perceive a great degree of overlap between the training of group and individual counselors and as a result have made little formal comment about the education of the group counselor. It is interesting to note that in a survey reported a few years ago (Gazda, Duncan and Meadows, 1967), about one half of the group counselor educators polled reported that they were essentially "self-taught," that is, they had limited formal preparation.

Even though the training of group counselors has not received proper attention in the past, the issue has not been totally neglected, as evidenced by the sample of literature in this chapter.

That all is not well with group counselor training programs is reflected in Kemp's recently expressed concern that existing preparation programs are "too shallow, too narrow and too dogmatic" (Kemp, 1970, p. 236). Along the same vein, Muro argues that one course in group counseling is not sufficient preparation for prospective group counselors. In his article "Some Aspects of the Group Counseling Practicum," the author outlines and discusses a viable and concrete approach, placing emphasis upon the group practicum.

Anxiety on the part of fledgling counselors is widely recognized as an inevitable occurrence. This initial anxiety usually abates as a counselor's experience accumulates and his confidence increases. Beginning group counselors, however, seem to be burdened by anticipatory anxiety to a considerably greater degree than counselors who are being trained to deal with clients on a one-to-one basis. Meyer Williams, in his perceptive contribution, "Limitations, Fantasies, and Security Operations of Beginning Group Psychotherapists," discusses the effects of personal and social limitations, fantasies, and security operations of novice therapists upon their functioning within a group context.

Lakin, Lieberman, and Whitaker ("Issues in the Training of Group Psychotherapists") stress the importance of a trainee's cognitive understanding of group operations. In addition, the authors emphasize the importance of incorporating a number of different training experiences to meet the needs of the developing group therapist. They go on to list and discuss a number of exemplary training experiences.

The articles in this chapter highlight the unique aspects of group counselor/therapist training; unique, that is, in contrast to programs designed to train persons who will be working with clients on an individual basis. Sensitivity to the special needs and anxieties of developing group counselors would seem to be an essential characteristic of the group counselor educator and supervisor.

The training of group counselors has been sadly neglected. It is hoped that the counseling profession will endeavor to become more responsive to the special training needs of neophyte group counselors.

References

Gazda, G. M., Duncan, J. A., and Meadows, E. M.: Group counseling and group procedures: report of a survey. *Counselor Education and Supervision, 6*:305-310, 1967.

Kemp, C. G.: *Foundations of Group Counseling.* New York, McGraw-Hill, 1970.

Mullan, H., and Rosenbaum, M.: *Group Psychotherapy.* New York, The Glencoe Press, 1962.

Additional References

Abrahams, L.: Action group training techniques. *Group Psychotherapy, 21*:151-154, 1968.

Davis, F. B., and Lohr, N. E.: Special problems with the use of cotherapists in group psychotherapy. *International Journal of Group Psychotherapy, 21*:143-158, 1971.

Finney, J. C.: Double reversal group psychotherapy: a method of teaching and treatment. *International Journal of Group Psychotherapy, 18*:100-103, 1968.

MacLennan, B. W.: Simulated situations in group psychotherapy training. *International Journal of Group Psychotherapy, 21*, 1971.

McGee, T. F.: Supervision in group psychotherapy: a comparison of four approaches. *International Journal of Group Psychotherpy, 18*:165-176, 1968.

Mullan, H.: Training in group psychotherapy: a symposium. II. The training of group psychotherapists. *American Journal of Psychotherapy, 12*: 495-505, 1958.

Stuckey, B., Garrett, M. W., and Sugar, M.: Group supervision of student companions to psychotic children. *International Journal of Group Psychotherapy, 21*, 1971. (in press).

Yalom, I. D.: *The Theory and Practice of Group Psychotherapy.* New York, Basic Books, 1970, pp. 374-380.

Yalom, I. D.: Problems of neophyte group therapists. *International Journal of Social Psychiatry, 12*:29-52, 1966.

SOME ASPECTS OF THE GROUP COUNSELING PRACTICUM*

James J. Muro

As early as 1961, a policy statement of the American Personnel and Guidance Association (APGA, 1961) recommended preparation and experience in group work as part of the counselor's minimal preparation. More recently, the ACES Committee on

* Reprinted from *Counselor Education and Supervision, 8*:371-377, 1968, with permission of the American Personnel and Guidance Association and the author.

Standards (ACES, 1967), also called for counselor educators to provide students with appropriate work in group counseling to include a supervised practicum experience. While most university preparation programs comply with the spirit of these recommendations by requiring all counselor candidates to take at least one course in group work in guidance and counseling, little evidence can be found in graduate school catalogues to indicate that a specialized group counseling practicum is a required offering. Recent professional literature indicates that counselor educators exhibit a strong interest in the nature and importance of the practicum (Berger, 1963; Delaney and Moore, 1966; Dreikers and Sonstegard, 1966; Ohlsen, 1966); however, most of these discussions are concerned with the supervision of individual counseling.

Since the supervision of the group counseling practicum is a somewhat neglected topic in the literature, this paper is an attempt to focus on some of the specialized aspects involved in group supervision. In addition, a model worksheet designed to aid the counselor educator and counselor candidate is included.

Pre-practicum Orientation

The counselor candidate who enrolls in a group practicum should be thoroughly grounded in counseling theory, have actively participated in small group life, and have completed a supervised individual practicum. A logical sequence of these experiences for the beginning counselor is enrollment in formal course work in individual and group counseling theory, an individual practicum, and an experience similar to the T-group approach of the National Training Laboratories. An effort should be made to blend the didactic and experiential phases in a meaningful way in order that the counselor candidate is able to merge the intellectual concepts gathered in theoretical courses with the more affective approach of the T-group.

The counselor candidate is likely to approach his initial venture into group work with a marked degree of apprehension. Stein (1962) warns that preparation for group work is quite different than preparation for individual experiences since the group experience is likely to be highly frustrating, anxiety arousing, and marred with slow progress and disappointing results. In a similar vein, Berger (1963) asserts that students who are not anxious "must be sick" in that anxiety is the coin of the realm. Such anxiety is a result of the candidate's own general anxiousness and his resistance to the group experience.

Small group meetings between supervisors and counselor candidates prior to the initial group session can alleviate some of the fears of graduate students. Candidates review the mechanics of group counseling, role play as counselors and clients, and are encouraged to initiate any topics that may be of concern to them. Other specific considerations of the pre-practicum group are modifications of Levin and Kanter's (1964) approach to working with the beginning group therapist:

1. Group relations are examined with emphasis on the attitudes the counselor holds toward groups. Since a high percentage of the graduate student population in guidance is recruited from the ranks of classroom teachers, a pedagogical rather than a counseling approach seems to prevail when the beginner finds himself with more than one client.

2. Fears of facing a group are discussed and the difficulties of integrating material from more than one client receive careful attention.

3. The nature and possible causes of group silence, anxiety, hostility resistance, goals, and other phenomena unique to the group situation are reviewed.

4. Since the aggressive client is probably the most disruptive influence on a group, the destructive potential of aggressive clients and methods of handling such aggression constitute important pre-practicum topics.

Numerous other topics are initiated by the practicum students. In some respects, the pre-practicum group frequently moves in the direction of a counseling group, thus providing a natural bridge for the counselor candidate to assume the counselor role in his own group.

Format for Group Supervision

Critical issues in the supervision of the individual practicum are also concerns for the group counseling supervisor. The questions of grades, nature of the supervisory relationship, and off-campus practicums are frequent topics in professional journals, and further elaboration of these would be superfluous for the purposes of this paper. There are, however, some special problem areas in the supervision of group counseling that should be identified.

1. *Observing the Counselor Candidate.* In some respects, group counseling seems to be a child of the 60's. Physical facilities for counseling on many campuses were designed under the premise that counseling was essentially a one-to-one relationship. As a result, the practical problem of observing the group counselor through one-way vision screens often make direct observation of the counselor candidate impossible since counseling offices are rarely large enough to contain more than three individuals.

Unless the counselor educator relies solely on auditory accounts of the group proceedings, his only approach to actual observation of the student may require that he be physically present in the counseling room. Care must be taken, however, to prepare the group for the presence of an "outsider" lest the presence of the counselor educator disrupt the group process. The responsibility for preparing the group for a non-participating observer must fall to the counselor candidate. Grotjahn (1951) warns that the attitude of the counselor is vital in preparing the group for an observer and that the group will permit observation only if the counselor sincerely indicates to the members that an observer is desired. Counselor candidates who consciously or unconsciously fear evaluation may transmit such anxiety to group members who in turn will reject the presence of the supervisor.

While it may seem an improbable task to get the counselor candidate to actually "want" the supervisor to enter the counseling group, his anxiety about direct observation can be reduced if he can function as an *observer of the counselor educator* at work. In the structure of the group practicum at the University of Maine, counselor educators counsel at least one group along with the students. After groups are formed based upon general considerations in the literature (Bramer and Shostrom, 1961; Joel and Shapiro, 1950; Luchins, 1964; Ohlsen, 1966; Slavson, 1947, 1954), each student is provided with at least one opportunity to observe the supervisor. Subsequent visits by the supervisor to the groups counseled by candidates seem to promote less anxiety, and provide material for fruitful comparisons of orientation, philosophy, and technique.

2. *Group Theory.* Counselor candidates are urged to evaluate their efforts within the framework of theoretical guidelines. Lister (1967) has recently noted that few counselors discuss their work from any recognizable framework and calls for counselor educators to minimize theory aversion in graduate students. Although the logic of his views would probably be supported by most counselor educators, the group practicum supervisor is somewhat handicapped in this area in that few group counseling techniques were derived from formal theory. Nevertheless, counselor candidates seem to benefit from a supervisory approach, requiring them to formulate hypotheses about their counseling utilizing principles from group dynamics, group therapy, social psychology, and the application of individual theory to the group situation. Current research in these fields can also be employed as supervisory guidelines.

3. *Nonverbal Data.* The importance of nonverbal factors in group and individual counseling has been stressed by numerous writers (Berger, 1954; Fromm, 1951; Ganghoin, 1961; Luchins, 1964; Reusch and Kees, 1956); yet a discussion of these with counselor candidates is difficult when the counselor educator does not directly observe the group. Tape recordings of the proceedings do not allow the practicum supervisor to determine what postures were assumed, what facial expressions were evident, and what individuals were taking no part in the discussion. At least two possibilities exist to make supervision more effective in the absence of direct observation.

The most obvious of these is the use of closed circuit television, and if such facilities are available each counselor candidate should attempt to have one session videotaped. Kinescope recordings of these tapes allow for even greater flexibility for supervisory discussions of nonverbal cues and discussions of nonparticipating clients. However, the cost and general unwieldiness of these devices, coupled with problems of confidentiality because of the presence of technicians and cameramen, make them generally impractical in many situations. A technique suggested by Pile (1958) can provide additional data about the group that can be helpful in supervision. Following each session, group members and the counselor candidate complete 3 × 5 inch index cards summarizing the main things that occurred during the session. This procedure accomplishes five purposes:

1. The thoughts of nonverbal participants can be determined.
2. The amount of content and its parts which seemed important to the clients and the counselor can be determined.
3. The degree and kind of individual selectivity in reporting content is revealed.
4. An indication of the amount of material assimilated by the group is available.
5. Interpersonal perceptions are revealed (Pile, 1958, pp. 10-11).

Completed cards are discussed and then filed as a continuing record of the group proceedings. In addition to providing the counselor candidate and supervisor with an evaluation of a given counseling session, changes in client and counselor perceptions as the group develops can be ascertained.

4. *Group Development.* Bach's (1954) observations of the developmental phases of the therapeutic growth process (initial testing, leader dependence, familial regressive, associative comparing, fantasy and play, in-group consciousness, and the work group) provide a useful model for the study of development in counseling groups. Since the movement of a group through these phases could be at least in part attributed to successful counseling practices, a subjective "group log" related to the developmental process of the group can be an effective supervisory technique. Candidates are asked to write weekly accounts of their group in terms of developmental phases and support their observations with data gathered from the counseling tape.

It should be noted that a crucial point for the counselor candidate arrives when the group moves through the initial testing phase and begins a period of leadership dependency. Typical client behavior at this time is one of direct verbalization to the counselor coupled with minimal involvement of other members. Neophyte counselors must be helped to recognize this critical point in group life and respond with comments directed back to the group as a whole, questions or other verbalizations designed to draw other members of the group into the discussion. Failure to do so can seriously hamper the mutual giving and receiving of help among members, one of the key benefits unique to the group situation.

5. *Reports.* Required written reports of counseling sessions by counselor candidates is a common supervisory practice. Hill's (1961) contention that a "group is like a snowflake in that no two are alike" is an indication of the difficulty of summarizing reports of group counseling within a rigid format. The ever-present danger of the "technique tail wagging the relationship dog" must be reckoned with when the counselor is asked to give reasons for a specific interpretation, clarification, reflection, or other group technique unless the technique is considered within the context of the relationship. While a detailed format for written evaluations of group proceedings would be too lengthy to present here, it is useful to have counselors respond to the following areas in written form:[*]

1. Group, individual, and counselor goals.

2. Tentative hypothesis about the group as a result of the session.

3. Special problems as they relate to the group (silence, anxiety, motivating factors, prejudice, confidentiality, resistance, etc.)

4. Group norms.

5. Group structure.

6. The clients (member roles, of Lifton, 1966).

7. The counselor, his techniques and methods of operation.

In addition, a checklist adapted from Corsini and Rosenberg's (1955) study of the mechanisms of group psychotherapy is a valuable supervisory aid. In their review of over 300 articles related to group therapy, ten classes of mechanisms that were commonly discussed by therapists were identified. This taxonomy

---

[*] See Lifton, W. M.: *Working With Groups.* New York, John Wiley and Sons, 1966.

with appropriate modifications to bring it into the general framework of a counseling group as opposed to a therapy group provides a framework for supervision that requires the student to "think group." Counselor candidates are given the form prior to their initial group experience to serve as a guideline for an examination of group process and dynamics. When used in conjunction with the tape recording of the session, the counselor can identify specific sub-areas of group functioning and relate them to his own philosophy, orientation, and self-evaluation. An example of an abbreviated form of the check sheet will serve as an illustrative example:*

1. *Acceptance.* Implies a warm, friendly feeling in the group.
   a. Group identification.
   b. Isolation.
   c. Acceptance by the group.
   d. Supportive relations, etc.
2. *Universalization.* Refers to the concept that others in the group present problems similar to ones own.
   a. Recognizes similar problem in others.
   b. Discovers he is not unique.
   c. Client learns that his behavior is duplicated by his peers, etc.
3. *Reality Testing.* Refers to the concept that "real things" can be tested in a group.
   a. Provides a testing forum.
   b. Outlet for frustrations.
   c. Defenses can be tested, etc.
4. *Altruism.* Refers to the concept of the desire to help others.
   a. Advice by client.
   b. Suggestion by client.
   c. Encouragement, etc.
5. *Emotional Attachment.* Similar to the concept of transference in therapy group. Existence of strong emotional ties to the counselor or other group members.
   a. Client to client attachment.
   b. Client to counselor attachment.
   c. Flow of emotional support, etc.
6. *Spectator Gains.* Through this mechanism, people are helped by listening to and observing others.
   a. People client can imitate.
   b. Client listens to himself objectively.
   c. Testimony of other clients, etc.

---

* *Ibid.*

7. *Intellectualization.* A process of learning or acquiring knowledge in the group which can lead to insights.
    a. Interpretation.
    b. Explanation.
    c. Understanding defenses of others, etc.
8. *Interaction.* The concept of relationships within the group and the client benefits attributed to the relationships.
    a. Relationship to counselor.
    b. Contact with other clients, etc.
9. *Ventilation.* The release of feeling of group members.
    a. Release of hostilities in a socially accepted way.
    b. Release of anxiety, etc.
10. *Miscellaneous.* Group mechanisms not readily classifiable under the other nine categories.
    a. Sharing mutual responsibilities.
    b. Rivalry.
    c. Sublimation, etc. (Corsini and Rosenberg, 1955, pp. 407-09).

Summary

While the interest in group work is reflected in policy statements of the American Personnel and Guidance Association and the recent edition of the ACES Standards, the supervision of group counseling has been a somewhat neglected topic in professional literature. Supervision of the group practicum should include a brief pre-practicum orientation session designed to combat neophyte counselor anxiety about group work.

A suggested format for group supervision includes mutual counselor educator counselor candidate observations, emphasis on group theory, a study of nonverbal data, a log of group development, and written reports. A checklist modeled after Corsini and Rosenberg's report of mechanisms of group therapy is presented.

References

Association for Counselor Education and Supervision: Standards for the preparation of secondary school counselors—1967. *Personnel and Guidance Journal,* 46:96-106, 1967.

American Personnel and Guidance Association: Standards for the preparation of school counselors, *Personnel and Guidance Journal,* 39:402-407, 1961.

Bach, G.: *Intensive Group Psychotherapy.* New York, Ronald Press, 1954.

Berger, M. M.: Non-verbal communication in group psychotherapy. *International Journal of Group Psychotherapy,* 8:161-171, 1958.

Berger, M. M.: Problems of anxiety in group psychotherapy trainees, In Rosenbaum, M. E., and Berger, M. M. (Eds.): *Group Psychotherapy and Group Function.* New York, Basic Books, 1963.

Brammer, L. M., and Shostrom, E. L.: *Therapeutic Psychology.* Englewood Cliffs, New Jersey, Prentice-Hall, 1961.

Corsini, R. J., and Rosenberg, Bina: Mechanisms of group psychotherapy: process and dynamics. *Journal of Abnormal and Social Psychology, 51:* 406-411, 1955.

Delaney, D. J., and Moore, J. C.: Student expectations of the role of the practicum supervisor. *Counselor Education and Supervision,* 6:11-17, 1966.

Dreikurs, R., and Sonstegard, M.: A specific approach to practicum supervision. *Counselor Education and Supervision,* 6:18-26, 1966.

Fromm, E.: *The Forgotten Language.* New York, Rinehart, 1951.

Ganghoin, Betty: Non-verbal communication in counseling. *The School Counselor,* 9:28-30, 1961.

Grotjahn, M.: Special problems in the supervision of group psychotherapy. *Group Psychotherapy,* 3:309-315, 1951.

Hall, C. E., and Lindzey, G.: *Theories of Personality.* New York, John Wiley, 1957.

Hansen, J. C., and Moore, G. C.: The off-campus practicum. *Counselor Education and Supervision,* 6:32-39, 1966.

Hill, W. F.: Group psychotherapy lectures. Lecture No. 1. Idaho State College, 1961 (mimeo).

Joel, W., and Shapiro, D.: Some principles and procedures for group psychotherapy. *Journal of Psychology,* 29:77-88, 1950.

Johnston, J. A., and Gysbers, N. C.: Practicum supervisory relationships: a majority report. *Counselor Education and Supervision,* 6:3-10, 1966.

Levin, S., and Kanter, S. S.: Some general considerations in the supervision of beginning group psychotherapists. *International Journal of Group Psychotherapy,* 14:318-331, 1964.

Lister, J. L.: Theory aversion in counselor education. *Counselor Education and Supervision,* 7:91-96, 1967.

Luchins, A.: *Group Therapy: A Guide.* New York, Random House, 1964.

Ohlsen, M. M.: Adapting principles of group dynamics for group counseling. *The School Counselor,* 13:159-162, 1966.

Pile, E.: A note on a technique designed to aid in studying the process of group psychotherapy. *Group Psychotherapy,* 11:211-212, 1958.

Ruesch, J., and Kees, W.: *Non-verbal Communication.* Los Angeles, University of California Press, 1956.

Schoch, E. W.: Practicum counselors' behavior changes. *Counselor Education and Supervision,* 6:57-62, 1966.

Slavson, S. R.: *The Practice of Group Psychotherapy.* New York, International University Press, 1947.

Slavson, S. R.: A contribution to a systematic theory of group psychotherapy. *International Journal of Group Psychotherapy*, 4:3-29, 1954.

Stein, C.: Emotional needs of professional personnel in the training of psychodramatists and group therapists. *Group Psychotherapy*, 15:118-122, 1962.

LIMITATIONS, FANTASIES, AND SECURITY OPERATIONS OF BEGINNING GROUP PSYCHOTHERAPISTS *

MEYER WILLIAMS

Literature concerning the training of group psychotherapists and particularly focusing on the everyday problems of trainees attempting to master this highly complex and personally taxing treatment approach is sparse. Slavson (1943, 1964), Powdermaker and Frank (1953), and more recently Mullan and Rosenbaum (1962) have delineated and discussed some of the general problems from an educational and supervisory standpoint. Geller (1958) and Levin and Kanter (1964) have commented more specifically on actual training experiences and have suggested considerations from a supervisory standpoint. This paper is offered as an addition to the above contributions and will explore the effects of personal and social limitations, fantasies, and security operations of beginning group psychotherapists upon their group work.

The comments which follow are based on observations of fifty supervisees who have undergone training with the author in the last fifteen years. They are the product of direct contact in intensive supervisory sessions, cotherapist participation, and didactic group psychotherapy seminars occurring in both a neuropsychiatric and a general hospital setting, as well as in institutional outpatient settings in more recent years. The subjects of these observations were advanced psychology trainees, psychiatric residents, social workers, and staff members in these specialties, all of whom had had at least one year's previous training in individual psychotherapy and most of whom had been in group

* Reprinted from the *International Journal of Group Psychotherapy*, 16:150-162, 1966, with permission of the American Group Psychotherapy Association and the author.

therapy training with the author for at least one year. Most supervisees were involved in carrying out intensive group psychotherapy (three to five sessions per week, inpatient; one session per week, outpatient) for periods ranging from six months to two years. All were being trained along group-dynamically oriented lines.

Before presenting my observations and commentary, some framework should be provided regarding the general orientation for therapy given to these supervisees and its implications for group therapist characteristics and behavior. Briefly, the approach taught was that group psychotherapy is a small-group sociopsychological treatment procedure wherein the therapeutic power or agent lies not primarily in the therapist, but potentially in the collective capacities of a group of peers striving together for greater personal understanding and social maturity. It is the therapist's task to weld this group of suffering strangers into a strong cohesive social and therapeutic body by means of purposive catalytic activities and techniques. Such a collective entity, once genuinely established, provides both a vehicle for increasing and deepening examination of individual feelings and conflicts and an experimental ground for interpersonal development. To be effective, the group's transaction must occur in a relatively unstructured atmosphere in which free verbal and emotional expression is the cardinal rule, yet in which individual integrity and dignity are also safeguarded.

Looking at group psychotherapy this way, the demands on the neophyte therapist can appear overwhelming, and for some they were so. All saw group psychotherapy as demanding much more of the therapist than individual therapy and as exposing them to the threat of more direct personal and professional evaluation than most other treatment activities. Needless to say, in the beginning, anxiety was always high and defensive reactions to it abundant. The problems which arose were multiple, but this paper will be confined to three related aspects, namely: (a) inability to assume an effective group-dynamically oriented therapist role (b) fearful fantasies regarding group attitudes and behavior toward the therapist, and (c) adoption of special pseudotherapist roles as security operations against personal threat.

Therapist Role Limitations

The problem of assuming the role of a group-dynamically oriented group psychotherapist appeared on a number of levels. First, some rather socially immature and inexperienced supervisees were far from socially perceptive and verbally facile individuals. Their life history suggested little movement toward groups, little leadership experience, more comfort in one-to-one situations, and a lack of flexible communicating in common social situations. They were traumatized by the openness of feeling and unrestricted communications required in group situations, even by the lack of physical barriers, such as a desk between the patients and themselves. Moreover, the absence of opportunity to have a special relationship or privacy with each patient, as they might in individual therapy, caused them to become highly constricted and to feel exposed. They tended to fear constant scrutiny and evaluation by their patients, and all spontaneity was dampened by their need to be cautious and correct. Their groups tended to disintegrate or the therapist found some reason to withdraw from group therapy activities.

Second, other supervisees, less socially limited in the above manner, nevertheless were frequently insensitive to group process, despite much didactic preparation and supervision. They promoted multiple individual patient relationships with themselves but could not promote or allow interaction among group members, consequently blocking group development and movement. Without the necessary group-centered catalytic action on their part, which implies faith in and genuine commitment to group process, their groups tended to become a concurrent series of watered-down individual therapies. In reality, these supervisees feared a group-dynamic approach because they saw it as threatening their self-esteem and personal control by diminishing their authority. They could not relinquish authority or work at moderating their role as the focal person in the group. Consequently, their groups failed to develop or to feel their own strength and cohesiveness. Such supervisees could only operate as didactic group therapists.

Third, many supervisees, though sensitive to group process,

varied in their ability to carry out the group therapist's requirement of being able to handle, as well as withstand, a number of intense transferences at one time, even though these were diluted by the presence of other group members. This was particularly true when multiple transferences involved the concurrent pressures of extreme hostility, dependency, and eroticism from different patients. It was also difficult for many of these supervisees to be faced with an intense collective group transference attitude, usually in the form of strong hostility or dependence. Reactions varied from highly restrictive dealing with transference material to total shift or regression from therapist-group-centered interactions to old, more comfortable, therapist-individual-centered interactions with group members. The therapist's reactions here were distinguished from specific countertransference problems in that they appeared to relate to unresolved problems regarding the assumption of parental roles as well as a lack of leadership experience. Sharing of transferences with cotherapists and intensive supervisory support tended to modify these problems.

Finally, there were a number of supervisees who, unlike these three subgroups, were indeed capable of developing a group with high morale and cohesiveness. Their difficulty appeared to be inability to utilize their groups as effective therapeutic instruments or media for therapeutic work with individual members' specific problems and conflicts. As long as their groups dealt with group feelings and common problems, these therapists were effective and restrained their activity, allowing the group to be interactive. However, they were negatively reactive to any sign of subgroup development or any demands by individual patients for group consideration of more specific personal problems or feelings. Such efforts were either blocked, rapidly compromised, or ignored, frequently with a spasm of activity on the therapist's part. Interestingly, these supervisees were generally socially active and popular individuals in their personal lives. They made contacts easily, talked well, intellectualized readily, and usually presented a fine veneer of social sophistication. Yet, virtually all had a common characteristic: a resistance to examination of their own inner conflicts and a need to see all problems as interpersonal only. Above all, most enjoyed such strong narcissistic gratification from their feelings of acceptance as group leaders that they perpetuated the stage of "group ego" formation, seeking only to enlarge this information as if it were the sole goal of group therapy. Personal therapy, stressing character analysis, was helpful in allowing some of these supervisees to become more effective group psychotherapists.

Fearful Fantasies

As one works with many group therapy supervisees, certain common therapist fantasies come to light, which are quite helpful to an understanding of many facets of the therapists' ineffectiveness or early problems with their groups. I have dubbed these the "fearful fantasies" since they all have in common marked anxiety in regard to specific threatening therapy situations which conceivably could come to pass but which, in reality, infrequently do. Some of these fantasies are entrenched strongly and secretly in the minds of almost all beginning group psychotherapists, and must be brought to light and dealt with in supervision. Six of the most common fantasies observed by the author will be discussed.

Virtually all beginning therapists harbor a frightening fantasy of encountering unmanageable resistance during the early group sessions. Such fantasies are evident in statements or questions such as, "What if they don't talk?" or, "What if they just sit and look at me?" or, "What if they keep asking how talking to other patients as sick as they are can help them?" When the underlying fantasy comes to light, the therapist's feelings of social impotence and his personal doubts regarding the group approach become evident. Usually, he is so impressed by, and anxious over, the massed individual psychopathology confronting him in the group, that he loses sight of the underlying communality of human feelings and thought processes. Frequently, during supervision, it becomes apparent that the therapist himself is resistant to the notion of being treated in a group and projects this resistance upon the patients. Thus, while giving lip services to the rationale of group therapy, he finds himself trying to carry out a procedure which is ego-threatening to him and in which he does not, in actuality, have faith.

Related to the above, is the fantasy of losing control of the group. Here the supervisee often comments: "This patient talked for the whole session and no one could shut him up," or "They just ignored any comments I made," or "I couldn't get them to stay with anything." In supervision, this beginning therapist reveals little leadership experience and often shows concern over his own aggressiveness, which he confuses with hostility. He is fearful of asserting himself and of group confrontation, and frequently rationalizes this in adherence to a theoretical therapy model stressing permissiveness. He interprets the catalytic activity of the therapist as one of relative inaction, so that his interventions with the group are weak, and aggressive patients step in to fill the vacuum. When, with increased experience, he begins to see that firm and frank dealing with shared group phenomena brings group cohesiveness and movement, he may begin to enjoy his role as therapist and, if he is characterologically able, he moves out from behind his passive defense.

Many budding group therapists raised in restrained middle-class environments with emphasis on suppression of hostile expression are much preoccupied with the fantasy of excessive hostility breaking out in their groups, particularly hospitalized groups. They raise questions such as, "What if they disagree and start a fight instead of talking?" or they anxiously complain, "They all seem mad at me because I don't answer their questions," or "I can just feel that something terrible is going to happen" (i.e. that the patients will harm him). As suggested, the therapist's own overconcern about, and oversensitivity to, hostile expression makes him unable to gauge the true level of hostile expression in his patients. Not infrequently, he projects his own ego-alien hostile feelings onto his patients. Moreover, it often becomes apparent that these therapists have the same unfounded fear as the public at large, namely, that psychiatric patients as a group are violent. The lack of communication which exists early in the group tends to reinforce this notion, since it is interpreted by the therapist as stemming from hostility rather than the patient's social fear. Strong supervisory efforts to get the supervisee to recognize the potential for group control which lies latent in his group, but which can easily be mustered, can reduce concern.

Obviously, if such fantasies remain unaltered, group movement will be thoroughly impeded by suppression of hostile feelings in the group and by the therapist's failure to deal actively with negative transference.

Another fantasy which arouses immense anticipatory anxiety in new therapists is that of possible acting out by group members. The new therapist afflicted with such fantasies will frequently question: "What if a sexual affair develops between two of my patients?" or "What if he threatens to leave treatment if the group criticizes him?" or "Should I continue him in the group if I think he's potentially suicidal?" Reflected most frequently by fantasies of acting out are two underlying problems: (a) an unspoken concern about what colleagues and members of other disciplines might think about the therapist should the patient act out, and (b) an unfounded hope that therapeutic change can occur without mobilization of strong affects and their potential risks. Young therapists harboring these acting-out fantasies frequently do not yet understand the powerful influence of group members in stressing responsible behavior in order to maintain group integrity and continuity. In addition, they tend to neglect the extratherapeutic relations and arrangements necessary for good group therapy to proceed. Consequently, they look upon their colleagues, and particularly the administration, as critics rather than allies. Perhaps of greatest importance here is the necessity for neophyte group therapists to learn that change always involves risk and that it is only in an emotionally charged atmosphere where acting out is a possibility that new, more adaptive behavioral patterns can emerge and be tried out. In fact, for some patients, acting out may be a sign of progress. Only critical personal experiences, as well as long-term group experiences and a secure supervisor to lean on during initial, trying times, reduce the new therapist's anxiety.

Fearful fantasies of overwhelming dependency demands on the therapist are another variety of concern developing in new therapists. These are sometimes concealed in statements such as "They're an awfully sick bunch of people," or "They keep asking me why they are sick," or "They tell me I should tell them what to talk about." In all these instances, the beginning therapist usually feels much burdened and put upon by his group. Sometimes, there is real basis for these feelings, particularly if he has done a poor job of composing his group and ended up with a majority of passive-dependent and verbally impoverished patients. Quite often his problems are the result of his own need to maintain authority and control. Thus, he unwittingly comports himself in such a manner as to discourage interaction among group members and to block the emergence of neurotic patient leaders. His group, consequently, continues in the traditional dependent medical model, namely, "You're the expert, so cure me." Also troubled by dependency fantasies are those young therapists who confuse responsibilty for treatment with total responsibility for the patient. Such omnipotence sparks fantasies of overwhelming demand when the young therapist imagines or actually faces six to eight suffering souls in the cold light of the group situation. If he can foster real group development, he will learn that the group and many of its members also have a strong sense of mutual responsibility as well as personal assets to support one another, and that, while they may be able to live better with him, they can generally survive without him.

To complete this discussion of fantasies, comment will be made on perhaps the greatest fearful fantasy of all beginning group psychotherapists, that of the fantasy of group disintegration. Recently, listening to the beginning of a recording of an outpatient group therapy session, a fairly routine procedure in our training program, the author heard one cotherapist say halfjokingly to the other prior to the group's members arriving, "I wonder if anyone will show up today." More frequently, the author hears in supervision such depressive comments as "I don't think I'll have a group left after this session." Themes of this nature are most commonly heard from therapists in the early sessions but may reappear at any time when the group's feelings have been running high, usually in opposition to group interpretation or during multiple transference struggles. In reality, the author has seen very few new groups disintegrate where adequate attention has been given to group composition and patient preparation and, of course, therapist preparation. The persistence of this fantasy is generally a function of the new therapist's underlying feelings of impotence being stimulated by his lack of experience and faith in the group process. Such feelings of impotence are readily mobilized by early group resistance and tend to break through the omnipotent fantasies many new therapists secretly maintain to bolster them through the initial group sessions. Close scrutiny of the therapist's comments at such times will reveal that he is usually struggling with a mixture of guilty and hostile feelings toward his patients. He generally speaks more easily of his guilty feelings (his felt inadequacy) than of his hostile feelings (his resentment over their resistance). In either case, the fantasies of group disintegration emerge—either patients will leave him because he is inept or, projecting his hostility, he feels they will leave him because they resent him for not being what they want him to be. Since one cannot do therapy or promote adequate group process without patients, the group's greatest threats to the therapist is not to come to the next session. Until sufficient group development has taken place to allow the new therapist to see that in the long run, group members do not come for the therapist alone but also for the emotional support and understanding of the group, he may have to proceed by borrowing faith and technical guidance from his supervisor.

Security Operations

Having commented on some of the built-in limitations in personal and social development which make some beginning therapists relatively ineffective and the fantasies which frighten most new therapists, consideration of the characteristic security operations of beginning therapists in carrying out group therapy will be discussed. These usually entail the unconscious adoption of specific roles to reduce personal threat and to satisfy primary personal needs. Powdermaker and Frank (1953) remarked on some of these tactics and, hopefully, this paper will elaborate on and add to their list. In the author's experience, these therapist roles can be classified according to three overriding needs which become apparent during supervision, namely the need to control, the need to avoid self-exposure, and the need to be liked. Doubtless, the reader will see how much related to therapist personal characteristics and fearful fantasies these needs are.

First, the need to be in control as a response to the threat of the group will be examined. This need is satisfied by the adoption of a consistent authoritarian leadership position which may range from relative benignness to strict tyranny. Classic examples are found in the types best classified as "The Doctor" and the "Benign Authority." "The Doctor" is typically a psychiatric resident or staff man, one who not infrequently enters the therapy situation wearing a white coat with a rubber hammer protruding from his pocket. He typically is drawn into lectures by his group on physical symptoms, drug treatment, and psychiatric symptoms, all material with which he feels comfortable and which allows him to dominate the group since he is usually more knowledgeable than his patients in these areas. In supervision, he defends his approach by indicating that, after all, he is a doctor and it is not his fault that patients relate to him in this way. He rationalizes that he must establish a relationship to get therapy under way, and this way seems natural and to his patients' liking. If he is not too rigid and insecure, he soon begins to see the contradictions in his approach and takes off his armour (the white coat) and stops lecturing. Those who cannot give up this security operation end up denouncing group process or running psychiatric information programs under the rubric of group psychotherapy.

More difficult to detect is the security operation best named the "Benign Authority." The cardinal sign of his effect on his group is that his group members are active, businesslike, and noncontroversial, but they move very little and express little real affect. Study of the "Benign Authority's" interventions shows him to be most accepting and tolerant of group members' participation until they show affect. Here he is bound to step in, consistently minimizing or neutralizing all expressions of feeling by focusing on content and "reality." His patients soon appreciates that he regards expression of feeling as bad or sick and adopt a level of discussion based on fact or, even worse, banalities. In essence, the "Benign Authority" communicates to his patients, "If you want to be in my favor and get my help, don't make waves." In supervision, the "Benign Authority" is usually calm and sure and justifies his approach as one stressing the highest level of personal and social adjustment of his patients, specifically rational thinking and reality-consciousness. Only long and patient supervision and growing realization on the therapist's part that his group likes him but does not move, allows such therapists to begin to see how they are controlling the group situation to restrain the strong affective expression which basically is frightening to them.

A second need stimulating a whole gamut of related security maneuvers is the need for the therapist to remain unexposed. This need can be so severe that, on occasion, the author has encountered the new therapist whom he calls "The Sleeper." "The Sleeper" is so fearful that the group will see him as a limited human being and professional that he engages in total psychological withdrawal within the group, namely, dozing or actually falling asleep during group discussions. The presence of an active cotherapist facilitates this withdrawal. More commonly, one sees the type best termed "The Underactive One." This therapist busily gives the appearance of intense listening to his group members and may even step out from behind this façade from time to time when patient discussions lag to get the patients talking again. His rationale in supervision is that he is listening and refraining from interfering with group process. Of course, in time it becomes apparent that his group is not moving but is engaged in superficial bull sessions which he approvingly promotes. Then the real fear of truly interacting with his group emerges, and his doubts about himself, which he is sure the group will see, are voiced.

Related to the underactive one who fears personal exposure is the type easily recognized as "The Professor." "The Professor" is not infrequently a psychology trainee or full-fledged psychologist who sits in his group in a tweed jacket, calmly smoking a pipe, and acting primarily as a commentator on the group scene before him. The cardinal characteristics of his remarks are that they are highly intellectual, objective, textbook-like, and removed from the patient's level of communication. If the patients talk of "being pissed off," he speaks vaguely of hostility; if they speak of "screwing," he uses the term sexual intercourse. During supervision he justifies such language usage as "raising the group to a higher level of communication and teaching them objectivity."

He is usually hard put to understand why his patients remain distant from him or even kid him on occasion (as one group did by all coming to a session smoking pipes), since he consciously is utterly sincere, avidly interested in group dynamics from a theoretical basis, and is highly permissive in allowing his group to talk about anything. With a supervisor who speaks basic English and placement in a group with the "cowboy" type of co-therapist who interacts affectively and freely with the ebb and flow of group process, some of the less defensive therapists of this variety slowly open themselves to their groups and to the satisfactions of real emotional exchange. Others are doomed to be intellectual commentators on the group scene but never participants in it.

Protective operations relating to the need to be liked are the most difficult of the three categories to alter. Therapists presenting this set of defenses give every outward evidence of friendliness, altruism, dedication, and tolerance. Their need for love and personal acceptance unconsciously supersedes all other needs. Their range of roles is from that of missionary to fellow patient. Two common types will be discussed. The first may be classified as "The YMCA Therapist." This supervisee interprets instruction in group techniques as methods of promoting good fellowship and friendliness. His groups exude positive feelings, and his patients somehow feel that improvement lies primarily in positive thinking and conformistic behavior. Therapists masquerading in this role minimize pathology in their groups, see good in all their patients' maneuvers, often refuse to believe in unconscious processes, and are quick to rationalize away acting out or the persistence of maladjustive behavioral patterns in their patients. In return, their group members frequently feel and comment on what a nice, understanding fellow their therapist is and how devoted he is to them. In essence, a private contract is made by this type of therapist with his group in which they conceal their pathology and negative feelings in the group in return for the therapist's love. The therapist, in turn, feels loved, valued, and, most importantly, unthreatened. Attempts to expose this unwritten contract in supervision frequently end up with the therapist feeling that his supervisor is hardhearted and prone to see only the badness in people. Since many dependent and suggestible patients will show transient symptom reduction and even pseudo personality change in such a group atmosphere, the therapist will be even more convinced of the correctness of his approach. Only long-term life experience with a few real personal traumata plus personal therapy tends to make some of these individuals aware of the basis of their therapeutic stance, which is more appropriate to religious leadership than to group psychotherapy.

Lastly, in this need to be liked by the group, there is the all too frequent "I-Am-One-of-You Type." This is a therapist whose need for personal acceptance is so great that he literally tends to reduce his position to that of just another patient in the group. Initially, he insists that everybody call everybody, including himself, by first names. Early he begins to share his own personal feelings with the group and to join in with personal material. At first, his group of patients, if not too heavily made up of patients with paranoid inclinations, tend to give him what he wants: acceptance and the feeling he is a nice guy, not distant or authoritative like many of his colleagues. In time, when they sense the absence of real direction and his overinvolvement in the treatment, they end up resenting him, just as they do themselves, as weak, insecure, and fearful of taking firm stands and making decisions. In supervision this therapist espouses theories about democratic approaches to patients and the need to feel like a patient in order to understand and gain rapport with his patients. After seemingly initial success, he commonly gets emotionally overinvolved with some of his patients, who begin making inappropriate and unwelcome demands upon him both in and out of the treatment. Unable to gratify them, he finds love changing to hate, and, in his impotence, he usually turns in a most dependent manner to his supervisor to be rescued or becomes quite emotionally disturbed. In more severe cases it has been necessary to substitute other therapists or to terminate the group, and, not infrequently, to refer these overinvolved therapists to personal therapy.

Training Recommendations

What to do about all these problems is obviously a topic which merits much thought, experimentation, and volumes of exposition. However, the writer cannot refrain from listing a number of general recommendations. In his experience these problems can be minimized by:

1. Group and social experience prior to group psychotherapy training, such as experiencing leadership in clubs and on committees in nonpsychiatric settings plus vigorous involvement in milieu therapy programs in psychiatric settings.

2. Personal psychotherapy, including, if possible, concurrent group psychotherapy, and if not possible, group process workshops.

3. Thorough didactic preparation emphasizing group dynamics and group process prior to undertaking group work, and formal group review concurrent with it during the first year.

4. Prior clinical experience in intimate, long-term patient contacts.

5. Undertaking group psychotherapy with a competent, experienced cotherapist before engaging in it independently.

6. Close supervision by an experienced supervisor, with supervision starting well before group work so that a working relationship has already been established.

7. A successful group psychotherapy experience early in training. This experience will have the greatest possibility of taking place if the above recommendations are implemented and early experience occurs in a carefully composed group having maximal group-dynamic potential for cohesiveness and movement. Success for the beginning group therapist is no accident. It should be a carefully planned and prepared eventuality which in the long run will have great effect on moderating many of the problems discussed in this paper.

References

Geller, J. J.: Supervision in a hospital group psychotherapy program. *International Journal of Group Psychotherapy*, 8:313-322, 1958.

Levin, S., and Kanter, S. S.: Some general considerations in the supervision of beginning group psychotherapists. *International Journal of Group Psychotherapy*, 14:318-331, 1964.

Mullan, H., and Rosenbaum, M.: *Group Psychotherapy.* New York, Free Press of Glencoe, 1962.

Powdermaker, F. B., and Frank, J. D.: *Group Psychotherapy*. Cambridge, Harvard University Press, 1953.

Slavson, S. R.: *Introduction to Group Psychotherapy*. New York, The Commonwealth Fund, 1943.

Slavson, S. R.: *A Textbook in Analytic Group Psychotherapy*. New York, International Universities Press.

ISSUES IN THE TRAINING OF GROUP PSYCHOTHERAPISTS *

MARTIN LAKIN, MORTON A. LIEBERMAN, and DOROTHY STOCK WHITAKER

Probably the most significant factor in the shaping of group therapists is that most formal programs for training group therapists emerged from and are still conducted in institutions where the primary emphasis is on individual therapy. Even when an institute has been established exclusively for the purpose of training group therapists, the supervising personnel are likely to have been trained in the former type. Although exceptions exist, the tendency is for most training programs to rely heavily, if not exclusively, on individual supervision as a training device, with the trainee assuming the role of apprentice.

In recent years, the use of groups for therapeutic purposes has both diversified and proliferated. More persons in the mental health and related professions are conducting groups; diverse patient populations are becoming increasingly involved; and group activities, while not therapy in the traditional sense but with therapeutic purpose, are increasing; yet training has not been appreciably altered to meet these changes. These developments suggest that some rethinking about the character of appropriate training for those who intend to use groups to help people would be in order.

In undertaking this rethinking, we think it inappropriate to prescribe a specific training program. Indeed, considering the diversity referred to above, no single program of training could be expected to meet the needs of all trainees. The trainees start from different professional backgrounds and bring with them dif-

* Reprinted from the *International Journal of Group Psychotherapy*, 19:307-325, 1969, with permission of the American Group Psychotherapy Association and the authors.

ferent skills and background knowledge. They are likely to apply their training to quite different patient populations in different settings.

While eschewing prescription, it has seemed to us useful to bring forward for consideration a series of training issues likely to be present for any would-be group therapist, and consequently necessary for any training program to take into account. Our procedure in this paper, therefore, will be to discuss a series of general training needs and to consider a number of both traditional and innovative training procedures in the light of their potential contribution to these needs.

Any therapist who undertakes this task is bound to produce a list of needs and issues which reflects his own views about the nature and conduct of group therapy; therefore, let us be explicit about our views. Our position is that the therapy group creates its own social system with properties distinct from those to be found in individual therapy (Lieberman, *et al.*, 1969) and that the practice of group therapy should take into account the ways in which these unique group properties channel change processes within the individual. Ideally, the therapist should be alert not only to the needs, conflicts, and defenses of each individual patient, but also to these individual dynamics as they are expressed in and influenced by the milieu of the group. One of the important roles which the group therapist must fill—which has no counterpart in individual psychotherapy—is that of the "social engineer." By this term we mean that the therapist must be alert to group forces and must monitor and attempt to influence these forces so as to generate a constructive and therapeutically beneficial milieu for his patients.

We assume that the overall goal of a group therapy training program is to familiarize the trainee with the character of the group as a therapeutic milieu and to train him to understand the experience of the patient who comes to it. Also, the program must provide appropriately guided opportunities for each trainee to test himself in the role of group therapist so that he can decide whether to develop a personal investment in doing this form of therapy and how, if he decides affirmatively, to become effective in its practice.

Part I. Training Needs

1. *The trainee needs to make explicit his own implicit help-giving model and generate a model appropriate to the group situation.* No one who reaches a point in experience at which he enters a professional training program can have failed to establish his own personal view of what a helper is like and how he behaves, and what a helpee is like and how he behaves. The image of the helper is likely to be related in some way to ideas of the helper as teacher, parent, doctor, or to an image of how a therapist or analyst would behave. Similarly, the image of the person who is helped may have been shaped by experiences as a child, medical patient, student, etc. Some model of this relationship doubtless exists for every trainee. Perhaps the model is an amalgam of earlier experiences, or possibly even incorporates a reaction against some of them, but it is certain to bear some relationship to personal experiences of helping and being helped. Most likely, the helping model is largely implicit. Often, it involves some definite ideas about how much of an expert, social equal, authority, intimate, and social model, and how emotionally expressive the therapist ought to be.

The issue of the trainee's help-giving model is particularly important because the model we visualize as most appropriate to the group is not likely to be generated by the typical trainee's personal or professional experiences. Specifically, the model we suggest as most appropriate for group therapist training focuses on the management of social forces and the utilization of group resources. These foci are not characteristic of the traditions from which most therapists stem. The therapeutic model which is shared by the helping professions is usually a medical model in which the patient is sick and in need of something to be done for him. An alternative in recent years has been a "hothouse model" in which psychotherapy fosters a relationship which serves as an artificial climate designed to promote growth. A third model may be only half facetiously called a "powerhouse" model; it is one in which positive persuasion is used to deal with the problems the patient presents. All three of these models emphasize the therapist's role as a unique savior or authoritative expert, and their respective emphases do not take into account those natural processes occurring in groups which are most potent for change. Thus, it seems to us that any group training program must look carefully at the assumptions it has or that the student brings with him about the help-giving process and the role of the helper.

2. *The trainee needs to understand the unique character of the group as a medium for therapy.* Certain phenomena which one finds in groups can occur when a number of persons meet together in a face-to-face situation. Others, though not present in all small groups, are likely to emerge in a therapy group because of the special stress placed upon the individual in his role as a patient. Specifically *group* phenomena include the following:

a. The group's capacity to define reality through consensus. Unanimous opinions on the part of the patients—about the therapist, each patient, what is right and proper, etc.—tend to be felt by each person as real, convincing, and compelling. The therapist needs to be aware of the power of a group consensus so that he can cope with his own feelings should he become the object of the group's unanimous scorn, admiration, or curiosity, and so that he can monitor the situation when some antitherapeutic or erroneous view of reality is being lent credence by unanimity.

b. The group's capacity to establish standards for behavior and to try to impose them on its members. Here, the need on the part of the therapist is to understand the necessity for shared standards in the group, the various attempts patients will make to impose these on reluctant members, and the conditions under which such pressured individuals are and are not likely to conform. Again, the need is for the therapist to monitor the standards which emerge permitting or encouraging those which he regards as furthering the therapeutic process and interfering with or challenging those which he regards as antitherapeutic.

c. The group's capacity to cast various of its members in particular roles. Sometimes a group and a particular member will collude together to place that member in the position of an isolate, a destructive person, a spoiled child, or even an expert, and sometimes the position which a person thus comes to occupy restricts the therapeutic movement which could otherwise occur.

Alternative behaviors must not even be considered. The therapist needs to be alert to such possibilities so that he can avoid unwitting collusion with such a patient and the group fixing him into nontherapeutic positions.

d. The group's capacity to offer its members warmth and a sense of belongingness. This capacity has both positive and negative potential effects. For the patient who feels isolated, alienated, or unacceptable, the group's capacity to offer warmth and belongingness may provide a way back into the human race. However, the patient who comes to value this above all else may reduce his risk-taking to a point where the therapeutic gain ceases to occur. The therapist needs to recognize the quality of the cohesiveness present in the group and its meaning for each of the patients.

e. The opportunity for direct interaction with peers. Unlike individual therapy, the group offers opportunities to practice new behaviors within the boundaries of the therapeutic situation itself, with peers. That is, a patient may try out more direct ways of expressing anger or warmth, or he may confess to traits which he has hitherto considered unacceptable or reveal past experiences of which he has been ashamed. In each instance, he will have the opportunity to see and experience for himself the reactions of others who, like himself, are not bound by the conventions of the therapist's role. This can constitute a constructive form of reality testing. Sometimes, the special relationships which spring up among patients, or the trying out of new behavior, have been regarded as "acting out within the group." This can indeed occur if the group provides merely an opportunity for the discharge of feelings. The therapist must learn to sense the distinction between useful reality testing within the group and "acting out," which prolongs and reinforces neurotic patterns, and develop skill in helping patients turn the latter into the former.

f. The patient's capacity to collude in erecting defenses. When confronted by a threat which is experienced in common, the patients in a group are capable of collaborating, usually without being at all aware that they are doing so, in erecting shared defenses. They may, for example, keep a trivial conversation going as a way of avoiding their real concern; they may scapegoat one of their members; they may maintain a stubborn silence; they may psychologically wall off or exclude a difficult patient. Such defenses can be powerful and intractable. It is necessary for the therapist first of all to be able to recognize when such processes are occurring, then to sense when to intervene with some prospect of success.

g. Fears of revealing vs. fears of concealing the shared hopes and fears of the patients. The patients are likely to see the therapy group as a potential source of help. Their hopes are placed in the group and in the group therapist. They are likely to assume, or they soon learn to believe, that in order to be helped they must talk about their feelings and problems. This tends to generate fears of the consequences of such frankness: fears of being ridiculed, condemned, or rejected. Such fears can be massive and primitive, especially during the early phases of the group, and they lead to the erection of various individual and group defenses. The group therapist needs to understand the profound character of such fears so that he does not become too impatient or press too hard and so that he recognizes and nurtures the early signs of mutual trust and confidence as they emerge in the group.

3. *The trainee needs to understand the relationship between dyadic and group therapy.* This is particularly important because many potential group therapists learn in the first instance to become therapists by dealing with one patient at a time in individual therapy. There is some tendency, then, for them to transfer the attitudes and skills learned in the two-person setting to the group without critically examining their relevance and limitations. It is helpful, therefore, to identify and make explicit the relationship between the two forms of therapy, identifying those attitudes and behaviors appropriate to both settings and those which may be appropriate to the one and not to the other. Examples of attitudes and behaviors appropriate to both settings include attitudes of respect toward the patient, honesty in one's expressions, and understanding of the dynamics of individual personality. Other therapist attitudes and behaviors require revision in the group setting. For example, the group therapist must learn to attend to the interactions of pairs, subgroups, and the

group as a whole, rather than focusing on his own relationship with each patient; he must adopt a different position vis-à-vis power, centrality, reality-defining function, etc.; he must enlarge his repertory of therapeutic and managerial tactics in order to exploit the group situation positively.

4. *The trainee needs to become empathically aware of how the patient feels.* The patient is in some sense a "target" in the therapeutic group. Patient colloquialisms—"being on the hot seat," "on the griddle," "it's your turn today"—frequently express experiences that are not always felt to be supportive or reassuring. Group treatment *means* the utilization of group forces developed when a collection of patients meets as a unit over time, and these forces are bound to exert occasional pressures toward conformity, to exercise regressive influences, and even to develop scapegoating as a technique of dealing with collective anger, guilt, etc. The power of these forces is not unidirectional; they do not always operate in the most helpful way. Particularly if the trainee is unaware of the operation of these forces, he is unlikely to be able to ensure their constructive use. He may even unconsciously or inadvertently facilitate their expression in a way that hurts rather than helps. We feel that it is operationally important and ethically imperative that training enhance to the degree possible the trainee's awareness of how the patient feels in the group. How does the patient feel when he takes certain role positions—when he is the most active or the most passive, when he initiates the discussion, when he reveals painfully intimate details of his most personal relationships? How does the patient feel when under attack by several other members simultaneously, when his veracity, sincerity, or even his intelligence are questioned? The trainee should know what the individual experiences when he occupies the position of scapegoat or isolate, or when group anger is directed in his way. There are moments when the entire group seems to demand revelations that the patient is unprepared to make or when approval is expected which the patient does not wish to give. Particularly panicky feelings assault the patient when he feels alone, cornered, or deserted— even by the therapist. Waves of despair move through a group when one of its members reports a personal failure or when several share the patient's feelings of hopelessness.

If the therapist can empathize with the patient's feelings under the conditions we have described—all of which occur at one time or another in a group's history—he is less likely to be thoughtless or unwittingly cruel in his own activity, and less impatient or contemptuous of his patient's defenses. Without the ability to assume the role of the patient in a group, the trainee's potentiality for irresponsible behavior is no less than that of any of his patients; with it he will be able to help his patient experience the group forces as aids. In his empathic responsiveness to his patients, he may model for them an ideal of ethical interpersonal responsibility which is a key factor in healthy relating.

In many ways, achieving and sustaining empathy with the individual in a group is more difficult than in a dyad. The reason is, of course, because of the multiplicity of empathic demands being expressed. For any therapist there is a tendency to collapse the "I-thou" of the dyad to the "I-it" of collective experience (a factor which steers some patients and therapists away from encounters with groups). Overcoming this tendency requires an extra effort in the face of the group forces which influence the therapist much as they do the patient. Constant monitoring of the individual-in-the-group is difficult but imperative for the group therapy trainee.

5. *The trainee needs to become aware of and resolve or control his fears of the group.* In consequence of the special features of the group, the group therapist is likely to be particularly vulnerable to certain kinds of fears and apprehensions. For example, a group of patients may develop a shared belief or consensus about the therapist which the therapist cannot accept or finds threatening. They may decide that he is incompetent, inexperienced and not interested in the group, etc. Because consensus lends credence to such beliefs, the therapist feels their impact strongly, (most emphatically of course, if the group's opinion coincides with covert fears of his own). To take another example, the therapist, sensing the sometimes powerful character of the group affect, may fear that strong emotions will erupt which he will not be able to control, or, because of the capacity of the group to collaborate to establish shared defenses, he may fear the erection of implacable group defenses against himself. He may be disturbed or dismayed to find that he is not the sole source

of therapeutic help in the group, indeed that on many occasions the group seems to do very well without him. In consequence, he may feel robbed of his appropriate role. It will doubtless disturb him to find that episodes occur in the group which he does not understand and which have him at a loss to know how to be helpful. Many therapists, even experienced ones, find it difficult to be the target of unanimous hostility, multiple demands for help, and the like. Not all therapists are vulnerable in the same way or to the same degree, of course, but it is hard to imagine a therapist who is wholly untouched by these concerns. If a therapist operates out of fear, without realizing it, he will make errors. If he recognizes his fears, he is more likely to control the behaviors which would otherwise be generated solely by the fears.

6. *The trainee must have an understanding of how persons are helped in a group.* Lacking such understanding, the therapist proceeds on an ad hoc basis and is likely to miss critical opportunities to make helpful interventions. He may even work destructively, against the therapeutic process, without realizing it. Two kinds of faulty models are typically utilized by inexperienced persons. One is that the trainee transfers to the group whatever model he has found useful for understanding the events of individual therapy, a model that is usually inadequate, for it focuses on dyadic relationships and fails to take into account the specific dynamics of the group. The other is an uncritical acceptance of a kind of "mystique-of-the-group," which assumes that, in some unspecified way, merely being in a group will generate therapeutic benefit to all the members.

Although a comprehensive and satisfactory model of group therapy which takes specifically group phenomena into account does not yet exist, a number of theories about therapy in groups provide some basis for thinking about the behavior specific to them. We have in mind the ideas of Bion (1959), Foulkes and Anthony (1957), and Whitaker and Lieberman (1964). If the trainee is exposed to these, he can test for himself how and to what degree they illuminate what happens in his groups, and the kinds of interventions and activities on the part of the therapist they suggest.

7. *The trainee must learn to operate as a therapist.* The ultimate goal of training is to produce a therapist who can grasp what is going on in the therapy group, have some feeling for the internal experience of each patient, and behave in a way which will help both the group as a whole and every patient in it to move in a constructive and therapeutically beneficial way. Training should, moreover, develop skills to do this right on the spot in the immediate situation, while the interaction is going on.

8. *The trainee needs to become aware of his own natural preferences, embedded in his own personality, for a therapeutic role.* To this point we have been concerned with the social roles of helper and helpee (tinged as these must be with idiosyncratic personality characteristics); now we wish to make explicit the question of each trainee's personal therapeutic style. It should not be surprising that the group therapist, no less than the group patient, will try to develop for himself a role or position in the group which he finds comfortable and rewarding. For the therapist, this means that he may feel most comfortable when he is more—or less—central, powerful, intimate, distant, open, secretive, self-effacing, and expressive. A therapist may operate selectively to screen out or to encourage certain kinds of behaviors or discussions. One thinks of the therapist who always turns off hostility as being "too dangerous for the patients," of the therapist who distances himself by restricting his participation to one long and complex comment at the end of each session, of the trainee who insists on being called by his first name in order to "reduce the humiliation of being a patient." It is obviously desirable for the trainee to become aware of his personal preferences for what they are, so that he may avoid elevating them to the dignity of being justified by theory. Hopefully, personal needs which lead a trainee to establish a role for himself which works against the therapeutic process can be recognized and modified or controlled. Occasionally, a trainee may be fixed in a personal style which is inappropriate to a group, although he might be an adequate helper in other therapy forms. If this is recognized and its implications faced, it may lead the trainee to pass up the role of group therapist in favor of one which is more congenial to him.

Part II. Training Procedures

If this list of issues indicates a series of training needs, how are these needs to be met? Some commonly and not so commonly employed training procedures include (a) didactic teaching, in which the trainee listens to lectures or reads books; (b) participant learning, in which the trainee is placed in the position of patient or group member; (c) vicarious exposure to groups through tapes, films, transcripts, or the observation of live groups; (d) role-playing and exercises; (e) apprenticeship learning, in which the trainee is a co-therapist or therapist under supervision; and (f) seminars and discussion groups. We shall take each of these in turn, discussing their relevance to the training needs and some of the considerations and problems involved in their utilization.

1. *Didactic teaching, in which the trainee listens to lectures or reads books.* Didactic teaching tends to be de-emphasized in training programs, perhaps because of the recognition that conducting a therapy group is a skill and that a skill is something which must be learned through practice and not primarily through reading. Still, there is a place for this kind of learning in a training program. No doubt, the most economical way of being exposed to a set of ideas about a subject is to read about them in books or articles or hear about them in a lecture. Two of the training needs mentioned earlier can be partially fulfilled in this way: the need for some model of how persons are helped in groups, and the need to understand the unique character of the group as a medium for therapy.

If didactic teaching is to be included in a training program, three questions arise concerning its use. The first of these has to do with selection of articles, books, or topics. Is a single, internally consistent approach to group therapy to be presented? Does the instruction present a limited number of conceptual approaches, different but compatible in outlook and emphasis? Or does it present the full range of views and theory, exposing the student to all of the unresolved contradictions and controversies? A second issue concerning didactic teaching has to do with timing. Should a trainee be exposed to conceptual ideas about groups before or after he has had personal experience as a patient, as an observer, as a therapist? The third point concerns the use of didactic teaching in conjunction with other methods. Should the material which is read or heard then be discussed in seminars? Can a theory best be tested and assimilated by applying to groups what has been observed or conducted? Can exercises be devised to help the trainee compare and evaluate different theoretical approaches?

It is not unusual for students to be more confused than helped by exposure to diverse theoretical ideas and to controversy. The decisions about when and how didactic teaching is to be introduced, and how it is to be supplemented, are crucial in determining whether diverse ideas will contribute to confusion or clarity.

2. *Participant learning: the trainee as patient or group member*. Placing trainees in therapy groups, T-groups, or study groups is being done with increasing frequency. The use of group therapy for training is based on the assumption that what is to be learned has to do with the personality characteristics of the learner. It is assumed that the learner has certain lacunae or certain maladaptive patterns which must be confronted, modified, or at least brought under conscious control in order for him to become an effective group psychotherapist. In groups the prime learning task is viewed as permitting the student to experience the member role so that he adds this perspective when he begins to function as a therapist. In some groups the learning is centered about experiencing the group *qua* group, and a major learning task is to understand the group as a social system. In practice, the effects of these kinds of group experience overlap: the patient in the therapy group learns something about group processes; the participant in a T-group or study group may recognize and revise maladaptive patterns.

A trainee who is placed in a group as a patient is not in actual fact in the position of a patient. He is not as anxious or as troubled as a bona fide patient, he is not pinning his hopes on the therapy or the therapist in the same way or to the same extent, and he knows that the therapy group is part of his training and can thus use the "game" aspect of the situation to defend or distance himself in a way which is not available to the patient. An opposite hazard for some persons is the possibility of becoming too involved in the situation so that they truly use it for therapeutic rather than learning purposes; that is, they do not distance themselves *enough*.

The T-group (training group) or study group is a bit different: the trainee is not defined as a patient but as a participant or group member. He is not necessarily expected to correct maladaptive patterns as a result of the experience, but he is expected to become more aware of and sensitive to group events and phenomena by experiencing and simultaneously observing and thinking about them. The relevance of such an experience is not limited to therapy groups, for they are equally relevant to staff groups, classrooms, and the like, in fact to any small face-to-face group.

Although training in none of these types of groups is precisely like being a bona fide patient in a therapy group, the groups generate similar feelings and experiences. For example, they can provide the trainee with an understanding of what it feels like to be in a group interaction when the familiar structuring aspects (agenda, hierarchy, task, etc.) are lacking and when initial expectations seem almost deliberately to be ignored (the patient's complaints are not solicited nor is a curative program prescribed). Such experiences can provide ample opportunities to be in the role of the isolate, the deviant, the scapegoat, or to be the target for strong group feelings such as hostility. Being in these positions means that one can learn experientially what it *feels* like to be in them. From the participant-observer vantage point the trainee can learn about the operation of powerful pressures which generate conformist responses or spread unpleasant emotionality and how difficult it is to withstand or to modify these.

As a therapist one is the authority, but as a member of such a group one contends with the authority. How one relates and is perceived as relating from these different perspectives can be an "eye-opener." Unfortunately, it is an experience which surprisingly many group therapists fail to have in the course of training.

There is more to this issue than effectiveness and knowledgeability. When the trainee feels that upon him as group member devolves a share of the responsibility for the conduct of the group, that his behavior is visibly influential in its up and down swings, and that he can be as vulnerable as the patient, he understands more fully what being a group patient means and he can be more responsive to his group patients.

In our view, however, the experience of being in a group is not enough. Opportunities to reflect, think over, and study are necessary in order to grasp the complexities of the group situation, the nature of one's own participation and feelings, and the impact of oneself upon others and others upon oneself. Perhaps the issue is more easily resolved in a T-group or study group, for here reflection about the process is seen as a legitimate and necessary part of the process itself. In a therapy group the problem is more difficult, for there is always the argument that to stop and reflect about the process is to interfere with it. In either case, such devices as post-mortems and tape-listening could conceivably be used.

3. *Vicarious exposure to groups through tapes, films, transcripts, or the observation of live groups.* It is possible to set up learning situations which simulate the real thing, through showing films, playing tapes, reading transcripts, etc. The advantage to the trainee is that he can do one thing at a time: rather than being required to understand and grasp the import of the group interactions *and* respond on the spot *and* be responsible for the conduct of the group, he can concentrate on the single goal of attempting to understand. Tapes and films have the advantage of being able to be stopped: a trainee can hear or see an episode which the supervisor considers critical or difficult to handle, the tape or film can then be stopped and the situation discussed. The trainee can be led to think about the kind of intervention which is appropriate, or the kind which might be a mistake, and in either case predict the likely consequences for the group and specific patients. One can then resume the tape or film and discuss what actually *did* happen. The disadvantage, of course, is that the material is "cold"; the trainee does not experience the situation in the same way that he would if he were actually in the real situation.

Observing live groups, participating in groups, and being the therapist for a group constitute very different perspectives from which to try to relate to group therapy. The latter two involve the trainee is not defined as a patient but as a participant or group to "figure out" his strategies. They flow more or less spontaneously, they may be excellent or poor, but they are usually instantaneous responses to the demands of the situation. Observing a group is quite different in its emphasis upon the cognitive: the observer is far freer to engage in diagnostic speculation; indeed this is one advantage of observation. But by this very "objectification" of the patients who are interacting, the observer comes to regard them as actors, as players in a fascinating drama. Consequently, one of the temptations of the observer role is to "script" the patients, to anticipate certain behaviors and to be disappointed if the predictions are unfulfilled. Observing, particularly through one-way vision screens, tends to reduce empathic responses to individual patients to the extent that it generates the tendency to see members predominantly as functional parts of a unit.

Nevertheless, it is certainly true that no adequate substitute exists for the conceptualizing vehicle of group observation. The "caveat" we mentioned can be taken account of by making sure that trainees have opportunities to rotate through more than just one of the training media, with experiencing, directing, or vicarious exposure, such as observation, used as supplements to one another.

True, the observer does not have the responsibility of acting. Also, he cannot stop the action and reflect on it; he must wait at least until the session is over. If he is in the same room with the group, he cannot discuss events as they proceed, and he must to some extent control his nonverbal reactions so as not to distract the group. If he is watching from behind a one-way screen, he can comment as the group moves along, although again he cannot stop the action. However, in either situation, he can check afterward with the therapist, comparing his formulations of the meaning of events with those of the therapist, questioning the therapist as to his intentions, comparing impressions of the impact of interventions on the group, etc.

4. *Role playing and exercises.* A wide range of exercises and role-playing situations can be devised, keyed to a number of

training needs. For example, a group of trainees can be asked to write down problems they anticipate they will have as group therapists. They are then grouped into pairs and asked to share as much as they can of these problems with their partners. Following this, they are asked to form themselves into a large group and share the same problems. This exercise has the two-fold purpose of, first, getting the trainees to reflect about their potential problems as group therapists, and, second, enabling them to experience the different quality of sharing under pair and group conditions.

A group of trainees can be asked to role-play a therapy group, with one of their members acting as therapist. Such a simulated situation can be surprisingly realistic if each person taking the role of a patient is asked to keep in mind a particular patient whom he knows well and to behave in character with that person. After a short period of role-playing, the trainees form themselves into a discussion group to talk over what occurred in the group and how the therapist dealt with the situation. The exercise can then be repeated with someone else assuming the therapist's role. Many variations of this exercise are possible: for example, by varying the instructions to the group, typical problems can be presented, such as an apathetic group, a dominating patient, and the like. During role-playing, a trainee can practice conducting group therapy in a live situation without actually having to assume responsibility for an ongoing group of patients.

Another possibility is for trainees to be divided into pairs to observe a therapy group through a one-way screen. Each pair is asked to observe the group interaction from some particular theoretical point of view. Afterward, they can compare their formulations and consider whether and in what way the adoption of differing theoretical approaches would have led to different behavior on the part of the therapist.

Another exercise has been successfully used for training purposes by one of us. Each of the trainees in a group of seven was given the therapist's role for a period of two hours. However, the "action" was halted periodically—every twenty minutes or so—for a "clinicing" session with two senior therapists who observed the group. Feedback by the supervisory therapists could be used by the trainee-in-therapist-role to try out various strategies of intervention as he saw the opportunity to make them.

The above should be regarded merely as examples, for the possibilities are almost endless. One caution, which is particularly applicable to role-playing, should be mentioned. If an atmosphere of mutual trust and acceptance has not been established within the group of trainees, and if unresolved problems are still present having to do with competitiveness, resentment of the training staff and the program, etc., a role-playing situation can constitute an invitation to act out. The role-playing episodes then lose their value as a training device and become merely an opportunity for catharsis or for establishing nonconstructive solutions (scape-goating, ridiculing group therapy, and the like) to problems existing within the trainee group itself.

5. *Apprenticeship learning, in which the trainee is co-therapist or therapist under supervision.* Many technical variations are possible here. The trainee may function as a co-therapist with the supervisor; two trainees may function as co-therapists; or the trainee may conduct a group on his own and have a supervisory session for every therapeutic session. The discussion between the supervisor and the trainee(s) may be based on verbal reports drawn from memory, on verbal reports drawn from notes, on a tape of the session, or the supervisor may have observed the session or parts of it through a one-way screen. Many of the problems of supervision are not specific to group therapy but are familiar also in supervising individual therapy: problems of keying the supervision to the ability and skill level of the trainee, establishing the boundary between supervision and therapy, dealing somehow with the dilemma that one can only discuss what has happened in the past and yet needs to prepare the trainee for dealing with the unpredictable future.

The supervisory model for the group therapist trainee will more than likely be the dyadic one, in which event the authoritarian and authoritative relationship engendered by our usual training modes will be in conflict with many of the potent aspects of the group itself. Let us examine the question of "reality definition," for example. In the therapeutic group there are many contending sources and some of these afford fresh looks at old problems or novel perspectives on long-term dilemmas. By contrast, a "this-is-the-way-I-do-things" approach sets up apprenticeship and imitative tendencies. The supervisor's experience and know-how are assimilated as craft and as value, but the trainee is not liberated to try and err. We do not mean to imply that individual supervision of group therapy trainees is a mistake but to suggest that such supervision in the absence of supplementary or even countervailing group supervisory experiences can only stamp in a mentor's approach and not exploit the range of possible group learning experiences.

6. *Seminars and discussion groups.* Discussion is likely to appear as a supplement to almost any of the training devices discussed so far. A book is better assimilated if it can be discussed with others; to observe a therapy group without a chance to discuss one's impressions afterward with others is relatively sterile.

Apart from these supplementary uses, however, at least one other possible use of a discussion group comes to mind. It was suggested earlier that to place a trainee in a therapy group leaves something to be desired, for it can never approach the real experiences of fear and hope which are felt by a bona fide patient. Yet everyone has had the experience in his or her life of despair, hope, fear, etc., and of the very sorts one expects to occur in a therapy group. Everyone has had a variety of group experiences. It could be very useful through group discussion to reach back to experiences in one's own life (e.g. first day at school, etc.) to help one to empathize with the experiences of the patients.

Discussion groups can fulfill two quite different purposes: first, to assimilate intellectually something to which one has been exposed, and second, to recall and explore situations which one has previously experienced. In the first instance, the discussion group must supplement something else. In the second instance, it can stand on its own, with appropriate input from a discussion leader to steer it in the most useful direction.

Part III. Designing a Training Program

We have listed the issues involved in the training of a group therapist and we have described their relationship to the problems of skills and attitude development. We have predicated the consideration of these upon the central idea that the processes of group psychotherapy are unique and distinctive in many ways from other forms of therapy. It should be clear that much of the learning of technique and the didactic experiences which the mental health professional gets in his other training activities has no necessary transfer to group therapy practice. On the contrary, there is the likelihood that practices that are good and sufficient in work with a single patient may be inimical to the successful conduct of a group.

We have alluded to such aspects as the many-to-one relation, the difficulty of achieving one-to-one empathy in a group setting, the ubiquity of group forces, and the multiperson orientations of the therapist. Even the hallowed supervisory practices of dyadic psychotherapy may require "unlearning" in assuming the group therapist role effectively.

In the face of this difference in emphasis, the training institution must be willing to ask itself how seriously it has invested in group therapy training, whether its training program adequately recognizes the discontinuities of the various therapies and is willing to devote the time, manpower, and other resources necessary to do a good job of training.

Having listed a set of training needs and discussed a series of possible training procedures and their relevance to the list of needs, there still remains the problem of designing a training program: deciding which procedures are to be used, in what order, in what combination, and to what end. Having said in the beginning we did not intend to prescribe a training program, we shall not do so now because many combinations and orders of priority are possible. What is suitable to one trainee population may not be applicable to another. Also, the supervisor-apprentice relationship can appropriately be regarded as one of a number of possible training devices, one which comes at the end of a series of other training experiences rather than one which comes at the beginning or which constitutes the only training procedure.

In designing a program of training, it is important to recognize that many training needs can be touched upon or dealt with within a number of training contexts. Often, no single training context is exactly suited to a particular need but can make some contribution to it. As an example, consider the need to become aware of one's own fears in a group. Such awareness could emerge in the course of participating as a patient in a therapy group, or as a member in a training or study group; it may emerge in exercises; it may become apparent only when the trainee assumes responsibility for a group for the first time. The same may be said of many of the other needs which we have identified. All this suggests that the value of a program does not lie exclusively in its design—suitable training experiences introduced in a suitable order—but in the attitudes and teaching skills of the training staff, for if the mentors are aware of the training needs, they will be alert to opportunities to meet them in whatever training context. Offering a variety of training experiences can be expected to increase the likelihood that a number of training needs can be touched upon, but the real effectiveness of operation of group therapy practice will depend on the extent to which the training staff is sensitive to the training needs of the learner and can effectively exploit the full range of training procedures to this end.

References

Bion, W. R.: *Experiences in Groups.* New York, Basic Books, 1959.

Foulkes, S. H., and Anthony, E. J.: *Group Psychotherapy.* Baltimore, Md., Penguin, 1957.

Lieberman, M. A., Lakin, M., and Whitaker, D. S.: Problems and potential of psychoanalytic and group-dynamic theories for group psychotherapy. *International Journal of Group Psychotherapy,* 19:131-141, 1969.

Whitaker, D. S., and Lieberman, M. A.: *Psychotherapy Through the Group Process.* Chicago, Atherton Press, 1964.

Chapter 8

PARAPROFESSIONALS: THEIR ROLES
AND FUNCTIONS

Pₐᵣₐₚᵣₒfₑₛₛᵢₒₙₐₗₛ have been used in schools, hospitals, research and training centers, university counseling centers, and the ghetto. They serve such diverse populations as psychiatric and retarded patients, college dormitory residents, emotionally disturbed children, and the disadvantaged. People representing varied backgrounds, from college students to mothers, have provided assistance in their role as support personnel. To add to its credibility, professional organizations have recognized the existence and growing importance of this movement by drawing up selection and training guidelines. And finally, descriptions of programs utilizing paraprofessionals, as well as studies investigating the efficacy of employing them, are being found in the literature with increasing frequency.

Thus, little doubt exists that the use of paraprofessionals represents a bona fide expansion of the counseling horizon with implications for counselor educators and supervisors. The roles and functions of paraprofessionals, however, have come under considerable attack. One point of view is stated in no uncertain terms by Gust in the following passages: "I believe that as producers of both counselors and support personnel, counselor educators must respect the function of counseling as being restricted to the professional. . . . Unless counseling remains as the professional counselor's function alone, and unless the professional counselor's autonomy in his function is safeguarded from the supervised functions of support personnel, I fear that the present confusion might lead to chaos" (Gust, 1968).

C. H. Patterson, in basic accord with Gust, suggests further that paraprofessionals should engage in circumscribed counseling-related functions. In his article "Subprofessional Functions and Short-Term Training," Patterson discusses the different roles and functions served by the professionally trained counselor and the paraprofessional.

It should be noted that Patterson and Gust's point of view reflects the American Personnel and Guidance Association position as outlined in their professional policy statement, "APGA Support Personnel for the Counselor: Their Technical and Non-technical Roles and Preparation" (see Chaper 2).

Carkhuff in his contribution, "Differential Functioning of Lay and Professional Helpers," argues that lay helpers can acquire counseling skills within a reasonably short period of time. Carkhuff's article is in sharp contrast to Patterson's as he challenges the adequacy of existing counselor training programs. He documents his contention that lay counselors compare favorably and in some cases outstrip products of counselor training programs in their facilitative skills. The author further states that counselor educators employ irrelevant criteria in selecting counselor candidates as well as teach them material that bears little relationship to the development of facilitative relationships.

Patterson and Carkhuff, two of the leading contributors to the literature, appear to be clearly polarized and in direct opposition regarding the extent of responsibility to be granted the paraprofessional. Data relative to how counselor educators and supervisors *in general* perceive this issue has not been available. Jones and Cox's study, "Support Personnel: Attitudes Toward Functions and Training Responsibility," offers some helpful information in this regard. They asked counselor educators to respond to a list of seventeen functions and (a) indicate if they are appropriate for support personnel, and (b) specify who should assume training responsibilities for each of the seventeen functions. In general, the respondents' perception of the role of support personnel is consistent with the APGA policy statement.

At a time when selection criteria and training activities for professional counselors remain in a state of flux, counselor educators and supervisors have embarked on a promising venture designed to integrate paraprofessionals into the counseling profession. At the very least, this enterprise is expected to pose significant challenges in the years ahead.

References

Gust, T.: Support personnel vs. the counselor. *Counselor Education and Supervision,* 7:153, 1968.

Additional References

Berenson, B. G., Carkhuff, R. R., and Myrus, P.: The interpersonal functioning and training of college students. *Journal of Counseling Psychology,* 13:441-446, 1966.

Brown, W. F., and Zunker, V. G.: Student counselor utilization at four-year institutions of higher learning. *The Journal of College Student Personnel,* 7:41-46, 1966.

Carkhuff, R. R.: *Helping and Human Relations: A Primer for Lay and Professional Helpers, Vol. 1, Selection and Training.* New York, Holt, Rinehart and Winston, 1969.

Carkhuff, R. R.: *Helping and Human Relations: A Primer for Lay and Professional Helpers, Vol. II, Practice and Research.* New York, Holt, Rinehart and Winston, 1969.

Dendy, R. F.: *The Training of Undergraduate Residence Hall Assistants as Paraprofessionals: An Integrated Didactic-Experiential Model Using Video-Taping and Interpersonal Process Recall.* Unpublished manuscript, Michigan State University, 1971.

Haase, R. F., and DiMattia, D. J.: The application of the microcounseling paradigm to the training of support personnel. *Counselor Education and Supervision,* 10:16-22, 1970.

Harvey, L. V.: The use of nonprofessional auxiliary counselors in staffing a counseling service. *Journal of Counseling Psychology,* 11:348-351, 1964.

Holzberg, J. D., Knapp, R. H., and Turner, J. L.: College students as companions to the mentally ill. In Cowen, E. L., Gardner, E. A., and Zax, M. (Eds.): *Emergent Approaches to Mental Health Problems,* New York, Appleton-Century-Crofts, 1967.

Matarazzo, J. D.: Some national developments in the utilization of nontraditional mental health manpower. *American Psychologist,* 26:363-371, 1971.

Salomone, P.: The role of the paraprofessional: present and future. *Rehabilitation Research and Practice Review,* 1:1-4, 1970.

Schlossberg, N. K.: Sub-professionals: To be or not to be. *Counselor Education and Supervision,* 6:108-113, 1967.

Schroeder, P., and Dowse, E.: Selection, function and assessment of residence hall counselors. *Personnel and Guidance Journal,* 47:151-156, 1968.

Sobey, F.: *The Nonprofessional Revolution in Mental Health.* New York, Cole Press, 1970.

Tomlinson, T. M., Barthol, R. P., and Grott, H.: Responses of non-professional therapists to chronic schizophrenics. *Psychotherapy: Theory, Research and Practice,* 6:256-260, 1969.

Truax, C. B., and Lister, J.: Effectiveness of counselors and counselor aides. *Journal of Counseling Psychology,* 17:331-334, 1970.

The utilization of support personnel in rehabilitation counseling. *Studies in Rehabilitation Counselor Training.* Joint liaison committee of the council of state administrators of vocational rehabilitation and the rehabilitation counselor educators (No. 7), 1969.

Verinis, J. S.: The ex-patient as a lay therapist: Attitudes of group members toward him. *Psychotherapy: Theory, Research and Practice,* 7:161-163, 1970.

Wolff, T.: Undergraduates as campus mental health workers. *Personnel and Guidance Journal,* 48:294-304, 1969.

SUBPROFESSIONAL FUNCTIONS AND SHORT-TERM TRAINING*

C. H. PATTERSON

The demand for counselors in various fields has exceeded the supply for many years. This demand is presently increasing more rapidly with the development of new government programs, such as those under the Economic Opportunity Act of 1964. It is estimated that there will be 30,000 new counselors needed in the next few years.

In the face of such a demand, there is pressure, and temptation, to attempt to meet the need by shortcuts, such as the reduction of the period of counselor preparation. The summer NDEA institutes are an example of the acquiescence of professional educators to such demands. The CAUSE program is another. Even the easy acceptance of academic year institutes is a compromise in the face of professional recognition that two years is the minimum time in which a person can be adequately prepared for counseling.

The argument for such programs is made in terms of the immediate need for counselors. An eight- to ten-week program supplies persons for jobs much sooner than a two-year program. Two things must be noted here, however. First, such persons are not adequately prepared for counseling and are not and should not

* Reprinted from *Counselor Education and Supervision,* 4:144-146, 1965, with permission of the American Personnel and Guidance Association and the author.

be called counselors. Second, the earlier availability of such persons may appear to meet an immediate need but (a) over a period of time there will be no more persons available than if a two-year program were provided, since at the end of two years adequately prepared counselors would be produced at the same rate as eight- to ten-week persons; and (b) the setting up of short-term programs delays the development of long-term programs and makes it necessary to wait longer for adequately prepared persons. In addition, the field becomes filled with inadequately prepared persons, most of whom will not continue their education to the point where they are adequately prepared. Low standards are thus perpetuated.

The establishment of short-term programs for the preparation of persons for counseling is thus clearly professionally undesirable. There is another partial solution to the urgent need for providing counseling services to the increasing number and variety of clients. This is an approach which has developed in other professional fields. It consists in identifying and defining functions which can be performed by individuals with lesser skills and/or preparation than the fully professionally prepared person. These individuals are often called aides or assistants, e.g. nurse aide, dentist's assistant, teacher's assistant.

It might appear that this is the approach being taken by the Department of Labor in its CAUSE program, since the term counselor aide is used. There is a significant difference, however, between the proposed counselor aide and the use of the term aide in most other professions. In most professions, the aide is a terminal position, and not a promotional position. The nurse aide does not become a nurse following experience or further training, unless the aide enters into the standard program for nurses' training. In contrast, the counselor aide in the CAUSE program is viewed as becoming, with experience and *without any further training* (Kranz, 1964) a counselor. This is something which it would hardly be expected that the United States Employment Service of the Department of Labor, with its experience in job definitions and classification, could condone.

Since the term counselor aide has been misused by the Department of Labor, it seems desirable to avoid its use in the designation of individuals who might perform subprofessional functions related to counseling, in a terminal position. It is suggested, however, that a partial solution to the manpower shortage in counseling, as in nursing and teaching, could be provided by the employment of such subprofessional persons in counseling agencies, including schools.

The APGA Professional Preparation and Standards Committee considered this solution in relation to the APGA Policy Statement on "The Counselor: Professional Preparation and Role." At its June 1964 meeting, the following relevant statements were made:

> The total complex of functions of a counselor consists of professional competencies which are in part built upon certain basic technical skills. The amount of training required for individuals to perform various technical skills may vary considerably. Certain of the skills, such as interviewing for data collection purposes only, may require a relatively short period of training while preparation for the professional competency of test interpretation would obviously require a much longer period of time.
>
> It is recognized that there may be job situations requiring only certain technical skills and it would be possible to train individuals for these specific skills in limited periods of time. The amount of training would have to be fully compatible with the specific needs of the job situation. Furthermore, the expectations of job performance of individuals receiving such training should be limited to *only* those specific skills for which they are trained and for which competent supervision is provided. Extension of their functions should be limited to tasks compatible with their own abilities and personal characteristics and for which the necessary additional training has been received. Qualified individuals should be encouraged to undertake planned graduate programs leading to the point of their ultimately becoming a professional counselor [APGA, 1964].

One of the apparent points of disagreement among some counselor educators regarding subprofessional assistants or technicians is that some see this individual as a person who is on the way to becoming a counselor. The position taken here is that (a) there is precedent for establishing terminal subprofessional positions; (b) the nature of the training for such positions, while they may include some of the parts of the preparation of a counselor, is not identical with the first part of such preparation; (c) the kinds of persons selected for such positions may differ from those selected to prepare for counseling, and if potential counselors were selected for such positions, they would soon leave to enter upon preparation for counseling, or, if they could not do so, would not be satisfied in the work to which they would be limited; and (d) the use of such positions in recruitment of persons for counselor preparation programs is thus not desirable. It is suggested that the counseling profession should give serious consideration to the establishment of subprofessional positions in which individuals could function as technicians and assistants to fully trained counselors, following appropriate preparation for such functions.

References

American Personnel and Guidance Association. *The Relationship of Short-Term and Specialized Programs to the APGA Policy Statement, "The Counselor: Professional Preparation and Role."* Report of Professional Preparation and Standards Committee, June 1964.

Kranz, H.: A crash program to aid disadvantaged youth. *The Guidepost,* 6:3-6, 1964.

DIFFERENTIAL FUNCTIONING OF LAY AND PROFESSIONAL HELPERS*

ROBERT R. CARKHUFF

A number of programs involving (*a*) short-term accelerated training for professional counselors (such as Natoinal Defense Education Act, NDEA, and Counselor-Advisor University Summer Education, CAUSE, Institutes) and (*b*) the employment of nonprofessional practitioners have been proposed and implemented to meet ever-growing social service needs. Concern over the development of these programs has taken two principal directions: First, speaking for many in the helping professions, some writers have expressed concern over the dangers of lowering professional standards and have stressed the employment of lay persons *only* as aides and assistants to free the professional from clerical and other more menial duties (Carkhuff, 1966; Odgers, 1964; Patterson, 1965; Rosenbaum, 1966; Schlossberg, 1967).

* Reprinted from the *Journal of Counseling Psychology, 15*:117-126, 1968, with permission of the American Psychological Association and the author.

Second, another group has emphasized the direct counseling contributions which lay persons can make and has explored the potentially unique advantages of selected subprofessions (Gordon, 1965; Holzberg, 1963; Reiff, 1966; Reiff and Riessman, 1965; Reissman and National Institute of Labor Education, 1964). The development of these "lower level" programs has, in addition, become the concern of the major national associations concerned with guidance, counseling, and therapeutic activities. The American Personnel and Guidance Association (1964) and Kennedy and Strowig (1967) have acknowledged the limited contributions (at maximum, short-term interviewing, at minimum, clerical assistance) of subprofessionals, with the proviso that these persons be encouraged to continue further professional study. The American Psychological Association (Hoch, Ross, and Winder, 1965), in turn, has, with some apparent ambivalence, assumed a relatively open stance, suggesting that psychology ought to keep an open mind, letting the results speak for themselves" (p. 51).

At least in part because of their concern for protecting the public at large from potentially harmful practices, professionals have assessed the processes and outcomes of lay training and treatment. The following set of propositions summarizing the research of lay training and treatment programs (Carkhuff, 1967) is presented in the hope of "letting the results speak for themselves." In so doing, the results of subprofessional training and treatment programs will be contrasted with those of professional training and treatment. It is hoped that the summary nature of the propositions will establish the groundwork for generating a series of tentative hypotheses concerning the differential processes of lay and professional training and treatment.

Efficacy of Training

While a number of lay as well as professional training programs have been implemented, only a few have systematically assessed their effects in terms of process variables related in previous research to a variety of indexes of constructive client outcome. Those that have assessed dimensions such as the counselor's communication of empathy, warmth, regard or respect, and genuineness or congruence, and, to a lesser degree, dimensions, such as concreteness or specificity of expression, self-disclosure, and openness (the outcome research which is summarized in Carkhuff and Berenson, 1967, and Truax and Carkhuff, 1967) have yielded the following conclusions:

1. There is extensive evidence to indicate that lay persons can be trained to function at minimally facilitative levels of conditions related to constructive client change over relatively short periods of time. Both carefully screened college graduates interested in school guidance activities and unselected volunteers from the school, hospital, and community at large demonstrate change in the direction of more facilitative functioning on dimensions related to constructive client change or gain in training periods ranging from 20 hours to 1 year (Berenson, Carkhuff, and Myrus, 1966; Carkhuff and Truax, 1965b; Demos, 1964; Demos and Zuwaylif, 1963; Gunning, Holmes, Johnson, and Rife, 1965; Hansen and Barker, 1964; Jones, 1963; Kratochvil, in press; Martin and Carkhuff, 1968; Munger and Johnson, 1960; Pierce, Carkhuff, and Berenson, 1967; Webb and Harris, 1963; Wrightsman, Richard, and Noble, 1966).

2. There is little evidence to indicate that professional trainee products are being trained to function effectively on any dimensions related to constructive client change over very long periods of training. The evidence on the communication of facilitative dimensions related to constructive client change (Bergin and Soloman, 1963; Carkhuff, Kratochvil, and Friel, 1968), as well as the ability to judge the personal characteristics of others (Arnhoff, 1964; Kelly and Fiske, 1950; Taft, 1955; Weiss, 1963), for graduate trainees screened primarily on intellective indexes yield negative results over periods ranging from 4 years upwards. Although the results in one intermediate type professional 2-year rehabilitation counselor training program were positive (Anthony, 1968), the initial level of trainee functioning was so low that the final level of trainee functioning was still lower than the initial level of most professional trainees in other programs. Thus, the results, while statistically significant, should be interpreted cautiously.

3. Comparative statistics indicate the greater effectiveness of lay over lower level guidance training programs in eliciting con-

structive trainee change on those conditions related to constructive client change. While there are few directly comparable studies, in general, following training, on both identical and converted indexes, lay trainees function at levels essentially as high or higher (never significantly lower), and engage clients in counseling process movement at levels as high or higher, than professional trainees (Anthony, 1968; Berenson, *et al.*, 1966; Bergin and Soloman, 1963; Carkhuff, Kratochvil, and Friel, 1968; Carkhuff and Truax, 1965a; Martin and Carkhuff, 1968; Pierce, *et al.*, 1967).

Of course, the fact that one program can demonstrate the movement of its trainees on indexes (even those related in previous research to constructive client change) while another program can give no evidence of any significant movement (even on indexes unrelated to any meaningful criteria) does not of necessity indicate immediate and direct translations to client benefits in favor of the former group. In order to break free of possible circularity in our efforts, we must assess the effects of the consequent treatment engaged in by the trainees of both groups.

Efficacy of Treatment

Again, although ongoing treatment programs, lay as well as professional, are of necessity much more numerous than the training programs, few have systematically assessed their effects. However, where the varied assessments of the efficacy of the helper's treatment offering have included those made by outside experts—the helper's supervisors and co-workers, the patient's ward attendants, and significant others—as well as reports by the patient himself, and where the client outcome criteria have included hospital discharge and recidivism rates, assessments of psychological functioning and total adjustment, social-interpersonal behavior, communication and cooperation, self-care and mobility, reaction time and verbal fluency, and indexes of sexual-marital and educational-vocational functioning, as well as the more traditional testing indexes, the following conclusions emerge:

1. There is extensive evidence to indicate that lay persons

can effect significant constructive change in the clients whom they see. There is evidence to indicate that hospitalized neuropsychiatric patients (Anker and Walsh, 1961; Appleby, 1963; Beck, Kantor, and Gelineau, 1963; Carkhuff and Truax, 1965a; Colarelli and Siegel, 1963; Glasser, 1965; Greenblatt and Kantor, 1962; Holzberg and Knapp, 1965; Kantor and Greenblatt, 1962; Poser, 1966; Siegel and Colarelli, 1964; Tudor, 1952; Warme, 1965), outpatient neuropsychiatric patients (Magoon and Golann, 1966; Mendel and Rapport, 1963; Rioch, Elkes, Flint, Udansky, Newman, and Silber, 1963), normals situationally distressed or otherwise (Brown, 1965; Harvey, 1964; Zunker and Brown, 1966), and children (Guerney, 1964; Guerney, Guerney, and Andronico, 1966; Wahler, Winkel, Peterson, and Morrison, 1965) demonstrate significant constructive change as a consequence of their contacts with lay persons.

2. Professional graduate programs have not yet demonstrated the relevant evidence for the translation of their training efforts to client benefits. The lack of empirical demonstration of the positive effects of professional graduate programs is perhaps due not so much to the inability to do so as to the universal reluctance of these programs to make enlightened and systematic inquiries into their training efforts. Ironically, that benefits do accrue to patients treated by professional helpers can be inferred from the data of Eysenck (1965), Levitt (1963), and Lewis (1965). These data, while indicating no average differences between treatment and control groups of adult and child patients, also indicate that approximately two-thirds of patients do improve over a 1 to 2 year period. The fact is that constructive change does occur in both treatment and control groups. Perhaps we must devote more attention to studying the control group members, who, although not assinged to professional helpers, may have found nonprofessional helpers.

3. In directly comparable studies, selected lay persons with or without training and/or supervision have patients who demonstrate change as great or greater than the patients of professional practitioners. While the number of comparable studies is limited, with both outpatients and inpatients, lay persons effect change on the indexes assessed at least as great or, all too frequently,

greater (never significantly less) than professionals (Anker and Walsh, 1961; Harvey, 1964; Magoon and Golann, 1966; Mendel and Rapport, 1963; Poser, 1966; Rioch, *et al.*, 1963).

Questions and Explorations

The results raise a number of unanswered questions. Are the results, for example, attributable to differences in (*a*) the trainees themselves, (*b*) the selection processes, (*c*) the training personnel, (*d*) the training programs proper, (*e*) treatment procedures, (*f*) any of the above, or (*g*) all of the above? In the interest of casting further illumination on these results, let us explore what evidence there is in all of these areas.

Trainee Personnel

Indications are that, in general, lay counselors are less intelligent and intellectual, less educated, and from lower socioeconomic classes than professional counselors and therapists, who by virtue of education and vocation are upper class. In addition, it would appear that lay persons are motivated to help by other than the overdetermined needs of the professional to find position, status, prestige, money, and perhaps some "handles" on his own psychological difficulties, among other things, within the helping role. Perhaps the lay person is simply motivated to help because he is most in contact with the need for help, for himself, for others. How do these differences translate to the helping process? Here, interestingly enough, we have extensive base-rate data to indicate that the typical professional trainee at the beginning of training is functioning at significantly higher levels of those dimensions related to constructive client change than is the typical lay person (summarized in Carkhuff and Berenson, 1967). The fact that the professional trainee is functioning at higher levels prior to training and lower levels following training, both in relation to lay trainees and himself (Bergin and Soloman, 1963; Carkhuff, Kratochvil, and Friel, 1968), implies that something deleterious to his level of functioning on those indexes related to client change may happen to him over the course of training. In summary, we can conclude that both the means and the intentions of prospective lay helpers are more humble and direct, or honest, at the beginning of training than the means and intentions of prospective professional helpers.

Trainee Selection

While the process of professional trainee selection is quite stable, the selection processes of lay training programs vary widely, from essentially unselected populations involving self-selected volunteers to very carefully selected helpers. However, although the selection procedures of at least one lay program Rioch, *et al.*, 1963) closely paralleled those of graduate programs, the screening efforts by the promulgators of most lay programs are typified by the work of Harvey (1964) and his colleagues, who made an intensified attempt to select "persons who exhibit a sincere regard for others, tolerance and ability to accept people with values different from one's own, a healthy regard for the self, a warmth and sensitivity in dealing with others, and a capacity for empathy" (p. 349). The professional training programs, in turn, are dominated by highly intellective indexes of selection, primarily grade-point average (GPA), complemented by Graduate Record Examination performance. However, even though the professional trainees' higher levels of functioning on facilitative dimensions suggest a relationship between intellective indexes and level of functioning, within the range of levels of functioning of candidates for graduate school, there is little or no relationship with GPA (Allen, 1967; Carkhuff, Piaget, and Pierce, 1968). This finding is consistent with that of Holland and Richards (1965), indicating the independence of academic performance from real-life indexes of achievement. Further, within graduate school, there are tentative indications of a slightly negative relationship between GPA and the levels of trainee functioning on indexes relevant to constructive client change (Bergin and Soloman, 1963). Thus, while professional selection indexes appear, at best, irrelevant to effective counseling and therapeutic functioning, it can be concluded that lay trainees, ranging from self-selected volunteers to carefully selected psychologically healthy persons, are able to effectively employ the training experiences which are provided them. With the thought in mind that there is no necessary reason why high levels of intellectual functioning should present a handicap to the acquisition of improved interpersonal skills (Berenson, *et al.*, 1966; Carkhuff and Truax, 1965b), we turn to consideration of the training programs and their promulgators.

Training Personnel

Base-rate data indicate that experienced practitioners, including those conducting our professional training programs, are functioning at less than minimally facilitative levels. Indeed, they are functioning at levels commensurate to or lower than professional trainees at the beginning of graduate training (summarized in Carkhuff and Berenson, 1967). Further, there is evidence to indicate that just as clients converge on the level of functioning of their counselors (Pagell, Carkhuff, and Berenson, 1967), so do trainees converge on the level of functioning of their trainers (Pierce, *et al.*, 1967): Trainees of high-level functioning trainers demonstrate uniformly positive change; trainees of low- or moderate-level functioning trainers demonstrate little, no, or deteriorative change. It can be inferred that the level of functioning of the professional trainer may account in large part for the negative results in studies of graduate training. While the work of Hansen (1965) suggested that NDEA guidance institute trainers may be functioning at levels higher than the pretraining expectations of trainees (and this has implications for either the high level of functioning of these trainers or the low level of expectations of the trainees), there is no direct evidence concerning the level of functioning of the lay trainer.

Training Program

The lay training programs are, by and large, simple, rather homogeneous programs geared to producing counselors who can effectively relate to persons in need of help and facilitate their positive movement. In the limited time available, the focus seems to center around two phenomena: (*a*) sensitivity training or the acquisition of interpersonal skills, and (*b*) the change in the personality and the attitudes of the trainee himself. Thus, these programs are built around the core conditions of understanding, regard, and genuineness, both in their didactic teaching for helping and the experiential base provided the trainee. By contrast, the professional training programs are highly complex, hetero-geneous, often apparently self-neutralizing admixtures of science and art and research and practice, often with little to bridge the yawning gap.

While the results of lay programs exhibit trainee gains on those dimensions related to client change, the professional pro-grams exhibit a drop in the level of trainee functioning over the course of graduate training, with the largest drop seeming to occur from the first to second year (Carkhuff, in press; Carkhuff, Kratochvil, and Friel, 1968; Carkhuff, Piaget, and Pierce, 1968). Although practitioners, with experience, appear to recoup some of their losses in functioning, there are direct suggestions that they may never again function at the level of those conditions re-lated to constructive change with which they entered graduate school (Carkhuff and Berenson, 1967). Two follow-up evalua-tion studies also indicated that those who drop out of professional training tend to be functioning at higher levels of facilitative conditions than those who stay in. There is, however, evidence to indicate improvement in the ability of graduate trainees to dis-criminate the levels of conditions offered by other counselors (Carkhuff, Kratochvil, and Friel, 1968). While there is no evi-dence to relate discrimination to client change, the direct im-plication is that the main effects of graduate training are related to the development of discriminators, rather than communicators, in a world needy for communicators. It can be concluded, then, that lay training programs attempt to use the little time which they have available to effect as great trainee changes as they can on indexes related to counselee and trainee change. Professional programs, in turn, appear to use the great time which they have available to them to effect trainee change on indexes unrelated to counselee or trainee change. Simply stated, lay programs simply try to prepare people to help people. Among the many things which graduate training attempts, one thing which it apparently does not prepare people to do is to help other people.

Treatment

Again, while professional programs have failed to produce tangible evidence of their translation to client benefits and, indeed, evidence that they are concerned with researching their training efforts, assessments of lay counselor programs have yielded positive results. The professional practitioner all too often focuses upon highly elaborate, highly cognitive systems in treating his client: His efforts are role dominated, and it is frequently his theories and techniques that are on the line in counseling— not he, the counselor. By contrast, the lay counselor has less expertise; he is more in contact with his uncertainty, less sure and less formulative; he has only himself (and, sometimes, his supervisor) to rely upon, and often tries only to stay with and "be with" the client. However, the lay counselor is also unencumbered by the professional role conflicts which disallow his full and intense involvement and entry into the life activities of another person. In summary, the person of the lay counselor and the treatment which he offers appear to have the following distinctive advantages when compared to his professional counterparts: (*a*) the increased ability to enter the milieu of the distressed; (*b*) the ability to establish peer-like relationships with the needy; (*c*) the ability to take an active part in the client's total life situation; (*d*) the ability to empathize more effectively with the client's style of life; (*e*) the ability to teach the client, from within the client's frame of reference, more successful actions; and (*f*) the ability to provide clients with a more effective transition to more effective levels of functioning within the social system. In short, the lay counselor, when appropriately employed, can be the "human link" between society and the needy. Here there is some evidence concerning the differential effects in counseling of both race and social class (Banks, Berenson, and Carkhuff, 1967; Carkhuff and Pierce, 1967), a necessary link which professionals are not now adequately filling.

Extensions and Implications

The helping professions have asked critical questions concerning the effectiveness of lay training and treatment programs. A review of these programs indicates (*a*) that lay persons can be trained to function at minimally facilitative levels of conditions related to constructive client change in relatively short periods of time, and (*b*) that lay counselors can effect significant constructive changes in clients. An inference that we might draw is that whatever allows one individual to help another is not the sole and exclusive province of professional helpers. In fact, the lack of significant differences between treated and untreated groups in the Eysenck-Levitt-Lewis data may be accounted for by the possibility that some of the patients in the "untreated" control groups sought out the help of untrained lay persons. Of course, all of this is not to say that any form of psychological treatment is significantly more effective in eliciting constructive client movement and outcome greater than other forms of activities. In order to determine this, studies are needed which incorporate treatment control groups of patients which meet for the same amount of time for different kinds of activities (Anker and Walsh, 1961).

Perhaps the main value of lay counseling research is in pointing up the need for similar research of our professional training and treatment programs. While many, in defense of their programs, particularly those in psychology, have stated that they are not training people to help people, we do not believe this to be a tenable position. If, however, they are primarily training researchers, then we believe that, at a minimum, the first order of investigation should be to assess the translation of professional training to treatment benefits. We can no longer afford—at the expense of our clients—the luxury of assuming the effectiveness of professional treatment.

For the present, it appears that both the trainees and the trainers, the procedures by which they are selected, and the training and treatment procedures are all potential sources of the differential results of lay and professional programs. However, there is absolutely no reason in the world why professional programs cannot be effective in enabling their trainees to function at higher levels of those conditions related to client change; in fact, there is evidence from at least one one-semester program to indicate that graduate students can do very well indeed (Carkhuff and Truax, 1965b).

Interestingly enough, whereas it is traditional to look upward to the next highest rung in the status hierarchy in order to emulate their models and, hopefully, to achieve their successes, the highest rung—the medical profession and, particularly, psychiatry— is already seriously considering the extensive employment of lay personnel (Coggeshall, 1965; Creech, 1966 Joint Commission on Mental Illness and Health, 1961; Lief, 1966), and at least one school—the University of Pittsburgh School of Medicine—is seriously considering instituting an accredited training program in lay mental health counseling. It is imperative that the professional programs in guidance, counseling, and clinical psychology, as well as psychiatry and social work, not only look downward to the "lower level" programs for their own distinctive contributions, but also to incorporate the simple emphasis upon core conditions conducive to facilitative human experiences and the simple procedures for training people in discriminative and communicative skills. It certainly would be congruent with the client's perception of what is helpful to him in counseling (Deane and Ansbacher, 1962; Lorr, 1965; Matarazzo, 1965; Miller, 1965; Spiegel and Spiegel, 1967).

All of this is not to say that there are no problems in lay counseling. Of the programs which are here reviewed, at least one treatment program assessing unselected and untrained hospital attendants (Sines, Sliver, and Lucero, 1961) yielded no positive results. In addition, there are problems involved in the recruiting of lay helpers and implementing lay programs (Weiner and Brand, 1965), including those involving consultation and role definition (Warme, 1965). Finally, there are problems involved in assessing the long-term effects of short-term programs. For one thing, the trainee products frequently will return to an environment which will not support and reinforce their activities (Meadow and Tillem, 1963; Munger, Myer, and Brown, 1963). Lay counseling training and treatment activities may run counter to many of the prevailing traditional forces in the helping profession and the community at large. Reluctant verbal acknowledgment and assent may give way to unconscious undermining in the face of the real possibility of lay practices. Already, for example, the critics of programs demonstrating the greater effectiveness of lay helpers over professionals on indexes selected by professionals are saying that with time the effectiveness of the lay persons will wear off (Rioch, 1966; Rosenbaum, 1966). With the question, "What happens to the professional counselor over time?" we encourage these critics to research the long-term effectiveness of both lay and professional helpers.

Further examples of problems resolve around the question of employing lay persons as clerical assistants in order to free counselors for counseling duties. While this would seem to make sense for effective helpers, it appears premature. We simply do not know if our counselors are effective. Even if the counselors were freed of their administrative responsibilities (most of which are of highly dubious value in the first place) and did indeed engage in more counseling activities (which may be highly unlikely in the second place), we would only be perpetuating more of the same practices (which are of unknown or questionable efficacy in the third place). There will be no new learning in this for a profession which needs to learn very much about itself, very much indeed.

The dangers of professionalization, in part as we have described them in our explorations of professional programs, but much more extensive in terms of professional concerns for image, status, and spheres of influence, will beset the potent practitioner, lay and otherwise. On the one hand, there are those who have worked for and acquired recognition of various master's and doctoral programs who will be threatened. On the other hand, there are already those who argue for a master's program in lay counseling for college graduates. There may come a day when, ironic as it seems, there will be proposals for doctoral programs in lay counseling.

Finally, while the results of lay programs point upward to the need to explore and, if necessary, reconstruct our professional programs, they also point downward to indigenous personnel within the populations of persons receiving help. We are talking about the "helper therapy principle" by which persons in need of help may be selected and trained to offer help. At a minimum, there is evidence to suggest that indigenous persons giving help demonstrate constructive change themselves, as a consequence of being cast in the helping role (Holzberg, Gewirtz, and Ebner, 1965; Holzberg, Whiting, and Lowy, 1964; Knapp and Holzberg, 1964; Riessman, 1965).

References

Allen, T. W.: The effectiveness of counselor trainees as a function of psychological openness. *Journal of Counseling Psychology, 14*:35-40. 1967.

American Personnel and Guidance Association, Professional Preparation and Standards Committee. *The Relationship of Short-Term and Specialized Programs to the APGA Policy Statement, "The Counselor: Professional Preparation and Role."* Washington, D.C., APGA, 1964.

Anker, J. M., and Walsh, R. P.: Group psychotherapy: a special activity program and group structure in the treatment of chronic schizophrenics. *Journal of Consulting Psychology, 25*:476-481, 1961.

Anthony, W.: *The Effects of Professional Training in Rehabilitation Counseling.* Unpublished manuscript, State University of New York at Buffalo, 1968.

Appleby, L.: Evaluation of treatment methods for chronic schizophrenia. *Archives of General Psychiatry, 8*:8-21, 1963.

Arnhoff, F. N.: Some factors influencing the unreliability of clinical judgments. *Journal of Clinical Psychology, 10*:272-275, 1954.

Banks, G., Berenson, B. G., and Carkhuff, R. R.: The effects of counselor race and training upon Negro clients in initial interviews. *Journal of Clinical Psychology, 23*:70-72, 1967.

Beck, J. C., Kantor, D., and Gelineau, V. A.: Follow-up study of chronic psychotic patients "treated" by college case-aide volunteers. *American Journal of Psychiatry, 120*:269-271, 1963.

Berenson, B. G., Carkhuff, R. R., and Myrus, P.: The interpersonal functioning and training of college students. *Journal of Counseling Psychology, 13*:441-446, 1966.

Bergin, A., and Soloman, S.: Personality and performance correlates of empathic understanding in psychotherapy. *American Psychologist, 18*: 393, 1963.

Brown, W. F.: Student-to-student counseling for academic adjustment. *Personnel and Guidance Journal, 43*:811-817, 1965.

Carkhuff, R. R.: Training in the counseling and therapeutic processes: requiem or revielle? *Journal of Counseling Psychology, 13*:360-367, 1966.

Carkhuff, R. R.: *The Effects of Lay Counseling: Evaluation and Implications.* Paper presented at a conference on innovations in rehabilitation counseling, State University of New York at Buffalo, March 1967.

Carkhuff, R. R.: A nontraditional assessment of traditional programs. *Counselor Education and Supervision,* 1968.

Carkhuff, R. R., and Berenson, B. G.: *Beyond Counseling and Therapy.* New York, Holt, Rinehart and Winston, 1967.

Carkhuff, R. R., Kratochvil, D., and Friel, T.: The effects of graduate training. *Journal of Counseling Psychology, 15*:68-74, 1968.

Carkhuff, R. R., Piaget, G., and Pierce, R.: The development of skills in interpersonal functioning. *Counselor Education and Supervision,* 7:102-106, 1968.

Carkhuff, R. R., and Pierce, R.: The differential effects of therapist race and social class upon patient depth of self-exploration in the initial clinical interview. *Journal of Consulting Psychology,* 31:632-634, 1967.

Carkhuff, R. R., and Truax, C. B.: Lay mental health counseling: the effects of lay group counseling. *Journal of Consulting Psychology,* 29:426-432, 1965 (a).

Carkhuff, R. R., and Truax, C. B.: Training in counseling and psychotherapy: an evaluation of an integrated didactic and experiential approach. *Journal of Consulting Psychology,* 29:333-336, 1965 (b).

Coggeshall, L. T.: *Planning for Medical Progress Through Education.* Evanston, Ill., Association of American Medical Colleges, 1965.

Colarelli, N. J., and Siegel, S. M.: *A Re-evaluation of the role of the Psychiatric Aide.* Progress Report, Project Grant OM-770, National Institute of Mental Health, 1963.

Creech, O.: Medical practice in 1990. *Bulletin of the Tulane University of Louisiana Medical Faculty,* 25:229-238, 1966.

Deene, W. N., and Ansbacher, H. L.: Attendant-patient commonality as a psychotherapeutic factor. *Journal of Individual Psychology,* 18:157-167, 1962.

Demos, G. D.: The application of certain principles of client-centered therapy to short-term vocational counseling. *Journal of Counseling Psychology,* 11:280-284, 1964.

Demos, G. D., and Zuwaylif, F. H.: Counselor movement as a result of an intensive six-week training program in counseling. *Personnel and Guidance Journal,* 42:125-128, 1963.

Eysenck, H. J.: The effects of psychotherapy. *International Journal of Psychiatry,* 1:99-178, 1965.

Glasser, W.: *Reality Therapy: A New Approach to Psychiatry.* New York, Harper & Row, 1965.

Gordon, J. E.: Project CAUSE, the federal antipoverty program, and some implications of subprofessional training. *American Psychologist,* 20:334-343, 1965.

Greenblatt, M., and Kantor, D.: Student volunteer movement and the manpower shortage. *American Journal of Psychiatry,* 118:809-814, 1962.

Guerney, B.: Filial therapy: description and rationale. *Journal of Consulting Psychology,* 28:304-310, 1964.

Guerney, B., Guerney, L. F., and Andronico, M. P.: Filial therapy. *Yale Scientific Magazine,* 40:6-14, 1966.

Gunning, T. J., Holmes, J. E., Johnson, P. W., and Rife, S. M.: Process in a short-term NDEA counseling and guidance institute. *Counselor Education and Supervision,* 4:81-88, 1965.

Hansen, J. C.: Trainees' expectations of supervision in the counseling practicum. *Counselor Education and Supervision,* 4:75-80, 1965.

Hansen, J. C., and Barker, E. N.: Experiencing and the supervisory relationship. *Journal of Counseling Psychology,* 11:107-111, 1964.

Harvey, L. V.: The use of nonprofessional auxiliary counselors in staffing a counseling service. *Journal of Counseling Psychology,* 11:348-351, 1964.

Hoch, E. L., Ross, A. O., and Winder, C. L.: Conference on the professional preparation of clinical psychologists. *American Psychologist,* 21:42-51, 1965.

Holland, J. L., and Richards, J. M.: Academic and nonacademic accomplishment: correlated or uncorrelated? *Journal of Educational Psychology,* 56:165-174, 1965.

Holzberg, J. D.: The companion program: implementing the manpower recommendations of the Joint Commission on Mental Illness and Health. *American Psychologist,* 18:224-226, 1963.

Holzberg, J. D., Gewirtz, H., and Ebner, E.: Changes in self-acceptance and moral judgments in college students as a function of companionship with hospitalized patients. *Journal of Consulting Psychology,* 28:299-303, 1964.

Holzberg, J. D., and Knapp, R. H.: The social interaction of college students and chronically ill patients. *American Journal of Orthopsychiatry,* 35:487-492, 1965.

Holzberg, J. D., Whiting, H. S., and Lowy, D. G.: Chronic patients and a college companion program. *Mental Hospitals,* 15:152-158, 1964.

Joint Commission on Mental Illness and Health: *Action for Mental Health.* New York, Basic Books, 1961.

Jones, V.: Attitude changes in an NDEA institute. *Personnel and Guidance Journal,* 42:387-389, 1963.

Kantor, D., and Greenblatt, M. (Eds.): *College Students in a Mental Hospital.* New York, Grune & Stratton, 1962.

Kelly, E. L., and Fiske, D. W.: The prediction of success in the VA training program in clinical psychology. *American Psychologist,* 5:395-406, 1950.

Kennedy, E. G., and Strowig, R. W.: Support personnel for the counselor: their technical and nontechnical roles and preparation. *Personnel and Guidance Journal,* 45:857-861, 1967.

Knapp, R. H., and Holzberg, J. D.: Characteristics of college students volunteering for service to mental patients. *Journal of Counsulting Psychology,* 28:82-85, 1964.

Kratochvil, D.: Changes in values and interpersonal functioning of nurses in counselor training. *Counselor Education and Supervision,* 1968.

Levitt, E. E.: Psychotherapy with children: a further evaluation. *Behavior Research and Therapy,* 1:45-51, 1963.

Lewis, W. W.: Continuity and intervention in emotional disturbance: a review. *Exceptional Children, 31*:465-475, 1965.

Lief, H. I.: Subprofessional training in mental health. *Archives of General Psychiatry, 15*:660-664, 1966.

Lorr, M.: Client perceptions of therapists: a study of therapeutic relations. *Journal of Consulting Psychology, 29*:146-149, 1965.

Magoon, T. M., and Golann, S. E.: Nontraditionally trained women as mental health counselors-psychotherapists. *Personnel and Guidance Journal, 44*:788-793, 1966.

Martin, J. C., and Carkhuff, R. R.: The effects of training upon trainee personality and behavior. *Journal of Clinical Psychology, 24*:109-110, 1968.

Matarazzo, J. D.: Psychotherapeutic processes. *Annual Review of Psychology, 16*:181-224, 1965.

Meadow, L., and Tillem, K.: Evaluating the effectiveness of a workshop rehabilitation program. *Personnel and Guidance Journal, 42*:541-545, 1963.

Mendel, W. M., and Rapport, S.: Outpatient treatment for chronic schizophrenic patients: therapeutic consequences of an existential view. *Archives of General Psychiatry, 8*:190-196, 1963.

Miller, T. K.: Characteristics of perceived helpers. *Personnel and Guidance Journal, 12*:353-358, 1965.

Munger, P. F., and Johnson, C. A.: Changes in attitudes associated with an NDEA counseling and guidance institute. *Personnel and Guidance Journal, 38*:751-753, 1960.

Munger, P. F., Myers, R. A., and Brown, D. F.: Guidance institutes and the persistence of attitudes. *Personnel and Guidance Journal, 41*:415-419, 1963.

Odgers, J. C.: Cause for concern. *Counselor Education and Supervision, 4*: 17-20, 1964.

Pagell, W., Carkhuff, R. R., and Berenson, B. G.: The predicted differential effects of the level of counselor functioning upon the level of functioning of outpatients. *Journal of Clinical Psychology, 23*:510-512, 1967.

Patterson, C. H.: Subprofessional functions and short-term training. *Counselor Education and Supervision, 4*:144-146, 1965.

Pierce, R., Carkhuff, R. R., and Berenson, B. G.: The differential effects of high and moderate level functioning counselors upon counselors-in-training. *Journal of Clinical Psychology, 23*:212-215, 1967.

Poser, E. G.: The effect of therapists' training on group therapeutic outcome. *Journal of Consulting Psychology, 30*:283-289, 1966.

Reiff, R.: Mental health manpower and institutional change. *American Psychologist, 21*:540-548, 1966.

Reiff, R., and Riessman, F.: The indigenous nonprofessional. *Community Mental Health Journal*, No. 1, 1965.

Riessman, F.: The "helper" therapy principle. *Social Work, 10*:27-32, 1965.

Riessman, F., and National Institute of Labor Education: *New Approaches to Mental Health Treatment for Labor and Low Income Groups.* Report No. 2, National Institute of Labor Education, Mental Health Program, New York, 1964.

Rioch, M. J.: Changing concepts in the training of therapists. *Journal of Consulting Psychology, 30:*290-292, 1966.

Rioch, M. J., Elkes, E., Flint, A. A., Usdansky, B. S., Newman, B. G., and Silber, E.: NIMH pilot study in training mental health counselors. *American Journal of Orthopsychiatry, 33:*678-689, 1963.

Rosenbaum, M.: Some comments on the use of untrained therapists. *Journal of Consulting Psychology, 30:*292-294, 1966.

Schlossberg, N. K.: Sub-professionals: to be or not to be. *Counselor Education and Supervision, 6:*108-113, 1967.

Siegel, S. M., and Colarelli, N. J.: Gaining more from research experience. *Mental Hospitals, 15:*666-670, 1964.

Sines, L. K., Silver, R. J., and Lucero, R. J.: The effect of therapeutic intervention by untrained therapists. *Journal of Clinical Psychology, 17:*394-396, 1961.

Spiegel, P. K., and Spiegel, D. E.: Perceived helpfulness of others as a function of compatible intelligence levels. *Journal of Counseling Psychology, 14:*61-62, 1967.

Taft, R.: The ability to judge people. *Psychological Bulletin, 52:*1-23, 1955.

Truax, C. B., and Carkhuff, R. R.: *Toward Effective Counseling and Psychotherapy: Training and Practice.* Chicago, Aldine, 1967.

Tudor, G.: A socio-psychiatric nursing approach to intervention in problems of mutual withdrawal on a mental hospital ward. *Psychiatry, 15:*193-217, 1952.

Wahler, R. G., Winkel, G. H., Peterson, R. F., and Morrison, D. C.: Mothers as behavior therapists for their own children. *Behavior Research and Therapy, 3:*113-124, 1965.

Warme, G. E.: Consulting with aide-therapists. *Archives of General Psychiatry, 13:*432-438, 1965.

Webb, A. J., and Harris, J. T.: A semantic differential study of counselors in an NDEA institute. *Personnel and Guidance Journal, 42:*260-263, 1963.

Weiner, H. J., and Brand, M. S.: Involving a labor union in the rehabilitation of the mentally ill. *American Journal of Orthopsychiatry, 35:*598-600, 1965.

Weiss, J. H.: The effect of professional training and amount and accuracy of information on behavioral prediction. *Journal of Consulting Psychology, 27:*257-262, 1963.

Wrightsman, L. S., Richard, W. C., and Noble, F.: Attitude changes of guidance institute participants. *Counselor Education and Supervision, 5:*212-220, 1966.

Zunker, V. G., and Brown, W. F.: Comparative effectiveness of student and professional counselors. *Personnel and Guidance Journal*, 44:738-743, 1966.

SUPPORT PERSONNEL: ATTITUDES TOWARD FUNCTIONS AND TRAINING RESPONSIBILITY*

LAWRENCE K. JONES and WRAY K. COX

For some years now, a number of professions have considered the use of support personnel in a variety of health-related services. Discussion regarding the use and training of support personnel for counselors in the public schools has recently caught the attention of those directly related to this profession. The American Personnel and Guidance Association (1967) published a tentative statement of policy on the role and preparation of support personnel for counselors. Problems central to the training and use of support personnel have been discussed by Hansen (1965), Patterson (1965), Wrenn (1965), Gust (1968), and Strowig (1968). Recently, Beale (1969) surveyed the opinions of junior college counselors and counselor educators regarding appropriate duties, supervision, and preparation of "counselor aides" functioning in community junior colleges.

Most writers tend to agree that support personnel who are adequately trained and who have a well-defined role can make a significant contribution to the work of the counselor. The crucial issues, of course, are what their functions should be and who should have the responsibility for their training. To contribute to this ongoing dialogue, the authors felt it would be helpful to survey the opinions of heads of counselor education programs regarding these issues. More specifically, this study attempted to answer the following questions:

1. What functions do heads of counselor education programs feel are appropriate for support personnel working at the secondary school level?

2. Who should have the responsibility for training the support person to perform appropriate functions?

* Reprinted from *Counselor Education and Supervision*, 10:51-55, 1970, with permission of the American Personnel and Guidance Association and the authors.

3. To what extent are institutions with counselor education programs currently engaged in the training of support personnel?

Procedure

The *Directory of Counselor Educators 1967-1968* (Trexler, 1968) lists 372 colleges and universities that prepare guidance counselors. The sample for this study consisted of 200 heads of counselor education programs from these institutions randomly selected so that each of the five Association for Counselor Education and Supervision regions was proportionately represented. Heads of counselor education programs were selected because they represent positions of leadership in this field.

A questionnaire sent to each of the respondents asked them to identify any of 17 functions commonly performed by counselors they thought were appropriate for support personnel working at the secondary school level. For any particular function identified, they were to indicate who should have responsibility for training the support person for that function: counselors, counselor educators, or city-state directors of guidance. Chi-square ($d = .01$) was used to test the significance of their agreement or disagreement. The respondents were asked if they were currently engaged in the training of support personnel. They were invited to comment on the study and the questions it raised.

Results

Of the 200 respondents selected, 128 (64.0 %) replied to the questionnaire. This number represents nearly one-third of the total population.

There was considerable agreement among the respondents about the appropriateness of a particular function (Table 8-I). *Referral to outside agencies* and *providing teachers with information regarding pupils* were the only functions on which there was no significant agreement.

Those who agreed on the appropriateness of a particular function generally agreed on who should be responsible for training the support person to perform it. The only exceptions were the *job placement* and *referral to outside agencies* functions.

A small number (11.7%) of the respondents are currently engaged in training support personnel. A number of others reported

TABLE 8-I

ATTITUDES OF HEADS OF COUNSELOR EDUCATION PROGRAMS TOWARD THE FUNCTIONS AND TRAINING OF SUPPORT PERSONNEL

Function	Appropriate?*		Responsibility for Training†		
	% Yes	% No	% Counselor	% Counselor Educator	% State or City Director
1. Assisting in research.	96.5	3.5	51.4	30.5	18.1
2. Information-gathering and processing.	95.5	4.5	58.2	30.7	11.4
3. Group test administration and scoring.	94.7	5.3	37.9	50.0	12.1
4. Secretarial tasks.	93.4	6.6	81.1	10.2	8.7
5. Routine follow-up of counselees.	91.6	8.4	70.5	23.5	6.0
6. Scheduling.	87.0	13.0	74.3	9.7	16.0
7. Information resource for students and parents.	77.3	22.7	47.6	37.1	15.3
8. Fact-finding interviewing.	75.6	24.4	36.4	51.1	12.5
9. Job placement.	74.9	25.1	44.2	35.7	20.1
10. Orientation.	74.7	25.3	65.9	21.6	12.5
11. Providing teachers with information regarding pupils.	48.1	51.9	53.1	35.9	11.0
12. Referral to outside agencies.	42.2	57.8	33.9	26.7	39.4
13. Parent conferences.	36.9	63.1	32.6	55.1	12.3
14. Test interpretation.	34.7	65.3	11.1	75.5	13.4
15. Group counseling.	27.4	72.6	11.4	80.0	8.6
16. Administering individual intelligence tests.	25.8	74.2	12.1	78.7	9.2
17. Individual counseling.	25.4	74.6	15.1	75.7	9.2

* $p < .01$ for all functions except 11 and 12.
† $p < .01$ for all functions except 9 and 12.

that they were planning to establish a training program in the near future.

Interest in the functions and preparation of support personnel among the respondents was widespread. Of those who wrote comments (62.5%), nearly half specifically expressed interest in this problem and felt it was an important professional issue.

Discussion

There was significant agreement among the heads of counselor education programs in their attitudes toward the appropriateness of support personnel functions, with the exceptions previously cited. The reasons for the lack of agreement on the two is conjectural. It is interesting to note, however, that the APGA policy statement (1967) specifically mentioned referral as a recommended support personnel function. The disagreement regarding support personnel providing teachers with information on pupils may be the result of its ethical implications.

In general, the respondents' perception of the role of support personnel is clear and consistent with the APGA policy statement (1967). There is also close similarity between their perceptions and the functions satisfactorily performed by support personnel in the Counselor Assistant Project in the Rochester, New York, area (Salim and Vogan, 1968).

There was also significant agreement on the responsibility for training support personnel to perform each function (with the exception of job placement and referral to outside agencies). The counselor is perceived as having the major responsibility for training support personnel in all of the appropriate functions except group test administration and fact-finding interviewing. These were considered the responsibility of counselor educators. The minority who believed that functions 13 through 17 were appropriate agreed that counselor educators should have the training responsibility. This may point to a trend among counselor educators of accepting the position that lay people can be trained for core counselor functions, as suggested by Carkhuff and Truax (1965).

This study has implications for the training of school counselors. If support personnel are going to be used in substantial numbers, their proper use, supervision, and training should become an integral part of counselor education programs. This would help the counselor differentiate between his role and that of his support person, enabling him to avoid the problem of role confusion that some consider serious (Hansen, 1965; Gust, 1968; Salim and Vogan, 1968).

Munger (1968) has expressed concern over the general disinterest among most counselor educators concerning the use and training of support personnel. This is not confirmed by the comments made by the substantial number of respondents in this study. Nevertheless, institutions are beginning to train support personnel and it is clear that counselor educators will soon have to crystallize their thinking and make decisions relevant to the issues raised in this study.

In the near future it appears that crucial decisions will be made regarding the functions and training of support personnel. It therefore seems imperative that the attitudes of counselors toward these questions be surveyed. Their on-the-job experience will be an invaluable contribution toward making these decisions and their involvement will lend support for the use of support personnel. A study similar to this one directed toward counselors should be the next step toward resolving these issues.

References

American Personnel and Guidance Association: Support personnel for the counselor: their technical and non-technical roles and preparation. *Personnel and Guidance Journal,* 45:856-861, 1967.

Beal, R. M.: Counselor aides in community junior colleges: duties supervision, and preparation. *Dissertation Abstracts,* 30:126-127-A, 1969.

Carkhuff, R. R., and Truax, C. B.: Lay mental health counseling: the effects of lay group counseling. *Journal of Consulting Psychology,* 29:426-431, 1965.

Gust, T.: Support personnel vs. the counselor. *Counselor Education and Supervision,* 7:81-82, 1968.

Hansen, D. A.: Functions and effects of "subprofessional" personnel in counseling. In McGowan, J. (Ed.): *Counselor Development in American Society.* Washington, D.C., U.S. Department of Labor and U.S. Office of Education, 1965.

Munger, P. F.: Support personnel. *Counselor Education and Supervision,* 7:81-82, 1968.

Patterson, C. H.: Subprofessional functions and short-term training. *Counselor Education and Supervision, 4*:144-146, 1965.

Salim, M., and Vogan, H. J.: Selection, training, and functions of support personnel in guidance: the counselor assistant project. *Counselor Education and Supervision, 7*:227-236, 1968.

Strowig, R. W.: Prospects for use of support personnel in counseling. *Guidepost, 11*:5-6, 1968.

Trexler, L. (Comp.): *Directory of Counselor Educators 1967-1968.* Washington, D.C., U.S. Government Printing Office, 1968.

Wrenn, G.: Crisis in counseling: a commentary and a contribution. In McGowan, J., (Ed.): *Counselor Development in American Society.* Washington, D.C., U.S. Department of Labor and U.S. Office of Education, 1965.